Extensions

SUNY Series in Contemporary Continental Philosophy

Dennis J. Schmidt, Editor

Extensions

Essays on Interpretation, Rationality, and the Closure of Modernism

Stephen H. Watson

State University of New York Press

Published by
State University of New York Press, Albany

© 1992 State University of New York

For information, address State University of New York Press,
State University Plaza, Albany, N.Y., 12246

Production by M. R. Mulholland
Marketing by Dana E. Yanulavich

Library of Congress Cataloging-in-Publication Data

Watson, Stephen H., 1951-
    Extensions : essays on interpretation, rationality, and the
closure of modernism / Stephen H. Watson.
        p.   cm. — (SUNY series in contemporary continental
philosophy)
    Includes bibliographical references and index.
    ISBN 0-7914-1191-5 (alk. paper). — ISBN 0-7914-1192-3 (pbk. :
alk. paper)
    1. Philosophy. 2. Hermeneutics. 3. Methodology.   I. Title.
II. Series.
B72.W38 1992
100—dc20   91-38857
                                                          CIP

10 9 8 7 6 5 4 3 2 1

Acknowledgments

Portions of this work have been presented in a number of contexts, as indicated, and conference participants, colleagues, and reviewers all contributed to the result. The flourishing of continental philosophy in North America occurs not simply in a number of departments, not only in the give and take between a number of disciplines, but in a number of societies that foster it. Among the latter that should be mentioned in connection with this volume include the Society for Phenomenology and Existential Philosophy, the International Association for Philosophy and Literature, the Canadian Society for Hermeneutics and Postmodern Thought, the Merleau-Ponty Circle, and the Heidegger Conference. It is obviously impractical then to list everyone who has contributed to this work, but I should like to single out colleagues along the way— Tom Ewens, Ann Ashbaugh, Gary Gutting, Karl Ameriks, Richard Foley, Gerald Bruns, Fred Dallmayr, and Fred Crosson—as well as those from whom I have always learned much—John Sallis, Jacques Taminiaux, Hugh Silverman, Charles Scott, and Jack Caputo. Thanks for bringing this work to publication should likewise be given to Dennis Schmidt.

Chapter I, "Abysses," was originally presented at the Society for Phenomenology and Existential Philosophy and appeared in *Hermeneutics and Deconstruction*, ed. Hugh Silverman and Don Ihde (Albany: SUNY Press, 1985). It is reprinted here with permission of the publisher.

Chapter II, "Aesthetics and the Foundation of Interpretation," appeared in its original version in the *Journal of Aesthetics and Art Criticism*, 45 (1986) and is reprinted here with the permission of the editor.

An early version of Chapter III, "Hegel, Hermeneutics, and the Retrieval of the Sacred," was first presented at a conference on hermeneutics held at Conception (Missouri) Seminary College, February 1990. Parts of this paper in turn were presented at a conference on the concept of person, Mansfield College of Oxford University in September 1991.

Chapter IV, "On the Agon of the Phenomenological," first appeared in *Philosophy of the Social Sciences*, 17 (1987). It is reprinted here with the permission of the editor.

Chapter V, "The Dispersion of Dasein," was presented to the Canadian Society for Hermeneutics and Postmodern Thought held at McMaster University in May 1987.

Chapter VI, "Between Truth and Method," appears in this version for the first time. Originally presented at the Center for Twentieth Century Studies as "Reason and Interpretation: On the Deconstruction of Hermeneutics Strategies," it acquired its current title in a version presented in a conference on hermeneutics at the University of Dayton. In various versions it was presented in a number of places before assuming its final form as presented in the Heidelberg Philosophische Seminar on the work of Hans-Georg Gadamer in July 1989. The appendix on Strauss and Gadamer was presented in a second Heidelberg seminar on Gadamer and the Greeks in July of 1991.

Chapter VII, "On the De-Lineation of the Visible," was presented in an earlier version to the Merleau-Ponty Circle in September 1987, at the University of Rhode Island.

Chapter VIII appears in print here for the first time.

An early version of Chapter IX, "The Philosopher's Text," was presented at the ninth annual meeting of the International Association for Philosophy and Literature in May 1984. That version appeared in *Literature as Philosophy/Philosophy as Literature*, ed. Donald C. Marshall (Iowa City: University of Iowa Press, 1987). It is reprinted here with the permission of the editor.

Chapter X, "On the Rationality of the Fragment," has been presented in a number of contexts, including addresses to the philosophy departments of Purdue University and Canisius College, in 1990 and 1991. It likewise appears in print here for the first time.

Funding from a number of institutions assisted in making this work possible, including the National Endowment for the Humanities, the Center for Twentieth Century Studies of the University of Wisconsin—Milwaukee, the Colgate University Research Council, and the Institute for Scholarship in the Liberal Arts, the University of Notre Dame. Additionally, a grant from the Philosophy department made possible Rev. Brian Miclot's assistance in the final production of the manuscript and index.

Finally, granted the number of works referenced in the text, it was deemed infeasible to provide a master list of abbreviations. Abbreviations found in specific chapters centering on the works of one figure (Chapters III, IV, VI, VIII) consequently are provided along with the notes to each. For the same reason I have restricted citations to standard English translations where available, correcting them as necessary.

Introduction:
Time, Narrative,
and the Dialectics
of the Phantasm

1. Prologue: On the Crisis of Theory

Often enough, contemporary debates associated under the rubric of continental philosophy have given the impression of demanding that one be either for or against reason. The result issues, to use Hegel's term, in a certain *Hexenkreis* of rational dilemmas. On the one hand, it has been claimed, either one find grounds for ultimate rational assent or give up doing philosophy, and on the other, either one stop talking about reason, judgment, and justification or risk never being able to glimpse truth without blinders. Hence the ultimate accusations of the proponents, either that in lieu of appeal to demonstrable warrant one is a decisionist or that simply accepting such criteria implies a calculative reduction which reduces truth to "the empire of judgment." Moreover the paradoxes seem only to multiply. For example, proponents of decidability demand that we give up the search for the Good for the sake of rational warrant, whereas those strongly committed to substantive accounts of Being (or its transcendental kin, Truth and Justice) seem happy enough to pronounce what is at stake to be an 'impossible phenomenon.' And, often enough such antagonists too give the impression of merely having bailed out: hence the question of what comes after philosophy.

The 'thesis' of the writings that follow is that things are in fact much more complex, that the issues which arise in this domain are both theoretically and historically embedded. As a result the hope that one could *solve* the issue of rationality becomes almost doubly suspect, perhaps neither a desideratum nor a possibility—and yet *not* in any case because either philosophy or reason has come to an end. The very idea of the ending of philosophy is, after all, as fictitious as the hope that one might, equipped with an algorithm for its adjudication, indicate or *decide* it.

On the other hand, like other issues associated with this ending, issues governing the reappropriation of humanism for example, the fact that such an issue arose at all is indicative of a certain remove from origins, a matter, after all, that accompanied the translations of 'humanism' from the outset.[1] And, it is indicative moreover that metaphysics ('humanist' or otherwise) would not receive the homogeneous replies that once seemed to suffice, not because we have overcome them (necessarily) so much as the very idea of either reinstating or overcoming them remained itself insufficient—"logically," as the positivists used to say. What would it mean to assert against reason? Which proposition would suffice, and when would we depart from its orbit? And yet, on the other hand, the hope for an adequate theory, definitive, foundational, and apodictic in the classical sense seems equally absurd.

Indeed, we face—still—*meditations hegeliènnes*, questions concerning pure essentiality and pure difference, the problem of categorization and the equivocity of determination.[2] Those who followed Bolzano (and there were many if one considers the pivotal role that Frege and Husserl have in staking out the protocols of twentieth-century thought) now find the very idea of a meaning-in-itself, an idea-in-itself, a truth-in-itself, an objectivity-in-itself—in short, the idea of a theory-in-itself—the height of a certain nonsense and subjectivism. Indeed the very idea of a theory without competitors, actual or possible, now seems itself irrational, verging on something like the eternal return of this crisis itself.[3]

The hegemony of theory always requires this alterity. It requires that the hegemony of theory be capable of being placed into question, that from a standpoint other than its own, it be acknowledged as definitively indefinite. If we gain warrants for our own practices by acknowledging their 'perspectival' character, we do not gain truth—even if we gain warranted claims to truth, and even if only in the form of claims to assertability, ones that of necessity then await their own crisis. Hence the ultimate disjunction between certainty and truth. And the strategy by which this split might be denied, the hope that this alterity might be dissolved, the hope that the heterogeneity of theory might be exchanged for simple rational hegemony (i.e., certainty) is in a sense what made the concept of ideology an entirely modern notion. As Lefort aptly noted, a recognition affecting the ideology of theory at all levels, what was at stake in all ideological forms involves a "sequence of representations which have the function of re-establishing the dimension of society 'without history' at the heart of historical society."[4]

It is in this sense that claims to 'logical analysis' as a sufficient solution for such problems, in any case, smack of a certain ideology that by now has turned parodic. We have learned this if we have learned nothing else, that if, as Wittgenstein put it, "logic must take care of itself," it will not take care of anything else. Nor will anything else, for that matter take care of itself—neither, to use a language that once seemed clear, the syntactics nor the semantics of theory. And, like the complexity of the theories engendered by this complication, neither syntactic nor semantic analysis alone will yield sufficient results to these questions. Clearly, if it is not true that everything is a text or that all truth has become a fable, it is still true that in the strict sense there seems nothing left to 'analyze' outside of them: no logical simples, no atomic facts, no pure 'takings', no pretheoretical particulars, no essences, no meanings-in-themselves. There are more than two dogmas to empiricism. Still, if in the end the 'empirical' is a function of a 'posit,' a narrative, and the practices that accompany it, this of course is not to say that it is any less 'empirical' let alone philosophical. But it is to acknowledge that to be an empiricist in any of its labryinthian possibilities is no less and perhaps no more complex than to learn how to read.

Substantial (i.e., metaphysical) resolutions to theoretical problems seem hopelessly fictitious in this regard, albeit perhaps not without their own inextricable virtue. If it is true, after all, that no theory escapes its imaginary origins, it is precisely the 'fictionalization' of truth that makes truth possible. And yet knowing *that* does not solve the *problem* of its fictionalization: of its *not* being simply commensurate with the real. If it is true that intelligibility takes precedence over act, and if reason is parasitic on narrative, paradigm, and practice, it is true too that to think that all events are equally intelligible, or without conflicting 'intelligibility' is naive—if not 'metaphysical' in the pejorative sense.[5]

'Knowing that' was never biconditionally equivalent to 'knowing how,' nor was theory to practice, nor were the 'takings' of certainty to the perdurance (and, to speak Heideggerean, the "withdrawal") of truth. There remains a certain underdeterminability in the figuration of theory, a certain excess of the imaginary over the real. All of which is to say that the judgment of truth will not be ascertained without risk or without, in any case, overlooking the interpretative excess that both overdetermines and undercuts certainty. The dangers of theory in this regard become nondefeasible.

Hence the problem of interpretation. Popper already pointed out, however, the risk of interpretation—one, as will become evident, in which reason openly depends on what exceeds it, demanding in fact that one wager one's own 'uncertainty.' Hence its epistemic shortfall: if it is true that all theories are interpretative, it remains true too that not just any interpretation is true. Moreover, to put it bluntly, interpretations are not theories.[6] Nothing in fact would be more incoherent than to claim to provide (or to demand) a theory of interpretation, except perhaps to demand equally that there be a science of all science. In this regard interpretation, as Gadamer realized, is less a method, than an event. Indeed, as Jean-Luc Nancy has rightly put it, it involves an event without *arche* or *telos* that silently circulates throughout the texts and practices of philosophy.[7] The problem of interpretation surfaces perhaps, again like 'humanism,' only when the assertions of philosophy have broken down, a certain excess that both accompanies and undercuts the very possibility of assertion. And, it should be added, the problem of this excess accompanied 'humanism' from the outset: part and parcel of the question of translation across the margins and in default of tradition. The humanists' confidence, after all, had less to do with the self-assertion of the subject of reason than with the courage of the translator in the extensions of the letter. If it concerned both, the latter involved an event and the former a strategy—a difference that, as the history of renaissance humanism attests, became increasingly apparent as it became engulfed in the issue of the will. The problem of the will, after all, divided Luther and Erasmus no less than it would Nietzsche and Heidegger.

Neither the will nor time can make claims true however. It is one thing to claim that all truths are historical, that is, to deny that truth arises outside of a particular context among competing possible interpretations, and another to claim that the diachronics of such conflicts constitutes truth, that is, to commit oneself to history as the *arbitrator* of truth. The best critics of those enamored by interpretation always realized this.

Nonetheless, if Popper once more concluded an investigation of the historicism with which interpretation had become increasingly connected by denying it theoretical status, the recognition was not limited to external criticism. Heidegger had drawn similar conclusions fifteen years earlier, almost a decade before *Being and Time*. If again and again it would prove unwieldy for him, Heidegger realized from the outset that what was at stake remained a matter *otherwise* than theory, not because theory might improve on it, but because it requires that theory preclude it. The enterprise of certainty requires this closure and its exclusion of interpretative excess: "indeed the sciences must remain closed if [they] wish to perform their proper function."[8]

Moreover if he realized too, prior to Husserl, that in this closure the 'European' sciences were brought into internal crises, he likewise realized that it was by such crises that theory advances. Indeed, *pace* the hermeneut's commitment to the perdurance of tradition, "such crises do not take place in the historiological sciences only because they have not yet reached the degree of maturity necessary for revolutions."[9] Far from improving on or substituting itself for 'science,' the hermeneutic "as," 'intentionally' traced in this excess would involve less a return to origins than an attempt to think beyond strict theory. As Cavaillès too would argue vis à vis Husserl's foundational pretensions: "[H]ere there is no longer a return to origins but an orientation according to the flux of a becoming which presents itself as such only by the intelligible enrichment of its terms." It relies instead precisely on this excess, a practice that proceeds only because of its "indefinite plasticity."[10] And, even Popper would realize the inevitability of its return, acknowledging himself that at the margins of theoretical certainty there remains the problem of what withdraws from the decidability of theory, recourse to which, he acknowledged, could be accomplished precisely (and only) by means of interpretation.

What is at stake in what follows are explications that concern the remainder of 'hermeneutics' and the complications of reason. Although they cannot be taken to constitute or outline a theory of interpretation, neither are they intended to be definitive and conclusive, but instead indicative of the complexity by which one traces its event. If they are not without broader effect, they remain 'continental,' a classification too often perhaps accepted without question—though it still may not be hard to say what is at stake in the practices associated with this term that have arisen since Kant and Fichte in the works of Husserl and Heidegger, Merleau-Ponty and Sartre, Gadamer, or Arendt, Adorno, and Habermas, Foucault, or Derrida. This domain—doubtless now fragmented—once fell under the rubrics of 'transcendental logic.' Its claims concerning the indispensability of our narratives and philosophemes regarding the subject, world, the question of embodiment, and so forth now however interface in ways which, though systematic, always turn out to form less than a system.

2. On the Narratives of Dasein

The practice of hermeneutics was besieged, if not from its beginning, then doubtless at its end, by a certain agonistics: one that, in complicating both its logical status and theoretical scope, afflicts the significance of its incursion within the history of the modern. And perhaps appropriately, this is nowhere more explicit than in its most 'radical' attempt theoretically to discipline the status of interpretation— an attempt to overcome the metaphysical past to reconfront its task, perhaps even its 'call,' its *hermeneia*, within 'science' (*episteme*).

Heidegger's *Being and Time* opened by citing the *Sophist*, almost plagued by the ancient narratives that it seemed intent on destroying.[11] That Plato should have entered the Heideggerean text was surely not accidental, granted not only the latter's insistence on returning to the origins of Western metaphysics, but equally the Platonism of its own time—one that, after all, could count not only both neo-Kantians and logicians like Frege or Natorp among its adherents, but phenomenologists like Husserl as well. Still, Heidegger's text was intently hinged: divided by a certain attraction and repulsion, situated between repetition and overcoming, between the destruction and the retrieval of its metaphysical past.

From the outset, the investigation had been intentionally directed on Plato's wake, in the attempt radically to ground the ancient science of Being qua Being. Like the *Sophist's* expulsion that forms its preamble, *Being and Time* sought to surpass narrative for the sake of science. The problem of Being would be grasped, Heidegger claimed, without "telling a story [*erzählen*]" and yet without "*falsification.*"[12] The science of Being would dissolve all entities from their attachments to myth precisely to grasp Being in its purity. What Heidegger called the *doubling*, the *Verkoppelung* of the phantasm, might then be equally dissolved, thus overcoming the semblance (*Scheinung*) of appearance for the sake "of that which already shows itself [indeed radiates (*ausstahlt*)] in the appearance as prior to the phenomenon." [13] Still, when the science of Being that Heidegger sought had finally been reestablished in the existential analytic of Dasein—in accord with his own account of the rational and of *logos* as relational, as 'making manifest'—he still sought *verification* 'behind it,' in *muthos*, that is, in the myth of care.[14] It was precisely this move that the *Sophist* seemingly had forbidden: that reason might depend on myth, that narratives might underlie propositions, that philosophy and literature might be inseparable—and that understanding and imagination, far from being distinct, might be in complicity, in spite of all classical endeavors to split their differences for the sake of truth.

Instead, Heidegger ultimately concluded that the narratives of the everyday, like the temporality or 'historicity' to which they remained bound, were insurmountable: "we cannot trace those 'sentences' to theoretical statements without essentially perverting their meaning."[15] Notwithstanding the importance of its attempts to surmount the 'ontic' oblivion of Being, Heidegger's hermeneutic strategy shared a good deal in common with other turns toward the everyday, the near, to the prerequisites of the conventional, and even to ordinary language, as has been noted often enough. Nonetheless, this was also a radically different turn. Far from being the fulfillment of Reason, this turn involved the recognition of classical Reason's ultimate failure, along with the invocation of all that exceeds its limits. Neither the task of translation nor the task of explanation and theoretical reduction would find its requisite completeness. *Logos* and *muthos*, in short, were inextricably bound together. It forced a refusal to divide reason and narrative, a demarcation that had seemed necessary even to Heidegger himself. The problem of the ultimate vindication of reason now seemed out of reach to him, the confrontation of an assertion that stood in conflict not only with itself but with the whole rhetorics of *philosophia*, a genre that from its inception had contested the possibility of a truth other than the strictly univocal.[16]

No more telling evidence could be cited for the strength of this challenge than Heidegger's own abandonment of the project of the critical science that motivated *Being and Time*, notwithstanding the fact that it had been precisely the problem of oblivion (that is, the oblivion of Being) that had been its motivation. If Heidegger's preoccupation with what always already remained unthought, with the 'nothing' that escaped assertion, seemed still to smack, almost positivistically perhaps, (if not of the non-sense of which Carnap would accuse it, then) of "a silence whereof one cannot speak," his text continually belied itself.[17] Heidegger's own meta-narratives continually, perhaps unavoidably, circulated through his texts.

As early as 1919, arguing against Natorp, Heidegger had already denied the simple correlation between 'theory' and 'description,' convinced of a realm in which description extended beyond, convinced, moreover, that all 'theory' had been undercut in this rupture.[18] The later Heidegger, however, risked abandoning this rupture, along with its *Rücksfrage* for sake of the *ekstasis* of *poiesis*, stepping outside the vagueness of historiography to reinvoke a time in which *logos* and *muthos* were *not* in opposition.[19] Ironically however, it was not a solution, despite its opposition, without complicity with neo-Kantism as such. Despite his appeals to the fecundity of 'tautology,' Heidegger's declarations on the speaking of language (*die Sprache spricht*), or the eventing of the appropriative event (*das Ereignis ereignet*), the waying of the way, the calling of the call, or the infamous nihilating of the nothing (*das Nicht nichts*) still smacked of the self-grounding of science—if not the positivist reliance on the fecundity of tautology, then the Ich=Ich of classical transcendentalism. We will still need to sort this out. But, in any case, as Popper would remind the positivists—as much as Derrida would the phenomenologists—there remained in all such "antimetaphysical fervour" a certain utopian optimism, perhaps even a transcendental subreption, all of which suggested a certain "Father-killing."[20]

In fact, beyond the 'explicit' myth of care to which *Being and Time* appealed for "confirmation" of its analytic, there remained not only the narratives of "the Augustinian (i.e., Helleno-Christian) anthropology" that the author admitted had 'grown on' him in explicating Dasein, but also those other, apparently less 'philosophical' narratives that structure the Heideggerean text (inter alia, the narratives that concern all that escapes within the 'uncanny' nothing itself, the fourfold, the unthought, and ultimately the 'narrative' of *Ereignis* itself).[21] But throughout, *Being and Time* itself seemed compelled to disclaim this connection with narrative. "Strictly taken" as he quite strictly put it, these narratives, uncannily and curiously, have "nothing to tell."[22] And when the project had ultimately been abandoned in favor of responding to the voice of Being, which would call through the poetic speaking (*Dichtung*) of language, things seemed to fare no better. In the end, the disequilibrium between *logos* and *muthos* would, after all, be more truncated than put to rest; the unity it invoked would be irretrievably interrupted, depending on the exposition of an event that exceeds it.[23] The critical importance of Heidegger's project in this regard may well amount ultimately to having truncated the issue of Being's transcendence as much as having solved it, having opened up, that is, the complex field of the *Seinsfrage*, the risk of its herm*ēneuein*, and the complex status of both assertion and explication with respect to it.[24] And it is doubtless just for this reason that the effect of Heidegger's work may be intransigent. If Heidegger may not be the only figure who can lead us here, there will be no easy way around him.

Although Heidegger may still be cited too often as exceptional within the philosophical canon, polemics concerning the problem of interpretation generally have been similarly infatuated with beginnings and endings. Theorists almost everywhere in contemporary philosophy have claimed that they have finally solved the problem of interpretation or—precisely because it is, after all, a problem of interpretation—the 'problem' of anything else is declared to be finished. Hence we find the ad absurdum arguments on all sides (and in a number of fields; e.g., in philosophy of science, legal theory, or literary criticism) where interpretation and adjudication seem so stringently to demand opposition.

3. *Circulos in Demonstrando*

Like much having to do with this circularity ('hermeneutic' or otherwise), such claims may at best be true about what is affirmed and false about what is denied. The confusion that results, in any case, remains essential to, perhaps haunts, issues surrounding interpretation. Whereas theoreticians in various quarters are in agreement that reason is a matter of tradition, that judgment is as much a matter of viewpoint as evidence, and hence that rational assent is as much a matter of history as logic, such agreement does not *license* either reason or tradition, either in themselves or against alternatives. Foucault's discontinuities, Benjamin's images, Kuhn and Feyerabend's incommensurabilities, Derrida's deferrals, or Wittgenstein's uncircumscribables, far from being the traces of the exhaustion of contemporary thought within irrationality, are all in themselves the constant reminders—if not the very demarcation principles—of this alterity, with the vagaries of judgment that ensue. If these authors mutually reveal the interpretation behind assertion and the complexity involved in making 'truth' historical and context dependent, it seems to force a recognition that in the end would not so much *solve* the classical problem of truth as it would risk perhaps dissolving it.

Reminding ourselves that we do not have the freedom simply to choose our 'traditions' or 'perspectives' neither makes our present ones true in themselves nor warrants the closing down of our options: real, imaginable, or otherwise. Those following the critical tradition like Habermas or Davidson may be right to press the necessity of accounts of judgment and criteria regarding the rational (insisting in fact that the very idea of a conceptual 'schema' or point of view presupposes "a common coordinate system"[25]). Still, it does not follow from the fact that we require such homogeneous and unchallenged criteria, either that we in fact have them, or even that if we presuppose certain criteria de facto, we are thereby vindicated with respect to our dependence on them. What is attested to instead is the extent to which we lack an account of the rational that affirms the complexity at stake in the confrontation between 'procedural' and 'substantial' accounts. After all, if narrative is the medium in which all truth is chronicled, it remains equally thereby inextricably 'fictionalized,' the medium of theoretical construction: to speak Kantian, an extension into the unknown. Both the risks *and* the obligations implied by our judgments remain insurpassable in this regard, affecting, as no one better than Hannah Arendt realized, not only the epistemic realm, but both the "essential character and amazing range" of judgment "in the realm of human affairs" generally.[26] It involved, however, an event that would not respond to the requisites of 'strict science.'

Indeed strictly taken, we lie besieged between demands that could be satisfied only by an ideal chronicler, on the one hand, or by the pronouncements of an omniscient interpreter, on the other. If the warrant for our truth claims is always a matter of 'historicity' or 'tradition,' there still remains the possibility of *lapsus judicii* between reason and origins, between assertion and tradition and the problem of the latter's legitimation; there remains the question of what Heideggereans recognized as the *traditionis traditio*[27]. The rationality of any tradition's claim to truth, after all, always remains provisional. It is in this sense that even Gadamer declared (appropriately, against Leo Strauss) that "It is in no sense settled (and can never be settled) that any particular perspective in which traditionary thoughts present themselves is the right one."[28] We pursue a 'science of infinite tasks' whose regulative ideals are still to be vindicated—and whose claim to 'objectivity' in this regard remains inevitably, albeit perhaps transcendentally, illusory. Such claims remain "woven," as the *Sophist* had realized, in the difference between transcendental 'ideality' and empirical 'reality.' The asymmetry between verification and proof, the dialectical and the demonstrative, the hermeneutic and the aphophantic, thus runs deep. It is precisely in this regard that the order of interpretation remains, as existentialists like Sartre emphasized, 'ambiguous': neither "purely logical" nor "purely chronological," but itself the intertwining of reason and cause, of the intentional and the historical.[29] Hence as Merleau-Ponty put it, the very idea of an ultimate 'refutation' or 'verification,' the notion of a truth-in itself becomes nothing less than barbarous (*barbare*).[30]

4. Discipline and Interpretation

From its inception the practice of interpretation, 'hermeneutic' or otherwise, has been forced to contend with the complexity of its own 'disciplining.' Moreover, appeals to the classical tradition in hermeneutics that descends from Schleiermacher notoriously fail as solutions for the questions of justification that it confronts in the wake of philosophical modernism. In the first place, as has been seen, to cite Schleiermacher as progenitor here has always been something of a fable. Schleiermacher was not, in fact, the 'origin' of hermeneutics, nor did he attempt to present hermeneutics as a general theory of understanding, but (at most) as a discipline of applied philology, a practice for disambiguating texts—one, moreover, that the generalized research program of contemporary 'hermeneutics' itself has called into question. Further, his attachment (even simply as a philologist) to the movement of German romanticism makes any attempt to see his account of interpretation as 'scientific' paralogical at the outset. Indeed, German idealism, its own frequent self-delusion notwithstanding, was not a movement bent on either simply mirroring or completing the strictness accompanying the science of nature (i.e., mechanics, as it had become), but, again, of thinking *otherwise* than it. Those who in retrospect would view German idealism's attempt to privilege certain disciplines that had been submerged in the Enlightenment (aesthetics, history, religion), like its 'idealism' generally, to be the result of certain logical confusions, perhaps pay testimony to their lingering allegiance to positivism as much as they do to the former's "obvious" shortcomings.

Even when Dilthey presented hermeneutics as an antidiscipline, perhaps even a 'counterscience,' to speak Foucauldian, or as a competing methodology for the successes of the natural sciences, this too remained testimony to a belief left over from the Enlightenment itself: a commitment regarding, if not the 'dogma,' then at least the cultural hegemony of science.[31] Whereas Dilthey remained convinced from the outset that the natural sciences needed a 'competitor,' and that any alternative conceptual practice would need to seek its justification before the court of appeal of the natural scientist, we are finally prepared to say that both assumptions were mistaken. It would be as mistaken, that is, to think that the 'natural' sciences, even on this positivist account, somehow needed a competitor in the proper investigation of its objects as it would be to restrict justification to what Kant had already declared to be the "sciences properly and objectively so called."[32] If, as Gadamer rightly realized, "Today it seems to us that the dispute between Husserl and the Vienna Circle would have gone against both sides," the effect of this recognition is far reaching: questions concerning the interpretation of reason will be neither easily decided nor easily dismissed.[33]

Contemporary discourses regarding the status of interpretation are in fact no less complex in this regard, and too often rebuked with the charge of irrationalism. For example, although Derrida, perhaps closest among Heidegger's followers, continually insisted on the limits of philosophy and the necessity of thinking beyond it, what he demanded equally is *not* that one abandon justification, but that one view justification always from "within a topic and an historical strategy. . . never absolute and definitive."[34] Rather, it would be necessary to come to grips with all that was entailed (both epistemically and metaphysically) by the failure of the search *pour les fondements* that had underwritten philosophical modernism. Similarly, Foucault's insistence on understanding rationality 'strategically,' refusing to separate justification from the machinations of power, never led him to challenge what he called verified truth *tout court*. In the end, he refused to be aligned either with skepticism or relativism. Rather, as Foucault claimed, "It is senseless to refer to reason as the contrary to nonreason."[35]

In both cases it was not a question of critically recognizing the failure of irrationalism, as Michel Serres put it, but of insisting on the very irrationality of rationalism itself.[36] And it is precisely in this respect that all three insisted on seeing the object domains of reason as 'texts,' accessible only by means of what Barthes called a *cubist* or structuralist method, as "an object decomposed and recomposed," an operation wholly in act, dis-articulating all reference to the real in transforming its truth into a "simulacrum reconstructed." Still, if so, it was again less to dissolve certainty than to grasp the syntagmatic structure of truth and the narratological context and structure of reason itself.[37] The very attempt simply to distinguish text and evidence, judgment and construct, and again in the extreme, reason and myth, seemed to be misplaced. As Hans Blumenberg rightly *re*emphasized, it is *not* reason that is at stake even in the demarcation of science and myth. If "[n]o one will want to argue that myth has better arguments than science... nevertheless it has something to offer that—even with reduced claims to reliability, certainty, faith, realism, and intersubjectivity—still constitutes satisfaction of intelligent expectations."[38]

Even in granting myth this pragmatic justification, however, Blumenberg perhaps still remains too cautious, because the point is that the 'myths' and 'narratives' by which we articulate the real are neither eliminable nor exhaustive. And, although this need not affect either the 'certainty' or the success of science (as Foucault put it, the ideological component to science need not simply conflict with its 'objectivity'), the appeal to a "reduced" rationality does not affect its impact either within or without science.[39] If science indeed has less to do with the elimination than with the transformation or the 'refiguration' of myth, and if, strictly taken, the 'rationality' of neither science nor myth is in question, then neither the realist (in the classical sense) nor the romantic can take comfort. Neither Schelling nor Comte can be vindicated in this recognition—or, in any case, we would require both the myths of history and the myths of science.

5. Against Demarcation

The fact that this 'reduction' still seems to plague our narratives with a 'diminished' sense of the rational no doubt attests to the entrenchment of the belief that science will someday overcome them. Moreover, confronting the problem of myth's defeasibility as much as that of narrative's reliance on it for its feasibility has always depended on admitting the impossibility of this reduction—perhaps every bit as much as 'science' demanded it. But if the question is not one of strictly demarcating the rational in either domain, what truncates this difference more centrally concerns the status of the underdeterminability in question.

In one sense, of course, just as with the question of the rational, the problem of underdeterminability does not divide the letters and sciences, as Quine was as much aware as Barthes.[40] In neither domain however would it be simply a matter of reason being at stake. Although coherence may not be a victory easily arrived at, even it may not be decisive. As an ultimate criterion of the rational, that is, coherence comes too cheaply. In this respect, ironically, the problem of interpretation in both domains is not so much that there are too few justifications, but that there may be too many sufficiently 'good' ones finally to decide. This is not to say that we cannot tell bad readings from good ones (the tolerance of the text is clearly not absolute). Still, if the potentially infinite excess of interpretations cannot force a text to say, or an object to be, what it neither says nor is, neither for the same reason can any lay claim to being, definitively or finally, absolute.

In the end, it may be less the existence than simply the significance of this plethora that is strategically contested. Moreover, in this light there remains a certain vindication perhaps for what classicists like Gadamer continue Platonically to call the "countermovement" of reason and poetry.[41] Instead of dissolving the undecidable, hermeneutics (along with the archive from which it emerges) has always appealed to its abundance, to the "distending" of signs, to use Barthes's term, as a virtue.[42] Accordingly, Hegel's speculative proposition became for the philosopher the absolute dissolution of difference within identity, drawing Popper's ire that it involved both "an assault upon the law of contradiction" and "a loose and wooly way of speaking."[43] For Mallarmé, however, within its 'rhythm,' there was a "special source of attraction for the poet of *poésie pure*," the rupture of the *aleatoire*, to use Sartre's terms, a poetics whose fulfillment embodied its own nothingness.[44] Still drawing on an ancient archive concerning the *explication* or unfolding of the absolute, Hegel himself attempted to integrate this Other into the text of philosophy precisely by combining its *ekstasis* with the absolute certainty of *Wissenschaft*, a movement through which "substance is implicitly subject" and "consciousness is explicitly the Notion of itself:"[45] that is, substance—one whose exposition was the task of *Wissenschaftlehre* to provide (realize) and thus to confirm or ascertain.[46] In this regard, if Gadamer could claim that Hegel was "the first to actually grasp the depth of Plato's dialectic," the solution attempted by means of it was neo-Platonic.[47] From the outset, it involved a solution that contested the modernist archive that Hegel also sought to complete in his attempt to make the very *ekstasis* of the finite self certain. Ultimately, therefore, it must both be affirmed that "the *querelle des anciens et des modernes* is fought out monumentally in Hegel's philosophy" *and* that Hegel never fully grasped the *querelle* itself, but simply tried to resolve it.[48]

In fact, both Gadamer's and Heidegger's radicalizations of Dilthey's program would further, and explicitly, attest to this past not only in their retrievals of the *Seinsfrage*, but also in their attempts, thereby, to overcome *both* the ultimate 'scandal' of philosophical modernism's demand for proof *and* what *Being and Time* at the outset acknowledged to be the "genuine philosophical embarrassment of the dialectic."[49] Both authors confronted the problem of interpretation by dwelling on the difference on which it relied, recommitting its underdetermination to the polysemy tolerated within the analogical, an event the medievals aptly described as one midway between pure univocity and pure equivocity.[50] Assertion itself thus became nascently and equivocally *pros hen*, a pluralization and dissemination of 'Being' itself. The turn to interpretation, true as much for Nietzsche as for Plato's *Ion*, is not so much a reduction of the epistemic to the relative as it is one that relied upon what exceeded it.[51]

This 'reliance,' however, could neither *solve* nor dissolve the modernist's search for truth. Although "Being can be said in many ways," it does not, after all, follow that *any* way that it is 'said' is true. Such appeals themselves rested on a certain *muthos*, one that would be succinctly stated in Plotinus' own invocation of a *diaphora* through which "difference everywhere is good."[52] And yet the dogma that the difference—or its underdeterminability, and its dependence on the *ekstasis* of imagination—might somehow be simply avoided either by the proofs of experiment or those of deduction in retrospect appears equally mistaken.

In fact, whereas those in the wake of Husserl or Heidegger might refuse to dissolve the *Scheinung* of the appearances in the plethora of signs, it would not be possible to save even science itself from a similar reliance. The failure of reductionism would force again the affirmation of what Kant still called *analogies* that make all articulation of identity and difference within experience possible.[53] Popper would speak accordingly in this regard of the uncertainty attending the method of trial and error, as an extended form of dialectic, one that likewise attests to the complex origins of experimentalism and the problem of the *interpretatio naturae*.[54] But the mistake in Popper's grasp would not be found in his attempt to defend the necessity of critique, in the strictness of his own criticism of the positivist's 'dogmatism' of the facts, in his reservation with regard to historicism, nor in his admission of the fecundity of myth in rational practices, but simply in his refusal to allow evidence that could not be demonstrated—decisively tested—to be reasonable (and still, in this sense, 'true'). His mistake lay, that is, less in his commitment to rigor than in his lingering attachment to logicism.

6. Dialectic and the Canonizations of Excess

Notwithstanding the failures of the models invoked for their own practices, what was at stake in the practices that hermeneuts constantly (if not consistently) traded on did not simply involve the *Errinerung* of a tradition, or a *sensus communis*, or even an unquestionable natural order that might found reason, as much as an account of the rational that extends beyond grounds, beyond a preestablished certainty. It would not be a question of allowing theory simply to "be allied with the undemonstrated." Instead, as Cavaillès rightly realized, in thinking so, "[w]e again meet the Platonic reserve against *dianoia* and its attempt to lend hypotheses to the visible world."[55] Rather the *Seinsfrage* marked the opening of an excess in which thought, precisely in depending on it, acknowledged both its transcendental necessity and transcendental deferral, the rupture of an event that was both more than and less than truth, and one in which rigor and multiplicity could not be opposed.

Still, even were we to suspect, with thinkers as diverse as Gadamer or Cavaillès that this step beyond which all interpretation risk taking must still be aligned with the classical tradition's invocation of dialectics, it is precisely the retrieval on which the latter trades that has been called into question. Rather than a resolution of the rational, the history of 'dialectic' must be seen as a history of an ever-recurring step into the unknown, one whose complexity doubtless still needs to be traced and unraveled—from Plato and Aristotle through the neo-Platonists and pseudo-Dionysius, to the explications of Cusanus, the logic of appearance in Lambert (or illusion in Kant), or beyond it, the speculative science of Hegel and its aftermath: Nietzsche's perspectival interpretationism, Heidegger's attempt in reinvoking it to refound the science of Being, or Sartre's and Adorno's refusals of its totalities. What would likewise need to be examined, however, are the complex relations by which, throughout this history, and despite its fecundity, the practice of dialectic constantly maintained its links with the very metaphysics that it fostered. From the outset, it might be argued, dialectic remained either subsumed beneath the figures of pure form or invested circularly within those of narrative itself: relying, that is, either on paths opened up by the Greek's *episteme* of *mathesis*, on the one hand, or on the grand synthesis which had underwritten the pure narratives (*semes*) of the scholastics' *septenium*—to be replaced in its modern version with the constitutive representation of enactment.[56]

It was not accidental, therefore, that Descartes had undermined dialectic precisely by invoking the Enlightenment's demand for certainty at its origins: "The dialecticians think of governing human reason by prescribing certain forms of reason for it"—nor that, granted his own deductive protocols he consigned it as a result to the literary and the rhetorical.[57] Even Heidegger would similarly link it, epistemically and politically, to a certain dictatorship. Dialectic in its modern guise would

indeed manifest itself as a certain *Diktatur*, made possible by a certain
loss of questioning, one that is part and parcel of modern technology
and its calculative reduction of *episteme*.[58] But here too as Toulmin
realized at the Enlightenment's end, undertaking the retrieval of dialectic
anew, "Not to mince matters, *episteme* was always too much to ask."[59]
Instead, the step beyond, risked but not solved through this extension,
would remain unsteady before such demands, haunted by conceptual
constraints before which modern retrievals would indeed be complex.

Granted the strictness of these protocols, Hegel's renewed
dialectical attempt to elevate reason once more to the Absolute, still
connecting it with the most rigorous forms of demonstration, could
occur only at the cost of the Golgotha of the spirit, behind the back
of consciousness (and, one might claim, of the critical moment that
accompanied the phenomenologically evidential itself).[60] Moreover,
notwithstanding his own criticism of Hegel's logicism, when Husserl
too attempted to construct anew a 'scientific phenomenology' on its
own terms, now a systematic, but descriptive, inventory of 'essences,'
he required a similar surpassing through which the (bound) contingency
of originary appearance might, through "figurative reactivation," result
in an unbound and determinate ideality.[61] Both, however, would be
confronted with a similar epistemic (and demonstrative) shortfall in their
attempts to extricate their verificationist commitments from the vagaries
of temporal (and historical) contingency.

7. The Phantasm and the Ruins of Being

Contemporary versions could not but show the shortfall of these
failures. The early works of Walter Benjamin, for example, had betrayed
their effect in confronting such a phenomen-ology. "What differentiates
images from the 'essences' of phenomenology" is just their deferral
within "an historical index."[62] Rather than a mere occasion, the doxastic
event or object of intentionality, it would become necessary to explicate
a *Sinn* both inextricably bound and inaccessible to reductive adequation.
Instead, and fully aware of its scholastic origins, Benjamin claimed that
"truth is loaded to the bursting point [and] (This bursting point is
nothing other than the death of intentio. . .)."[63] In fact, in the strict sense,
what remains of this rupture is inextricably linked with the *distentio*
of the phantasm itself, now broken free of the assured movement on
which both intuition and dialectic had relied. Far from being "Spirits
falling into time" its *Zugrundgehen*, "the existent Notion itself," as Hegel
put it, or the iteration of objective truth, as Husserl put it, for
Benjamin—precisely in the disequilibrium of immanence and withdrawal—the "image is dialectic at a standstill."

It is just in this sense that Heidegger equally thought the techniques of dialectic steal past the phenomenon, missing the withdrawal at stake. It would require accordingly a new account of the event of the phantasm. Far from providing the simple correlate of an intellectual *actus*, it would involve instead the fragmented trace of what exceeds adequation.[64] "The image," as Levinas too would state in this respect, becomes "both a term of the exposition, a figure that shows itself...and a term which is not at its term." Ventured and defrayed within ontological difference, "exposition implies a partition of the totality of being," its truth always deferred, always promised—always in the strict sense still mythic.[65]

To think that the issues governing the emergence of the phantasm (or its reduction) could be localized within the treatises of "phenomenology" would of course be to forget the generalized economics of the issue's emergence in early twentieth-century thought, not only in Husserl's precursers—Brentano, Wundt, or Stumpf—but equally those to whom he seemed originally opposed—Mach, Schlick, Russell, or Carnap. And, to think that such reductions could be accomplished, either, to speak Kantian, "from above" or "from below," whether by reflective adequation or by the constructions of logical atomism, inevitably amounted on all accounts to a matter of transcendental illusion. If one grants Husserl, however, as even his critics would in the end, with having embarked on the most rigorous investigation of this science of observables—"a discipline," as Derrida put it in this regard, "of incomparable rigour"—it is true too that the outcome of such a phenomenology was far from the fulfillment of the science Husserl had sought in the *Logical Investigation's* Prolegommena that had received such widespread acclaim.[66] In this regard, the phenomenology of Reason ultimately arose, as Merleau-Ponty already realized, less to fulfill the science of the visible than to dwell within its ruins.[67]

From the outset in fact the *phantasma* had been seen to be similarly equivocal, "an indefinite plurality," as even Plato knew: ambiguous, as Aristotle attempted to define it, "like sensuous contents except that they contain no matter."[68] In fact the event becomes doubly indefinite: an indefinite multiplicity for each individual and an indefinite multiplicity of individuals constantly provoking the need to interpret.[69] Moreover, even those modern versions intent on remaining with the appearances and the phenomenological ultimately concurred. Instead of the immediacy of self-certainty and transcendental representation, the experience of the phantasm would depart from the realm of immanence, laden with the boundaries of its own theoretical genesis, the question of its history complicated, as Merleau-Ponty and Cavaillès both already insisted, by "the thickness of duration."[70] If the articulation of such a phantasm still seemed incumbent and paradoxical, posited in a middle realm between *synthesis* and *diaresis*, what nonetheless remains evident is that limiting its rationality to the realm of the demonstrable would, precisely in depending on more than we know, miss the space that had been opened up by acknowledging its risk.

At best, reacknowledging a certain insurpassability of the 'phantasm' could occur now only by realizing in the same moment both what authorizes and limits its 'transcendence.' To readmit what Adorno had called the ecstatic potentials of dialectic, transformations or interpretations from within but extending beyond the schematics of Kantian anticipations,[71] it would still be necessary to grant to Popper and the positivists at least this much: to appeal to an ultimate *telos* for resolution, however emotionally satisfying, "is an appeal to abandon all rival moral opinions and the cross criticisms and arguments to which they give rise."[72]

The 'teleology' in question would be, in Kantian terms, purposiveness without a purpose, an extension without ultimate *arche* or *telos*. And yet, to claim that in default of demonstrable conclusions, the rationality and truth that it invokes have come to an end, would surely carry its own dogmatism. Even Popper realized, as others like Strauss (or the early Husserl) opposed to historicism did not, that the hermeneutic question arises not within the failures of historicism, but as its rational extension.[73] Here, that is, matters would remain staunchly underdetermined, matters of reflective judgment, based upon what Popper too called a "preconceived point of view" and guided provisionally by matters of interest.[74]

Still, granting an extension of the truth predicate beyond the limited constraints of positivism—acknowledging what Adorno aptly described as a domain that "jars like discordant music in the positivist's ear," that is, an extension, "imperfectly present in objective circumstances"—would require confronting the inevitable limits of judgment which that extension relied on from the outset.[75] In fact, such an agonistic would not simply be episodic within contemporary theory. Here, as elsewhere, those like Popper were too often driven by this evidential shortfall simply to align the irrefutable with the false, doubtless (again unlike Kant) for lack of an evidence *other* than the strictly demonstrable.[76]

8. On the Critical Tribunal

Kant in fact becomes privileged (and doubtless contested) within this sphere, less because the critical tribunal solved the issues at stake within the Enlightenment, hence forcing time and again a "return to Kant,"[77] than because his works bear witness to its irresolvable complexity. Refusing to affirm the conflict of the faculties, he was led to demarcate what was in retrospect a certain "heterology" of the rational. Still in accord with the Enlightenment, Kant modeled first philosophy (or 'epistemology' as those short sighted in his wake would call it) on an account of the rational as demonstrable (still subsuming the figures of reason beneath the pure forms of geometry). Nonetheless, unlike those in fact more stalwartly committed to 'Enlightenment' and the proofs of representation, he was led to reinvoke the 'tolerance' at stake in the plurality of rational practices, to vindicate the extension at work in those domains that differ with respect to it (practical, aesthetic, teleological, historical, anthropological, religious, etc.) and hence to render the metaphysical unity of reason itself "problematic." The problem of reason in this regard from the outset was precisely a problem of extensions, its crisis the search for univocal *Erweiterungs-Grundsätze*.[78] And, even if Kant still insisted on the demand for "complete systematic unity," it was a unity at best presumptive and deferred, guided by an analysis that was from the outset both experimental and anticipatory.[79] The unity of science, was, in a sense—as Hegel would insist—precisely its disequilibrium, that is, a unity in "movement... unfolding becoming" and thereby inherently unstable.[80]

The venture through which the appearances might be 'saved,' one which continuously haunted philosophical modernism, depended precisely on the tolerance or plasticity of the phantasm itself, a certain affirmation of illusion (*Schein*), thereby an admission of the narratives of reason and the retrieval of dialectic as a domain of the probable. In this regard if, in fact, as Paul Ricoeur has said, narrative is the domain of the *Als ob* (indeed the *'als'* itself of the hermeneutic), then the Transcendental Dialectic is in this regard the reintroduction of the narratives of Reason beyond the canons of enlightenment.[81] But it is so precisely insofar as narrative is from the outset a certain venture that, far from being positively well founded, is equally the articulation of a certain *nègatité*, to use Sartre's term.[82]

The opening that this extension affords then remains, irresolvably, ambiguous. If Nietzsche would claim (as would Reinhold and Carnap) that Kant demurred before the science of the Enlightenment, he would still be called, by no less a hermeneut than Gadamer, "the all shatterer of rationality"[83]— perhaps even in the same moment that Heidegger would claim that "the problematic of 'being and time' flares up for the first and only time in Kant."[84]

9. The Genre(s) of Theory

Finally, it becomes similarly incumbent to mark the deformation that (implicitly or explicitly) has accompanied the treatise of philosophy itself. If it is necessary to raise anew the question of the bond between *muthos* and *logos*, between imagination and time, between text and tradition—and once again the question of that between rhetoric and philosophy—then the question of the genre of theory itself doubtless becomes complex. Insofar as this heterology bespeaks a certain pluralization of the rational, there follows not only a certain fragmentation of the philosophical *topos*, but a certain fragmentation of the classical philosophical treatise itself, an agonistic that concerns not only truth and certainty, text and demonstration, but also that of form and content, system and fragment. If Heidegger urged us in this regard to measure the difference between a Plato or an Aristotle and a "narrative section from Thucydides" to reveal "the unprecedented character of those formulations which were imposed upon the Greeks by their philosophers," so much more difficult does the attempt become to circumscribe that genre at its 'end.'[85] What results is a 'treatise' that lacks encompassing genre in precisely the same sense that it lacks ultimate foundation, divided not only between analysis and synthesis, but equally between the 'stylistics' of proof and those of the essay, that of demonstration and that of exposition. Here, as Aristotle realized at the outset, 'dialectic' belongs to the realm of the probable, linked inextricably to the narratives of opinion.[86] His hope was that reason could ultimately, and demonstrably, be separated from this realm. And all his allegiances notwithstanding, what Kant would likewise realize was that reason would instead be linked inextricably to this *doxa* precisely in rendering its dreams of totality illusory.

Again, this is not to say that we lack warranted judgment. It is perhaps (and surely more explicitly) to truncate again what Aristotle already blinkingly recognized elsewhere: the bond that unites *mimesis* to *poiesis*. What we can (perhaps both at least and at most) demand of those who would commit truth to time and meaning to its origins is that neither be timelessly locked up therein. Nonetheless, although we are not then barred from but propelled toward the 'abyss' of judgment and legitimation, both the requisites of dialog and those of judgment remain at risk, more a matter of dialectic than of assertion, opening a domain that belongs as much to *doxa* as to *episteme*—as much to semblance as demonstration. Like empty demands for universality, then, neutral demands for 'clarity' turn ideological in this regard. The upsurge of the rational here remains fragmentary: local, specific, and subjunctive. Or such is the overriding risk of the investigations whose 'topic' is united here. If in the order of demonstration "reason comes to an end," as Wittgenstein put it, it is also true that the task of adjudication, as he likewise realized, does not; both open themselves precisely in the margins that extend beyond theoretical closure.

The texts that ensue remain hinged on this difference, committed both to the rationality of the letter and to its ultimate dispersal, to the acknowledgment of a truth that is momentary because historical through and through—and the recognition, thereby, of the failure of systematics and its treatise as completeness. In its wake they affirm the provisional, the openness of interpretation, and the virtues of what lies beyond that genre and its discipline. Moreover, they thereby conflate both the ancients and the moderns, the humanist and the experimentalist, acknowledging both the risks in applying past truths and those inherent in devising new interpretations for our present truths, ones that never simply escape the confines of the fragment and the aphorism, as many commentators have noted (in both affirmation and denial). But here the hermeneut and the humanist again join hands— precisely in the problem of the letter, the literary, the issue of translation, and, what Nietzsche, in praising the aphorism called the "art of exegesis."

Hence nothing would be more fallacious than to consent in all this to the charge of irrationalism, nothing more shortsighted than to miss the complex history that unites truth and its expression, unites form and content with respect to it. As Arendt rightly realized, "The true danger threatening the tradition did not come from those who did not believe it capable, sight unseen, of carrying new content but rather from those who bombastically or sentimentally wrote in it as though nothing had happened."[87] Whereas the 'aphoristic' pronouncements of much of twentieth-century thought are often (and not incorrectly) paired with (if dismissed in terms of) an avante garde tradition that descends from romanticism, both must likewise be paired with philosophical modernism's most stringent demand for rigor, along with its accompanying break with the metanarratives and genres of the ancients—or as Bacon put it, precisely in raising the problem of interpretation, the need for equipping the intellect for "passing beyond the ancient arts."[88]

It is just in this regard that Bacon (every bit as much as the writers of the *Athenaeum*) raised the problem of interpretation: denying the systematic completeness of the sciences and the masks attending any method, whether by deduction or by enumerative induction, that might bring it about. Consequently, like those following him—not only in recourse to experimentalism, but the reliance on the fecundity of interpretation (the point is, they have been inextricably linked from the outset)—Bacon refused the attempts of a systematic genre that would simply parade scientific results as if they seemed "to embrace and comprise everything which can belong to the subject...the form and plan of a perfect science."[89] It is just in this regard that the history of philosophical modernism still remains to be written.

Abysses

Kant had proceeded some 600 pages into the first *Critique* before he had reached this problem of abysses. He had faithfully followed out the Enlightenment's search for foundations, its peculiar form of the *recherche de la vérité*, as it was called. He had deployed the schemata of the Enlightenment's beliefs. Transcendental arguments, always, at least in Kant, were regressive. *"If knowledge is to be possible"*—it postulated a complete picture of knowledge as well as possibility. And, no one doubted it—let alone Kant, for whom Newton, Galileo, and Euclid provided the texts for an archive of pure reason. The systems, the *principiae* were introjected: the schemata for synthesis—the bringing of the manifold of sensation into a unity, the necessary unity of knowledge, of concepts, of judgment, and thereby, of objects. And, consistently, self-critically, and the anathema to all neo-Kantianism, Kant's *Dialectic* would not allow these grounds to go themselves ungrounded. Reason seeks the conditions of the conditions, a higher unity that might ground the certainty of the understanding. The search for grounds, for justification, for legitimation, for necessity is not tangential to what had gone before: it is necessary. A final grounding is requisite that might satisfy the search, providing a complete determination or ground for logical and ontological possibility such that it might be affirmed, finally and ultimately, that "everything which exists is completely determined."[1] Being thus could be claimed to be fully rational, that is, both orderly *and* intelligible.

It was Kant's peculiar twist, *trope* perhaps would be adequate here, to have recognized that this project, the project of all *metaphysica rationalis*, was part and parcel theological. The foundation that would found logic and ontology must also be inherently theological. In short, as he put it, the project of rationality was *onto-theo-logical*. The object of this search would contain by *implication* the sum total of all possibility. It would be the *omnitudo realitatis*. Because all particularity (manifoldness) would be a limitation of it, it would be the primordial being (*ens originarium*). As the condition of the conditions it would be the highest being (*ens summum*). And, because everything that is conditioned is subject to it, it would be the being of all beings (*ens entium*).[2] With this ultimate grounding *metaphysica rationalis* would have found completeness. Bacon's foundations would have finally hit bedrock. Transcendental logic as a logic of truth would have been vindicated. Objectivity would have finally been assured in accordance with a necessity that had driven the search after truth since Plato's dialectic.

Kant recognized this was fundamental to the project of pure reason, unavoidable to the problem of certainty; implicit to the problem of bringing the dispersion (the manifoldness, the divided being) of a finite knower to certainty. It was, consequently, fundamental and unsurpassable. *Natural* was Kant's word for it, and it would bring Hegel's response that it still smacked of an indefensible psychology.[3] And yet, equally unavoidable was the fact that this search implicitly contained as well a certain *delirium*. Its search involved an illusion, that transcendental ideas could receive the *Sinn und Bedeutung*, as Kant was the first to call it, of what he also called *experience*.[4] Such a Being, albeit necessary and inevitable to Reason's search, was merely a *focus imaginarius*. But it was not merely a necessary delusion, in the sense of the *postulates* of practical reason, somehow. It was a delusion that struck at the heart of Reason itself. This was the delusion of its project, the failure of the foundation that ultimately justified what had gone before. It was, after all, the ground of all grounds. And Kant, despite all his commitment to philosophical modernism and the heroes of the Enlightment, did not fail at least to blink, to use a Nietzschean phrase, at what he had wrought: "Unconditioned necessity, which we so indispensable require as the last bearer of all things, is for human reason the veritable abyss."[5] *"Der wahre Abgrund,"* the combination expresses the paradox, the undecidable of German idealism. *Wahre Abgrund*. True abyss. The truth of grounding, to be *without* grounds. A truth that arises *from* grounds: to be without, to be *Abgrund*. It is a peculiarity of German, Hegel believed, a "delight to speculative thought"—and he referred in fact in this context to this word—to have a "twofold meaning." And, it must be kept in mind throughout.[6] Heidegger appealed to it as well, saying at the same time that, "we must avoid uninhibited word-mysticism."[7] If it does not occur in English (abyss) or French (*l'abîme*), it is there in their etymological past (*a byssos*).

II

Notwithstanding the circumflexes and peculiarities of 'those who come after' Kant, he does not merely mention this word with twofolded meaning, but bends it again, fully cognizant of what had transpired. It involves, he claims, a thought that "(w)e cannot put aside, and yet cannot endure. . ." Namely, that:

> All support here fails us (*Hier sinkt alles unter uns*); and the *greatest* perfection, no less than the *least* perfection, is unsubstantial and baseless for the merely speculative reason, which makes not the least effort to retain either the one or the other and feels indeed no loss in allowing them to vanish entirely.[8]

It is a curious passage: a thought that cannot be put aside—namely, that of the ultimate ground, the ultimate truth, the true *Abgrund*—and at the same time, a thought that cannot be endured. And yet, speculative reason "makes not the least effort" to retain the order that it implies. Kant's whole effort in the succeeding pages will be to reinstate the shell of *metaphysica rationalis* as a hypothesis: what cannot be determined will be regulated, reflected, understood 'as if' it were so.

The end result circles back on one of the axioms of Kant's position, but in this text it is stated in a form whose anticipations are over-determined. "The thing itself (*die Sache selbst*) is indeed given, but we can have no insight into its nature."[9] That is, in a radical split between the phenomenal and the noumenal, between the a priori and the a posteriori, we are barred from the thing's essence, divided by the appearance of the sensation, that event that both 'gives' the thing and withdraws it. And this sensation, consequently, just is that "element in the appearances...that can never be known *a priori*, and that therefore constitutes the distinctive difference between empirical and *a priori* knowledge," one that "cannot be anticipated."[10] The thing itself *ist gegeben*, but as divided, and screened beyond, as appearance and its other that is given without appearing, just as the positivity of the appearance itself remains divided already between the a priori and the a posteriori, as effect in the distinctive difference that constitutes it: dividing, ultimately, the thing itself from our grasp, dividing all presence from within, and finally, dividing the finite subject internally, interminably.

And yet in the preceeding passage, where all support fails, speculative reason seems content to let the play of imagination loose. Speculative reason, for just a moment in blinking before this opening, seems content, as he put it in the *Anthropology*, to have that state of affairs in which the "imagination runs riot," as it is "richer and more fertile in ideas than sense."[11] And the corresponding state, the noesis, if you will, might be characterized by what Kant calls "amentia (*Unsinnigkeit*)...the inability to bring one's idea into even the coherence that is necessary to make experience possible."[12]

Kant's abyss did not sink from sight in those who come after him. Schelling was perhaps right that this "abyss" that "all men are warned of" is a consequence of "mechanistic philosophy...in its highest expression."[13] There is a sense perhaps in which *metaphysica rationalis* and the postulate of complete determination could be systematically (if not successfully) completed only under the hypothesis of mechanism —as Laplace and those who come after him understood. Consequently, Schelling attempted to do away with the hypothesis, transforming

Naturphilosophie from within. "[P]ursuing speculative philosophy into its bottomless abysses in order to dig out its deepest foundation," he hoped to mine an abundance whose possibility could be questioned no further.[14] The abyss which resulted was then construed to be both the *Urgrund* of freedom and the emergence of a new transcendental cosmogony. The metaphysics that resulted was however neither more successful nor more rational—if it did rely on the very underdeterminability Kant's analytic had sought to escape.[15] Even Kant's mechanistic schemata were, after all, just his interpretation, his proviso on *finitude*. And the point was that others were possible, that no finite cognitive act could ultimately determine or ground. Consequently, although acknowledging that what was at stake involved precisely a transformation in our view of the *Cosmos* (*Weltanschauung*), what the Copernican turn itself enforced—the sublimity of the starry heavens above notwithstanding—was precisely the failure of such solutions. "The observations and calculations of astronomers have taught us much that is wonderful; but the most important lesson that they have taught us has been by revealing the abyss of our *ignorance* that otherwise we could never have conceived to be so great."[16]

Hegel, on the other hand, remained more convinced by Schelling than Kant. Armed with the metaphysics of *Realizierung*, he attempted to overcome the problem of this abyss, by regulating it in the economics of *Aufhebung*, that other German word whose polysemia was to bespeak a speculative truth. In the *Science of Logic*, recounting in fact the chapter on grounds, Hegel stated:

> [T]his end itself, *this falling to the ground* (*Zugrundgehen*) of the mediation, is at the same time the *ground* from which the immediate proceeds. Language...combines the meaning of this *downfall* (*Untergang*) and of ground; the essence of God, it is said, is the *abyss* (*Abgrund*) for finite reason. This it is, indeed, in so far as finite reason surrenders its finitude and sinks its mediating movement therein; but this *abyss*, the negative ground, is also the *positive* ground of the emergence of simply affirmative being, of essence that is in its own self immediate; mediation is an *essential movement*.[17]

Hegel's *Abgrund*, as one might expect, is controlled, an economics of truth with its own economics of signs. The negative is implicitly the positive, the negative and positive in the economics of *Aufhebung*. One always buys the whole package in Hegel. On the basis of it in the *Lectures on Philosophy of Religion*, with Kant clearly in mind, Hegel was content to reinstate the ontological argument.[18] In a sense, however, the *Logic* had always already presupposed it, the function of Kant's onto-theology. It was, after all, "the exposition of God as he is in his eternal essence before the creation of the world."[19] And, within it the same economics that regulates positive and negative mediates inner and the outer, the sensible and the intelligible, the phenomenal and the noumenal.

III

For Nietzsche, consequently, Kant became "*a delayer par excellence,*" who sees but does not see "what stands at the door."[20] Only recently, perhaps, have we begun to see Nietzsche as post-Kantian, notwithstanding all that he himself stated. If Hegel was able to transform Kant's abyss into infinite self-affirmation, Nietzsche intended to cut loose all intention to *ground*. Indeed post-Kantian in this respect, in the words of Kant, Nietzsche maintained "not the lease effort to retain either the least or the greatest perfection." Nietzsche entered the abyss, neither to despair, nor simply to nihilate (it is, after all, nihilism that stands at the door), but to affirm infinitely its groundlessness, its heterogeneity, to use a Kantian term.

Just like those others normally called *post-Kantian*, Nietzsche had little use for the notion of the *Ding-an-sich*: "The sore spot of Kant's critical philosophy has gradually become visible even to dull eyes: Kant no longer has a right to his distinction 'appearance' and 'thing-in-itself.' "[21] The thing-in-itself involves "the scientific prejudice," the last of the prejudices of the Enlightenment to be dissolved:

> Against the scientific prejudice.—The biggest fable of all is the fable of knowledge. One would like to know what things in themselves are; but behold, there are no thing-in-themselves! But even supposing there were an in-itself, an unconditioned thing, it would for that very reason be unknowable! Something unconditioned cannot be known; otherwise it would not be unconditioned![22]

The scientific prejudice is precisely this belief in unconditioned facts, unconditioned grounds. But it is a consequence of Kant's *Abgrund* that there are no such unconditioned grounds. And the grounds that buttress Kant's architectonic are no less implicated in this failure: "The categories are 'truths' only in the sense that they are conditions of life for us: as Euclidean space is a conditional 'truth.' "[23]

What arises then is a play of conditions from which one cannot escape. This itself, in fact, is identified by Nietzsche as the new "infinite." The perspectival character of existence extends indeterminately—*in indefinitum*, as Kant would say.[24] Whether existence without interpretation makes any sense cannot be decided, for to decide it we would have to get around our own perspectives, interpretations, etc. But "(w)e cannot look around our own corner."[25]

Truth then must be put in scare quotes, variously characterized by Nietzsche now as a 'reduction,' a 'fiction,' a 'lie'; as 'ugly,' an 'inertia,' an 'error,' 'falsification,' a 'schema,' the 'greatest error ever committed,' 'nonsensical,' a 'seduction'—but in any case a failure, one that accompanies a belief in knowledge-in-itself, a world-in-itself, and especially an in-itself that might be set over against a 'for-us,' a fiction, falsity, and so on. Furthermore, it is not a question of positing appearance over against the in-itself or the real, a positive over against its negative limit, the dissolution of the positive and the negative into some third more real thing, removing thereby the screen between accident and essence. Abolishing the system of exclusion that constituted the element that differentiated the 'real' dissolves its opposite, the 'positivity' of the apparent as well.[26] What results, then, is another infinite play of affirmations.

Nietzsche's affirmation, however, transgresses the affirmations of Hegel, or even those of the tradition that precedes him. Hegel had himself blinked at this chasm precisely before introducing its dissolution by means of *Aufhebung*. Speaking of the problem of grounds that link the determinations of reflection, binding *explanans* and *explanandum*, he declared: "In fact one finds oneself in a kind of witches circle (*Hexenkreis*) in which determinations of reflection, ground and grounded, phenomena and phantoms, run riot in indiscriminate company and enjoy equal rank with one another."[27]

Nietzsche instead refused to reduce the Other to the Same. It is, rather, the affirmation of difference, of chance, and the possibilities of the 'irrational' that are to be faced. Reason itself has become unquestioned belief. Moreover, there is a refusal to reduce all attributes to a univocity. A refusal, therefore, of ontology, of 'Being.' All now is interpretation and exegesis. The world itself, in short, has become an abyss. Nietzsche's abyss, however, is neither a negative ground for a positive emergence (as was Hegel's) nor one that can countenance a philosophy that proceeds as if it had not been met (as did Kant, whose regulative employments following the failure of foundations made him in this regard a 'scarecrow,' for Nietzsche). It is a chasm of infinite alterity, the infinite return of this Other without a Same. It is the return of the Other, of becoming, of the identity of difference. "That everything recurs is the closest approximation of the world of becoming to a world of being."[28] The confrontation of all this is in fact Zarathustra's mission. Facing this perfect circle, this eternal return that refuses all reduction, Zarathustra proclaims at the decisive conclusion of part III, "I call you my most abysmal thought!" (*Dich rufe Ich meinen abgrundlichsten Gedanken!*)[29]

What remains then, Nietzsche proclaimed, is merely the infinite play of life itself, precisely as this play of alterity[30] Otherwise stated, what remains, or rather becomes without being, is precisely the will to power. And, it is the will to power that infinitely interprets. In this sense, nature—as well as the problem of its 'synthesis'—becomes a play of forces, one that, to borrow from Kant's characterization of the moral law, 'possesses us rather than we possess it.'

IV

Just as Schelling and Hegel had transformed the material into the spiritual from within, Nietzsche transformed the paradigm of mechanism in arriving at the will to power, a monadalogy now without center:

> The victorious concept "force" by means of which our physicists have created God and the world, still needs to be completed: an inner will must be ascribed to it, which I designate as "will to power," i.e., as an insatiable desire to manifest power; or as the employment and exercise of power, as a creative drive, etc.[31]

Still, it is not the case, certainly, that Nietzsche is to be taken as a physicist. The account of the will to power is not simply a new *Naturphilosophie*—if it cannot be understood without it. Drawing on the distinction between explanation and interpretation, however, Nietzsche becomes one of the first philosophers to consider (or fear) that, far from reserving a justified domain of enquiry for the *Geisteswissenschaften*, the problem that emerges with interpretation is one regarding the 'universality' of interpretation itself. Neither domain, consequently, would function as a grounded domain of enquiry. Physics, too, might turn into interpretation. "It is perhaps just dawning on five or six minds that physics, too, is only an interpretation and exegesis of the world (to suit us if I may say so!) and *not* a world-explanation. . ."[32] Rather than providing the instantiation of classical certainty and justification, physics, too, would become an interpretation of the infinite affirmation of the eternal return. It too would posit a sign for the process in which it participates, without being able to look beyond its own corner: "The mechanistic concept of 'motion' is already a translation of the original process into the sign language of sight and touch."[33] Scientific discourse would be part of the infinite series of translations and interpretations of the 'original process' in which language tropes the world of becoming. And, 'truth' persists within it only as a rigidified effect in this 'mobile army of metaphors.'[34]

Will to power is itself original assertion, a force that, Nietzsche himself was willing to trope, belonged to every body in that each "strives to become master over all space and to extend its force (—its will to power) and to thrust back all that resists its extension."[35] But all, in any case, share in the life force of interpretation (again attributed synonymously to all bodies): "the essential priority of the spontaneous, expansive, form-giving forces that give new directions. . ."[36]

And all evaluations here must proceed accordingly, affirming what enhances, liberates, breaks down, experiments, enjoys uncertainty— all, in short, that refuses to confine the will to power within the myth of knowledge and the correlate that similarly bifurcates the world into good and evil. Indeed, in one of those loaded statements that perhaps overcomes the tradition by twisting it, that ruptures truth while connecting it to the moral or the immoral, that denounces logic by connecting it to force, that delivers all justification to its practice, Nietzsche proclaimed: "The criterion of truth resides in the enhancement of the feeling of power."[37]

V

This shift haunts the legacy of the Nietzschean (and perhaps Kantian) text, dividing it from within. But what is its status? Does this *'Wahre Ab-grund,'* this deflected truth that enjoins force in Nietzsche, that defies logic for practice, that exchanges the timeless for the contextual, does it form a correction for truth or its dissolution? Does it mark a limit, a transformation, or a simple substitution?

Ordinarily, as Martin Heidegger noted, such a question would be 'monstrous' (*ungeheuerlich*).[38] There is a whole archive in Western thought for dealing with the skeptic, the sophist, the misologist who would give up truth for rhetoric, for 'persuasion,' in short, for force. Moreover, it might be argued that Heidegger himself did not face the issue seriously enough. "Truth" in any case, has become a problematic marker. And faced with recent events even in post-Kantian fortresses of certainty, that is, philosophy of science and epistemology (but equally elsewhere), it might appear that the question of truth in any strong sense now just needs to be forgotten—for the sake of the artist's faith, Nietzsche might say, but as well, because we simply cannot escape our practices or paradigms. If, consequently, we cannot get around the issue of certainty, perhaps we can just get rid of it, because we can at least straighten out our references, if not truth: our assertibility conditions, if not justification in the strict sense. Beyond this scope, the problem of truth or Being simply seems to make no sense. And, all of this seems to authorize the substitution of *pragmata* for truth, reminding us as well that the history in which Nietzsche participates still needs to be written along with those others who would claim of truth that it is the expansive or the 'expedient,' as James put it.[39]

What haunts the interpretation of post-Kantian thought in this regard is just the status of the *primat* it grants to the practical. It is a primacy that, marking the limits of speculative thought, unleashes the scepter of its nihilism. It occurs perhaps for the first time in that conflict between classical science and classical metaphysics outlined previously that issues in Schelling's proclamation resounding throughout the nineteenth century's commitment to practice; namely, that "Will is primordial being."[40] This *primat* granted to practical reason, to *praxis*, and to *Realizierung* marks both the end of metaphysics and the need for its overcoming. '*Ueberwindung*,' a Nietzschean word, is to be found equally at the center of later thought: explicitly, in Heidegger or Derrida, certainly, but also in Wittgenstein or Carnap, who used it in 'overcoming' Heidegger.[41] Implicitly nonetheless it occurs in any number of thinkers who have felt of late the effect of history and its 'conditioning,' becoming worried once more that 'physics,' just as much as what came 'before' it, 'metaphysics,' may be a form of *eisegesis*.

VI

Nietzsche had overcome the scientific prejudice, the prejudice of foundations and, ultimately, metaphysics itself by an appeal to that which underlies it, the force that it constrains, the will to power. Enhancement, like efficacy or expediency, was seen to underlie truth, and thus 'truth' and 'truths' were seen as transferences or rigidified effects of the forces or practices from that they merge. Hence, Nietzsche claimed in 1885, "logic does not stem from the will to truth," but from a fundamental falsification that stems itself from will to power.[42]

But what sense can this claim that denies claims, this assertion that denies 'assertion' make? Martin Heidegger, who has perhaps faced this issue in Nietzsche's text as strongly as anyone, provides an exacting comment for this passage:

That is surprising. According to Nietzsche's own conception, truth is indeed what is firm and fixed; but should not logic emerge from this will to fixate and make permanent? According to Nietzsche's own conception, it can only derive from the will to *truth*. If Nietzsche nonetheless says, "Logic does not stem from the will to truth," then he must unwittingly mean "truth" in another sense here: not in *his* sense, according to which truth means error, but in the traditional sense, according to which truth means agreement of knowledge with things and with reality. This concept of truth is the presupposition and principal standard for the interpretation of truth as semblance and error.[43]

In what sense is this 'truth' to be understood in Nietzsche? Is it to be understood as what 'truly' is, or as what is valid in all judgments or life? In calling truth a lie what must be presupposed? Nietzsche himself had claimed that logic was, at best, an organon, or, within the problematic of force or of willing, an imperative. And consistent with this, in a move not unheard of *vis à vis* the collapse of correspondence theories, he turned to coherence, and once again to practice, and what was 'taken' as true. The claim that the axioms of logic are *adequate* to reality therefore "contains no criterion of *truth*, but an imperative concerning what *should* count as true."[44] Still, Nietzsche reminded us that such a world is not the real world but the apparent one, the one that must also be abolished if we are to surpass Kant.

"Truth" then is to be seen as the attempt to master multiplicity. "The character of the world in a state of becoming," however, Nietzsche stated, is "incapable of formulation," is "false," and "self-contradictory." Knowledge and becoming exclude one another. "Consequently, 'knowledge' must be something else: there must first of all be a will to make knowable, a kind of becoming itself must itself create the deception of beings."[45] Truth becomes "truth"; knowledge becomes "knowledge." And, the will to power becomes. But it is just here that Heidegger grows uneasy. Why are there no scare quotes around this 'will to power,' this marker for becoming that "creates reality" through the axioms of logic? And, what in the end is the relationship between the signs of Nietzsche's metaphors and the becoming they indicate? What in the end is the relationship between this becoming and these 'lies,' these falsehoods that are, terribly, Nietzsche's truth? What voice speaks from *Ecce Homo* to proclaim with the same deflection, "[T]he truth speaks out of me—but my truth is *terrible* for so far one has called lies truth."[46] What Sphinx proclaims three years earlier all the while that there is no truth, that "[t]here are many kinds of eyes. Even the sphinx has eyes—and consequently there are many kinds of 'truths,' and consequently there is no truth."[47]

VII

Nietzsche nihilated Being for the sake of what becomes. He turned the truth of Being to a fable, its verification into falsification. Heidegger, however, had refused this simple transformation that would exchange one side of the polarity for the other, Becoming for Being. Kant, as has been seen, had similarly bifurcated the world into the sensible and the intelligible, the real and the apparent, a dichotomy that Nietzsche had attempted to overcome. Yet, at the same time, Kant himself was unable to simply limit reason to the apparent, to the sensible, to the experience of physics. No more, then, could the bifurcation hold in Kant's own text. Human reason was inherently, 'naturally' metaphysical. It inherently surpassed the limitations that reason placed on its own endeavors. What can be thought inherently transcended what reason might be certain about. "Being," which Kant attempted to confine to mere position, to mere positing, problematically and yet indeterminately extended always further than any possible conceptualization or schematization.[48] Inherent to Kant's position, then, as Heidegger argued in his work on Nietzsche, is precisely a notion of Being that eludes the classical determination that would grasp it as *ground*, as *stasis*, as receptacle of all predicates. In this regard, in this overcoming that lies beyond but within metaphysics, Kant's abyss is likewise the abyss of Being itself.

> But the celebrated "universal" significance of "Being" is not the reified emptiness of a huge receptacle into which everything capable of transformation can be thrown. What misleads us in the direction of this notion is our long-accustomed way of thinking that thinks "Being" as the most universal determination of all and that therefore can admit the manifold only as the sort of thing that fills the vast empty shell of the most universal concept.[49]

Metaphysics at its end could no longer conceive Being as a set of predicates in terms of which all entities might receive determination. It could no longer fulfill the requisites of *metaphysica rationalis*. It would instead be forced to face the indeterminacy or underdetermination of Being with respect to all positing, but *also* to affirm the overdetermination of Being and—in accord with an ancient archive—an abundance that transcends all predication. What becomes 'imperative' for Heidegger, then is precisely to grasp this Janus head (*Doppel-gesicht*) of Being and the discord it initiates between representing and understanding, between using and relying on, between retaining and forgetting, and finally saying.[50]

The overcoming of metaphysics is consequently not to be found in the creativity whereby the will to power would make manifest the becoming of beings. It is rather the thought of ontological difference between Being and the emergence of beings, that ontological differentiation that was for Kant a natural disposition, the differentiation of categorization and what always eludes any and all presentation.

Surpassing the failure of metaphysics, then, means precisely remaining open to the surpassing in Being itself, remaining open to the otherness in which Being itself erupts or departs. In fact, on this account, what constitutes human authenticity in its own most or most proper possibility involves precisely remaining open to what is disclosed in the encounter with Being. Truth becomes then not a fable, an entity without time, nor even a being in itself. Rather, it involves remaining free within the revelation of Being, a freedom that is itself the letting-be of Being in its Otherness.[51] And, it is precisely this freedom before Being, this surpassing that calls on human response, this difference that beckons human freedom. Freedom remains consequently both ungrounded and yet (the paradox retains a certain Hegelian overtone) acquires foundation precisely in what withdraws from its grasp. In *Vom Wesen des Grundes*, a text that directly concerns this problem of foundations, of grounding, Heidegger states:

> Freedom is not a ground in any *one* of the ways of grounding, as we are always inclined to think, but is the grounding unity of the transcendental dispersion of grounding. As *this* kind of ground, however, freedom is the abyss (*Ab-grund*) of Dasein, its groundless (*grundlos*) or absent ground. It is not as though the only kind of free behavior were groundless (unmotivated) behavior. Instead, as transcendence, freedom provides Dasein, as "potentially for being," with possibilities that gape open before its finite choice, i.e., in its destiny.[52]

Heidegger's abyss then became the event of Dasein's freedom, an event that it receives in transcendence. This freedom is, therefore, as much receptivity as spontaneity. Human Dasein is 'thrown' into freedom, a word still with Nietzschean overtones.

And yet, this thrownness belies Nietzsche. This Being that perpetually escapes is not created, not simply 'effect,' nor is its force simply one form of Becoming. There is Being. *'Es gibt Sein,'* Heidegger pointed out is again another fortuitous idiom ('There is Being,' 'It gives Being') whose twofold meaning portends the necessary overdetermination of speculative thought—and Being itself, as has been seen. And it opposed all that Nietzsche stood for. As the latter proclaims clearly and consistently in *Thus Spoke Zarathustra:* " 'It is given' (*Es gibt sich*)—that is also a doctrine of submission. But I tell you, you comfortable people: *it is taken* (*es nimmt sich*) and will be taken more and more from you."[53]

VIII

Although it is true that no one has more forcefully faced the challenge of what has been limited here to Nietzsche's question, Heidegger's treatment is not uncontroversial. Jacques Derrida, for example, despite his differences with Heidegger's Nietzsche books, using words he employs sparingly, characterized it as "Heidegger's mighty tome (*le grand livre de Heidegger*)."[54] Gilles Deleuze, on the other hand, claimed that "Heidegger gives an interpretation of Nietzschean philosophy closer to his own thought than to Nietzsche's."[55] Both may be true, even though they still disagree.

Derrida's interrogation of the Heideggerean reading of Nietzsche has centered precisely on the machinations of authenticity in the Nietzschean abyss. First of all, however, it should be said that he has in fact affirmed the problematic of the Heideggerean question. For example, commenting on Nietzsche's claim that the truths of his books remain *his* truths, Derrida began: "The very fact that 'Meine Wahrheiten' is so underlined, that they are multiple, variegated, contradictory even, can only imply that these are not *truths*. Indeed there is no such thing as a truth in itself. But only a surfeit of it. Even if it should be for me, about me, truth is plural."[56] There can be no ultimate decidability in the exchange between the true and the false. But again, Derrida queried, what sense can be made of 'truth' if there are no 'truths-in-themselves'? Once this abyss has become pluralized, all oppositions become in the strict sense indefensible. Moreover, Derrida claimed, this includes the opposition of an 'authentic' or 'inauthentic' response, reading, or hearing of 'Being.' 'Being' and 'beings,' what exceeds and what erupts, presence and absence become lost in an infinite labyrinth of exchanges. Still, the gift of Heidegger's *Es gibt* is, seemingly, precisely that proper, that standard, that origin in terms of which one may still, in accord with the scientific prejudice, adjudicate between the authentic and the inauthentic, the true and the false, between what gets revealed and what gets covered up.

Heidegger hoped to restore the authenticity of the origin, of Being, by a recourse to a property of the abyss of Being itself: "The noble or the worthy Appropriation of the origin is the unique release as Appropriation of freedom, which is unconcealment of concealment, because it belongs to the abyss, *das Eigenthum des Abgrundes*."[57] Derrida aptly questioned whether Heidegger's whole understanding of Being, of its withdrawal of the abyss itself, does not have built into it a privilege, a proper, a bifurcation that is itself indefensible, that remains, in line with its speculative (Hegelian) ancestry, positive. In all this it remains, Derrida charged, despite all the critical resources of the ontological question, pre-critical: "in its relation to the signified, in the return to the presence of the spoken word, to a natural language, to perception, to consciousness, and its phenomenological system."[58]

Still, one must tread carefully even on this site, granted the Derridean choice of markers here. The very meaning of *critical* and *precritical* itself, after all, emerges only from the history of transcendentalism. It is not, again, the case that this history is being dissolved— even if it is to be overcome—as is evident from a text in *Of Grammatology*:

> I believe that there is a short of and a beyond of transcendental criticism. To see to it that the beyond does not return to the within is to recognize in the contortion the necessity of a pathway (*parcours*)....Without that track, abandoned to the simple content of its conclusions, the ultratranscendental text will so closely resemble the precritical text as to be indistinguishable from it.[59]

And yet, for Derrida, this ineffaceable within of the transcendental text already contains its beyond in what exceeds it. Like Kant's own unconditioned necessity, indispensably required as the last bearer of all things, the first ground of transcendentalism too becomes the veritable abyss. Speaking of the event of freedom's appropriation, an event that Heidegger himself equally describes as Being's expropriation (*Enteignis*) of itself in its withdrawal, Derrida stated:

> Finally, then, once the question of production, doing, machination, the question of the event (which is one meaning of *Ereignis*) has been uprooted from ontology, the property or propriation is named as exactly that which is proper to nothing and no one. Truth, unveiling, illumination are no longer decided in the appropriation of the truth of being, but are cast into its bottomless abyss

as non-truth, veiling and dissimulation. . . .The property of the abyss (*das Eigentum des Abgrundes*) is necessarily the abyss of proper-ty, the violence of an event that befalls without Being.

Perhaps truth's abyss as non-truth, propriation as appropriation/a-propriation, the declaration become parodying dissimulation.[60]

The truth of grounds hence becomes the abyss of truth. It is, that is, the abyss of truth as nontruth, the dissolution of all truth, of all immediacy, of all origins. In a sense Derrida has forsaken the Heideggerean text for its Nietzschean ancestry—but wholly on Heideggerean grounds. Still, in defining truth as revealment, as *aletheia*, even if no final interpretation renders a sign complete, did not Heidegger himself *guarantee* truth, because there is nothing more primordial to being *Da-sein*—as revealing, disclosing?

Even Heidegger himself had wavered before this abyss. It was, he related in his 1964 UNESCO address (and Derrida's preceding text depends on it), "inadequate and misleading to call *aletheia* in the sense of opening, truth."[61] In this hasty identification, truth and Being are still too much thought together, thought too much within the coupling that links together the opening of presence with the simple *correctness* of statements and judgments, too much abstracted from the event itself. Being, after all, withdraws without fully presencing, without, therefore, being fully 'adequatable.' It is precisely in this sense that Derrida's abyss is Heidegger's as well. Where is truth to be placed in this event that appropriates and 'depropriates' at the same time? Heidegger's own query, following his own destruction and retrieval of the Greek origins of the tradition, that is, takes us to this limit itself:

Aletheia, unconcealment thought as the opening of presence, is not yet truth. Is *aletheia* then less than truth? Or is it more because it first grants truth as *adequatio* and *certitudo*, because there can be no presence and presenting outside of the realm of the opening?

This question we leave to thinking as a task.[62]

IX

But then what is to be made of the belonging-together of Being and Truth? What is it that remains undecidable in *aletheia*? And, what is it that remains insurpassable, that leads this abyss, this *Ab-grund* to be connected time and again with the problem of truth or its loss?

In 1927 Heidegger in fact had seemed sure of all this:

> *Why must we presuppose that there is truth?* What is 'presupposing'? What do we have in mind with the 'must' and the 'we'? What does it mean to say 'there is truth' (*"es-gibt Wahrheit"*)? 'We' presuppose truth because 'we' being in the kind of Being that Dasein possesses, *are* 'in the truth'. . . . It is not we who presuppose 'truth'; but it is *'truth'* that makes it at all possible ontologically for us to be able to *be* such that we 'presuppose' anything at all. Truth is what first *makes possible* anything like presupposing.[63]

A strange passage. One that marks again the passage of truth to 'truth,' fully cognizant that this truth as well cannot be the truth of *certitudo* or *adequatio*. And it enframes, also, the same appeal to transcendentalism and its *conditio sine qua non* with which Heidegger had met Nietzsche's own quotation on truth.

But then why is it not classical, this appeal to the *'es gibt'* once again? Is this not an appeal to grounds, the 'presupposing' that 'subject' and 'object' are always already in harmony? Should we not hear Nietzsche's roar that the appeal to a subjective necessity does not prove 'truth,' that roar that was to shake Kant's faculties and synthetic a priori judgment to the ground?[64] Is not Dasein's "presupposing" to be taken, after all, *as* Dasein's? After all, it was Heidegger, too, who was quite willing to say that " 'There is' truth only in so far as Dasein is and so long as Dasein is."[65] *Es gibt* or *es nimmt*? Constituted or revealed? The problem remains, it might be said, assuming the Heideggerean genre once more, "undecided," the legacy of the undecidable Transcendental Ideal.

What remains true, however, is that this 'truth' which always already includes its own deferment cannot ground this abyss, but derives from it. Similarly, it cannot solve the problem of modernism and its search for unequivocal grounds or foundations. Reason in the end functions beyond foundations. All judgments are conditional, 'presuppose' a prior framework, and the ensuing 'truths' are by no means commensurable de juris. There is clearly no truth in itself, any more than there could be a knowledge in itself.

And these other, remaining 'truths,' this labyrinth without decidability? Here, as Heidegger consistently claimed, "A skeptic can no more be refuted than the Being of truth can be 'proved,' "[66] Scare quotes again; 1927 again. Notwithstanding his later, perhaps hasty characterization, Heidegger's 'truth' never was the truth of modernism, the truth of proof, of certainly, of adequation. If his story then sometimes flirted with neo-Kantianism in its search for the *conditio sine qua non* of truth, the resulting quoted, troped 'truth' was in this respect perhaps 'already' Nietzschean. And his later works would depart from *Fundamentalontologie* faced with the abyss at which it unavoidably arrived. Fourteen years later, in "Recollection in Metaphysics," he would claim little else in stating that the truth of Being cannot be proven and "is inaccessible to every explanation,"[67]—at least not from the perspective of beings, of totalization, foundation and completeness. One must look rather to that thought of what exceeds: "What 'is' Being? May we inquire into Being: as to *what* it *is*? Being remains unquestioned and a matter of course, and thus unthought. It holds itself in a truth that has long since been forgotten and is without ground."[68]

The question is whether this is enough and what sense is to be made of it. Is not one person's abyss another's ground, one person's listening another's response, one person's authenticity another's inauthenticity, and even one person's *es gibt* another's *es nimmt*? Has not Heidegger simply exchanged reason for taste, philosophy for poetry? Recall that Carnap, too, praised Nietzsche in his *Ueberwindung*, precisely for having realized that metaphysicians were bad artists who masked their emotional commitments.[69] Now finally we were in a position to clarify science and send the metaphysicians to art school. A modernist concern, perhaps, retaining its commitments to the purity of reason and the univocity of methodology but also one that stands at the center of understanding rationality after their default.

X

Heidegger's response is first a claim about the modernist project itself and its commitment to a "technical scientistic view of language,"[70] reducing 'Being' to a frame, a metalanguage through which reality might become pictured or, under the guise of the latter's failure, in an appeal to ontological relativism, claim that—as Quine put it—'to be is to be a variable.' It forgets, thereby, the ontological difference in an antinomy, to speak Kantian, that grants either too much or too little, "both" sides claiming "more than it knows."[71] Further, from Heidegger's standpoint it thereby functions on the ground of nihilism as, "the essence of nihilism is the history in that there is nothing to Being itself."[72]

Still, the other side of what Heidegger called philosophy's "most extreme counterpositions," termed by him "the speculative-hermeneutical experience of language," cannot provide a simple or easy alternate. If language here is the 'house of Being' the place of the occurrence of the '*es gibt*', it must involve anything but the simple Absolute of the idealist tradition *it* stands on. Heidegger, certainly, had learned the failure of that event of Will, of realization, that would get around Kant's dilemma. There is no final proof in all this for Heidegger, not even the proof of practice.

Rather, it is the thought of Being—and its difference—that are to prevail now. "Thought" is a speculative mark that may still descend from the machinations of German idealism, however. It is, as Phillipe Lacoue-Labarthe has noted, "the word of greatest proximity to Hegel," and consequently, "the word of greatest danger."[73] For if Being is to be authentically disclosed and divided, it is to be received in thought[74]— 'speculative hermeneutical' thought, two words that, in other arenas, Heidegger might have rejected. If, however, Heidegger dissolved the proof of this Being, if he forced the recognition that there is no final foundation, no final proof for the matter of thought, this does not deny that there is a strictness to thought. Using characterizations that echo to Husserl's notion of *Strenge Wissenschaft*, and a text that Heidegger claimed is "much too neglected today,"[75] he stated:

> This multiplicity of possible interpretations does not discredit the strictness of the thought content. For all true thought remains open to more than one interpretation—and this by reason of its nature. Nor is this multiplicity of possible interpretation merely the residue of a still unachieved formal-logical univocity which we properly ought to strive for but did not attain. Rather multiplicity of meanings is the element in which all thought must move in order to be strict thought.[76]

And ultimately, this strict thought, underdetermined, incomplete, groping, interpretative, remains 'true' thought precisely to the extent that it responds to this Being without proof. Notwithstanding the failure of science or the failure of metaphysics, then, Heidegger remained committed to "thought," to *strictness*, to the matter of thinking every bit as much as Hegel with his own "element of thought" (*Elemente des Denkens*)—and all the baggage of its metaphysical commitments: to the intelligible or the spiritual versus the sensible, the inner versus the outer, the essential versus the accidental.[77]

Still, this 'strict' thought cannot remove itself from its own contingency, presuppositions, possibility, and historicity—which is why *aletheia*, as Heidegger ultimately realized, must mean more than truth (*Wahrheit*), must mean more than the safeguard of Being, as he sometimes allowed. There remains the problem of abysses. There remains the problem of alterity, that risk that turns all perception, all

Wahr-nehmung, as Heidegger ironically liked to hyphenate it, into a mere phantasm. It is this perhaps that inextricably haunts phenomenology, like all commitments to the immediacy of the given; namely, in a fundamental repetition of Kant once more, that "the thing itself (*die sache selbst*). . .is and remains inscrutable." In this respect there remains the Nietzschean question, overdetermined in its reference, and unavoidable in its force:

> "Is seeing itself—not seeing abysses?"[78]

And, what holds for the pure seeing of the given must likewise stand perhaps for Heidegger's 'matter of thinking,' which, he believed, can remain in the former's disappearance. Certainly this is why the Heideggerean text for all its strength remains problematic and, as no one knows better than Jacques Derrida, a bit comic in the 'strictness' of the disclosure of its *magnum mysterium*.

Still, it is not a question of alternatives, of oppositions: the logic itself has become overdetermined. A simple dismissal here would be fallacious in its implicit appeal to a story about certainty and the sure progress of knowledge that has been put in question. We should not, consequently, dismiss the Heideggerean text too fast. Heidegger perhaps does not say it often enough; often enough, he says the opposite. But he too knew the theoreticians's dilemma that concerns the abyss of truth and freedom: "Whether the realm of the truth of Being is a blind alley or whether it is the free space in which freedom conserves its essence is something each one may judge after he himself has tried to go the designated way, or even better, after he has gone a better way, that is, a way befitting the question."[79]

Aesthetics and the
Foundations of
Interpretation:
Schelling and the
Überraschung of the
Work of Art

In a famous proposition that reflected a history, a science, a metaphysics, and a performative that did not question themselves, Hegel in the Preface to the Phenomenology of Spirit declared: "Lacking strength, Beauty hates the Understanding for asking of her what it cannot do."[1] It was the axiom for what Martin Heidegger would still call a century later "the most comprehensive reflection on the nature of art that the West possesses—comprehensive because it stems from metaphysics."[2] Moreover, Heidegger himself epilogued his own text, "On the Origin of the Work of Art," in turn one of the most famous in twentieth-century aesthetics, by citing three more propositions from Hegel concerning the decline of art:

> Art no longer counts for us as the highest manner in which truth obtains existence for itself. One may well hope that art will continue to advance and perfect itself, but its form has ceased to be the highest need of the spirit. In all these relationships art is and remains for us, on the side of its highest vocation, something past.[3]

Although Heidegger declared that the truth of Hegel's propositions on art still remained to be decided, he himself at one point seemingly decided against 'modern art,' declaring, in a posthumously published interview in Der Spiegel, that "we are left in the dark as to how modern art perceives or tries to perceive what is most proper to art (das Eigenste der Kunst)."[4]

What is it that art lacks, by which it stands now in a state of decline? Beauty is without force, "lacking in strength," and more specifically with regard to Hegel, lacking "the energy of thought," the "tremendous power of the negative." Beauty lacks reality. It lacks, that is, 'realization,' that which was for Hegel, with a certain outlook on pragmatics, "the magical power that converts (thought) into being." Art proceeds unaware that truth can be won "only when, in utter dismemberment, it finds itself."[5] Beauty, in short, lacks a proof; it remains merely fanciful before this need for proof. Before reason's critical tribunal, art, on the contrary, will always remain "a priori helpless (hilflos)," as Adorno put it, thinking nonetheless that this was precisely its virtue.[6]

II

If Hegel's assertion can be seen to culminate a certain metaphysical position on the work of art, it arises nonetheless only at a particular

point within its history. The proof in question already commits itself
to a certain transcendentalism as well as a strict commitment regarding
the demonstrability of the rational. Hegel's *Phenomenology* is the enclave
to a systematic science that barred the possibility of any epistemic
content falling beyond its boundaries. It involved a ban that was perhaps
unthinkable prior to the rise of modernism, a commitment limiting
rationality to strict demonstrability and rational proof—rather than, for
example, a *theoria* and a *telos* that ultimately came to rest in *contemplatio*.
There is perhaps no greater symptom of this modernism and the
shattering it portends than Kant's critical system. Kant's third *Critique*
showed metaphysics in fact in ruins, underwritten by an epistemic
commitment to *mathesis* and its modern offspring, the *principiae* of
scientific idealization. At the same time however it recognized a
'provocation' before the work of art—an event that, although sensible,
and nonconceptual, provokes thoughts (*denken veranlasst*) into reflection,
into play, "without however any determinate (*bestimmter*) thought, i.e.
any *concept* being capable of being adequate to it."[7] The underdetermination in question and the *inadequation* that ensued barred any simple
rules of correspondence for translating the work of art into thought or
words. Unlike logical attributes that simply *represent* what lies in the
conceptual, "aesthetical attributes," as Kant called them, "arouse more
thought than can be expressed in a concept determined by words."[8]
They "enliven (*beleben*) the mind by opening it out [literally providing
an *Aus-sicht*] to an illimitable field."[9] Rather than a field of thought based
on representation, on *Darstellung*, on what can be encompassed within
the unity of a concept, and consequently on the *homoiosis* between
concept and object, the underdetermination here forces thought to have
recourse to imagination. Beyond the simple forms of univocal discourse,
it enforces, that is, a certain *ek-stasis* on thought. Rather than facilitating
a simple substitution between thought and concept, the work of art
enforces the deferral of representation within reflection. And it involved
an event provocative enough that Kant could find no better words for
the description of its *Aussicht* than to appeal for its characterization to
the metaphysical past. The third *Critique* characterizes the encounter
with the work of art precisely as "purely contemplative" (*blöss
kontemplative*).[10]

Still, Kant could say no more. Notwithstanding the metaphysical
appeals of his 'post-Analytic' considerations, he was incapable of going
beyond an almost nostalgic attribution. The *Aussicht* could not seemingly be made rational. In fact, Kant in the end almost removed all
rational overtone from this 'contemplation.' If it remained the case that
the experience of the work of art is not restricted to a faculty or to taste,

but is ascribed to the thing, its *ascription* would be at best only subjunctive. The one who perceives the beautiful "speaks of beauty *as if* it were a property of things."[11] Consequently, Kant would place the experience within the dialectical regulation of the *Als ob* and, thus, within the sphere of transcendental illusion. Notwithstanding all that the *Aussicht* of the aesthetic had opened up, Kant's last word with regard to it remained determined and decisive: "The judgment of taste is not cognitive" (D)as Geschmacksurteil ist kein Erkenntnisurteil."[12] And, all thought based on *Erkenntnistheorie* would thereafter make the same assignation, barring the work of art from its domain and substituting the investigation of its subjective experience for the work itself.

III

Hegel's Preface to the *Phenomenology* without question shares Kant's ban regarding this excess. It was in fact subtitled, "On Scientific Cognition." And if it were true that on other matters Hegel saw himself disagree *toto coelo* with Kant, when it came to art, in fact, Hegel's *Asthetik* had at least the same effect, treading on similar commitments regarding the rational and the ensuing ban concerning the work of art. What was the Hegelian system, after all, if not the system of systems, the attempt once and for all to provide the form and content of an absolutely presuppositionless system, providing even the foundation of science with its own immanence?[13]

And yet, one might be tempted equally to claim that what Hegel seeks to finish off only concerns an *arche* much more ancient, an *exclusion* of the work of art that is active as early, perhaps paradigmatically, in the Platonic text. In the *Republic* Plato himself already described the *agon* between poetry and philosophy as ancient or archaic.[14] And, whereas the *Ion*, on the other hand, reinstates the poet to an elevated position, granting him or her a kind of insight into the divine, it is an inspiration that is totally irrational, an inspiration through that the poet is not in his right mind, "out of his senses and the mind is no longer in him."[15] And because poets utter their incantations not by rules of art, the *techne* involved is simply magical, sophistical, in fact, betraying a content totally exceptional to the rationality of the *polis*. If Plato grants the poet an exceptional grace, as the interpretor of the gods, in fact it is only in a way that *defuses* his or her gift—a gift that stands outside the art of dialectics, beyond *episteme*, an art capable of saying anything and defending nothing.

The specific target of Hegel's condemnation, nonetheless, is Friederich Schelling, a voice that for the most part remains silent, overshadowed within the history (and perhaps the metaphysics) of aesthetics. Still, if it is true, as Heidegger claimed, that Hegel presents the *apotheosis* of metaphysics and its work of art, its most comprehensive reflection, a speculative optics that claimed "(p)ure self-recognition in absolute otherness,"[16] then Schelling, however briefly as will be seen, presents its utter provocation, an *Augenblick* that itself remains irrecuperable.[17] And, this remains true even for the Heideggerean text itself perhaps. Although Heidegger was quick to place Schelling's later philosophy within the *Geschick* of metaphysics and to decree the latter's claim that Will is primoridal being, the bellwether of the nineteenth century, he remained remarkably silent on Schelling's aesthetics—both in relation to the history of metaphysics and its overcoming (*Überwindung*).

In a letter to his (then) friend, Hegel, written in 1795, Schelling wrote: "[P]hilosophy is not yet at an end. Kant provided the results. The premises are still missing."[18] Nonetheless, if there were a certain agreement regarding what was to be concluded, the nature of the premises and the meaning of their implication would in the end bring about an ultimate *agon* between the two philosophers concerning the beautiful and, more generally, the relation between *Anschauung* and *Erkennen*. In fact Kant had bequeathed his progeny the problem of what he calls in the third *Critique* an "immeasurable gulf" (*unübersehbare Kluft*)[19] between the sensible and the intelligible, one that had generated philosophical antinomies in the attempt to account for the origins of experience, the relation between freedom and necessity, and hence the nature of morality and metaphysics in general. The rift between the litigants of these antinomies was in fact immeasurable, incommensurable, and consequently undecidable on theoretical grounds. The decision was made then to allow each its own domain, granting the realm of the practical a certain priority in rational *recherche*, so long as it did not trespass its limit.

Still, Kant searched for a bridge, if for no other reason, as he stated in the Introduction to the third *Critique*, than the domain to which he had granted privilege 'demanded' it: "The concept of freedom is meant to actualize (*wirklich machen*) in the world of sense the purpose proposed by its laws."[20] Kant hypothesized:

There must therefore, be a ground of the *unity* of the supersensible, which lies at the basis of nature...[A]nd the concept of this ground, although it does not attain either theoretically or practically to a knowledge (*Erkenntnisse*) of the same, and hence has no peculiar realm (*kein eigentumlichen Gebiet*), nevertheless makes possible the transition from one mode of thought according to the principles of the one to that according to the principles of the other.[21]

Hegel denied that such a paradox concerning this ground lurked for science. He was in fact absolutely convinced that Kant had implicitly solved his own problem, artificially setting up limits and then surreptitiously surpassing them in discovering the Absolute. The solution was already posed in the problem. The fact that the concept of freedom is meant to actualize the purpose its law proposes in the world of the sensible, in the strictest of Kantian senses that it proposes to *realize* its purpose, meant that the proof of its reality would be precisely in making *aufgehoben* the opposition—and in recognizing only itself in absolute otherness.[22]

The problem of the work of art, the problem with 'beauty,' its weakness, as Hegel put it, is precisely its inability to transform itself before reality, precisely the helplessness by which it remains bound to a 'foreign' content. In fact, the work of art has no laws and no concepts to realize. And, were it in fact to recognize itself in its other, were strict correspondence to arise before its object, it would precisely no longer *be* art, but simple presentation; that is, *Darstellung*. In the strict sense of the word there are no signs in art. Art merely occasions or provokes—rather than translates—the language of thought into an expressive stratum. Indeed it could be said that art figures or '*symbolizes*' rather than actualizes thought, if that too did not presuppose a concept or thought to be figured, both of which the work of art lacks. And, that is for Hegel precisely its weakness. It is anything but coincidental, as shall become evident, that Schelling's last letter to Hegel (November 1807), containing a terse reply to the *Phenomenology's* Preface, would have misgivings about Hegel's misuse of his notion of Idea, in particular invoking with regard to it a false opposition between 'concept' and intuition.[23]

IV

Schelling's own *System of Transcendental Idealism* (1800), nonetheless, coheres at first glance with the *Erkenntnislehre* that Kant bequeathed. It was a transcendental system, a science of knowledge that claimed a certain closure—a definitive completeness and determinateness, to invoke the Kantian predicates.[24] And yet the opening sentence of the Foreword testified equally that it would be "a system which completely alters and even overthrows the whole view of things prevailing" (1). Schelling realized in fact, despite what he called "the rigorous demonstration of its principles," that from the prevailing standpoint the work would contain "monstrous consequences." No less a figure than Schiller would concur: in the final chapter of the work, he declared, Schelling's conclusions concerning the status of the work of art destroyed transcendental philosophy and its commitment regarding a reflective ground.[25]

The outcome of the treatise attempted a *demonstration* of the unity of the elements of knowledge, a *monstre* concerning the unity of the subjective and the objective, consciousness and nature—a proof of how, as Schelling put it "the purely presentative" and "what can be presented" (5), consciousness and unconsciousness, can find unity. Moreover, in so doing, the unity of the theoretical and the practical would be established, the unity of consciousness' prescription of the laws governing its own actions as well as the laws governing phenomena. That is, such a unity would provide a legitimation for the domain that had been opened up by the third *Critique* and yet could not be raised to the level of knowledge.

The 1800 *System*, however, bars Hegel's solution for speculative metaphysics. Rather than providing a demonstration of the unity of subject and object, practical reason abolishes the object. "In the free act the identity of the two activities (objective factor and the subjective factor) must be annulled precisely in order that the act may thereby appear as free" (220). Schelling thus barred the voluntarist solution that would in Michel Foucault's term result in a certain "theologization" of man in the nineteenth century.[26] The abolition of the other here remains, Schelling claimed, in an argument anticipating Marx's critique of Hegel, one in which the requisite identity was such that "the intelligence was conscious only for inner intuition, but for outer remained unconscious" (218). But, equally the unity cannot be simply demonstrated in thought alone. "It is utterly impossible for anything objective to be brought forth with consciousness" (219). From the standpoint of the theoretical, "man is forever a broken fragment" (216). Hence it would be necessary to surpass the reflective ground of transcendental philosophy. Schelling, in this regard in fact agreed with Kant, the ground of the unity between subject and object remains inaccessible to thought alone. The finite *Rücksfrage* cannot provide its own origins. Subjectivity cannot itself be the agency of objectivity. Rather, if the unity between the subject and the object is to appear, it must *appear* in the object. *Qua appearance*, then: "An intuition must therefore be exhibitable in the intelligence itself, whereby in one and the same appearance the self is at once conscious and unconscious for itself, and it is by means of such an intuition that we first bring forth the intelligence, as it were, entirely out of itself" (217–18).

The product of such a bringing forth, such a *poiesis* will share, therefore, both the characteristics of the products of freedom (in that it appears before consciousness as its own) and the products of nature, that are unconsciously brought about. Every organism, Schelling claimed, is a "monogram" of the identity in question but not as self-recognized. It remains one whose identity lies beyond it, that is dirempted before the gaze of an external judgment: reflection. The exhibition of this unity would then be precisely the underlying ground, the absolute for the two moments in question:

> This unknown, however, whereby the objective and conscious activities are here brought into unexpected harmony, is none other than that absolute which contains the common ground of the preestablished harmony between the conscious and the unconscious. Hence, if this absolute is reflected from out of the product, it will appear to the intelligence as something lying above the latter, and which, in contrast to freedom, brings an element of the unintended to that which was begun with consciousness and intention (221–22).

The product, reflecting the absolute from within itself, would arise precisely in completing the 'meting out' intimated in the Introduction to Kant's first *Critique*: "There are two stems of human knowledge, namely sensibility and understanding, that perhaps spring from a common but to us unknown root."[27] The common root here, the faculty of synthesis, the generation of transcendental Ideas would be similarly referred to by Hegel as "the faculty of speculation."[28] Its product, the work of art, Schelling claimed, "radiates back" (*widerstrahlt*) the inner unity of the two stems, accomplishing what no simple inner intuition can provide and thus "appearing to the intelligence as something lying above the latter": the unity of consciousness and unconscious, freedom and necessity, the inner and the outer, the principles of theoretical and practical reason.

It is precisely this "exhibited" identity, which no willing could provide, that is the "miracle" (*Wunder*) of the work of art, as Schelling called it. And the analysis of the artist, he believes, itself confirms what the work of art reveals. The testimony of artists, he claimed, is that they are involuntarily driven to create their works, satisfying an irresistible urge, in a manner that "free activity becomes involuntary"—proceeding, then, from a contradiction, "one that strikes *at the ultimate in him, the* root of his whole being" (222). Equally, as it strikes at the relation to the ultimate, so too, it ends "in the feeling of an infinite harmony" (223), a harmony that is involuntarily produced in accord with "things that he does not fully understand and whose meaning is infinite." It involves, Schelling stated in a fundamental repetition of Plato, a power that separates the artist from all other human beings, an intuition or inspiration that reveals the Absolute. And when Schelling discussed what he called the "obscure concept of genius" (222), it is in accord with Kant's notion of *intellectus archetypus:*[29] genius derives from neither of the two stems by that it is composed but rather "presides over both" in the generation of the Absolute. It involved then a phenomenon that, like Kant's moral law was in itself absolutely compelling, fixed of itself alone, *für sich selbst feste*, as the latter put it.[30] For Schelling, the work of art is a phenomenon that is equally, fully 'convincing,' the predicates having changed from the moral to the epistemic sphere:

> [E]very absolute concurrence of the two antithetical activities is utterly unaccountable (*nicht weiter erklarbar*), being simply a phenomenon which although incomprehensible (*unbegreiflich*) yet cannot be denied; and art, therefore, is the one everlasting revelation (*Offenbarung*) which yields that concurrence and the marvel (*Wunder*) which had it existed but once only, would necessarily have convinced us of the absolute reality of that supreme event. (223)

It marked an event involving thought's most extreme *ek-stasis*, invoking a recognition that must occur beyond concepts, the failure of the concept's grasp, *unbegreiflich*, a provocation that discloses its essence in a singular event, a universal-singular deferring the universality of the concept. It was the production, the *poiesis* of a *Wunder* before that intelligence would "feel itself surprised and blessed" (*überracht und beglückt:* 221).

And yet, as such, it traced the destruction of transcendentalism. If the work of art is a revelation, it is so precisely by what transcends any and all transcendental category, precisely because of its nonimmanence and withdrawal before the concept and transcendental representation. On the contrary, it was, Schelling claimed, the presentation of what remained unpresentable within the transcendental text insofar as it delivers consciousness over to its unconscious and "sets all the forces of the mind in motion in order to resolve a contradiction that threatens our whole intellectual existence" (226). Hence, art delivers reflection over to a provocation that is the revelation of all that escaped transcendentalism, overcoming the metaphysical *agon* that had stood at its origin. This was for Schelling the significance of the work of art's *Überraschung*.[31] Art no longer then could be seen as the madness of the gods, an excess before thought that could be defused within the philosopher's text. It was now in fact, Schelling claimed, its culmination, a *Faktum der Vernunft* that was the *sine qua non* of knowledge itself: art alone succeeds in achieving absolute objectivity and *"universal validity"* (232). An inversion of the metaphysician's understanding of the relation between the philosopher and the poet thus ensues: "Philosophy as philosophy can never become generally current. The one field to which absolute objectivity is granted is art. Take away objectivity from art, one might say, and it ceases to be what it is, and becomes philosophy; grant objectivity to philosophy, and it ceases to be philosophy and becomes art" (233). The philosopher presents in subjective intuition what the artist reveals objectively, not simply as a seeing, or a sign, or an intuition of the identity between the subjective and the objective, but as their *symballein*, their concurrence. The work of art then is precisely a symbol—but now a *symbolon* that is concrete, a 'bringing-together,' a *Zusammenbringen* as he would say in the *Philosophie der Kunst*, treading more literally on its etymological past.[32] It is one that, far from being the poverty of the subjective, is precisely the ground of identity, its concretization. Hence, the work of art's infinite repose, overcoming the 'infinite' "wavering between finite and infinite." There results "unchanging identity that can never attain to consciousness" and that is precisely in its enlivening and uplifting "a dark unknown force that supplies the element of completeness or objectivity to the piecework of freedom" (225).

Far from being the impoverishment of thought as Kant (and Hegel after him) claimed, the symbol is its fulfillment. And far from being the mark of its incompleteness, the symbol is the surpassing of all that remains subjective within the sign, within representation. And, far from being its overcoming, the philosopher's text, the text of representation, finds its destiny in what could never attain to thought within the sign (222). Schelling's 1800 *System* then culminates precisely in handing science over to art: setting up an opposition that no theory can overcome."So far as particularly concerns the relation of art to science, the two are so utterly opposed in tendency, that if science were ever to have discharged its whole task, as art has always discharged it, they would both have to coincide and merge into one—which is proof of directions that they are radically opposed" (227). As has become evident, then, having claimed that the "poetic gift...constitutes the primordial intuition" (230), Schelling decisively demoted the text of the philosopher. "For though science at its highest level has one and the same business as art, this business, owing to the manner of effecting it, is an endless one for science, so that one may say that art constitutes the ideal of science, and where art is, science has yet to attain to" (227).[33]

V

The text's position was inevitably, archetypally perhaps, the inverse of Platonism. And, perhaps Schelling knew it. If it remained the masterpiece of his philosophy, it culminated in a position that its author would begin to abandon almost as hastily as he adjoined it to the book as the concluding chapter. It was, after all, to turn Nietzschean, "image mad" or at least "thought mad," proceeding, "not merely by logical inference" but "with the immediate certainty of intuition," as the latter began *The Birth of Tragedy*, a book that was intentionally anti-Platonist, transforming all texts into shining images.[34]

Within two years the problem of metaphysical extravagance, the problem of the text's anti-Platonism, had apparently struck home. Schelling, in any case, had backed off from the position. In *On University Studies* he first attempted to defuse the conflict claiming that history had itself overcome the dichotomy between philosophy, the discourse of truth, and poetry, the discourse of *ekstasis*. Christian religion, he claimed, has created its own poetry and art and "thereby it has become possible to formulate a complete objective theory of art."[35] Plato unfortunately, Schelling stated, was unaware of a critical difference in poetry and its works. "Christian poetry. . .expresses the infinite as unmistakably as ancient poetry expressed the finite."[36] Plato's mistake then was *not* in elevating the text of philosophy against poetry, but in not anticipating the evolution and perfection of poetry itself. Nonetheless, such a *reflection* presupposed a theoretical position from which objective *poiesis* could be adjudicated. That is, it presupposed an objective and reflective theoretical-critical standpoint. It presupposed the priority of the representation over its content, the privilege of theory. It is just this ancient privilege that is reinvoked in Schelling's *Kehre*. Retaining for art the privilege of the real, he nonetheless granted to philosophy *identity* and ideality. Still attempting to retain his earlier formulation, he granted the ideal now to philosophy:

> Art although entirely absolute, although the real and the ideal are perfectly united in it, is to philosophy what the real is to the ideal. In philosophy the opposition between the two is ultimately resolved in pure identity; nonetheless philosophy is ideal in

relation to art. The two meet at the summit, and because both
are absolute, each can be the archetype of the other. That is why
philosophy enables us to gain the deepest insights into art. . .[37]

The identity then falls to the philosopher who is no longer overtaken
by the revelation of the work of art but finds his or her identity instead
confirmed. Subjective 'reflection' is not a reflection, a limit. The artist
remains unconscious in relation to the work of art, that is, the identity
of the product remains external, 'reflected outside' in the philosopher's
text. "[P]hilosophy, for all its inner identity with art, remains always
and necessarily science—ideal—while art remains always and necessarily
art—i.e., real."[38] Thus, the notion of art as the ideal and inner identity
of consciousness has been left behind. The artist will no longer provide
"the eternal organ and document of philosophy" (231), before which
the conceptual grasp of consciousness would always appear as inadequate, simply subjective. Rather, the destiny of this identity is now to
be found precisely in the judgment of the text of philosophy. The *Bruno*
in fact barred the artist from access to the absolute. "[S]ince the creative
artist does not recognize the divine, he will necessarily look like one
who defiles the mysteries, not their initiate and devotee."[39] It was in
a sense just what Pareyson called "*I problemi del Bruno*"[40]—and there
was a sense in which Schelling never returned from it in his later
writings.

VI

What was it that caused the inversion within Schelling's position
and its ensuing setting of art into decline? Schelling scholars, as Tilliette
has noted, have argued variously here, for the most part without
conclusive results.[41] There are reasons enough perhaps why it could
have been abandoned. One thing is certain, however. The position,
Schelling's *monstre*, was from the outset untenable. Whether or not he
saw it that way, whether or not he moved on to problems of greater
interest to him: the wavering of the writings initially following the 1800
System recoil from its *ek-stasis*.

In one sense Hegel had been right about Schelling's position in
the end. The claim concerning "the ecstasy of thought in which knowledge is the immediate knowledge of the absolute" remained incompatible with Schelling's *demonstration*.[42] Hegel realized in this regard that
there is an ultimate dissonance between the appeal to intuition and
the fact that, "Schelling often uses Spinoza's form of procedure, and
sets up axioms."[43] As if this *Faktum der Vernunft* could be axiomatically
'mediated,' when it was precisely the revelation of an incommensurable,

"an oracle to that we have to give way," as Hegel described it.[44] The work of art, in the strict sense *unbegreiflich*, has no judgment behind it, no proposition to manifest, no premises, and strictly speaking, no entailment. In the strict sense, the sense, that is, in which both Hegel and Kant agreed about art, "the *proving* of anything is thus abandoned."[45] Schelling's revelation stood beyond all strict proof, heuristic with regard to its truth, beyond, then, all strict demonstrability. Hence Schelling's *Wissen der Wissen* had no firm grounds on which to stand. The work of art could not solve the problem of *Wissenschaftslehre*. The aesthetic act could not provide "the unity of the true and the good," that had been sought as early as 1796.[46] What was revealed instead, as has been seen, was something quite different, a "phenomenon" that was "utterly unaccountable, being a phenomenon that although incomprehensible, yet could not be denied" (233). And Schelling himself never perhaps quite came to grips with it.

In the "Philosophical Letters on Dogmatism and Criticism" written five years before the 1800 *System*, he had likewise said that the work of art opened up "a quiet abandonment to the Immeasurable (*Unermessliche*)."[47] And yet it was not without the recognition of a certain contingency and its risk. Incommensurable with any final concept or description, it was not a phenomenon that could escape the possibility of what later phenomenologists would call *phänomenologische Streit*. And Hegel saw it too—". . . if this appears false (*falsch erscheint*) to you nothing further can be said. . ."[48] The proof in question would then fail, committed as it was from the outset to a strict conception of demonstrability, its *ekstasis* before the requirements of this *episteme*, would inevitably derive by a certain hubris. Its claim succumbed in fact to a certain 'dogmatism,' as he said in the earlier writing, a text that provoked perhaps an ironical return on its author:

> [D]ogmatism, if consistent, is bent not on contest but surrender,
> not on enforced but voluntary annihilation, on quiet abandonment
> of oneself to the absolute object. Any thought of resistance and
> of contentious self-assertion that has found its way into dogmatism
> comes from a system better than dogmatism. However, in consis-
> tent dogmatism, that surrender has a purely aesthetic side (*eine
> reinästhetische Seite*).[49]

Still, in the 1795 text Schelling had in a sense seen both the limitations as well as the accomplishments of such a position. Here "there seemed to be no danger that criticism would demonstrate more than the indemonstrability of your system"[50]—that is not to say either the falsity or the contradictory character of its assertion. And, if Schelling's 1795 text quite rightly did not openly affirm such an aesthetic 'dogmatism,' he was aware in any case that the problem of the position's indemonstrability would neither simply bar the event's 'clarity,' its 'provocation,' nor its status as a *Factum*, one that was, to speak Husserlian, "rationality motivated," and one whose authentic status or "legitimacy," consequently, could not simply be denied.[51] And that seemed sufficient for the evidence in question....

VII

The wonder perhaps is how Schelling ever thought otherwise—how he came to hold that the phenomenon in question *evoked a proof* that was in the strict sense decisive. Having disconnected this 'revelation' from science, from conceptual adequacy, from objective certainty, from the hope of ever overcoming the 'contradiction' between the finite and the infinite that confronts the imagination, what seems miraculous perhaps is that Schelling still believed that recourse to 'science,' to conceptual adequacy, to objective certainty, could be had. What he had claimed instead of the phenomenon was that "the unexpected concurrence" (228) beyond all grounds showed that the 'contradiction,' or better the incommensurability between the finite and the infinite, was "one that is not worth the trouble of resolving" (226). That is, the phenomenon was undeniable and yet not strictly demonstrable, not amenable to a demonstration that would, to speak Platonically, come through the *agon* of refutation unscathed. It was the recognition that, as Husserl would say of the logic of the phenomenological in general, *"adequacy and apodicticity* of evidence *need not go hand in hand."*[52] And if the evidence were 'clear,' without ever being capable of being made 'distinct' *simpliciter*, this did not entail that it could not undergo further 'clarification,' articulation, or revision. What was entailed was only that no definite, final, univocal, or strict judgment—no determinate reflection, in the Kantian sense—could be provided for it.

The wavering Schelling recognized concerning products of imagination undermined his claims with respect to them. It opened up, consequently, a certain equivocation in the classical dictum, 'de gustibus non est disputandum,' one that remained unthought in Schelling. De facto, dispute does in fact occur with respect to works of art. Decidability does not. Adequacy, univocal 'distinctness,' is never reached. Perfect adequacy would require, the Cartesians had declared, an intuition. Kant agreed, but denied finite intellects such presentation. Hence he declared the exposition of concepts to be at best probable.

But the work of art's *Aus-sicht* must be seen to open up *another* kind of *disputandum*, one that steps beyond a modernist's account of rationality dependent on strict demonstrability and unequivocal decidability.

Schelling could in a sense be unconcerned that the critical—objectivist program would condemn the experience in question to indemonstrability just because he realized something else was in question—an event that remained rational, if still in the strict sense undecidable. It was the realization that the criteria of decidability or of 'resolution' did not overcome the nature of the evidence, did not bring reasoning to an end with respect to it—if it limited its 'expoundability' to the 'equivocal.' The disputandum in question was rather a matter regarding an *interpretandum*. And, the work of art's *Aus-sicht* is the opening of, the necessity of, and what Heidegger would call the "strictness" of, interpretation—an *Aus-legung.*[53] Schelling at least in one sense had concurred, introducing the theoretical problem of interpretation at the heart of the 1800 *System*, enframing a problem that would haunt the legacy of German idealism thereafter:

> So it is with every true work of art, in that every one of them is susceptible of infinite interpretation (*Auslegung*) as though it contained an infinity of purposes (*Absichten*), while yet one is never able to say whether this infinity has lain within the artist himself, or resides only in the work of art. (225, translation altered)[54]

VIII

Equally the opening in question was one that classical 'hermeneutics' had always overlooked, an opening where incommensurability, undecidability, and the conflict of interpretation were strictly speaking insurmountable, subject to a fundamental contingency. The *interpretandum* here invokes the failure of conceptual commensurability, its opening out onto an other, an *Aus-ein-ander-setzung* that was in the strict sense (but only in the 'strict' sense) incomprehensible. Interpretation always underdetermined the object. Not only was it the case that 'we understand in a different way if we understand at all,' but the *interpretandum* was itself differentiated, withdrawing from the grasp of the concept, opening out onto what, as Schelling put it, remained "unexpected," the sundering of subsumption, an experience in that thought is 'subjected' instead to what escapes it. Artistically it was the encounter with the sublime, a surpassing that was an *Über-raschung* from which no concept could find the requisite resolution of Schelling's conclusion. The work of art, the *interpretandum*, far from providing the requisite homogeneity for a science of knowledge, was rather thought's utter provocation. It would always involve a heterogeneity that thought attempted but failed to subsume, to grasp. The *interpretandum* of necessity then left as many questions unanswered as those for which it provided answers. And, if it remained the case that it was to be granted a rationality and a justification which escaped the commitments of modernism and strict demonstrability, that is, if a 'logic' of interpretation with respect to it must be vindicated, it is true as well that it invoked a margin that interpretation must respect, and in this regard a fundamental unintelligibility.[55]

Hegel, as has become evident, could only deny it. As he claimed in the greater *Logic* regarding reflective judgment, "What is thus found only comes to be through being left behind."[56] Positing and presupposing at the same time, the *Aus-legung* of reflective judgment gets lost in a play of indeterminacy, again a "relation to otherness," that could not contain its own ground and could not be strictly grounded.[57] And if he too had thereby glimpsed the problem of interpretation, he denied it access to the Idea. The Symbolic Idea of art remains always on its own "undetermined," an abstract universal; arbitrary, estranged, "neither completed, nor to be completed."[58]

In this final denunciation Hegel may well have finished off a long history that would subsume the work of art beneath an Idea, providing, thereby, both its determination and adjudication, the destiny of the articulation of beauty (*kalon*), of what is most radiant (*ekphanestaton*) and its grace (*charis*), within the text of philosophy. If it can indeed be claimed that Hegel's condemnation is in this regard the determination of its most, or perhaps last metaphysical moment, Schelling's 'Idea,' on the contrary, however briefly, and for the most part unthought, was its *over*determination—certainly its spur, by a semantic density that always exceeded determination.

IX

In one of those apocalyptic texts that defines the genre of his *écriture*, Walter Benjamin stated, "[T]he aesthetic of the painter, the poet, *en etat de surprise*, of art as the reaction of one surprised, is enmeshed in a number of pernicious romantic prejudices."[59] What remains 'pernicious' about Schelling's own romanticism was the belief and the 'proof' it constructed that the *Über-raschung* in question could be overcome, that the work *solved*, indeed concluded ratiocination. It was a belief that, once having recognized the limits of the concept, reinstituted still a metaphysics of the work of art (perhaps metaphysics as such), seeing it once more simply as "the sensuous manifestation of the good," a *parousia* presenting now the *Uridentität* of subject and object.[60] It was the certainty that this claim itself would not be overtaken by an insurmountable undecidability. And, as such, it involved, as has been seen, a claim by which Hegel, "insiduously perhaps, is close by," as Michel Foucault put it, when "truly to escape Hegel involves an exact appreciation of the price we have to pay to detach ourselves from him."[61] Schelling still believed, that is, that the *agon* of interpretation could be undone—if nothing else in the claim that his own *récit* concerning the work of art provided the literal sign, the meta-récit for all that had been claimed to be strictly indemonstrable, the incommensurable that withdrew from any subjective grasp. What was pernicious then in Schelling's account was precisely the claim to have demonstrated that the proof regarding the incommensurable was not itself overtaken and held within that other incommensurability on which he depended— *inter alia* in preserving the withdrawal of the aesthetic from the concept of what he called *criticism*. It involved a profound forgetfulness—that this incommensurable/incommensurability was as well the site of an undecidability, one about which Jacques Derrida has written, perhaps himself still too paralyzed by it, that "[t]he philosopher, the chronicler, the theoretician in general, and at the limit everyone in writing is. . .taken by surprise."[62]

Still, that such a *surprise* would not destroy ratiocination is as obvious as that it could not complete it. With regard to works of art, as has become evident, it is, on the contrary, precisely what *invokes* the necessity of ratiocination by a sort of wonder that is as archaic and as perhaps unanswerable as metaphysics itself.[63] But it forces the recognition, as well, that the work of art will never be fully adequated, will need, consequently, to enforce on the concept a certain respect for what escapes and a certain respect for the failure of the critical project to account for it. And it is perhaps just in this respect, as Adorno put it, that "[o]n and through the trajectory of rationality, mankind becomes aware through art of what rationality has erased from memory."[64] Equally, it should be noted, Adorno saw it too; "the artist has to be surprised by what he creates," though he linked it to the experimenta-tion of art of the 1930s.[65] Nonetheless, it was for him (not without a certain repetition of Schelling's metaphysics) the expression of a more fundamental fact about works of art: "They seek to translate the memory of shudder (*Schauer*), incommensurable as it was in pre-historical times, into such terms as can be understood by man."[66]

X

Still, if the 'incommensurability' of the work of art remains insurpassable, and if in the strict sense, as has been seen, art remains, consequently, undecidable, and thus, 'helpless,' the question of art's decline, the charge of the modern's nihilism, or its altern, the call for a return to classical origins, can receive no simple endorsement. Not simply because both answers fall before the limits of a critique underwritten by healthy skepticism. Indeed, both answers in fact depend precisely on critique, depend on simple rules of correspondence and access to the keys for deciphering a code that does not exist. They must, that is, have already decided...

Schelling in fact too, in a sense had decided, already committing himself to a certain "melancholy" enshrouding works of art, convinced that the true time of art's flourishing, when its power was capable of informing a *mythos* that would provide a unity for cultural practices, was complete. Now, on the contrary, he claimed, "there is a breach (*Trennung*) seemingly beyond repair" (232). Even after the ecstatic proof of the 1800 *System*, it marked a final breach and failure within the text of art's elevation. It was, after all, a text that remained a *"Wissenschaft"* claiming to adequately and objectively render the work of art's incommensurability into concepts. And, this melancholy too perhaps marked the blinking recognition that art could not decide what could not be decided on other grounds. No more than theory could decide the work of art's provocation, could the latter decide, could it *conclude* theory. No *Konsequenz-ästhetik* could itself be grounded. And it meant as well that the work of art would not remain in any unaltered sense, at least, intelligible by means of the classical *concept* of the beautiful. Its truth could neither be simply subsumed nor subsume.

In fact three years before the 1800 *System*, Friedrich von Schlegel had already written, "The principle of contemporary art is not the beautiful, but the characteristic (*Charakteristische*), the interesting and the philosophical."[67] It was in a sense the decline, but certainly the logical entailment outlined by the failure of Schelling's *monstre* regarding the strict objectivity of the work of art: "take away objectivity from art and it ceases to be what it is, and becomes philosophy" (223). But it perhaps marked, equally, a failure within the concept of the beautiful itself. There is a sense in which the concept of the beautiful remained too ideo-logical, too assured, and to this extent, too metaphysical to simply capture the work of art. If a test of a theory's value is its predictive capacity, Schlegel's account gains explanatory force. The concept of the beautiful in fact increasingly disappeared from accounts of art, finding no univocal and ready application in the art of this century. If it remained true that those writing in the wake of its archive have provided still the best path for grasping the trace of an archaic lineage within the art of a Klee, a Chagall, a Schönberg, a Mies, a Rothko, or an Andre, their protocols have found no easy intelligibility in the modernist challenges of a Beckett, a Bacon, a Cage, a Warhol, or a Beuys, for whom the *propre* of art has been directly placed in question, spurred by a moment over which the beautiful seemingly could no longer hold sway. It involved a moment in which, rather, as Adorno perhaps rightly put it, the radiance had become black—and its artists, like Nietzsche's tortured Apollinian martyrs aware of disillusion remained terror stricken, horrified by all that idealization had apparently excluded.[68]

The difference between these figures, these two *topoi*, their dissonance, to reinvoke Adorno's musicological trope, is the *mise en abyme* of the modern itself, an indecision that bequeathes a certain tension to its heirs, a tension, moreover, that would always verge on simply turning eclectic, dissolving itself in the illusion that mistook the undecidable for the merely relative. The result amounted to disarming the force of art's voice, its summons, or *An-rede*, as Hegel blinkingly put it—and perhaps thereby its truth.[69] It involved, as has been seen, a truth for which modernism has always had a dearth of concepts, faced with the threat of an *ekstasis* that was as ancient as the question of the truth of art, and the question of art's sacred past.

Schelling too, fully in line with its overdetermination, still appealed to this past for interpretation. As has been seen, the evidence that the work of art manifests is one before which thought finds itself *uberrascht und begluckt*: blessed. The work of art never was a simple 'fact,' notwithstanding Schelling's commitments concerning what he called from the outset of the *System* its *Evidenz* (1). It is rather an *Offenbarung*, a revelation, a category for which modernism has no resources. Heidegger was perhaps not far removed from this site in tracing the *phainomenon* of phenomen-ology (and ultimately the aesthetic) back to the problem of *das Offenbare*, "that which shows itself, the self-showing, the revealed (*das was sich zeight, das Sichzeigende, das Offenbare*)."[70] It is a site to which Julia Kristeva too, closer perhaps to Benjamin, has had recourse:

> *Revelatio* translates *Apocalypsis*; is, uncovering, the unveiling of a truth, the vision of an impossible future, the annunciation of an explosion; thus a *gnosis*; knowledge (*connaissance*) but also a relation of intimation. Neither becoming philosophical (*aletheia*) nor wisdom (*sophia*), the revelation is the intimate irruption of a representation that places me at risk.. [71]

If Schelling himself would later demure from the path of this trope, in fact invoking the term's fully literal sense in composing a *Philosophie der Offenbarung*[72] and reconstituting its predicates strictly in the domain of the theological, his 1800 *Augenblick* struggled by means of it to articulate the work of art's *Anrede*. It was an *Anrede* whose evidence, one that "could not be denied," nonetheless could neither comply with strict proof, a provocation then that occurred without recourse to simple refutation, opening instead on another evidence that distanced itself from the critical tribunal, summoning the latter's respect precisely in its withdrawal. In so doing it forced a rewriting of what it is to commit the work of art, the *interpretandum* to a text, invoking an extension (*Erweiterung*) to engage the Kantian trope, that forced interpretation beyond all strict foundations—extending, thereby, the reach of the rational—in placing it at risk.[73]

Hegel,
Hermeneutics,
and the Retrieval
of the Sacred

In his 1821 lecture manuscript on the philosophy of religion, Hegel demarcated a split, a dichotomy, perhaps even an *antagonismus* that his lectures on this topic (and perhaps all others, it might be argued) would seek to surmount. "Les sciences exactes [stand] opposed to religion" (I:107). Reason and the Absolute stand dirempted, precisely in lacking an adequate account of their relation, their 'relegation.'[1] As has been widely recognized, pivotally at stake in Hegel's quest was an attempt to surpass the Enlightenment in order to retrieve what had been excluded by its demonstrative demands—all the while not succumbing to irrationalism. And, crucial to such an extension was nothing less than the status of truth, its investment in the rational community, and the transcendence through which both were founded—its status now much contested within contemporary polemics.[2] The task in retrieving what had been excluded by the paradigms of Enlightenment became for Hegel one of revealing the Absolute of 'religion' as philosophy, escaping thereby the oppositions that split demonstration from insight, concept and intuition, the mind and the eye, reason and revelation, *Glauben und Wissen*. Elsewhere, not without acknowledging their "brilliant success," he identified the exact sciences as those of the physical or natural sciences, further explicating their task as one of "ascertaining natural forces and laws" (Ency: §62). He realized too however that limiting the rational to the paradigms of the exact sciences could not occur without ultimate failure—in fact the failure whose trajectory the *Phenomenology* had traced in explicating their undoing by inversion. The explanatory search for the tranquil kingdom of laws suffers from the underdeterminability of understanding (HP: §150f). The Absolute that Reason requires remains still absconded in this realm. The attempt to identify the diremption of conceptual plurality with truth in the strict sense resulted in Hegel's own version of conceptual hell—the inverted world, a world where the difference between *explanans* and *explanandum* reigns supreme.

Correspondingly, the religions of modernity (either as public reason, i.e. that underwritten by the demonstrative demands of Enlightenment, or its denial, the subjective pietism of "private reason") remain religions of masks, ones in which the "supreme being is inwardly empty and dead" (I:126). The Enlightenment itself, accordingly, could be designated as "the ultimate pinnacle of the formal culture of our time" (III:344). With it, however, the finite has become cut loose from its moorings. In the wake of Spinoza and Schelling, who had similarly argued for the identity of philosophy and religion, we would require a new *Naturphilosophie*—or so would be Hegel's strategy in the

Encyclopedia. In fact even Fichte had declared in his own 1806 *Religionslehre*, a work characterized by Hegel in terms of its "stiff originality with the silent gathering of new ideas," that the need had arisen for the most radical or "profound (*teifste*) metaphysics and ontology."[3] And, as will become evident, from the outset it provoked a hermeneutics whose status remained unwieldy.

Equally from the outset, however, it was clear that this radical ontology could not form a mere correction for physics. Hegel himself in any case was aware of his own shortcomings, his own "lack of experience," as he put it, as a physicist (Let:334). The point at stake instead involved a refusal to allow the practices of the physical sciences to dominate the experience of the rational. It was incumbent on philosophy to think otherwise than physics—precisely to retrieve all that had escaped it. Hence the necessity of confronting religion anew.

Still, if "the time seems to have arrived" for philosophy to mend its ways with religion, "this linkage between them is nothing new" (I:153). Indeed Hegel himself—perhaps more than he knew—turned to the mythemes of the past, endorsing, for example, the neo-Platonism of the patristics, and claiming that with scholasticism philosophy had become identical with theology, and theology with philosophy. If he was openly willing to condemn his romantic colleagues "post-modern" return to the religions of the past (Let:154], he too would claim at least this much, that "the theology of the Middle Ages thus stands much higher than that of modern times." (HP:III:67) Here, as elsewhere in the Hegelian systematics, history was by no means simply the archive of our ruins, a gallery of images sublated. "Memory, the Mnemosyne of the ancients," to which he had appealed since the earliest Jena writings, is not "a dead temple" but must be made to disappear in order that its meaning may be conceptually grasped (HP:III:15). Memory is the site in which Reason itself undergoes a certain self-enlightenment and emerges from its own darkness, its own "nightlike pit" [Ency:§453], the condition of the possibility for knowledge as such—and the opening, thereby, of "the Holy place of Truth itself" (HP:I:63).

Knowledge depends on this encounter and its appropriation, not only on a calculative but substantial appropriation, and not only on *phronesis*, therefore, but *anamnesis*. "Not until knowing *inwardizes, recollects* [*errinert*] itself out of immediate being, does it through this mediation find essence," Hegel had argued in the *Logic* (WdL:390). Hence essence is past, timelessly past, being. And, religion becomes then itself an essential step in reason's liberation from the image, the eruption of *Darstellung* within *Vorstellung*, and the plastic manifestation of Spirit's figuration, its *Geistesgestaltung*.

II

For all of his idealist rage against materialism—here and elsewhere—the argument that would surpass the religion of modernity is not that of the irrationalist simply privileging what escapes physics and the realm of finite certainty. Nor is Hegel's argument even in the strict sense of the word simply 'antiempirical,' being, he claimed, fully verificationist in the end—even with regard to the rationality of belief itself.

The turn to *protodoxa* nonetheless remains always marginally dogmatic. Phenomenology in the end always results in the undoing of consciousness.[4] On its own, Hegel realized, philosophical faith loses all connection with legitimation. Pietism of any sort always loses its authority and objectivity—in his terms, the objectivity of the church. It admits equally "a belief in the divinity of the Dalai Lama, the ox, or the monkey—thus, so far as it goes, narrowing Deity down to the simplest terms, a 'Supreme Being'" (Ency:§63). The search for the logical simples of religion always misses the complex relation between semantics and syntactics.[5] The religions of the Enlightenment, in short, remain abstract.

The necessity that is required instead will surpass even that of demonstrative necessity, "the way that a geometrical theorem is proved." The latter, although a "subjective convenience," Hegel declared, remains insufficient precisely insofar as it remains "indifference toward the content" (III:246). Coherence, as he had learned from Kant and Jacobi, will not deliver the object. Instead it remains "bound within the circle of the rigid necessity of the finite," at best implicitly defining its object without sufficient proof: that is, the revelation of the transition to the real (WdL: 817). Hence the necessity of transcending reflection, mere thought forms whose claims in isolation remain essentially fanatical (III:243). Beyond the naïveté of pietism and the abstraction of reflection will lie consequently "the third estate of the community of philosophy" (III:247).

Appeals to the rational community here are, however, equally complex. Fichte, before Hegel, had claimed the transcendental need for communicative symbols to assure identity and coherence within rational assertion. The problem for him was whether the symbols should be understood in what he called the 'Catholic' mode, that is, as taking those symbols prejudged by tradition as ultimate, or whether, on the contrary, the symbols in question should be taken, if you will, counterfactually, in the 'Protestant' mode, "proceeding from the symbols into the infinite."[6] Schelling, on the other hand, equally criticizing "the imbecilic representatives of the Enlightenment" while holding that Catholicism could not be the whole of "a modern poesy and mythology," still claimed that, outside it, "one can expect *only* subordination to content, forced movement without serenity, and mere subjective usage," an event in which "mythology degenerates into an object for *use*."[7] Still, no one seems to have gone so far as Schlegel, for whom, rather than Sophocles or Shakespeare, "True idealism has gone on since Christ—in the fathers of the Church, the Scholastics and members of the sects."[8]

In fact, as has become evident, even Hegel himself would not simply disagree, however. And, it might be argued, no more than he could understand Schlegel in other matters did he understand him here. What is clear instead, in any case, is that he could not endorse what he described as the simple adoption of "past world views...as in recent times many have done for art's sake" (Aesth:606). Instead he claimed the rupture he identified both with Protestantism and the opening of the modern age (HP:§ III) to be at least this necessary, that it opened precisely in the epistemic refusal to confuse images and things (HP:I:73), forcing instead a venture beyond the symbolic both to appropriate and to vindicate its meaning.

Still, what the Enlightenment had missed—and Fichte included, for whom "the ego retains the significance of the individual" (HP:III:499) was the mediating role of the cultus itself; that is, the event delivering rationality from subjectivism (I:193). It would not suffice, consequently, with 'Protestantism,' to "require that human beings should believe only what they know" (I:456). Indeed Hegel is in this sense at least not unwilling to see the cult as essential to the rational in general, claiming that "philosophy [too] is a continual cultus" (I:447). Nonetheless, it is clear too that what binds the cult cannot be reduced to mere events, but the rationality of belief (I:192). Hence the "monstrous antithesis" that divides not only 'religion' but the modern age—the alternation (*Abwechslung*) or bad infinite that characterizes belief as well as the splitting (*Entzweiung*) of the self it affects (I:285).

III

The problem of this venture then can be specifically formulated as one of moving beyond the chiasm that both opens and undermines modernity—the crisis in legitimation awaiting the abstract solutions of the Enlightenment. It is the solution to this problem that the *Philosophy of Religion* declares to be the need of our time, one that extends not only throughout the philosophy of religion, but all those neighboring disciplines it interfaces: history, politics, the aesthetic, and philosophy itself. For all that his turn to history shares with romanticism, however, Hegel's claim is precisely the opposite. If legitimation requires the community, it is true too that the latter requires the former in transforming its mythic past. "The symbolum or *regulae fidei* itself is no longer regarded as something binding" (I:169)—the perdurance of the cultus itself is not on its own self-legitimating. It cannot itself, that is, escape the demand for legitimation.

In this regard, moreover, the nostalgia of romanticism for the lost origin becomes perfectly intelligible. There is, as Schelling realized, a breach with the old myths seemingly beyond repair. And, if Hegel was as convinced as anyone concerning the impoverishment of the *symbolon* vis à vis the demonstrative demands of Enlightenment, he realized too, against his romantic predecessors, that any reconciliation concerning *Glauben und Wissen* would need to acknowledge the demands of the rational—in his terms, the necessity of the exposition of the signs of reason beyond their symbolic vestige.

Precisely in this regard the breach in question turns logical, a matter that requires both more than explanation and more than mere experience. Instead, to render experience into concepts ratiocinatively by "inference and exegesis," that is, "to embark on the process of reasoning [and] reflecting," is to enter into "the process of interpretation" (III:258). It is this process that separates the task of legitimation from all historical philology. It is moreover the necessity that accompanies this exposition that separates theology, *Wissen* from historical description, and, consequently, the iteration of the truths of faith (*Glauben*) from simple repetition, simple "slavery to the letter," as Schelling put it.[9] Hence Hegel's ridicule of the irrational redundancy of theologians practicing the merely "historical attitude toward religion." The result, he declared, is comparable to "countinghouse clerks, who keep the ledgers and accounts of other people's wealth" (I:128). Instead, the legitimation of the past precisely requires the breach opened by interpretation.

> But where interpretation (*Interpretation*) is not mere explanation of the words (*Worterklärung*) but discussion (*Erörterung*) of the content and elucidation of the sense (*Erklärung der Sinne*), it must introduce its own thoughts into the word that forms the basis [of the faith]. There can only be mere interpretation when all that happens is that one word is replaced by another with the same scope. If interpretation is *elucidation*, then other categories of thought are bound up with it. A development of the word is a progression to further thoughts. (I:123)

Reflection in this regard, as Hegel put it in the *Logic*, both posits and presupposes at the same time, never simply a matter of "reading and repetition" (III:258). Consequently, "the argumentative always involves assumptions" (I:167), being free neither from the conflicts of interpretation nor the vagaries of ideology.[10] Commentaries acquaint us both with the object and "the mode of thought of their age." Here too, consequently, things remain underdetermined: "The most sharply opposed views are exegetically demonstrated by theologians on the basis of scripture, and in this way so-called holy scripture has been made into a wax nose. All of the heresies have appealed to scripture, as has the church" (I:123).

IV

The lectures on the *History of Philosophy* equally alluded to the problem indicated by this 'wax nose,' precisely in denying strategies of reformation that would confine the true spirit to that of the letter. Hegel realized equally that "we find what we look for, and [that] just because I make it clear to myself, I make my conception, my thought, a factor in it." Still, forcing an admission one does not find often in Hegel's text, he claimed that if the letter, the *Buchstab*, then depends on the Spirit, "it will depend absolutely on what the nature of the Spirit is, for spirits are very different" (*denn die Geister sind sehr verschieden*) [HP:III:13f]. In fact as the *Religion* lectures concur: "the most contrasting viewpoints have been elicited from the letter of the text because the spirit did not grasp it" (I:168). If Anselm had his presuppositions, so did Kant. The Medievals' appeal to the concept of perfection and the Moderns' appeal to the foundation of subjectivity, to "concrete humanity," Hegel realized, stand in this regard in strict confrontation (III:183).

The utter opposite of the immediate appeal to the appearances occurs then with the assertion of their denial, that interpretation of the Absolute transforms itself into the history of our errors, "for through comprehension the infinite is annulled and downgraded to the finite" (I:135). What results, that is, in accord with the protocols of exact science, is merely syntactic play, the play of transcendence itself dissolved within "the coherent connectedness of the determinate," merely a nexus of connections—and hence, "a system on its own account but without solid substance" (I:103). Even were the demonstrative demands of the Enlightenment fulfilled, they would, in one sense at least, immediately turn against themselves, undercutting the univocal character of the rational. As Hegel puts it: "the fact that there are a number of proofs already speaks against them, since a proof must on its own account be adequate and exhaustive if it is suited to the nature of the object" (I:144). The elevation to the Absolute instead will of necessity be interpretative, requiring as its most urgent condition the vindication of an interpretative access. "This spirit that interprets must legitimate itself" (I:168).

The experience of the Absolute, however, "the rationality of the Idea" (I:281) requires an extension beyond proof, requires the exposition of its elevation, the "quintessential movement of spirit" (II:726)—and requires, therefore, the vindication of interpretation: requires, that is, hermeneutics. Moreover, if Hegel saw dialectics as itself fulfilling this extension, not in naively denying the confrontation but in providing "a unification in which the different is not extinguished" (I:173), it is true too that dialectic comes at the end of demonstration—not, as Aristotle thought, at its beginning. As Hegel put it in discussing the work of Schleiermacher, "Dialectic is the last thing to arise and to maintain its place" (HP:III:508).

V

The problem of interpretation was not simply absent from Hegel's immediate predecessors, of course. And, even a cursory reading indicates the uneasy surpassing it demanded. In his *Religion Within the Limits of Reason Alone* (1793) Kant remained comfortable with the formal constraints of understanding. Troubled nonetheless by the demonstrative shortfall of the empirical, Kant could still claim both that revelation (*Offenbarung*) would require conceptual exposition and exegetical interpretation, while remaining at the same time confident regarding the requisite criterion for its explication. For Kant, however, the criterion was easily imported from the domain of pure practical reason, providing thereby "universal practical rules of a religion of pure reason."[11] Kant's confidence was in fact unambiguous. He was willing to admit that the criterion remained valid even in the instance of pure eisegesis. "Frequently this interpretation (*Auslegung*) may, in the light of the text (of the revelation), appear forced—it may often really be forced; and yet if the text can possibly support it, it must be preferred to a literal interpretation that either contains nothing at all [helpful] to morality or else actually works counter to moral incentives."[12]

Kant's immediate followers were stricken with his failure, one that doubtless followed the itinerary of debates on the spirit and letter of Kantianism itself.[13] Schelling however was direct on this issue. Although himself fully opposed to mere literary exegesis, precisely on the grounds that it divorced religion from its speculative truth, Schelling's 1802 *On University Studies* declared that Kant's moral reductionism "cannot be achieved without misinterpretation (*Missdeutung*)."[14] Similarly, having in his own *Critique of All Revelation* followed the strictness of Kant's view to their (apparent) conclusion, Fichte's 1806 *Religionslehre* turned more cautious in its views:

> As to the principle of interpretation (*Auslegung*) which I apply to this as well as to all other authors of the Christian Scriptures, it is the following:—so to understand them as if they had really desired to say something and so far as their words permit, as if they had said what is right and true:—a principle that seems to be in accordance with justice and fairness. But we are wholly opposed to the hermeneutical principle (*hermeneutische Princip*) of a certain party, according to which the most earnest and simple expressions of those writers are regarded as mere images and metaphors, and thus explained and reexplained away.[15]

To think that the authors of the Christian Scriptures did not intend to say something would be a curious thing, of course. As Gadamer has put it, hermeneutics (like any other assertion or intentional relation) must start from the position that a person seeking to understand something has a relation to the object.[16] Yet it points to the difficulty that confronts the interpretations at stake. As charitable as Fichte's claim was apparently, it could equally be claimed to be fully consistent even with the *Critique's* definition of revelation as invoking the problem of "translating (*Uebertragung*) something subjective into a being outside us...(an) alienation (*Entäusserung*) (which) is the real *principle of religion*."[17] Moreover, whereas Fichte's appeal to the literal perhaps undercut the reductionist pretenses of the Enlightenment (with regard to religion, for example, the possibility of miracles) at the same time it cut short the romantic's speculative conception of the symbolic as the unity of the finite and the infinite, the immanent and the transcendent, one whose neo-Platonic expositions surely remained pivotally at stake in the failure Fichte attempted to circumscribe.

Within the requisites of philosophical modernism religion would be inseparable from the risk of a certain fetishization, an act (intentional or otherwise) unmindful of the distance that separates the infinite and the finite, one Hegel would aptly describe as "the arbitrary selection of this or that as an idol" (II:291). Hence the problem of what Husserl had already recognized in analyzing the logic of intentionality as the ontological difference (*ontologische Unterschied*), the problem (and the *intentionality*) of parts and wholes, an event binding the conditioned and the unconditioned, "independent and non-independent contents."[18] Still, the *locus classicus* of romantic hermeneutics had been direct in its appeal to *Anschauung* to solve this antinomy between the inside and the outside, subject and object.

VI

When in 1805 Schleiermacher began the aphorisms that would originate modern hermeneutics, he began in the assurance that the problem of the plurality of meanings could be overcome only in the recognition that understanding is an act, a *factum*, and its accomplishment a matter of insight (*Anschauung*). Moreover he was convinced that its enactment was one by which "all the false dialectical distinctions among the various senses (*Sinnen*) can be avoided."[19] In fact in all this he would only be reiterating what he had already claimed elsewhere concerning the elevation of thought to the infinite, the event in which again "thousands might be moved religiously in the same way and yet each...might designate his feeling by different symbols."[20]

If since his 1799 *Reden* Schleiermacher too had sought to recapture the effective role of religion lost within the Enlightenment, again exchanging rational thought for intuition, his account remained bound by the subjective categories of the merely aesthetic. "True science is complete vision; true practice is culture and art self-produced; true religion is sense and taste for the Infinite."[21] Accordingly, here "everything is to be found immediately, and not proved from something else." The problem of ratiocination and justification; that is, "combination and connection belong to another sphere."[22] Religion for its part contains "a capacity for unlimited manysidedness in judgment," one, consequently, unencompassable by the demand for demonstration. If idealism is in need of religion, it stands unencompassable within the "miserable love of system."[23] Hence already in advance of Hegel's condemnation that, by separating the Absolute from the notion, "the glory of Philosophy is departed" in Schleiermacher's work, the latter had already recoiled from "the dominion of the mere notion" and "the mechanical erection of systems." Forty years later Schelling would again state Schleiermacher's objection. And yet Schelling refused just as strongly Schliermacher's tack. What was at stake instead involved a matter of exhibiting the rationality of revelation itself.[24]

It was, of course, precisely this chiasm between intuition and knowledge, belief and proof that had spurred the origins of the *Philosophy of Religion*. Indeed the relation between philosophy and religion was neither new to Hegel's thought, nor perhaps to any thought that would trace the internal transgression of modernism. The topic itself in fact formed the infrastructure of his itinerary, providing the matrix of reason's step beyond the abstractions afflicting the rational.

VII

Hegel's surpassing, however, was not without its own permutations and transformations and not without both the conflict and disequilibrium that underscored his account of the emergence of true harmony. The ultimate union by which philosophy and religion would culminate in Reason's realization, both as subject and substance, was, if not most or at least initially, one in origin that (in 1798 at least) was posited as a fulfillment *not* of Reason but of Faith. Moreover, if the dialectic on which this origin depended was already explicated, Hegel realized too that the proof of unity could not itself be strictly legitimated:

> [I]f it is shown that the opposed limited terms could subsist as such, that they would have to cancel themselves [or one another— *sich aufheben mussten*], and that even to be possible they presuppose a union (just to be able to show that they are opposed, the union is presupposed) then it is thereby proven, that they have to [*müssen*] be united, that the union ought to exist [*söllen*]. But that the union does exist, is not thereby proven, rather this mode of presence of the *Vorstellung* of it is believed [matter of faith]; and it cannot be proved. . .[26]

In short, granted the distinction between possibility and necessity, that is, the distinction of judgment itself, "Being can only be believed in" and "faith is not being but a reflected being."[27] Hegel's later exposition of the ontological argument would, of course, concur regarding the demonstrability thesis, but not about what he termed earlier the bound character of the reflection itself. What became all important was the event of the elevation in question, one that, far from being bound by the reflective *Voraussetzung* of its conceptual grasp, would yield a spiritual subjectivity that is "all-interpreting, all knowing" (*alles deutend, alles wissend* III:225).

This omniscience was not simply a matter of intuition or immediacy, being more perhaps a matter of "a longer way around," to use Plato's terms, one in which the religious was an essential moment. Equally, and for the same reason, the belief in question would not involve the simple demonstrative affirmation of a positive *credo*—in fact, far from it. If Christianity for Hegel provided the means for the fulfillment of both reason and religion, it did so not by the simple subsumption of reason beneath religion. If, finally, Christianity was in fact for Hegel absolutely rational, that is, "strictly adequate to the Idea," it was true too that it was so only insofar as it fulfilled adequate conditions of rationality, insofar, that is, as it provided the revelation of spirit to spirit, and insofar as revelation was itself open to "verification (*Bewahrheitung*) and absolute proof (*Beweis*)."[28] If Christianity was for Hegel, as it had been for Lessing and Schelling before him, the completion of mythology in the eruption of *logos* from *mythos*, allegory, and *Vorstellung* (I:399f), it was true too that it was never simply extricable from the "speculative good Friday" in which it emerged to overcome the "infinite grief of the finite"—and the demonstrative failures of the Enlightenment (FK:191).

In fact, the decisive moment of Christianity as religion for Hegel was in the end its undercutting of the 'positivity' of religion in this sense, providing both the mediation and the *Aufhebung* that had been glimpsed in the 1798 text. This need for reconciliation underlies the elevation Reason sought, fully aware of the cleavage between the finite and the infinite. It is just this recognition of the cleavage as absolute that most characterizes Hegel's account of religion and Christianity in particular—precisely insofar as it marks the interruption of 'pagan' myth.

> It (Christianity) has its very beginning in an absolute cleavage (*Entzweiung*) [and there is felt] need only in cleavage. Pagan religion contains (from the start) a more serene state of reconciliation. The Christian religion is not so serene; (it) awakens the need itself, takes its start from anguish, awakens this anguish, disrupts the natural unity of spirit (i.e. the unity of humanity with nature); it disturbs natural peace. (I:105).

Notwithstanding his 'positive' theological gloss concerning what he called *Christianity*, Hegel would, of course be neither the first nor the last to see the 'cleavage' at stake as the complex opening of Reason.[29] Pierre Duhem a century later would similarly see the cleft between the finite and the infinite as the opening of experimental reasoning in medieval accounts, a cleavage that, as Hegel too had claimed, underdetermines the finite's conceptualization of what escapes it, a cleft no appeal to the immediacy of the empirical might decisively overcome.[30] It was instead precisely this difficulty that ruptures all theory—as much as all *doxa*—from within. Again, there is the theoreticians' dilemma, one that involves something of an infinite return. There is no simple way into theory and no way out of it. And, theoreticians would endlessly attempt to account for the excess at stake by dissolving it. If Duhem, on the basis of this speculative excess attempted to render dogma objectively true—precisely because it would escape the vagaries of theory—critical theorists like Hans Albert would on the same grounds attempt to dissolve it.[31] Both, however, would still in a sense share in the same attempt. Both still remained committed, that is, to what Hegel criticized as the formalist idea of *Wissenschaftslehre* and its "attempt at a consistent system that would have no need of the religion and ethics that are foreign to it" (Nat:85). Instead, this *Aussersein* would remain irreducible, its practices both mining and undermined within the search to enframe it. Precisely in this regard, as Schelling had put it in 1806, "though in its search for laws science insists on conclusiveness, it has another side in which it is open and unlimited," one that marks, he declared, "the religion in science."[32]

VIII

Hermeneutics does not—either as a historical or a logical phenomenon— simply evolve out of this opening but presupposes it. This is not to say that either 'religion' or 'hermeneutics' might on its own accomplish what theory could not.[33] In fact, Nietzsche was right in this regard: if the *ekstasis* on which all theory depends were to be resubmitted to the demands of strict proof (*Strenge Wissenschaft*) then it would result *not* in the simple reinstitution of religion and the fulfillment of the Romantics' quest for a new mythology—now in the Enlightenment's wake, under the aegis of 'objectivity'—but instead simply the departure of the gods. Hegel's claim regarding verification and adequation, after all, would in the end be self-refuting, the attempt to make demonstrable what from the start it acknowledged eluded the strict demands of *Verstand*.[34] Even if in the end he thought Anselm "superior" to "the Kantian destruction of the proof" (III:179), Hegel at least realized too that the former's account was not a matter of proof but exposition—depending as much on freedom as necessity, on Spirit's elevation and extension beyond the underdeterminability of the finite. It acknowledged instead inevitably a "deficiency" (*ein Mangel*) with respect to all strict proof—and to ratiocinative representation (I:439).

In this regard, as Jean-Luc Nancy has put it, granted its dependency upon an 'infinity' that escapes from it, if the philosophy of strict science's last or ultimate thought would be the death of God, it is true too, he realized, that nothing would be more godless than a science of belief.[35] Not because it is irrational, but because *doxa* opens always (and only) by means of what Jean-Luc Marion has aptly termed a certain *principle of insufficient reason*, a certain *In-evidence*, to use Coleridge's term.[36] And, for the same reason, nothing would be more mythic than to appeal either to an empirical set of referents or a conventionally arbitrated set of propositions for its foundation when what was at stake involved an extension beyond both. The narratives by which the 'Absolute' becomes articulated in this event then could be neither dissolved nor ultimately vindicated; the possibility through which assertion became ventured instead is inevitably both interrupted and fragmented vis-à-vis its demonstrative deficiency.

Instead, the speculative or hermeneutic expositions that emerge would demand a more radical hermeneutics than such a science, a rationality whose transcendence and revelation would not exclude the "idea of inequality, difference and irreducible alterity"—and which for all that would "not entail the loss of rationality."[37] It would demand a relating, a *religare*—to speak Heideggerean, a "meting out"— that eluded the oppositions between the subjective and the objective, the rational and the sacred, explication and demonstration, theory and practice without sublating them.[38] In the moment of its decision, as Kierkegaard would realize, not without himself succumbing to irrationalism, the system would lie in fragments.[39] Yet this is, as the history of the fragment in philosophical modernism attests, both its comedy and its fecundity— but equally perhaps its rationality, as Hegel's own repetition attests. If, early on, Hegel articulated the unification that eludes proof as "a miracle that we cannot grasp" it is true both that he came to see that "these appearances, wild as they are, are rational" (III:288), and realized as well—in fact from the outset—that this rationality could not be limited to, nor contained by the limits of ratiocinative argument and finite consensus.[40]

As Schelling had realized, consciousness could not bring objectivity out of itself, depending precisely on what from the start escapes it, an event irreducible to any ego—or to any empirical community of egos. Hence, as Hegel saw, the necessity of "thought" to acknowledge its own defrayal, to acknowledge its own *Voraussetzung*, and in this sense once more to acknowledge itself as hermeneutic. The rationality in question, however, resists in the end his solution, the strict *adequatio* of *Realizierung*, of act and expression as much as it does any other— resisting in the end any and all attempts, to use Bataille's (Hegelian) term, of *substantialization*.[41] If instead the 'hermeneutic' opens precisely in dwelling on—openly, inextricably, and doubtless even despite itself—

the trace of all that exceeds it, interpretation of the event in question could arise only (and always) by acknowledging its own fragility. It would arise, that is, only by acknowledging both the extension and the limitations of the "speculative moment." Thereby, the hermeneutic gains warrant only by acknowledging what Hegel called elsewhere the *ambiguous* nature of what is called *experience*, but equally only in acknowledging—while relying on—the plasticity (*plastisität*) of exposition, differentiated within a site whose truth remains always in the end otherwise than proof (PhS: 39, 55).

Fully truncating the limits of the transcendental logic governing such 'adequation,' however, there would be those who would again point to its obvious folly, truncating, that is, the in-principle *in*adequacy, the excess on which the event of this figuration and its 'miracle' depends.[42] The miracle at stake was, to be exact, the event Hegel sought to trace from the outset—again from as early as the Frankfurt fragments—structuring the highway of despair that figures the Hegelian account of experience and that he hoped could be ultimately articulated by means of reconciliation and love, the life of the spirit. It proved to be overdetermined: both the site of Hegel's failure as well as his greatest venture—and in the end the site of what opens both the complex logic of its interpretations as well as the plasticity of the virtues it sought to make possible.[43]

The result would find broad ranging impact among Hegel's followers in all those realms in which his venture would affect theoretical modernism. Not only would the status of 'religion' be at stake, but equally the dichotomies re-ligated in the event at stake; that between the secular and the sacred, the political and the private, nature and culture, institution and conscience—or, in accord with the mythemes in which they had become invested, 'subjective' and 'objective' Spirit. The point is that the narratives by which we articulate this excess would be neither simply surpassed nor simply exonnerated—as 'theologians' as diverse as Bultmann or Rahner, Benjamin or Levinas, Habermas or Lyotard, Irigaray or Kristeva would attest. And all now would similarly be faced with the problem of interpretation as well as the transcendence it still ventured to articulate.

On the *Agon*
of the
Phenomenological:
Intentional Idioms
and the
Foundations of
Justification

One may accept the Brentano thesis either as showing the indispensability of intentional idioms and the importance of an autonomous science of intention, or as showing the baselessness of intentional idioms and the emptiness of a science of intention....My attitude, unlike Brentano's is the second.[1]

Quine's adamant rejection of the intentional in *Word and Object* comes rhetorically perhaps at its climax, in a chapter entitled "Flight from Intension" and in a section on "the double standard." It was a book that became the *locus classicus* of theoretical holism and ushered in, perhaps as much as anything else, the problems of the under-determination of theories and the incommensurability of conceptual frameworks into contemporary thought. And yet if, thereby, it provided weapons for their demise, it occurred still within the penumbra of positivism and the dream of unified science—and in this case its commitment regarding a certain materialism and the methodology of behaviorism. Notwithstanding what Wittgenstein too in this rupture had called the problem of "the variety of interpretation," Quine's theoretical webs, no longer free from what he termed "the beliefs of the moment," remained always underwritten by a certain metaphysical neo-Kantianism, committed still with ease to the 'unmediated' action of "external things on our bodies," the "surface irritations," the direct links of a sentence with "nonverbal stimulation," or what he called perhaps most comprehensively, "the specious present."[2] In so doing he satisfied a modern commitment regarding the necessity that science limit itself to the 'publicly observable' at a time when appeals for foundation within the unanimity of a 'scientific public' and the strictly 'observable' still seemed uncontroversial.

Accordingly, the true account of language and meaning, Quine held (a claim that seemed no less uncontroversial), contained damning consequences for intentional idioms and the theoretical accounts they spawned. The problem with intentional idioms and the theoretical accounts deriving from them, he decreed, confident of what constituted the rational and the scientific, and the demarcation principle that excluded their other, is that they betray a certain 'baselessness.' Their claims are ultimately illusory, ultimately, that is, unjustifiable. The claims that emerge in this domain cannot be verified, cannot be assigned a variable within the logical space of word-world relations. The link of intentionality, in fact, occludes the relationship—and many have taken that fact itself to provide the symptom, the ground, in fact, for demonstrating the existence of the intentional, a criterion by which language wears its intentional origins on its sleeve: beliefs, counter-factuals, the whole lot of those cognitive links that cannot be easily cashed out in some form of the ostensive and the extensional.[3] If the analysis could be successful, then linguistic analysis might itself provide an intentional proof, but perhaps one in the end whose significance would be no less controversial. The anti-intentionalists would always wonder here, as they did with the rise of linguistic analysis in general, whether anything has been grounded thereby. The existence of a particular linguistic idiom—however intransigent—concerning the intentional is simply fortuitous and contingent, positing an animism of the mental corresponding to an animism of the 'nonmental' that has been decisively rejected elsewhere, granted the bulk of scientific practice—a kind of mentalistic phlogiston. The objections of Popper, Hempel, and the rest against linguistic analysis in this regard perhaps should be taken seriously. If we could establish the existence of a nonreducible idiom here, a language game of the intentional that might provide the protocols of intentional 'theory,' would it in the end ever be more than tautologous, incapable of really providing an explanans of the events the theory was invoked to depict? The research program that sought out linguistic evidence, idiomatic criteria for the intentional, was in a sense question begging. Would it in the end have made a difference to the anti-intentionalist?

Still, it might be replied that such a charge has portentous returns lurking for a view seeking to strictly delimit the cognitive—one that affects all litigants. If the proponent of unified science had in fact provided a successful program, if correspondence rules had been established for translating 'mentalese' into the language of physics, what then? If the mental could be mapped onto physical relations, would that place its existence in doubt? If, for example, univocal causal relations could be established for these 'expressions,' would that eventuality in the end disconfirm their own evidence? Would it be possible in principle for a 'public,' 'objective,' 'material' 'observation' to disconfirm the object of intentionalese? Or is there not a categorical difference at work, one by which the hope of a uni-vocal idiom for behavior would be under-written by a simple category mistake, as the analysts called it, and the transcendentalists, a subreption? A successful materialism in this regard could at best demonstrate that intentionality is a 'worldly event' as well as an intentional event, approachable from either side of what Kant was the first to call an antinomy that opens up "two standpoints" from which to conceptualize these events.[4] Nonetheless, granted perhaps the materialist's ability to predict, to produce simplicity and unity within our rational practices, what could be gained by following what is apparently a path to nowhere, or at least a path into a bog "without certain foundations," to paraphrase Bacon, the oracle who, for the sake of the truth of experiment and against the idols of speculation, first broached the genre of modern foundationalism?

II

And yet, those who followed Brentano into the soft ground of intentional idioms thought anything but that the claims regarding these 'idioms' could not be fulfilled and that such a venture could not be epistemically solidified. If one follows Husserl, perhaps the most important, or in any case, the most influential of Brentano's followers, quite the opposite position occurs. From the outset of his work the 'theory' of intentionality carried extreme baggage as part of its claim. Not only, he held, could the idioms of intentionality and the description of its particular experience be justified, but all justification ultimately derived from it. Not only, that is, was the domain of the intentional not 'baseless,' but everything else was baseless without it. Analytic phenomenology, as it emerged in his *Logical Investigations* (1900), was in this regard to provide the foundations of 'pure logic,' its sources and validity. "Phenomenology. . .lays bare the 'sources' from which the basic concepts and ideals of pure logic 'flow,' and back to which they must once more be traced, so as to give them all the 'clearness and distinctness' needed for an understanding, and for an epistemological critique, of pure logic" (I:249–50). Pure logic for Husserl was the science of all grounded explanation, a "theoretically closed set of problems related to the Idea of theory," and as such the "condition for the possibility of science." That such a strict science was possible Husserl had no doubts. And just as Husserl had strong convictions about the need for ultimate foundations here, so too, he had strong optimism about the results to be obtained.

> Everything that is can be known 'in-itself.' Its being is a being definite in content, and documented in such and such 'truths-in-themselves.'. . .What is has its intrinsically definite properties and relations, and if it has natural, thing-like reality, then it has also its quite definite extension and position in space and time, its quite definite ways of persisting and changing. But what is objectively quite definite, must permit of objective determination, and what permits objective determination, must ideally speaking, permit expression through wholly determinate word meanings. To being-in-itself correspond truths-in-themselves, and to these last, fixed unambiguous assertions. (I:321–22)

In one sense the position was neither unique nor new. The formulations have antecedents in the work of Bolzano after whom both Frege and Husserl formulated their projects.[5] Moreover, the position was in a sense, as were other versions of unified science, neo-Kantian. Presupposing an analytic, an inventory of something called strict and exact science, Husserl sought out its conditions, *Erkenntnis aus dem Grunde* (I:225), an inquiry concerning "what makes science science." Yet, whereas most proponents of unified science were to follow what Kant called the *examples* of the physical sciences and the victories won by Newton and Galileo on the battlefield of metaphysics, Husserl's solution to the "playground of the endless quarrels" of theory (IP:17) was in fact to complete the discipline Kant had intended in the *Critique's* discussion of pure logic. Instead of modeling science on one or a set of factual and historical instances, Husserl intended to provide the epistemic ground for the possibility of *knowledge as such* (I:215). The result, Husserl claimed, would be a new and complex discipline, one, nonetheless, he was willing to claim by means of ancient standard, *Wissenschaftslehre* (I:60). This *Wissenschaftslehre* even went beyond Kant's notion of pure or general logic—which, the latter claimed, was completely independent of considerations concerning the critique of knowledge. *All* of the separate sciences, Husserl claimed, including logic, remained "incomplete," containing a "lack of inner clarity and rationality," so long as their foundation had not been clarified (I:58).

There remained a certain incoherence in simply accepting the "examples" of the positive sciences as having acquired rationality, a certain unqualified presupposition. Rather, the condition of the possibility for the emergence of science *as such* must first be established. The idea of pure logic, the "science" of grounds, must necessarily undergo a certain broadening or extension, Husserl claimed, an *"Erweiterung,"* a word, again, with Kantian overtones (I:246). Reason's intrinsic search for unity and foundations within the Kantian system equally forced a rational search for justification beyond the categories and principles of the understanding. Kant, nonetheless, ultimately understood the extensions involved as deductions, prosyllogisms, and episyllogisms leading to transcendental ideas that themselves were ungroundable (e.g., the paralogisms) and undecidable (e.g., the antinomies).

Husserl claimed similarly that the rationality of our cognitive practices depends on an ultimate grounding that would restore ultimate *theoretical* unity (I:225). The theories of the separate sciences remain "incomplete" (I:58) apart from the "justifying proof" (I:107) that established the normative claims of science as such. Nonetheless, their origin could not be simply a conceptual one, that is, not simply, inferentially based. Rather, it is the grounding of inference itself that is in question. Consequently, without the extension that would show the condition of the possibility of their emergence, reason would be lost in a set of infinite regressions. The grounding in question then could not simply be a 'premise.' "All grounds are premises, but not all premises are grounds. Every deduction is indeed necessary i.e. it obeys laws: but that its conclusions follow according to laws (the laws of inference) does not mean that they follow from laws that in a pregnant sense serve to 'ground' them" (I:229). Husserl's account of grounds in the end must involve something more basic than a mere postulate of a deductive system. For deductive systems to be necessary, to be "grounded," for science to be possible, *another* kind of necessity than deduction must be possible, and hence the necessity of an equally 'extended' definition for grounding: "Scientific knowledge is, as such, *grounded knowledge*. To know the ground of anything means to see the necessity of its being so and so" (I:227).

Whereas deduction is one way of 'seeing' the necessity of a state of affairs, it is not the only way—if in fact deductive grounds themselves are to be ultimately grounded. The basic propositions of the theory of knowledge are instead, Husserl claimed, to be obtained in a "purely intuitive fashion" (I:249) with a necessity that is categorically distinct from them. "The propositions that must here be affirmed will plainly be of a different content and character from the basic propositions and theorems of theories of the second group, from, e.g., syllogistic or arithmetical laws" (I:240). They would thereby overcome the problem of metaphysical regression. In this sense, not without a certain positivist ring, as he knew, the basis of "unities of sense" that underlie laws are claimed to be valid "not because we can deduce it from some metaphysical postulate or other, but because we can show it by an intuitive, completely indubitable procedure" (Id:129). Nonetheless, this should not be taken to mean that there is a single method or subject matter to the various sciences—but only that the necessity that underlies their 'showing' was itself identical. Husserl was in fact quite willing to allow a certain "heterogeneity" (I:230) with respect to the particular domains of the various sciences. What he did claim was that the necessity that constituted their status as rational, scientific, and grounded, remained univocal.

The "deeper ground" (I:248) necessitated here would arise through an intuitive clarification of the intentionality through which truth emerges, a clarification then of the *adequatio rei et intellectus*, as Husserl put in appealing to an ancient definition (I:254). It would do so by exhibiting the character of the relation between the acts and contents involved, that is, their intentional *interconnectedness*. Such is the task of phenomenology, as Husserl initially described:

> Our great task is now *to bring the Ideas of logic, the logical concepts and laws, to epistemological clarity and definiteness.* Here *phenomenological analysis* must begin. Logical concepts, as valid thought unities must have their origin in intuition: they must arise out of an ideational intuition founded on certain experiences and must admit of indefinite reconfirmation and of recognition of their self-identity, on the reperformance of such abstraction. (I:251–52)

The ultimate grounding of the sciences transgresses the field of scientific practice to establish the epistemic idealities founding their conventions. Moreover, in a move that clashes with a good deal of twentieth-century commitments regarding the epistemic and its justification, Husserl claimed in an alternate exposition that we must transcend even the linguistic conventions that are the expression of scientific 'acts':

> Otherwise put: we can absolutely not rest content with 'mere words,' i.e. with a merely symbolic understanding of words. . .such as we first have when we reflect on the sense of the laws for 'concepts,' 'judgements,' 'truths,' etc. . . .that are set up in pure logic. Meanings inspired only by remote, confused, inauthentic intuitions—if any intuitions at all—are not enough: we must go back to the 'things themselves.' (I:252)

The grounding in question then must go behind the conventional, the linguistic, the merely 'received' in order to describe the acts by which in "the attitude of reflection" they become constituted and adequated (I:255).

A primitive example of this is provided in the *Investigations'* examination of the simple proposition, "This paper is white." Husserl's claim is that there is a radical difference between the perceptual judgment of seeing white paper and saying "white paper" and the categorial intuition that must accompany the judgment, "This paper is white." In both cases, he claims, the fulfillment of the acts in question would involve a certain "coincidence with the part-percept." But in the second case, "[A] surplus of meaning remains over, a form that finds nothing in the appearance itself to confirm it" (II:775). This surplus of intentionality is the recognition of the part-percept *as* white, the categorial supplement to the particularity of perception. Ultimately, Husserl claimed, it is a supplement directed to the being of the percept itself, one that requires, consequently, a widening of sensuous intuition, that is, an "extended concept of perception" (II:786). The objects of these extensions, their species or essences as he would come to call them, can lie neither in the object (not being empirically verifiable) nor in the subject (which would turn their ideal qualities into real, psychological events). They arise rather in the categorial intuition of the objects themselves. Consequently, against Kant's charge that existence is not a predicate, Husserl agreed that in the real sense, in the "narrow" concept of perception, "being is absolutely imperceptible" (II:781). But because it arises, he claimed, as a necessary (and ideal) accompaniment of real perception, it can be claimed that "[T]he concept of Being can arise only when some being, actual or imaginary, is set before our eyes" (II:784). For Husserl, the extension involved was unproblematic. As he claimed in the *Idea of Phenomenology* (1908):

> They are there open to intuition. We talk about them not in just vague hints and empty intention. We inspect them, and while inspecting them we can observe their essence, their constitution, their intrinsic character, and we can make our speech conform in a pure measure to what is "seen" in its full clarity. (IP:24)

The potential of the investigative resources here in fact was seen as unlimited. And, the phenomenological research project itself underwent an extension paralleling the potential of the reserve underlying it. Husserl did not simply confine phenomenological description to the experiential essences underlying the strict propositional contents of categorial intuition. He believed that the essences in question extended throughout the sphere of experience. That is, Husserl believed that phenomenology potentially provided access not only to "being pure and simple" (IP:56), but also to a science of the experience of objects of all types. As such, phenomenology was to be divorced from any form of psychology, descriptive or otherwise (IP:5), and, in displaying the "sources of cognition" (IP:44) in all types, the phenomenological critique of cognition became synonymous with the subject matter of philosophy (IP:19). Thus, all forms of experience, adequate or inadequate, became opened to its gaze:

> *If we produce in free phantasy spatial formations, melodies, social practices, and the like, or if we phantasy acts of experiencing of liking or disliking, of willing, etc. then on that basis, by "ideation" we can see various pure essences originally and perhaps even adequately: either the essence of any spatial shape whatever, any melody whatever, any*

social practice, *whatever,* etc. or the essence of a shape, a melody,
etc. of the particular *type* examplified. (Id:11)

Husserl's name for this method that was to carry all of the rigor
of deductive inference as well as the burden of furnishing an absolutely
presuppositionless grounding is *essential intuition* (*Wesensschau*). Arising
out of Reason's ability to grasp the manifold possibilities of an entity,
essential intuition was to constitute a scientific method whereby, having
bracketed out all prejudices concerning a phenomenon's actuality,
proceeding by means of imaginative free variation, we could articulate
the identity of its essential possibility. Although the specific character
of the method emerges only in later works, as early as the *Investigations*
Husserl had described the site of the a priori as what essentially persists,
an object whose epistemic status cannot ultimately be denied or
suspended.

> The *true logical a priori*, therefore, concerns all that pertains to the
> ideal essence of understanding as such, to the essence of its act-
> species and act-forms, to that, accordingly, which cannot be
> eliminated (*was nicht aufgehoben werden kann*), as long as the
> understanding, and acts definitory of it, are what they are, i.e.,
> thus and thus natured, maintaining their *selfsame* conceptual
> essence (II:829).

It is this character of the ineliminable in what stands present to
consciousness that constitutes the evidence of phenomenology. As a
result of imaginative free variation the phenomenological essences
gleaned were both free from any ties to a specific instance or a set of
specific instances—as was the theory of abstraction—and yet tied to the
evidence of the possbility of the phenomena themselves, a necessary
and ineliminable identity that emerged precisely through their
divergences. "The essence then proves to be that without which an
object of a particular kind cannot be thought" (EJ:341). Phenomenological essences both transcend their instantiations and at the same time
relate precisely to them, as the essence *of* these phenomenological
individuals. It is this bond that constitutes the peculiar intertwining
of the empirical and the transcendental that constitutes the essentiality
of phenomenological experience, resulting in an object in turn "that
can be made the subject of true and false predication" (Id:10).

It was in a sense Husserl's answer to an ancient issue, that of first
premises. The problem can be seen already in Aristotle's notion of
epagoge, and like the latter, *Wesensschau* purports to provide an answer

to the problem of getting from particulars to universals. Husserl's reply was Platonist and Aristotelean at the same time, a seeing that transcends the particular but precisely by providing the essence of the "visible." Nonetheless, just like Aristotle's *epagoge*, such a seeing was not a demonstration, and hence its lineage to the problem of 'induction' by which it is usually translated. In fact, it is an *in-ducere* of a different sort, not simply a generalization, as Husserl believed in criticizing empiricist notions of generalization for falling short of the universality behind our claims.

The methodology of phenomenological investigation was to carry strong commitments. As a science of science it was to be absolutely necessary and indubitable—apodictic and adequate, as Husserl put it in reinvoking the predicates of Cartesianism. Its results, though not demonstrable in a strictly inferential sense, would exhibit the grounds of all rational practices. And by the same method, through a clarification of the phenomenological experiences of rational judgment, rationality itself would be ultimately clarified, so that 'reason' becomes subject to a phenomenology of reason. "[A]ll mediate grounding leads back to immediate grounding. With respect to all object-provinces and positings related to them, the *primal source of legitimacy* lies in immediate evidence, and more narrowly delimited, in *originary evidence*, or in the originary giveness motivating it" (Id 338).

III

The position was not without its detractors. The Foreword to the second volume, part two of the *Logical Investigations'* second edition (1921), mentions the challenges of a school of thought that would soon rise to fiercely contest phenomenology on the very basis of its claim to scientificity. Moritz Schlick's *General Theory of Knowledge* (1918), noting that phenomenology is a "widely propogated philosophical method today," devoted considerable space to a polemic against Husserl.[6] Although its author was ready to acknowledge that Husserl's distinction between the act and content of knowledge in the *Investigations* "contains an element that is factually correct" and assents, albeit reluctantly, to using the framework of intentionality to describe it, he denied that the distinction accomplished all that Husserl purported.[7] Rather than seeing the intentional relation as a relation of grounds, Schlick's argument aimed at disassociating the contents of knowledge from the intentional acts that 'underlie' them. He denied, then, that the relation accomplished the work for which it was claimed. In particular, he denied that intentionality opened up a realm of self-evidence by which consciousness could gain access to the ideal. "Logical structures are not real; they are not given as parts of aspects of mental processes."[8] Husserl, he claimed, on the other hand, thinks "the process of grasping as already having been determined by what is grasped," the latter regarded "as something at hand to which real thought processes can direct themselves."[9] In this, however, the relation remains fully obscured. "How these processes can fulfill their meaning function is precisely our problem."[10] And the answer, Schlick claimed is an old anathema, self-evidence. "But this ruins everything again: How do we *know* anything about an ideal self-evidence or about its possibility?"[11] In fact, Schlick claimed, Husserl simply entered into the vicious circle of Cartesianism. The priority of the 'evidence' of the *Ego sum* is not knowledge but simply a fact. It remains, as Descartes had admitted, grounded elsewhere, guaranteed in the veracity (the clarity and distinctness) involved in our idea of God. "Thus he was forever trapped in a circle. For the existence of the entity that assured him of the reliability of self-evidence was itself guaranteed only by self-evidence."[12] All Cartesianism, Husserl's included, must submit, Schlick claimed, to the same *petitio principii*, its proof always remaining extrinsic to it. The method of *Wesensschau*, therefore must remain only ancillary to knowledge.

> This method consists in imagining or bringing into experience, through intuition (of essences) or "Wesensschau" the objects to be known in all their aspects. But so long as the results of phenomenological analysis ends here, nothing is gained so far as knowledge is concerned. Our insight is not enriched, only our experience; what has been obtained is only raw material for cognition.[13]

Whether then phenomenology is in fact productive of *knowledge* is a question that still stands to be decided by a judgment that surpasses it. Phenomenology is merely productive of facts. It is, thereby, not even a "science of facts." To *claim* that the data is grasped as objective does not answer the question concerning whether it *is* objective. Husserl had confused (at best), Schlick held, drawing on a Russellian distinction, "mere acquaintance with knowledge."

Nonetheless, both Schlick and Husserl were in agreement, perhaps more than either realized, in their commitment regarding the justification of theories. It was, both agreed, a question of verification. "[T]here is indeed no other way to *establish* (*Konstatierung*) truth except through verification," as Schlick put it.[14] Still, in confusing acquaintance with knowledge, Husserl had not realized that theories could not be legitimated by reference to a mental act, but only by a process of verification that was strictly empirical; that is, not through relation to the 'subject' and the acts supposedly constitutive of 'objects' (denying that these acts condition them in any relevant sense), but solely in relation to the objects of which they are theories. In Schlick's account the pseudo-justifications of phenomenology would only mystify this process.

Husserl's Foreword in the *Investigations'* second edition begins with a flat denial of the charge that phenomenological contents do not pertain to epistemic and ideal, conceptual contents.

> On page 121 [of Schlick's first edition] of this work it is said that my *Ideas* "asserts the existence of a peculiar intuition, that is *not a real psychical act*, and that if someone fails to find *such an 'experience', which does not fall within the domain of psychology*, this indicates that he has not understood the doctrine, that he has not yet penetrated to the correct attitude of experience and thought, for this requires 'peculiar, strenuous studies.' " (II:663)

The response is adamant:

> The total impossibility that I should have *been able* to utter so insane an assertion as that attributed to me by Schlick in the above italicized sentences, and the falsity of the rest of his exposition of the meaning of phenomenology, must be plain to anyone familiar with this meaning. . . . Everyone, however, who has made these efforts, and who has risen to a very seldom exercised lack of prejudice, has achieved an indubitable certainty regarding the givenness of its scientific *foundation* and the inherent justification (*Eigenrechte*) of the *method* demanded by it, a method which here, as in other sciences, renders possible a common sort of conceptually definite work problems, as well as definite decisions as to truth or falsehood. (II:663-64)

It was a strong reaction to the criticisms of what Schlick's first edition referred to as the results of the *"wunderbare Reduktion."*[15] Schlick himself, it should be noted, however, softened the rhetoric in the second edition (1925), admitting in fact that he had indeed misunderstood the doctrine concerning the ideality of the results of phenomenological method:

> This was a misunderstanding. It arose because it seemed to me that after carrying through the *"Einklammerung"* ("bracketing") or

"Ausschaltung" of all that is real, as is required for the phenomenological *"Schau"* ("Intuition"), what would remain would not be a real process of consciousness, but only a mere abstraction. The clearing up of this misunderstanding leaves untouched the arguments set forth in the text.[16]

Certainly Schlick was correct here. The issues that divide them in the end concern *not* the ideality of phenomenological intuition, but rather its *objectivity*: that is, whether such products of 'fantasy' can constitute *knowledge*. Husserl's point, doubtless, as Schlick acknowledged, was well taken in correcting Schlick's account of the doctrine. But that recognition does not affect the charge concerning the illusion of its epistemic claims.

In light of this, Husserl's preceding amplification is an interesting one. He retained the Cartesian turn towards self-evidence, as well as the rider that access to the evidence in question depends on a purging of prejudice. Further, the strength of the claims made by phenomenological enquiry, he maintained, is supported by the strong corroboration of results. "Everyone" who has made the effort concurs. Finally, Husserl claimed that phenomenology is methodologically sound, providing a legitimate research program that is scientific, issuing in results that are unequivocal, "definite," and decidable. The justifications in question are characterized as inherent. Nonetheless, the problem of the method's 'strictness' and the unequivocal character of its 'showing' remains coupled to self-evidence in a manner that perhaps leaves Schlick's charge concerning the circularity of Cartesianism unanswered. The question of knowledge and self-evidence remains tied to a 'showing' and consequently dependent on a subject and the subjective. The question is whether this is sufficient (if necessary). And if the position cannot *demonstrate* this sufficiency, does it remain open to Schlick's charge?

Its failure in this regard would be a matter of no small importance. If Schlick's brief is warranted, then phenomenology could neither gain access to, nor strictly delineate the very theoretical domain it was intended to ground. Rather, the intentional relation would be precisely the occlusion of all subjective knowledge, resting simply as Schlick put it on "the insecure basis (*unsicheren Grund*) of a subjective psychological datum that lacks conceptual sharpness and may deceive us."[17] The question becomes then one concerning the manner in which the necessity of phenomenological claims is to be justified.

IV

The 'strictness' of the phenomenological method could not, as has been seen, be deductive. Husserl had realized it as early as the first edition of the *Logical Investigations*. And although he remained perhaps overly inclined towards the empirical in trying to align it with a descriptive psychology, following Mill's own "science of mental phenomena," he also realized, following, inter alia, Frege's critique of his earlier work, that he could not provide an empirical basis for what was an abstract or ideal question.[18] Even at its strictest phenomenology could not, Husserl realized, provide an explanation. It could not simply provide universal laws concerning events falling under causal, functional, or structural relations. Husserl, on the contrary, realized early that phenomenology would be something quite different. Phenomenology was to "shed light" (*Aufklärung*) on the idea of knowledge (I:265). It would provide grounds in the pregnant sense, ones that would not simply be premises but exhibit the sources from which their necessity arises, thereby understanding "the necessity of specific lower-level relationships in terms of comprehensive general necessities, and ultimately in terms of those most primitive, universal relational *laws* that we call axioms" (I:264)—ones that were exhibited then through phenomenological intuition.

The solution to the endless controversies that constituted metaphysics was to be had by a phenomenological extension that could be established neither inductively nor deductively. Nor could this "theoretical science of theory in general" (I:240) arise by any form of explanation as it is practiced in the "several sciences." Its demonstration was in a sense then exceptional to all rational practices and yet presupposed by each. The paradox concerning its theoretical status is in a sense 'unavoidable.' And Husserl perhaps glossed past it too fast in a passage deserving extensive citation:

> On our view, theory of knowledge, properly described is no theory. It is not science in the pointed sense of an explanatorily unified theoretical whole. . . .The theory of knowledge has nothing to explain in this theoretical sense, it neither constructs deductive theories nor falls under any. . . .Its aim is not to *explain* (*erklären*) knowledge in the psychological or psychophysical sense as a factual occurence in objective nature, but to shed light on the Idea of knowledge in its constitutive elements and laws. . . .This 'clearing up' (*Aufklärung*) takes place in the framework of a phenomenology of knowledge, a phenomenology oriented, as we

saw, to the essential structures of pure experiences and to the structures of sense (*Sinnbestande*) that belong to these....A pure phenomenological 'theory' of knowledge naturally has an application to all naturally developed and (in a good sense) 'naive' sciences, which it transforms into 'philosophical' sciences. It transforms them, in other words, into sciences which provide us with clarified, assured knowledge in every sense in which it is possible to desire the latter...(I:264–65)

Now one might be prone to construe such a program in a weak sense, claiming that the knowledge assured "in every sense in which it is possible" would merely provide a tentative basis where other theories failed. Phenomenology would arise to fill in the gaps in our rational practices, providing an intuitive basis when demonstrability came to an end—in accord again with weak readings of the method of *epagoge*. Nonetheless, the text mitigates against it. It is not, recall, the limit of justification and demonstration that is at hand, but rather, precisely to the contrary, their completion, their "fulfillment," albeit by a different method. "The real premises of our putative results must lie in propositions satisfying the requirement that what they assert permits of an adequate phenomenological justification, a fulfillment through evidence in the strictest sense" (I:266). But the question is, how is phenomenological exhibition and clarification a justification in the strictest of senses? And how does intuition provide the latter, unless the evidence in question just is ipso-facto self-evident? But then should it not in the end be indubitable? And what if it is not—as it was not, apparently, to Schlick?

If in the end the self-evidence in question is not such as to *prevent* dispute, if adequacy of articulation, *Aufklärung*, does not prevent disputibility, and if consequently, every phenomenological claim is open to denial, then how could it be 'strict'? And if not strict, then how could it be ultimately justified? And how then in the midst of all of these soft foundations, could phenomenology provide the basis for a "theory of theory," when at bottom it might indicate, rather, a fundamental *agon* within the phenomenological itself?

Such a recognition is not perhaps foreign to Husserl's writings, falling often under the rubrics of the problem of transcendental solipisism. The problem of constituting the alter ego, for Husserl the "supremely significant" problem of how it is that objective idealities, that is, the *certitudo* of the ideas, are intersubjectively 'reiterated' (CM:110) is a perennial one for Cartesianism. And it can be found quite early in Husserl's writings as well. Regarding the validity of logical principles, he stated:

I can compel nobody to see what I see. But I myself cannot doubt; I once more see, here where I have insight, i.e. am embracing truth itself, that all doubt would be mistaken. I therefore find myself at a point which I have either to recognize as the Archimedean point from which the world of doubt and unreason may be levered on its hinges, or which I may sacrifice at the peril of sacrificing all reason and knowledge. I see that this is the case, and that in the latter case—if it were then still reasonable to speak of reason or unreason—I should have to pack in all rational striving for truth, all assertion, and all demonstration. (I:159)

The *Ich stehe hier* of rationality is itself the *conditio sine qua non* of assertion and demonstration.[19] Without it, there can be no strictness, and yet its own strictness can be only clarified, 'shown,' but not, apparently— and this is the point—*proven*. In this sense, the fact that there is a problem of the 'other' within phenomenology is not a 'regional' or ontological problem concerning the contingent fact that there are other egos within the world. Rather it concerns the 'pregnant' but nonetheless equivocal grounds of phenomenology itself, the fact that the evidence involved allows of the logical possibility of other 'construals,' the fact that the *Ich stehe hier* remains one whose disputabililty remains open—the fact then that the accounts of phenomenological *Aufklärung underdetermine* their evidence, opening up, thereby, the problem of a logic of explication, of the interpretation (*Auslegung*) of the project of *Aufklärung*, when one would have expected just the opposite concerning the logic of this 'Archimedean point.'[20] One might have expected that the basis of apodicticity would have been absolutely adequated and not, as Husserl's position ultimately entails concerning its foundation, that *de scientia non est disputandum*.

The equivalence between apodicticity and adequacy explicitly posited for example in *Erste Philosophie* (35) in this regard is never more than simply *'posited,'* at best a regulative idea that lines the economics of pure logic. The "absolute certainty" of this *Wissenschaftslehre* in the end was only to be matched by the absolute indemonstrability of its origin, and consequently, in a traditional sense, the *in*adequacy of its foundation.

Ideas, as has been seen, cognizant of the ultimate digression of deduction, could still claim that phenomenological exhibition involved an unshakable foundation—"not because we can deduce it from some metaphysical postulates or other, but because we can show it by an intuitive completely indubitable procedure." In this text Husserl remained convinced of the link between adequacy and apodicticity. And yet the author's marginal notes betray a doubt, a dubitability. A question mark occurs in the margin, that portends events to come (Id:129n).

V

In *Cartesian Meditations* (1929) Husserl portentously, fatefully, and perhaps consistently in the end, distinguished phenomenological adequacy and apodicticity. He admitted in fact that apodicticity "can occur even in evidences that are inadequate" (CM:15). Absolute indubitability may be present even if the evidence in question may not sufficiently ground the belief, or in cases in which the evidence remains incomplete, partial, or not fulfilled "with strict adequacy" (CM:22). Equally, *Formal and Transcendental Logic* published the same year declared, "Even an ostensibly apodictic evidence can become disclosed as deception and, in that event, presupposes a similar evidence by which it is 'shattered' " (FTL:156). In that case we would be confronted with "a certain naïveté (the naïveté of apodicticity)" (CM:151). And yet, in one sense, at least, this is not a naïveté that was simply to be surpassed. Husserl did not, some of his commentators to the contrary, simply give up the notion of apodicticity, if he relented perhaps concerning the ultimately groundless character of his strictures regarding it. Rather, still consistent with the concept of the scientific that had underwitten his work since its inception, he relegated it to the status of a regulative idea. And, in a sentence that another marginal note depicts as still unsatisfactory, he stated: "[T]he question whether adequate evidence does not necessarily lie at infinity may be left open" (CM:15).

Why might such a statement be unsatisfactory? Well, inter alia, the whole status of the rationality of phenomenology depends on it and has depended on it from the beginning. In the *Investigations*, recall, the results of analytic phenomenology were "to admit of indefinite reconfirmation of and recognition of their self-identity on performance" (I:251–52). What this change concerning apodicticity and adequacy perhaps at long last admits is that such 'verification' can never, within a single instance, provide a point at which apodicticity finds absolute necessity. What the Platonist *Investigations* thought of as an infinite proceeding that Plato's *Republic* itself already described as one carried out "by means of the Eide themselves and proceeding through these"[21] must now be submitted to what Husserl called in the *Phenomenological Psychology* (1925) "the way of the cross of corrections" (PP:95). Without the conclusive strictness of the deductive systems for which it was intended to provide ultimate evidence, phenomenological 'knowledge' always confronted an insurmountable risk, even, as has been seen, at its most apodictic point: "[N]aturally it is characteristic of the performances of consciousness effected by experience itself that experiencing can fall to pieces in conflict and that the initially simple certainty of experience can end in doubt, in deeming possible, in deeming likely, in negation. . ." (FTL:235). But such a recognition ultimately could not help but have an impact on the strong claims of phenomenological evidence, once the revisability of the apodictic had been admitted. And it forced Husserl to raise radical questions concerning the character of the enquiry:

> What if each and every *truth*, whether it be the everyday truth of practical life or the truth of even the most highly developed sciences conceivable, remains involved in *relativities* by virtue of its essence, and referrable to *"regulative ideas"* as its norms? What if, even when we get down to the primitive phenomenological bases (*phänomenologischen Urgrunden*), problems of relative and absolute truth are still with us, and as problems of the highest dignity, *problems of ideas* and of the *evidence of ideas*? (FTL:278)

In that eventuality (which, as has become clear, is a necessary one, since claims to apodicticity are never ultimately decidable) phenomenological enquiry would be relegated to a certain relativity and a certain contestability that was, again to speak Kantian, "inextricable." The requisite *Urgrunden* that were to provide the basis of all necessity, epistemic and logical, were never free from a certain contingency, the risk of cancellation. As such, Husserl realized, the problem of truth approached phenomenologically could no longer be a problem of simply clarifying, of making adequate claims concerning apodicticity, but equally one of clarifying the evidence concerning the regulative ideas by which such claims were made. And, fulfilling this demand was no small matter, because the problem concerned evidence that was infinitely deferred, an idea whose evidence, which was to found all apodicitic evidence, was merely regulative—of necessity because its appearance (as absolutely adequated) was precisely impossible. The claim to an absolute foundation, necessity, and adequation in phenomenology was then, by a necessity that was equally absolute, based on an impossible phenomenon.[22] The essential 'ideas' of phenomenological enquiry could in principle not find strict and univocal verification. What turned all claims to apodicticity naive in this case were precisely the same rocks on which all positivism floundered, as Schlick, too, would learn from Popper, the problem of verification. "Indefinite reconfirmation" will not provide strict verification, *Be-wahrung*.[23] And, as Paul Ricoeur has likewise noted, this loss with regard to verification mitigated against all that Husserl had committed to intuitionism.[24]

VI

Phenomenology would not provide a science of strict foundations and determinability. In fact, the grounds of phenomenological description ultimately escaped it. Popper's charge against verificationism held against all of its forms. "Statements can be logically justified only by statements."[25] What he meant, as did Schlick in his charge against Husserl, was that a theory must be "conclusively decidable."[26] And phenomenology, it has become clear, in principle just is not. As a science of scrutible grounds, as a *Wissenschaftslehre*, the descriptive explication of the intentional—as Quine too rightly charged—was in fact in the strict sense "baseless." If phenomenology was taken then to provide a special source of a special kind of truth and a special kind of authority or guarantee for assertions, then its claims in the end would be as fictional as the other products of the imagination that were, Husserl claimed, simply "arbitrary" (Id:43).

Nonetheless, it may be wrong to think that that was all phenomenology amounted to in the end, just as it has become clear, too, in other domains that 'strict,' 'logical' justification may be an impoverished and perhaps ultimately impossible model for our rational practices generally. In fact after Kuhn (and perhaps, too, after Husserl) we may need to think of justification other than simply a practice (a *leistung* to use Husserl's term), that takes place only between and within statements. And, although the reduction of intentional idioms seemed to be justified, indeed necessitated by the failure of intentional descriptions to comply with the strict criteria of its claims, we may need to reconsider the status of the claims that arise here. Rorty has perhaps best seen this in underlining the failure in Quine's flight from intension discussed previously:

> Quine thinks this anti-intentionalism of a piece with his polemic against analyticity. But it is not. The author of "Two Dogmas of Empiricism" *should* have said that concepts and meanings are harmless if posited to give explanations of our behavior, and become harmful only treated as the source of a special kind of truth and of a special sort of authority for certain assertions.[27]

Nonetheless, it is true as well that Quine's charge, like in the end Schlick's before him, must hold against Husserl's program in its original sense—one that was foundational, ultimate, and unequivocal in its claims precisely to have provided a source for all other claims. And, analytic phenomenology thus in this regard could be justly accused of the dogma of analyticity. But it was a dogma that its author ultimately saw unfold before him and, consequently, a research program that inevitably deconstructed its own grounds. Phenomenology could not provide adequate and strict justification. In the end, there was, even Husserl admitted in *Formal and Transcendental Logic*, a certain "inconvenience" to phenomenological evidence: "The appeal to evidence ceases to be, so to speak, a trick of epistemological argumentation" (FTL:162). But it does so only because its evidence no longer remains in the strict sense argumentation at all, no longer remains, strictly taken, disputable. "One cannot," he wrote (against Wundt), "come to an understanding with someone who is both unwilling and unable to see" (ILI'56). But surely it is something of a fallacy for a research program based on 'seeing' to have taken the matter to have been 'shown,' let alone ultimately grounded or 'decided,' in the face of the possibility of radical dissent.

The question that remains then is whether there is any sense in which phenomenology offered justifications at all, or whether there is any way to provide reasons within the domain of the phenomenological—apart from those modeled on the foundationalism and the strictness that provided its demise. Husserl, the recognition of these limits notwithstanding, perhaps came to think—albeit blinkingly—that such was the case. Once the domain of the phenomenological had been liberated from its demonstrative idols regarding the absolute, he himself came to believe it finally opened up in fact the true wealth of its possibilities. In a statement that perhaps has self-referential overtones, he stated:

It is high time that people got over being dazzled, particularly in philosophy and logic, by the ideal and regulative ideas and methods of the "exact" sciences—as though the In-itself of such sciences were actually an absolute norm for objective being and truth. Actually they do not see the woods for the trees. Because of a splendid cognitive performance, though with only a very restricted teleological sense, they overlook the infinitudes of life and its cognition, the infinitudes of relative and, only in its relativity, rational being, with its relative truths. But to rush ahead and philosophize from on high about such matters is fundamentally wrong; it creates a wrong skeptical relativism and no less a wrong logical absolutism, mutual bugbears that knock each other down and come to life again like the figures in a Punch and Judy show. (FTL:278)

Such a 'phenomenology' would necessarily need to admit to the equivocal nature of its results and what Schlick aptly termed the *insecurity* of its grounds—at the same time denying Quine's simple decisionism in their outright rejection. It is not the case—even without strict decidability—that 'anything goes' within the practice of phenomenology. As Husserl stated in the *Investigations*—in what was perhaps his lasting insight.

Phenomenologically put: we are not wholly free (*nicht ganz frei*) to interpret a content *as* this or *as* that (or in this or that interpretative sense) and this has more than an empirical foundation—*every* interpretation including a significative one is empirically necessary—since the content to be interpreted sets limits to us through a certain sphere of similarity and exact likeness, i.e. through its specific substance. (II:741–42)[28]

Nonetheless, although the evidence of phenomenology may prohibit the possibility of anything goes here (if, that is, it may be the case that we are not *wholly* free regarding the viability of our descriptive construals), it remains true that there is enough play within the phenomenological to rule out the "univocity" of the strict discipline Husserl thought he had discovered. The equivocal character of the phenomenological grounds, rather, burdens its claims with a certain "provisional" character Husserl had initially reserved for the "putative theory" of the empirical (I:246), one that, moreover, precisely because of the lack of "definiteness for which we were striving," Husserl claimed, takes "on a painful and yet unavoidable relativity" (FTL:270). Although the claims of phenomenology are open to indefinite reconfirmation and to corroboration, to 'intersubjective' verification, they could not, even at their most apodictic, deny the possibility of cancellation.[29]

This means, of course, that they are in the strict sense "revisable." But the conditions of revisability and corroboration are as insecure as the method of "*Wesensschau*" on which they rely. Intentionality in this regard always remains itself a problem.[30] There is no strict relation—let alone control—between an *epoche*, the practice of free variability, and the results obtained. What will 'count' as a cancellation will, consequently, be openly controversial. *Wesensschau* in this regard always remains, as Husserl put it, a "hidden method" (FTL:200), always presumed, never fully adequated, never entirely extricable from the motivations of its horizons; a method, in short, whose own *Aufklärung* always remains underway.[31] And no claim would be free, therefore, from the possibility of potential competitors nor give rise to ultimate decidability regarding them. Whereas this may be more true here than elsewhere, it is, of course, the lot of refutation in general, as Popper in all honesty relented:

> In point of fact, no conclusive disproof of a theory can ever be produced; for it is always possible to say that experimental results are not reliable, or that the discrepancies which are asserted to exist between the experimental results and the theory are only apparent and that they will disappear with the advance of our understanding.[32]

Due to this lack of control, phenomenological claims will always remain potentially controversial and the results obtained, consequently, open ended. Husserl's claim that phenomenology was founded in a "strict method" (FTL:247) in this regard occurred perhaps too easily. In fact, granted the fate that had befallen the strong claims of its research program, it is only by force of habit that Husserl and phenomenologists after him could continue to call their research program "strict science," perhaps knowing all too well that its status as both theory and observation were too insecure to count for either, in any simple sense.

Still, the recognition of that insecurity and the risk involved, on the other hand, could not simply deny all 'phenomenological justification' (*phänomenologische Rechtfertigung*: I:266) nor deny that its claims were rationally motivated, even those regarding the apodictic, as Husserl related in *Ideas*—before the *Abgrund* concerning adequacy had been met head on: "The idea of an infinity motivated in conformity with its essence is not itself an infinity; seeing intellectually that this infinity of necessity cannot be given does not exclude, but rather requires, the intellectually seen giveness of the idea of this infinity" (Id:343). It remains the case, then, that the 'grounds' of this rational posit remain in the motivation within the concatenation of experience, even if those grounds remain soft and at the margins of our rational practices. But there is a sense, after all, in which that was from the outset the site of phenomenology, an "extension" to use the *Investigation's* Kantian term. That extension, nonetheless was not one that could be, as Husserl dreamed and hoped ultimately to "show," an extension to first foundations: the rationalist and Cartesian projects could not find simple fulfillment in phenomenological sources. And, phenomenology, therefore, would not solve what was unsolvable on other grounds. Its transcendentality amounted in the end strictly to a transcendental illusion, constituting itself precisely on what it accused others, on "false metabases" (Id:139).

Nonetheless, despite all its failures, phenomenology continually retains perhaps a certain recalcitrant role within our rational practices. It is, after all, an extension that incessantly questioned both the nature and limits of the 'empirical' on the basis of an *empeiria* that surpasses both, thereby opening up a field that the former excludes. In this sense it is perhaps an extension that occurs fully cognizant that neither the question of decidability nor the ultimate failure to provide requisite criteria for final adjudication closes down either its *Evidenz* or the risk of its rationality. If phenomenology were not in the end a science of first foundations it becomes in this regard inevitably perhaps a site of last resort, providing a domain of rational clarification extending beyond the strict confines of explanation and ontological commitment within the 'empirical' sciences. And in this sense it may be necessary equally to grasp the naïveté as well as the recalcitrance of its claims. As Max Scheler, perhaps the only phenomenologist to have considered the radical implications of *phänomenologischer Streit*, put it: "He who is always inclined to ask for a criterion first of all—a criterion of whether this picture is an authentic work of art, say, or whether any extant religion is true and which one it is—is a man who stands outside, who has no direct contact with any work of art, any religion, any scientific domain."[33]

The plea on behalf of direct access would always remain naive. Corresponding to the archaic *circulus in demonstrando* Husserl's project was invoked to overcome, phenomenology would "inevitably," to use Scheler's words, practice under the risk of its own circularity, a *"circulus in definiendo"* by which its appeal to immediacy would always appear viciously entrapped.[34] Thus, phenomenological *Aufklärung* could neither be transformed into Erklärung nor could it establish the necessity that was believed to underly both. But the claim that the recognition of this hazard simply ended the matter overlooked both the recalcitrance of its motivations as well as the equally inevitable naïveté with which the opposing claim, too, remained stricken.

Husserl himself doubtless increasingly abandoned the strategy of clarifying the phenomenological *Urgrunden* on the basis of the models of the formal sciences, extending the phenomenological analysis by further, almost infinitely (in accord with the infinity of the ideas that escaped it), articulating the conditions or motivations of its occurrence. Accordingly, the clarification of the acts of transcendental *analysis* were increasingly supplanted on the basis of the passive *synthesis* that it articulated and presupposed. Nonetheless, Husserl remained committed to the strict and unequivocal availability of *die Sache* before the tribunal of transcendental analysis—and doubtless therefore without in fact feeling compelled (again some of Husserl's commentators to the contrary) to modify his original views concerning the capacities for reflective equilibrium it required. But precisely in this regard, as Jean Cavaillès would soon put it with regard to transcendental logic in general, "the formal priority of analytic unity over synthetic unity consequently becomes at least dubious."[35] Unlike those more immediately in Kant's wake (or those immediately in the wake of Mach and Schlick), Husserl's increasing turn to the question of nature, to the problem of the incarnation of reason, the question of intersubjectivity, and the problem of history did not in fact place the reflective stronghold the logician seemed to require into jeopardy. What became increasingly evident was the impoverished character of his model of the rational and, consequently, the categories through which phenomenological 'clarification' had been articulated. All that Husserl assembled under "the great problems pertaining to a *world-logic*" (FTL:291) would require other resources for their 'explication.' In this regard, Husserl's 'positivism' would come back to haunt him, in fact fully retaining its debt to the modernism of Hume and Leibniz. As again Cavaillès rightly saw, and perhaps better than others, "if the *epoche*, in separating [the] transcendental consciousness from a consciousness situated in the world, removes the naive aspect and somewhat scandulous aggressiveness of logical empiricism and psychologism, they still lurk beneath the surface of phenomenological development."[36] In the end Husserl's failures were in this regard far less descriptive than logical, less 'phenomenological' than simply conceptual, and less 'scientific' than 'hermeneutic,' failures that he would bequeath to his progeny in the form of their own agon concerning their status.

Heidegger, the
Hermeneutics of
Suspicion, and
the Dispersion
of Dasein

I

Heidegger's texts remain interminably poised between *apophansis* and *poiesis*, judgment and interpretation, representation and analogy— perhaps thereby between the ancients and the moderns. It is just in this respect that the complications concerning their retrievals and destructions remain insuperable. Minimally it can be claimed Heidegger's texts will not be readily or ultimately subsumed. Granted moreover their rupture with the metaphysics they inscribe, the question of their unity or continuity with the past they transform becomes no less problematic. Hence, the question of their belonging-together in this regard, the question of their ad-judication, becomes then equally difficult. Elsewhere I have traced these texts' divergence concerning the history of analogy and judgment,[1] delineating their emergence and advance beyond the history they themselves delimit. One still faces however the question of articulating their remainder, a remainder especially overdetermined with respect to the archive now deliberately surpassed, and particularly regarding the economics of the *Seinsfrage* Heidegger instituted, that of the an-alogical past they hoped to retrieve and the 'sciences' it hoped to replace. Heidegger's most radical challenge in this respect became, as is often noted, Nietzsche—and doubtless the strongest advocate against Heidegger on this matter was Nietzsche's strictest interpretor, Gilles Deleuze. And this *Auseinandersetzung* brings to light, as will be seen, not only a confrontation between thinkers seemingly incommensurable, but equally discloses both the archive of their difference as well as its contemporary effect.

II

In an initial characterization of the entity Heidegger privileged in *Being and Time's* investigation of *Fundamentalontologie*, he stated, "Dasein's facticity is such that its Being-in-the-world has always dispersed (*zerstreut*) itself into definite ways of Being-in."[2] This dispersion, this diaspora that is articulated as part of the very facticity of Dasein itself, remained overdetermined in Heidegger's account. Its articulation in fact involved a problem that invoked a transcendence and withdrawal that exerted a certain attraction and repulsion on the construction of *Sein und Zeit*, on its assimilation of hermeneutics, and ultimately, perhaps, despite its undeniable advances, on the author's perceived failure concerning its accomplishment. On the one hand, it was precisely the event that this 'splitting' involved that was to underlie the hermeneutic project itself, manifesting an evidence that was insurpassable. If it were in the strict sense unfounded, it remained true, nonetheless, that "*[t]his vague (vage) average understanding. . . is still* a Fact (*Faktum*)" (25). On the other hand, the narratives of the everyday (§47, passim), split up, separate (*dispars*), and localized as they are, remain in fact precisely too vague and inadequate to strictly found the science of Being he still dreamed of founding in *Being and Time*, a science thought to remain already nascent and unexpressed (*unausdruchlich-naiv*) in the *Faktum* of the everyday, a preontological comprehension in need only of explication (*Explikation*). And, this word itself, as will become evident, may be neither unproblematically nor simply neutrally invoked in Heidegger's account. By its means he hoped—perhaps every bit as much as Husserl before him—that what remained always already nascently expressed within the local narratives of the everyday might still be brought to clarification and made secure, thus providing the basis on which Being might itself become understood, revealing thereby the articulation of the meaning of Being.

In this light the *Daseinanalytik* would provide the foundation that would make a *Wissenschaft vom Sein* still possible. It was, that is, to invoke the Kantian predicates Heidegger himself continually invoked, to provide an account of the unity, identity, and totality—the homogeneity—on the basis of which 'Being as such,' to invoke now the Aristotelean background of this *Wissenschaft* that Heidegger described as already "ancient," became grounded. And yet, precisely at the point at which *Being and Time* explicitly invoked this Aristotelean *arche* in retrieval of a *Wissenschaft vom Sein als Solche* (272)—in the conclusion to Division One's 'preparatory analysis'—it explicitly raises the possibility likewise of its *ultimate Destruktion*.

In fact the threat of this dispersion had haunted modern transcendentalism since Kant.[3] Granted everything that Heidegger had delivered over regarding this '*als*' in descending from the apophantic to the hermeneutic, one could wonder whether the *als soche* itself could ever again be vindicated—whether, that is, an account beyond the dispersal of Dasein's conditions could ever be 'grounded.' Indeed, this dissonance notwithstanding, Heidegger himself asks more directly whether the results of Division One were not simply "manifestly inconsistent" with such a *Wissenschaft*. That is, precisely at the culmination of the analysis which had explicated the "totality of Dasein's structural whole" in the phenomenon of Care—and confirmed it in the narrative of an ancient fable—Heidegger himself questioned the possibility of a science of Being. "If in care we have arrived at Dasein's primordial state of Being, then this must also be the basis (*Grunde*) for conceptualizing that understanding of Being that lies in care; that is to say, it must be possible to define the meaning of Being" (273).

In order for *Being and Time* to be successful vis à vis its foundational pretensions, the *Sorge* structure itself would need to provide the requisite homogeneity for overcoming the 'splitting' of Dasein's dispersion, tracing out the *diaphora* of the ontic and the ontological, the "ontological difference," as he had already conceptualized it. Still, Heidegger proclaims, what has been disclosed within the preparatory analysis is in fact radically incompatible with such a *Wissenschaft*: "The possibility of this entity's Being-a-whole is manifestly inconsistent with the ontological meaning of care, and care is that which forms the totality of Dasein's structural whole" (279).

III

In fact Dasein's being-underway, the task of its own self-articulation, precisely precludes the systematic totality and homogeneity that would make a philosophy of strict science possible. It precludes, that is, to invoke the Kantian requisites that structured all of transcendentalism in its wake, a science that could "guarantee, as following from principles, the completeness and certainty of the structure in all its parts."[4] Such a completeness that would ground and order all that is, was precisely what had to be foregone. If ontically Dasein is what is closest to us, "it is ontologically that which is farthest" (36). Even if it were true that it is itself the bridge, again to speak Kantian, between the ontic and the ontological, if, that is, "preontologically it is surely not a stranger" (37), it surely too does not follow that its knowledge will thereby ever be more than "inadequate," that is, vague and dispersed. The problem of the abyss (*Abgrund*) between *idea* and *ideatum* has not thereby been bridged. To claim, after all, that knowledge is a mode of Being, does not thereby make it true, as even—and perhaps especially some have argued—Spinoza knew.

Rather, the definition of Care as *"ahead-of-itself-in-already-being-in-a-world"* (236) that manifests the facticity of the 'average everyday' understanding of Being and the task, thereby, of its adequation, already in principle manifests its failure. Dasein never finishes the infinite task of *adequation* precisely because Dasein itself is never finished; that is, because the task of infinite adequation is precluded from a finite being. Hence, both the ultimate undecidability of its truth and the dispersion of its task: " *'There is' truth only in so far as Dasein is and so long as Dasein is"* (269). Dasein in fact never 'catches up' to the truth that it pursues and before which it always "falls" short. Hence, the inevitable falling behind that afflicts it and the "groundlessness and nullity of inauthentic everydayness" (223). Its overcoming required precisely a vindication of the fundamental ontology that escaped Dasein's theoretical reason. Only when Heidegger changed grounds, only, that is, when he had changed epistemic for the resolve of 'moral' certainty, could he reinvoke the possibility of the totalization that might overcome the impass, a move in fact, if it invoked both an archaic science and Kierkegaard for its predecessors, still smacked of the *Aufhebung* of Kant's second *Kritik* and the ensuing Fichtean ecstasies. Against the semblance of onto-theological *mimesis*, the figure of the divine man within us, as Kant put it, Dasein's possibility of existing as a whole possibility comes to the fore, in fact, only with the encounter with its own impossibility, that is, death. It comes to the fore only in confronting, "the possibility of the measureless (*maslosen*) impossibility of existence" (307), an encounter that wrenched one away from the everyday as a sufficient *Masstab* or criterion of intelligibility and forced one back on oneself, a forcing and "calling" that Dasein undergoes before the nullity of its own existence.

IV

Hence, precisely in confronting death as a possibility that cannot be outstripped, Dasein's possibility for being-a-whole is brought to light:

> Since the anticipation of the possibility which is not to be outstripped discloses also all the possibilities which lie ahead of that possibility, this anticipation includes the possibility of taking the whole of Dasein in advance in an existentiell manner; that is to say, it includes the possibility of existing as a *whole potentially for Being.* (309)

Still, Heidegger again rebuffs such an anticipation from any but the 'existential' standpoint—one that could not in fact overcome *lapse judicii* between the ontic and the ontological, and that could never ascend to the standpoint of what he called the *indifference* (*Gleichgultigkeit*) of apodictic evidence. Rather, the anticipation that this event called forth, and that would 'asymptotically' approach the actual, would instead involve another kind of certainty, which would "not mean that it is of a lower grade, but that *it does not belong at all to the graded order of the kinds of evidence we can have about the present-at-hand*" (309). That is, it could not belong to a *Ratio* in which apodicticity and adequacy go 'hand in hand,' one by which the apodictic and the demonstrable might be made formally equivalent. Of course, there was a sense, after all, that the claim (by the logic of the present-to-hand) was either trivially true or just false. 'Knowing that' we are going to die does not tell us much about what stands in between and knowing that the possibilities will be limited by that which is our own-most does not tell us much about them either.

Still, Heidegger realized, too, what had been withdrawn thereby. If by expecting the possible, "the possible is drawn into the actual" (306), it never coincides with it. Although anticipation, expectation, hope, and even the hopeless all remained viable options, even modes of possibility before the rocks of mortality, the thing itself remained withdrawn in the "in between" that constitutes the certainty of the present-to-hand and the anticipation of the appropriated ready-to-hand and risked within the dispersion that had haunted Heidegger's account since its initial invocation of a *Faktum* towards which all had been 'thrown.' Whereas Kant had been committed in all this to a 'Copernican' revolution that guaranteed the demonstrability of the rational, Heidegger, then, was forced to commit it to the contingency to which Dasein had been thrown, the Fichtean *Wechsel* (or *Schwingen*, as Heidegger put it), of world entry, and the task of its articulation in default of the strict demonstrability of the apodictic.[5]

V

Still, Heidegger did so not in demonstrating the foundations for a science of Being as such—vindicating *Fundamentalontologie*—but rather by 'demonstrating' in all this how the grounds of 'science' and Dasein's rationality were delivered over to conditions that escaped it. It is "[t]he ecstatic unity of temporality—that is, the unity of the 'outside-of-itself' in the raptures of the future, of what has been, and of the Present—[that] is the condition for the possibility that there can be an entity that exists as its 'there' " (401). The identity, unity, and homogenity that would transcendentally condition 'ontology', derive from beyond it. Moreover, it is the tracing of this 'beyond,' this excess and transcendence, that is at work in the very structural unity and differentiation of the *Sorge* structure, an *extensio animi*, to cite Augustine (and Heidegger did) that derives its unity not from its own 'spontaneity,' but precisely in its engagement of an excess that was itself measureless. Although Heidegger claimed that the notion of *Sorge* has Stoic as well as Biblical antecedents, he also declared that "[t]he way in which 'care' is viewed in the existential analytic of Dasein is one which has grown on the author in connection with his attempts to interpret the Augustinian (i.e., Helleno-Christian) anthropology with regard to the foundational principles reached in the ontology of Aristotle" (243n).

Aristotle's archaic science of Being as such itself introduced the problem of analogy in recognizing that Being could not be simply univocally defined. "Being is said in several ways," that is, the several ways of the categories (substance, quality, time, place, etc.).[6] The account affirmed a multiplicity that cut across all discourse and yet solved the Parmenidean problem of the many and the one, of unity and diversity, in thinking the heterogeneity in question as a unity of reference, *a pros hen logomenon*. Still, the unity involved is a "problematic unity of an irreducible plurality of meaning."[7] It was not, however, a 'figured' unity, as it would be for the medievals who would, beyond Aristotle's plurality, concern themselves with the 'distance' that separate the *ens finitum* and the *ens infinitum*, the *primum analogatum*, as Suarez put it in a way that would have an impact even on Descartes and Kant.[8] Still, if the latter developments, obviously, are crucial to hermeneutics and to Heidegger's account in particular, it is important first to recognize the significance that Aristotle's account of analogy is initially given in Heidegger's retrieval, a significance that is apparent as early as the opening pages of *Being and Time*.

Aristotle's understanding of the transcendence of Being as "a *unity of analogy* in contrast to the multiplicity of the highest generic concepts applicable to things," Heidegger claimed, "put the problem of Being on what was in principle, a new basis" (22). Its significance, however, is perhaps most straightforwardly evident in what he has to say regarding the modernist *refusal* of this problematic. In fact, Descartes's paradigmatic refusal to consider the question of the relation between the 'substance' vindicated in the court of representation and that of infinite substance itself is condemned as an "evasion" that is "tantamount to his failing to discuss the meaning of Being" (126). In all this he is, consequently, "always far behind the Schoolmen" and their complex discussions of analogy.

VI

Heidegger seemed in this regard simply to reinvoke the conclusion of his 1916 *Habilitationschrift* on the *modi significandi* of Duns Scotus, a book that, consequently, may be not simply the work of secondary importance that it is usually assigned. In that work analogy was claimed to involve the *Grundmarkmal* of the metaphysical. Moreover, it was asserted that this account of how "homogeneity and heterogeneity are intermixed in a specific manner" provides the means by which "alone...it will be possible to provide a satisfying response to the question of how the 'irreal', 'transcendent' meaning guarantees us reality and objectivity."⁹ If the *Scotusbuch* credits Husserl with reawakening the problem of speculative grammar, it is the medieval account of analogy that is ultimately invoked to solve the problem of signification and objectivity, that is, to *solve* the modernist account of strict science, perhaps not yet fully aware of how the two paradigms potentially conflicted. In both the *Scotusbuch* and in *Being and Time*, in any case, the simple account of immanence and objectivity, the truth of the present-to-hand as it would be called, is denied—the former to fulfill it in the medieval account of analogy and the rare solidarity experienced in the relation between God and His creatures as it becomes differentiated in the "plentitude of Spirit's historical productions": the latter, to return the problem of the present-to-hand to the transcendence of Dasein in explicating the preontological understanding nascent in narratives of the everyday.¹⁰

In both cases the accounts remain consistent, nonetheless, in proclaiming, again to speak Kantian, Being's "inscrutability." Still, if *Being and Time* itself refuses to deny the *Seinsfrage*, it remains true, too, that its invocation of Dasein's mortality is equally the shattering of the 'positive' transcendence that underwrote the medieval account of analogy, the ultimate refusal to affirm a resemblance between *idea* and *ideatum*, beings and Being, sign and signified. If the conclusion of the *Scotusbuch* endorses Hegel with a certain overenthusiasm as having provided an account of the transcendence of the Divinity in history, *Being and Time* at the outset accuses the retrieval of ontology at work in the *Science of Logic's* opening proclamation that Being is the "indeterminate immediate" as having still missed the *problem* of Being and its transcendence, viz. that Being cannot be reduced to a concept at all. Rather, "if it is said that 'Being' is the most universal concept, . . . it is rather the darkest of all" (23).¹¹

What perhaps should be granted to Hegel, nonetheless, is at least to have seen what was at stake in the rise of philosophical modernism. While the nominalist controversy had in fact left both the doctrine of universals and the doctrine of analogy in tatters, it would be a mistake to claim that it simply left the way open for the rise of modern science and the victory of empiricism. In fact, as has become increasingly evident among historians of science—but Hegel tacitly recognized it already—the foray to philosophical modernism is a somewhat twisted collection of elements. Hence, Hegel's account of the rise of modern philosophy delineating a struggle between the "two opposed tendencies" represented by Bacon (in whom the medieval problem of the *interpretatio naturae* is still evident but submitted to a new reading, that of the foundation of the sensible particulars) and Jacob Boehme (the mystic who would have great influence on German idealism and German romanticism). Moreover Hegel's narrative should not simply be seen as an application of the usual mannerist calculus awaiting *Aufhebung*.[12] Rather, it involves a complex and overdetermined history that largely still awaits to be written.

Nonetheless, what can be said about both the metaphysics of analogy and the rise of philosophical modernism is that the 'univocity of Being' remained in both cases unproblematic. If modernism in principle *ex*cluded the *Seinsfrage* for the sake of the certainty of the *speculum* of representation, neither its simple exclusion nor the distance the medievals depended on in their accounts interrupted the emergence of truth: that is, interrupted the continuity between *intentio* and *intentionem*, *idea* and *ideatum*, and what Michel Foucault has aptly in this regard called the *benevolence of the sign*.[13] Whether it were resemblance or re-presentation, at least in this respect, did not matter; the univocity of the 'objective' and the ultimate homogeneity of our knowledge were not in question. If they were in this regard in agreement, in fact the two positions were, nonetheless, radically incommensurate. The transcendence on which the analogical depends contests the truth of certainty for the sake of overcoming finitude. And, the proof of representation inevitably contests the 'beyond' on which analogy depends for its 'depth grammar.'

VII

Such a recognition underwrites the works of Gilles Deleuze, an oeuvre of which Foucault claimed—doubtless, inter alia because of the sophistication of the challenge it poses to the preceding account—that "perhaps one day this century will be known as Deleuzian."[14] Whether or not the latter is true, it is true nonetheless that its challenge (as well as Foucault's and many of the authors who have been collated under the title of *post-structuralism*) can be understood precisely in terms of the retrieval contested within the Heideggerean project that has been traced. Deleuze's philosophical texts radically contest the attempt to contain difference, whether it be difference conceived as an individual (the difference of a concept and of representation) or the difference of a species (the difference of generic continuity and analogy). Instead, difference itself, it is claimed, has never in fact been thought "as such."[15] And, in this regard the usually omitted history of the application and transformation of the analogical becomes crucial.

Still, Deleuze in fact presents at first glance an account that seems very close to Heidegger's own. He too privileges the work of Scotus as the culmination of the classical tradition (or 'positive theology') in its recognition of the 'neutrality' or univocity of Being (for which "being is said equally both of God and His creation").[16] Moreover, he likewise regards the Cartesian refusal and its substitution of the veracity of the *clarae et distinctae* as a failure to confront "what always already escapes," to speak Heideggerean. Deleuze's account however confronts what he claimed is a second transformation in the descent of the analogical, privileging Spinoza's refutation of Cartesianism and the transformation it originates in this problematic. If in standard accounts of the history of hermeneutics Spinoza is often privileged as an essential moment in its development, in Deleuze's account his works ultimately involve a crucial moment that essentially contests its descent. Moreover, while this privilege is of a piece with similar elevations of Spinoza in recent French thought (in addition to the works of Foucault, it occurs in those of Althusser, Lacan, Derrida, Serres, and even Ricoeur), it is Deleuze who has most directly challenged the archive of hermeneutics in Spinoza's name.

Deleuze's *Spinoza et le problème de l'expression* argues that the significance of the Spinozist account is first to have *negated* the classical hierarchies within Being. In it analogy ceases to underwrite the indifferent, neutrality of Being, instead becoming differentially articulated as an affirmative and unlimited plurality of attributes of which "each expresses the reality or being of substance."[17] That is, for Spinoza, analogy involves the affirmation of a difference—no longer simply a relation between genus and species—but the modification and expression, the 'differentiation' of substance itself. Further, in thus 'dehierarchializing' Being, it likewise challenges the priority of representationalism. The clear and the distinct do not, Spinoza claimed, provide a criterion of truth, but merely one of the 'veri-similar'—one, that is, that remains insufficient, lacking an account of causes, an account of the deriviation of substance.[18]

Spinoza's account in this regard radically breaks with the representationalism of the Enlightenment. But, coupled with its commitment to mechanism, Deleuze claimed, it radically transforms as well the more ancient archive of expressionism, dissolving the teleological structure that regulated the extensions of classical analogy, one by which—as Spinoza put it in an argument that Kant would repeat—"it mistakes for things the forms of imagination."[19] Hence, in summing up its effect, Deleuze stated: "The significance of spinozism seems to us the following; to have disengaged expression from any subordination with regard to an emanative or exemplary cause. Expression itself ceases to emanate as well as resemble."[20]

Thus, Spinoza denies in the end both the mainstay of representationalism, substituting for it a knowledge that depends on origins, as
well as that of the classical account of analogy, since it denies equally
the teleological 'causes' on which the latter depended. For Deleuze,
however, Spinoza's account ultimately remains incomplete, its commitment to substantialism still precritical. Identity, that is, still comes first,
always already presupposed, rather than being thought itself as
'expression.' The final extension would occur only in what Deleuze calls
the *Copernican revolution* of Nietzshe's eternal return.[21] Only here,
consequently, would the articulation of the analogical become complete.
But it would so, paradoxically, only by becoming dis-articulation, a
differentiation in which 'Being' becomes expression through and
through, a difference beyond ontological reference—and its truth,
consequently, "a mobil army of metaphors."[22]

In Nietzsche's work then, Deleuze claimed, the doctrine of analogy
comes full circle. The inner tension between analogy and univocity is
resolved precisely in the affirmation of univocity as the univocity of
difference. Nietzsche's eternal return becomes the recurring of difference
itself, a pluralism, that is, of *"differences sauvages."*[23] It admits, thereby,
the univocity of the different and the 'tolerance,' that is, the difference
at work even in the 'continuity' of species on which the analogical
always depended. As a result, the theater of representation became
radically decentered, a theater whose identity is neither guaranteed nor
grounded in advance nor whose essential structure could remain
classical, a structure governing the play of elements without itself being
in play. Instead, simple identity here becomes set into play within
differentiation itself, generating in the same moment the recognition
of the transcendental illusion of the former's simple 'affirmation': "The
same, the similar are fictions engendered by the eternal return. There
is there (*il y a là*), this time, no longer an error, but an illusion; an
inevitable illusion, which is the source of error, but from which it is
not able to be separated."[24]

What would deny this *ekstasis* of the different, what would, in
short, 'revalorize' the hierarchy of beings and reinvest their dispersion
in the economics of identity, must now be brought under a 'hermeneutics' of suspicion. Any reduction of this difference could occur only
as an eventuality in which the indeterminacy at stake might now be
subject to another 'transcendence,' an exteriority that was the function
of a certain overdetermination. Such evasions might occur, that is, only
by the *need* for the denial (and repression) of difference itself, forcing
the necessity of the recognition of a certain malevolence of the sign,
again to speak Foucauldian. Instead "the eternal return is the same of

the different, the one of the multiple, the resemblance of the dissimilar."[25] In fact, Deleuze argues, himself affirmatively quoting Nietzsche, it is precisely here that the significance of the will to power is to be found: "The pleasure of knowing oneself different, the enjoyment of difference."[26]

VIII

We should grant to Kant—or at least Deleuze does so continually—the credit for making this ultimate extension of the Copernican revolution if not necessary, then, to use Kant's language, "unavoidable." Although the transition that would pair Spinoza and Nietzsche may seem, prima facie, forced, the addition of Kant further specifies what is at stake. The failure of the transcendental Ideal in the first *Critique's* Dialectic, the failure, that is, of ontotheological completeness and the end of metaphysics as *Wissenschaft*, was, after all, equally the failure of all resemblance and similitude. More radically than even the Spinozist transformation, it undercut the foundation of all simple identity relations, introducing "a sort of in principle disequilibrium into the pure self of the I think."[27] Moreover, if this failure re-moved the ultimate foundations of our rational practices, it was not one that made possible a solution that might facilitate their ultimate retrieval—either by analogical or causally based accounts. That is, the Kantian categories remained in the end mere *Standpunkten* for the articulation of the horizon of intelligibility. And, they refused, thereby, the attempt to ultimately ground the *continuum specierum* on which the doctrine of analogy ultimately depended.[28] The *lex continui in natura* could not be demonstrated. Nothing could forbid the possibility, consequently, that the "rhapsody of perceptions ungovernable by rules,"[29] the rules (the *ratio*) of synthesis, that is, might not ultimately prevail. In all this Kant already anticipated Nietzsche: "Kant seemed armed...to reverse the image of thought."[30]

Still, one should not speak too fast of the irradication of the analogical here, the mistake in the end that in fact marked the ruin of Spinozism itself. If Kant denied the ultimate foundations of objectivity, precisely in so doing he traced the necessity of Reason's waxing analogical in its very inscription. While still attempting to contain the difference involved within a concept (albeit undetermined and 'reflective'), as Deleuze noted, Kant's account of the transcendental condition of the understanding and of judgment itself depended in fact precisely on the analogical. From the moment of its initial appearance within the first *Critique's* Principles of Pure Understanding (precisely,

that is, in the section entitled, "Analogies of Perception"), the problem
of reason's extension remains understood by means of the problem of
the analogical and the question of an anticipation that could be neither
algorithmically demonstrated (by mathematical proportion [*analogia*])
nor merely empirically predicted.[31] It remained, instead, the question
of a qualitative and regulative extension, an extension that was at best
an *expectio*, and one by which, as Hegel saw too, thinkers as diverse
as Kant and Philo must still be thought together.[32]

The appearance of this anticipation and the question of its delay
seems only to reinvoke the question of temporality, the problem of the
future, and the issue of the finite and existential appropriation of truth,
perhaps ultimately vindicating, thereby, the Heideggerean invocation
of another order of justification and the legitimation of Kierkegaardian
choice. It would seem, that is, to authorize a decision we must make
in recurring to the *Ursprung* of difference, one that is conditional on
a transcendental gift, the *Es gibt* of time itself. But it is just here that
Deleuze demurred. For Deleuze, the result of the Kantian 'inversion'
of Platonism is that, far from marking a transcendence "beyond" or
"within" the self, the diaspora in question is one in which "time is out
of joint," precisely because permanence, succession, and simultaneity
are no longer that which measure time, but are themselves mere modes
and relations of time itself. Radically unlike a similar (premodern)
Augustianian move that it now only faintly 'reflects,' here the problem
of transcendental analogy involves precisely the *failure* of *extentio* and
the origin of transcendental illusion, the ultimate fracture and heterogenity of the self. The self, here, as Deleuze put it, is simply one in
which "I am another."[33]

                              IX

The syntagm "After Kant" looks then radically different in the
Deleuzean text than it did in those of the positivists of Paris and Vienna,
or the idealists and romanticists of Jena and Freiburg.[34] It involved,
instead, a shattering and dispersion that had in a sense always lay
lurking in the inscrutability of the noumenon, but that could seemingly
be committed to the Cartesian refusal, or more archaically be traced
as the provocation of a depth that withdrew by transcendence.

In fact, this shattering raised once again the problem of the
phenomenon, the question of difference, and the status of the phantasm
itself as a difference that could not be reduced. It raised, that is, precisely
the necessity, following Nietzsche's own grasp of the *Dialectic*, to abolish
both the world of essence and the world of mere appearance, an event

by which "the disperse itself becomes the unity of measure and communication."[35] Rather than a dispersion that would be accommodated within 'Being,' the univocity remains that of difference itself, "the diaphora of the diaphora" and not, thereby, a diaphora that might bid Being forth, as Heidegger had hoped in still dwelling on this difference as 'ontological.'[36] Hence, the univocity of the 'same' across difference would not be the perdurance of what withdraws, as Heidegger still hoped. Against all *Identitätsphilosophie*, Deleuze proclaimed, it involves a difference that is—as "the first potency"—insurpassable.[37] What persists then is only the shining (*Scheinung*) of the simulacrum itself. Hence, finally, the utter reversal of Platonism and the teleologies of the "philosophical odyssey."[38]

In fact the problem of the phantasm Deleuze outlined is in this respect archaic to Platonism. Having just inscribed the *logos* of *logos* in the *Republic's* narrative of the divided line, an image that was to escape all imagining, Plato himself denoted the problem that concerns the sensible and its provocation (*parakletika*), "defining as provocative things that impinge on the senses together with their opposites."[39] What was in question then concerned precisely the problem of difference itself: "We see the same thing at once as one and as an indefinite plurality."[40]

For Plato it is this play of indeterminacy that is the origin of knowledge—"the need for judgment." And yet, ironically, this need likewise arises only by generating a demand, indeed a compulsion, to put an end to the difference that was its own provocation. It involved an underdetermination, that is, which "would compel the soul to be at a loss and to enquire by arousing thought in itself, and to ask, whatever then is the one as such [*auto to hen*]."[41] If difference itself provokes thought, the discipline that seeks the One compels the *reduction* of difference, precisely by the discipline of *mathesis*, that is, a discipline of indifference, the equality of the calculative. By its means this 'provocative' difference would be dissolved and the soul's "loss" overcome in the contemplation of true being and the one "as such."[42]

It is this subsumption of difference in presentation, it might be said, that in-forms the discourse of *philosophia* and its *theoria*. Moreover, it is this surpassing that has been denied in Deleuze's refusal to reduce the diaspora itself, a refusal that instead, as its inversion, becomes the strict affirmation of the phantasm, beyond resemblance, identity, continuity, permanence, and the hierarchy of representation—an affirmation, then, of the 'phantasm as such.'

X

The site of *Being and Time*, likewise, it must be acknowledged, arises with this very question of the phantasm, pursuing the *Destruktion* of the history of ontology with temporality as its clue, and in this regard what it likewise called in fixing on Kant's modernism, "Kant's shrinking back" before the imagination and the question of 'ontological synthesis' (45)...The method of this deciphering, of this hermeneutic of Being was however announced as 'phenomen-ological,' a method that, if it retained a certain proximity to Husserl would equally undertake a certain *Destruktion* of all that phenomenology had invested in the representationalism of Cartesianism. In fact, Heidegger is perhaps more direct in this regard than is often thought, granted the archive that both he and Deleuze share: "Everything that belongs to the species of exhibiting and explicating (*Art der Aufweizung und Explikation*) and which goes to make up the way of conceiving demanded by this research is called 'phenomenological' " (61).

In one respect, and even in Heidegger's own reading, this account of the phenomena in fact seems entirely 'unproblematic.' "Because phenomena, as understood phenomenologically, are never anything but what goes to make up Being, while Being is in every case, the Being of some entity, we must first bring forward the entities themselves...in the right way" (61). As on this account Being is constituted and grounded in the phantasm, the problem of ontology seems entirely straightforward, indeed merely an affirmation of the phantasm itself, to speak Nietzschean. Husserl nascently asserted the unproblematic character of this access in his phenomenological 'principle of principles,' vindicating the evidence of the given as a transcendental right de juris, and hence freely open to explication and intuition.

And yet, the status of explication is pivotal here—in fact summing up, as will be seen, the issue that has been in question. For Husserl, unlike for Heidegger and those who come after his retrieval of the *Seinsfrage*, the notion of phenomenological explication remains straight-forwardly Cartesian in method. Here, that is, 'clarification' belongs strictly speaking to the *Wissenschaft* of *adequatio* and to the presence of transcendental representation. Consequently, Husserl (like Kant before him, in this regard) simply understood 'explication' as 'analysis' and 'analytic phenomenology' as a research program modeled on the strict judgments of *apophansis* and the propositional identity of subject and object.[43]

But this is precisely what Heidegger denied in his account of explication, a denial that the *'hermeneutische als'* could ever successfully be retrieved within the apophantic. The narratives of the everyday could not be converted into positive knowledge, into "theoretical sentences," as he called it, without a certain transcendental illusion or "perversion," confronted with a totality that always already escaped categorial schematization (201). The elucidation involved required, instead, a refusal to simply assume the propositional attitude of the *theatrum philosophicum* of representation. Hence: "[T]he meaning of phenomenological description as a method lies in *interpretation (Auslegung)*" (61). The *logos* of phenomenology involved an engagement with a provocation that escaped decidability, a *hermeneuein*, as Heidegger would invoke an ancient archive, that escaped the discourse of philosophy and that would not answer, consequently, to the question of the simple opposition of the one and the many—nor whose 'expression' could be confused with simple 'description.' Here the phantasm could neither be reduced, disregarded, nor simply banned, as Husserl before Heidegger had hoped in removing the image from the domain of the phenomenologically present-to-hand. But this is precisely where the Heideggerean move differs, refusing to allow the *Aus-legung* of hermeneutic phenomenology to be reduced to analysis, but instead articulated as an event in which synthesis and analysis are intertwined in the opening of the phantasm and Dasein's *ekstasis*.

XI

Doubtless this appeal to 'hermeneutics' and its *ekstasis* involves a retrieval of discourses that have remained marginal in the history of philosophy, ones, moreover, to which the question of explication itself belongs. Doubtless too their confrontation remains essential for coming to grips with the status of the 'explications' of hermeneutics, as both those who contest it (like Deleuze) and those who would affirm it have agreed. Among the latter Gadamer, for example, devotes all of Appendix VI of *Truth and Method* to the claim that "the whole of our investigation shows why the concept of 'expression' must be purified of its modern subjectivist flavour and referred back to its original grammatical and rhetorical sense," one that derives from the neo-Platonic and mystical traditions and the problem of the emanation of the One and that in turn becomes "the basis of our critique both of 'art of experience (*Erlebnis*)' and of romantic hermeneutics."[44]

This history in fact is a long and twisted tale. Still, Hegel again may be invoked in order to grasp its crucial effect. In his own account of *ekstasis* in Plotinus—an interesting one granted the severity of his polemic against its manifestation in his contemporary Schelling—he claimed that the interest in *ekstasis* steps beyond the need for ratiocination and decidability, and in fact, no longer occurs by means of "an anxiety to explain and to lay out [*Auslegung*] (as in a deduction of matter or evil)...but rather to separate the soul...and give it its central place in simple clear ideas."[45] In all this there is no longer compulsion for demonstration and need for criteria (*Masstab*) to proceed. "Ecstasy is not a mere rapture of the senses and fancy, but rather a passing beyond the content of sensuous consciousness (*Vorstellung*)."[46] In it, he claimed, the separation of subject and object are rejected, a rejection, moreover, lost within the antinomy of "skepticism" and "dogmatism" of "modern times."[47] And yet, Hegel, doubtless as well still bogged down in that very antinomy himself, understood this pouring forth of the One and the *ekstasis* of *Geist* beyond *figurate* conception to be both the Idea and the Notion, that is, ultimately, nothing less than the *fulfillment* of representation itself, thought's '*Selbst-Darstellung*.'

The issue can, moreover, be further sharpened by focusing more specifically on the archive of explication—in fact even to the extent of concentrating the issue on a single author. Both Deleuze and Gadamer have privileged in this regard the work of Nicolas of Cusa. As Deleuze himself pointed out, the notion of *explicatio* has a long development, gaining prominence in commentators of Boethius in the school of Chartres in the twelfth century.[48] But it is especially in the work of Cusanus, he claimed, that the term "acquires rigorous philosophical status," making prominent as well issues that remain contested even within the present of contemporary hermeneutics. In his *Docta Ignorantia* (II.3), Cusa stated: "God is the complication [the enfolding] of all things (*omnia complicans*) in that all things are in him; and he is the explication [the unfolding] of all things (*omnia explicans*) in that He is in all things."[49]

For Cusa the explication-complication relationship furnished a resource for truth despite the looming onslaught of nominalism and the failure of accounts of knowledge by analogy. Despite the refusal of a positive or even analogical account of the relation between the finite and the infinite, as Gadamer put it in *Truth and Method*, discussing what he calls Cusa's *Explikationslehre*:

> The multiplicity in which the human mind unfolds itself is not a mere fall from true unity and not a loss of its home. Rather, there has to be a positive justification for the finitude of the human mind, however much this finitude remains related to the infinite unity of absolute being. This is prepared for in the idea of *complicatio*, and from this point of view the phenomenon of language also acquires a new aspect. It is the human mind that

both complicates and explicates. The unfolding into discursive multiplicity is not only conceptual, but also extends into the verbal sphere. It is the variety of possible appelations—according to the various languages—that potentiates conceptual differentiation.[50]

Heidegger had seemingly said little different in the *Scotusbuch's* account of the intensification of the individual's relation to and differentiation of the Absolute experienced in transcendence—its specific mixing of the homogeneous and the heterogeneous, as he put it. Moreover, if Cusa denied direct knowledge, as well as knowledge by analogy in this relation between Being and beings, what spurs this extension on, despite this failure, is again the encounter with a provocation that exceeds it. "Since there is no comparative relation to the Creator, no created thing posseses a beauty through which the Creator can be attained. But from the greatness of the beauty and adornment of created things, we are elevated unto what is infinitely and incomprehensibly beautiful."[51] This elevation was to provide access to all that might not be encompassed within the unity of a concept and demonstrated, an event that would be thereby not only 'before,' but 'beyond' demonstration—a tracing and interpretation of the extension of identity within difference, and precisely, thereby, the withdrawal of transcendence.

XII

Michel Foucault likewise has provided an analysis of this early Renaissance 'episteme,' one that he concentrates under the Hegelian title, "The Prose of the World." In a manner similar to Deleuze, Foucault claimed that this 'episteme' constituted a closed totality in which resemblance is extended throughout an infinite chain of signifiers.[52] Here, "resemblance never remains stable in itself; it can be fixed only if it refers back to another similitude, that then, in turn refers to others. Each resemblance therefore had value only from the accumulation of all the others, and the whole world must be explored if even the slightest of analogies is to be justified and finally take on the appearance of certainty."[53] Consequently, it remained a hermetic circle that, as he rightly saw, is "plethoric yet absolutely poverty-stricken." Hermeneutics and semiology were implicitly superimposed by means of the implicit bond of the ontological, the "secret similitude of entities." The result facilitated an "infinite accumulation of confirmations (*entassement infini de confirmations*) all dependent on one another."[54] But, following the strictness of the Cartesian criticism of resemblance, the benevolence of the 'depth' could no longer remain effective.

In fact, Foucault proclaimed, nothing except literature perhaps, and "even in a fashion more allusive and diagonal than direct," now remains of this depth, invoking once more the heroes of marginality and madness that emerged from *Madness and Civilization* (Hölderlin, Mallermé, Artaud).[55] And yet, if in all this, "throughout the nineteenth century, literature began to bring language back to light once more in its own being," it did so now without the assurance of the Renaissance. For now it emerged without that "primary, that absolutely initial word on which the infinite movement of discourse was founded."[56]

What stands in between, as Foucault pointed out—essentially in agreement with Heidegger—is that move which had transformed the system of signs originating with the Stoics from a ternary relation to a binary one.[57] By its means, consequently, language could be seen as a table of classifications and combination, and judgment an *ars combineatoire*. As a result, the *interpretatio naturae* could become a matter of representation and truth a matter of demonstration: thought a matter of analysis, and its assertion a matter of simple identity. And, what would not fit this paradigm became *excluded* as relative, a matter of taste, the subjective, the prejudicial, the fictional, and the feigning of hypotheses.

Nonetheless, for reasons perhaps now clear, that Foucault would cite the literary as its only remnant or would witness its 'reemergence' only there smacks perhaps not only of avante guardism, but verges simply on positivism, limiting, after all, everything that remained of its trace to the realm of the fictional. Moreover, it operated in this regard doubtless under the belief that distinctions between the scientific, the literal, and the imaginary, and the fictional could simply and categorially be made. It operated, that is, under the delusion that not only could there be no truth to 'fiction,' but no fiction (and no interpretation) to truth—presupposing, inter alia, that the literal and the fictional could be simply parsed. Here and elsewhere, perhaps still too much in Kant's (and the Enlightenment's) wake, Foucault attempted too strongly to separate explanation and interpretation—when the 'archive' in question implicated quite otherwise. In all this, instead, as has been seen, Foucault delimited not merely an 'episteme,' but—still to speak Kantian—a 'problematic' that neither simply originated in the sixteenth century, nor simply dissolved thereafter, nor whose "re-emergence" could ultimately simply be limited to the 'literary.'[58]

But this much is right, doubtless: the institution of modernist accounts of legitimation did result in the ultimate withdrawal—or 'exclusion,' perhaps—of the initial 'Word' that guaranteed the infinity of resemblance, precisely in the recognition that this *Ursprung* escaped ultimate and strict demonstration. And, likewise in the wake of the failure of the modernist search for demonstration and decidability, the trajectory of nominalism led ultimately to an infinite dissolution, the denial of which could only be viewed as a matter of suspicion. Hence the purges of "Marx, Nietzsche, and Freud." Still if, as has been seen, Deleuze's account cited Spinoza as their progenitor, it doubtless did so both because of his recognition of the failure of the teleological recovery of resemblances, by which classical expressivism had assured itself, as much as it was a commitment to the causal determinism and the visage of an all-encompassing explanation—one by which, after all, as Kant and Nietzsche realized, he still precritically construed the Absolute by extension, analogy, and thus, interpretation.

XIII

The author of *Being and Time* doubtless himself reinvoked the endless circle of expressivism, the circle he too has stipulated in fact as neo-Plotinian, one of the *ens a se* (being from itself) and *ens ab alio* (being from another)—or its remainder, that circle as hermeneutic.[59] But he likewise did so fully in acknowledging its failure and *ekstasis* as demonstration. From the standpoint of demonstration (the standpoint of scientific proof [*Wissenschaftliche Beweis*]), the circularity of explication, of condition and conditioned, of interpretation and context, will inevitably appear vicious and devoid of the strictness of demonstrative knowledge (*die Strenge der begrundenden Ausweisung*)—a recognition that occurs fully perhaps staring Husserl in the face. But thereby, appealing directly to the *Faktum* that has structured the evidence of narrative from the start, Heidegger proclaimed once more: "the Fact (*Faktum*) of this circle in understanding is not eliminated" (194). Hence, the famous claim: if we see this circle as a vicious one, we have misunderstood the act of understanding from the ground up, the preontological ground, Dasein's being-in-the-world of which understanding is always, nascently or not, precisely an *explication*.

Here, too, it might be said, as Heidegger stated in turning away from proofs for the external world (the issue, after all is the same), "the 'scandal of philosophy' is not that this proof has yet to be given, but that *such proofs are expected and attempted again and again*" (249). Instead, he proclaimed with a certain Nietzschean bravado: "If Dasein is understood correctly, it defies such proofs, because, in its Being, it already *is* what subsequent proofs deem necessary to demonstrate for it" (249).

Still, whether or not this 'assertion' is itself true depends on the retrieval of a preontological comprehension that was itself at stake, risked within the 'analysis' of the *Daseinanalytik*, a hermeneutic phenomenology that is as 'circular' as any (and all) interpretation must always be.[60] Consequently, this appeal beyond proof remained seemingly helpless before the Deleuzean objection that if Husserl were a 'Thomist' in his retrieval of Aristotelean intentionalism, Heidegger's appeal to a preontological awareness and a participation in Being to which "certainly we were not strangers" remained a naive retrieval that was ultimately simply 'Scotist.'[61] Thereby, it opens itself to the charge of having missed the threat of Nietzsche's challenge and what escaped those confines—that far from an 'explication' that might trace out the *transcendens* of Being, the difference in question might not be contained by a concept, a transcendental logic, nor even an 'ontological synthesis.' Heidegger's argument, instead, would never have seriously faced the Nietzschean risk. It would never have faced, that is, an eventuality in which, rather than a revelation of Being, "resemblance subsists but it is produced as the exterior effect of the simulacrum" and "identity subsists but it is produced as the law that complicates the series."[62]

If the 'justification' of the *Daseinanalytik* extended beyond proof, what became more and more evident, in any case, is the hubris by that *Being and Time* might be regarded as having *solved* the issue of *Wissenschaftlich Beweisung*, the retrieval of the science of being as such, and its hopes that by means of the hermeneutic circle, scientific themes might be made secure (*zu sichern*) (195). The result of *Fundamentalontologie*, after all, was, precisely to the contrary, that the facticity of Dasein, and consequently its *Faktum*, were *grundlos*. And, as a result, Spinozistic concerns regarding the projections of teleological explication could only fatally complicate the issue—as Heidegger would himself make evident in his own confrontation with Nietzsche. The scandal of philosophy would not be so easily overcome. In fact in the sense that Heidegger's explications might be taken (or have taken itself) to have *solved* the issue, to have made *explication* itself "secure," his account doubtless just failed, having discovered in the *Sorge* structure itself an entity that was profoundly incompatible with such a result. *Pace* its protests to the contrary, the circle *escaped* turning 'vicious' only by depending precisely on the *Augenblick* of a future and a measureless impossiblity on which its hopes were always already shattered, decentered within the circularity of its own facticity. In this regard it could neither simply nor outright deny the corresponding 'structuralist' claim that hermeneutics was merely an exchange of codes: structured, as Barthes put it, only by a certain rhetorics and its corresponding set of 'hermeneutemes,' one that always labored under its own peculiar transcendental illusion, that of the *decipherment* of truth.[63] Rather than a 'revelation' of Being, interpretation would then emerge only as an infinite play of texts. And, as Michel Serres claimed, the circle in question would then (functionally) reduce to merely "the application of the subset of one work to another, one space on another space" within an endless labyrinth of exchanges, the eternal return itself as *ars combineatoire*, its phantasm (and what it called its 'truth') a floating signifier.[64]

XIV

'Hermeneutic phenomenology'—two words that, for reasons now evident, could not be combined without a certain dissonance—was itself the displaying of Dasein's *dispersion*. In this regard it was the dis-play of a diaspora that has been inseparably linked both to modern transcendentalism and its archive.[65] If hermeneutics legitimately extended beyond the grounds of modernism, it never solved the latter's task of instituting the foundations of rationality in accord with a logic of demonstration. Heidegger's initial claim that phenomenology postulated a simple correlation between being and phenomenon, between the ontic and the ontological, remained in the strict sense doubtless naive and open to 'Spinozistic' objections regarding attempts to correlate the teleologies of the clear and the distinct with Being—and equally open then to the suspicions that might underlie and overdetermine such attempts.

Still, it remains true, too, as Deleuze likewise proclaimed at the outset, there is a "certain Nietzschean inspiration that is often present in phenomenology"[66]—precisely in the refusal of the claim that Being might be simply relied on as something strictly 'beyond' the phenomena, a refusal that doubtless, inter alia acknowledges the insurpassability of the modern, that is, the insurpassability of the critical enterprise. If Heidegger's account of Dasein's totalization as care is directed ultimately to the question of "transcendence" it is, after all, both generated by and resolutely returned to a concern for and even solicitude [*Fürsorge*] for 'beings'. It is this same resoluteness moreover that denies the simple affirmation of the appearance (of presentation, re-presentation, the judgment of the present-to-hand and its transcendental logic) to be sufficient, acknowledging thereby the withdrawal and distance that pervades the failure of the finite itself—that is, the disequilibrium of the phantasm, one that both pervaded as well as ultimately undercut the figuration of the analogical.[67]

If, then, the account must affirm the ultimate defoundation of the world of essence as well as the world of appearance, it does so in affirming the difference that is insurpassably their intertwining. Thereby, it likewise forced the rethinking of the "as" of metaphysical and representational characterization—precisely in acknowledging its complication. No longer would it be possible, as Heidegger himself ultimately recognized, simply to think "appropriation (*Ereignis*) as a species of Being."[68] Instead, in default of a guarantee that might maintain representation intact, a "transformed interpretation" resulted, one by which the *herméneuein* in question, the "sending and extending" that 'hermeneutic' appropriation 'explicates,' involved equally a "self-withholding" and "expropriation (*Enteignis*)."[69] Already the writings of the 1930s betray the complexity of this opening in their attentiveness to the joining and disjoining of figure, the work as fugue, and so forth—an event no longer quaranteed by a synthesis of recognition.[70] In this they approach without simply 'affirming' Deleuze's demand that we think an event in which "opposition, identity and even analogy are only effects produced by these presentations of difference."[71]

The phantasm that incites the *Rede* of the phenomenological exhibits, on the one hand, too little of 'Being' to ever be able to recuperate it. And yet, on the other hand, it exhibits too much, always saying de facto more than it actually intends, an ex-ceeding that occurs precisely in the venturing of its own doubling. It is precisely in this sense that 'hermeneutics,' now as the art of tracing, separating, holding apart—and as such, 'deciphering'—this difference becomes the affirmation of the depth and withdrawal of the phantasm itself.[72] The recognition that this difference entails the endless decentering of *Fundamentologie* likewise forces the recognition of the *in-substantiality* and thus the instability of the phantasm itself, a doubling in which analysis and synthesis, proximity and withdrawal, the visible and the invisible intertwine interminably and without resolution. If the sensible provokes the intelligible, as Plato demanded, the intelligible, as Kant replied, seeks the sensible for its *Sinn und Bedeutung*. The phantasm itself always remains a dis-articulation, an "exhibitive disparting" (*aufzeigendes Auseinanderlegen*), to use Heidegger's term, whose difference would always be in the strict sense undecidable.[73]

The evidence of the hermeneutic doubtless remains in this regard as Michel Foucault said of thought in general—claiming also that the question of *Was heist denken?* characterized Deleuze's project in general— "a perilous act."[74] And yet, the 'evidence' in question arose precisely by refusing to exchange what had become defounded within its past for another ground, a matter that both to those within and without the hermeneutic tradition presented the illusion of a simple nostalgic retrieval of an archaic classicism and its humanist past, a burden, along with the question of legitimation—granted the peril—that would be passed on to Heidegger's heirs.

Hermeneutics, as has been seen, could not simply situate its 'explications' on such grounds, in fact could not help but extend beyond the text of philosophy precisely in dwelling on the issue contested within it. In fact it was by affirming the dispersion contested within its past that its evidence became insurpassable, even if—*pace* Heidegger, that is, the Heidegger of *Sein und Zeit*—it did so only by cutting loose its own security to remain faithful to its 'claim'.[75] Deleuze, on the contrary, in recognizing the underdetermination of such an affirmation and its 'explication' would seek the route of alterity—and ultimately, of course, the route of an-archism.[76] But it was precisely against this possibility and its leveling that Heidegger ultimately remained 'resolute.' And, it was without question what remained contested in his 'task' and doubtless critical in the attempt to both articulate—and liberate—the figures of the everyday.

Between Truth
and Method:
Gadamer,
Traditionality,
and the Problem
of Justification
in Interpretative
Practices

Within the hermeneutic tradition and what remains left now as its trace there has always been what may be called a certain *classical dissonance*—classical, because it involves the delay of an epistemological research program whose grids shaped the rise of modern thought. The *practice* of hermeneutics, of textual *interpretation*, on the other hand, has always left those grids perpetually undone. Nonetheless, from the outset the justifactory status of the articulations that result was anything but clear, regarding either its archive, its assertion, or its contemporary remainder—all of which will be a stake in what follows.

In the *Compendium* of 1819, Friederich Schleiermacher gave two variations of the goal of hermeneutics, two heuristic goals for hermeneutic practices. A good deal of attention (by Hans-Georg Gadamer, among others) has been paid to what Schleiermacher called the *negative formula* (to avoid misunderstanding), that universalizes the hermeneutical problem. As a result, it is often claimed that hermeneutics is no longer seen as the narrow organon for deciphering obscure texts, but a general investigation of *Verstehen* itself, one that sees the problem of understanding as essentially one of interpretation. On the other hand, little enough attention is paid perhaps to Schleiermacher's *positive* formulation of its task: "IX. The rules for the art of interpretation must be developed from a positive formula, and this is: 'the historical and divinatory, objective and subjective reconstruction of a given statement.' "[1]

In this Schleiermacher returns to the grids of classical thought to found his project, expressive of the conscilience between romanticism and its modernist roots. Interpretation is a reconstruction; it is the re-presentation of the text's appearance—in reverse order. The interpreter *fuses* with the text, 'objectively' grasping the nature of the linguistic heritage it re-presents and subjectively grasping the statement "as a fact in the person's mind." The interpretation is to return to the immediacy of the creative act, just as Descartes was to return to immediate "simple and distinct" truths. And, ultimately this was to be achieved by a divination moving beyond the expressed sign, just as Descartes would have us by the *Via intuiti* found reason in the immediate; or Bacon, who introduced the philosopheme of foundations into the theater of the Enlightenment, hoped to "lead men to the particulars themselves."[2] In either case we have what Sellars has called the *myth of the given*, or Derrida, the *metaphysics of simple presence*: either the immediacy of the truths of reason (of mental meanings) is invoked or that of a world of sense particulars.[3] By this same myth, by an essential divination of the author's meaning, Schleiermacher's hermeneutics claims that there is ultimately no conflict between our practices, idioms, theories, grammars, genres, and so forth and those of the author: no difference between my idiolect and his or hers. Reason and truth might still remain everywhere one and the same. What started out conditioning meaning with interpretation ends by appealing to a myth that would, through an objective and subjective reconstruction, make interpretation unconditional.

Opposing this strain of hermeneutics that would lead us directly to the *science* of interpretation, one turns now almost as directly to the work of Friederich Nietzsche, who belongs to that other movement of the nineteenth century that had seen history as a proliferation of difference: the demise of man, classically understood, the demise of Reason, and the demise of the conceptual bases that had assured stability in Western thought.

> The biggest fable of all is the fable of knowledge. One would like to know what things-in-themselves are; but behold there are no things-in-themselves! But even supposing there were an in-itself, an unconditioned thing, it would for that very reason be unknowable! Something unconditioned cannot be known; otherwise it would not be unconditioned.[4]

One can believe the fable of the world of unconditioned truth and determinacy only by a peculiar form of 'forgetfulness.' The world of the true is a fable in which "a group of phenomena (are) selected and united by an interpreting being."[5] There are no unequivocal 'facts,' no simple 'truths,' but only the chaos of an infinite play of interpretations— never undone or reduced.

One would not be wrong, perhaps, in claiming the site of this conflict between meaning and interpretation, truth and context, observation and theory, the objective and subjective, as the site of postclassical hermeneutics. In fact, it may be the site of a much more general phenomenon that is postclassical or postmodern. In this regard, whether it is played out under the guise of 'hermeneutics' or not may be insignificant. But it is perhaps not insignificant that a variety of figures in fields originally alien to this domain have thought it important to play out their questions in relation to it: for example, Rorty, van Fraassen, Fish, or Dworkin; Barthes, Derrida, Eco, or Nancy.

This does not mean that hermeneutics has made an easy peace with this conflict, if it is often claimed to have made advances towards emerging from it. To bring both those advances and their hesitancy to light, one can focus on the relationship between interpretation, truth, and justification in what has become the *locus classicus* of twentieth-century hermeneutic theory, Hans-George Gadamer's *Truth and Method*.

II

But to begin with, such a reading should itself be legitimated, as *Truth and Method* is perhaps too rarely read this way—being typically read as a text that simply replaces or surpasses questions concerning methodology and justification with another, 'more primordial' discipline, fundamental ontology. Indeed Gadamer himself seems at first glance to charge Emilio Betti with *eisegesis* for questioning whether Gadamer has omitted raising the *qaestio juris* in this work on truth and method. But that it is no small matter to Gadamer can be gleaned from his opening statement to one of the central sections of this work: "Thus we can formulate the fundamental epistemological question for a truly historical hermeneutics as follows: what is the ground of the legitimacy of prejudices? What distinguishes legitimate prejudices from the countless others that it is the undeniable task of critical reason to overcome?" (TM:277) Unpacked, this passage manifests much. First of all, it shows not only a concern for the question of justification, but it does so in a way that is embedded in the language of the Enlightenment. Gadamer is concerned with the *foundational* question for a hermeneutics, one that involves the *grounds* for the legitimacy of interpretations. Moreover, even these are couched in the language of the Enlightenment that both Descartes and Bacon again share. We are involved with an investigation of our own *prejudices*. However, the notion of prejudice itself has undergone a transformation, one that marks for Gadamer a fundamental advance in hermeneutics. Against the Enlightenment, not all prejudices are to be exorcised from a legitimate (i.e., justified) hermeneutic practice.

Rather, there is an attempt on Gadamer's part to take what is at stake in the Nietzsche-Schleiermacher dilemma by the horns. Gadamer has given up the attempt to found hermeneutics in a psychologistic fusion between the intentions of reader and writer by means of a 'divination,' as had Schleiermacher, or empathy, as had Dilthey. Rather, what occurs in the hermeneutic event is a fusion in discursive horizons between reader and writer, and in particular what those horizons disclose.

This means, however, that in the end no interpretation ever reaches an epistemic or justificatory zero point, one never arrives at the null context, because what gets disclosed depends on the conditions of its disclosure (the interpreter's context). There are, in short, no

presuppositionless assertions. Neither the interpreter nor the interpreted ever completely surpasses the realm of their conditions, their
facticity. It is just this that forces, Gadamer claimed, a reformation in
the Enlightenment's position on truth and method, making possible
the retrieval of the humanist tradition it overshadowed.

Presuppositions, pre-judices (*Vor-urteilen*) are not something best
dissolved, but the *conditio sine qua non* of assertion. Unlike Descartes,
we cannot return to an immediate foundation. We are not, that is, in
a position that we can hope to "set aside all the opinions that (we) had
previously accepted among (our) beliefs and start from the very
beginning (*commencer tout de nouveau des les foundements*)."[6] Without
Descartes's rational Archimedian point, prejudice cannot be easily
identified as reason's contrary, simply as an Idol that is the source of
error. In fact the possibilities that any given tradition open up are not
just those for falsity, but those for 'truth' as well. Part of making an
interpretation is to carry one's roots along with it—context, presuppositions, paradigms, background assumptions, methods, conceptual
frameworks, and so on. Hence again, however, the proximity of
Nietzsche, the proximity of the 'fictionalization' of truth. And hence,
to use Gadamer's terms, the "borderline position of literature"—
precisely as "the place where art and science merge" (TM:159, 163).

III

To all this, accordingly, Emilio Betti sounded a familiar 'Western'
refrain (one that extends at least as far back as Aristotle's distinction
between fact and reasoned fact, occuring more recently in the distinction
between the *quid juris* and *quid facti* that structures Kant's *Transcendental
Deduction*).[7] In tying reason and tradition together, in tying *Urteil* to
Vorurteil, in refusing to allow—at least in principle—the ideal of
presuppositionless truth, it appears that Gadamer's *Truth and Method*
destroys both the substantives that are connected in its title. The search
for objectivity becomes lost in an irrationalism that relativizes truth and
delivers the question of method in a Hegelian fashion to a process that
takes place essentially behind the back of consciousness; the process
by which it is tied to a context—thus embedding reason within history,
and, in Kantian terms, trans-forming *cognitio et principiis* into mere
narration (*Erzählung*).

What is Gadamer's response here? In a letter written directly to
Betti (parts of which appear in later editions of *Truth and Method*),
Gadamer presented a response that relates directly to the ambiguity
at hand:

Fundamentally, I am *not proposing a method*; I am describing *what is the case*. That it is as I describe it cannot, I think, be seriously questioned. . . . In other words, I consider the only scientific thing is *to recognize what is*, instead of starting from what ought to be or could be. Hence I am trying to go beyond the concept of method held by modern science (which retains its limited justification) and to envisage in a fundamentally universal way what *always* happens. (TM:512)[8]

Read against the classical metanarrative on rationality this is doubtless a curious response. In a sense it starts out *not* refuting the claim that the analyses of *Truth and Method* reside on the level of the *qaestio facti*, on what is held, but affirming it. Gadamer from the beginning had been interested in the description of *what happens* in the hermeneutic event, in "what is the case." Still, a new qualifier is added at the end of the passage; Gadamer moves from "what is the case" to "what always is the case," to "what always happens." And, Gadamer's careful voyage for the *via media* between the Scylla of the Enlightenment's search for *les fondements* and the Charybdis of relativism must be sought here.

In this regard what follows in Gadamer's response should not be left out either, as it projects an even more forceful irony upon the classical text.

But what does Betti say to this? That I am, then, limiting the hermeneutical problem to the *qaestio facti* ("phenomenologically," "descriptively") and do not at all pose the *qaestio iuris*. As if when Kant raised the *qaestio iuris* he intended to prescribe what the pure natural sciences ought to be, rather than to justify their transcendental possibility as they already were. (TM:512)[9]

What in effect happens here, is a citation—even a certain grafting—of Kant made while Gadamer is wholly involved in 'overcoming,' in 'rehabilitating' Kant's distinction. The natural sciences "as they already were" contained an Enlightenment-based view of justification that could be wholly accommodated within the *qaestio facti–qaestio juris* distinction—precisely the one that Gadamer's 'concretization' has put into question. That is, Kant's view of rationality and the fact-reason distinction was not prescriptive of the natural sciences precisely because it was imported from a myth already operative in them—one for which now Gadamer tells Betti he is willing to allow only *"limited justification."* Here, in fact as elsewhere it remains the case for Gadamer that "the only 'objectivity'. . . is the confirmation of a foremeaning in its being worked out" (TM:267).

Kant himself however did not face Gadamer's question. Normative and descriptive simply coincided within the exemplars that structured the *experimenta crucis* of the Copernican revolution—a matter that would, consequently, always threaten to turn Kant's transcendental deductions circular. Reason and science really ought to be just as for Descartes and Newton, who believed objectivity in the end could be easily had without the interference of their own presuppositions or practices. They knew, in effect, more than any interpretation could provide.

And yet Betti's (and Aristotle's and Kant's) question remains. If Gadamer has enlarged and extended the classical, transcendental account by embedding it within its context and tradition, forcing thereby a certain contingency on it, what right does its claim to truth contain? If truth and method are mutually limiting, do they in the end cancel one another out? Is relativism the final word?

IV

What is Gadamer's response? As has been seen, if he does not simply give up doing philosophy in the 'modern' mode and its search for legitimation, he will not rest with its a-historical, de-prejudiced myth of the return to origins, to immediacy. Reason and authority, tradition and context cannot be simply opposed. The intrinsic involvement of reason in history, its character as finite interpretation, mitigates against this simple abstract opposition. We can neither, therefore, escape the ties of 'traditionality' nor simply hand rationality over to it.

> It seems to me, however, that there is no such unconditioned antithesis between tradition and reason. However problematical the conscious restoration of old or the creation of new traditions may be, the romantic faith in the "growth of tradition," before which all reason must remain silent, is fundamentally like the Enlightenment, and just as prejudiced. The fact is that in tradition there is always an element of freedom and of history itself. (TM:281)

Gadamer refused to abandon the failures of the Enlightenment for those of Romanticism, refused simply to abandon Descartes for Burke and Schlegel. He refused, that is, having recognized the impossibility of escaping history, to simply submit rationality to destiny, to fate, to 'progress,' to an overriding *telos*. But what is the relation between reason and historical practices then? And how can one avoid epistemic relativism, from turning the 'historicity' of truth into simple historicism? Reason is to be seen as linked with tradition—*essentially*. As Heidegger said before Gadamer, if we see this simply as a limitation on a faculty, we have misunderstood it from the ground up.[10] All of this by now is in a sense well known. But the ambiguity in this bond between reason and tradition would haunt not only Heidegger, but his followers—beginning with his earliest students, not only Gadamer, but those who would ultimately distance themselves from him, for example, Strauss or Arendt. As the latter realized, it involved a certain (Hegelian) retrieval of Augustine, elevating the problems of *memoria* and time.[11] Traditions would now be the *conditio sine qua non* of whatever it is that we are to call *knowledge*. Still, what is disclosed on the basis of a tradition could *not*, as the Enlightenment had made known, simply be a *function* of the latter. It could not be a simple processing of information through a unique table of categories—if this were the case, the diachronics of categorical transformation would become incomprehensible.

However enticing a coherence story about truth and justification might be in this setting (what is true is simply what 'makes sense' and accords with the inherent beliefs of our practices, theories, tradition, etc.), Gadamer, in any case, recognized it would not suffice unless we want to move from the Enlightenment's mistake to that of romanticism, unless we want merely to substitute one *foundation* for another. And to do this is to take everything the Enlightenment's account of rationality anchored in the thinking subject and hand it *tout court* over to the community (an equivocation that occurs naturally within the '*Geist*' of the German language, and the politics of German idealism perhaps depended on it). That is, this tack will not suffice unless we want to take the account of knowledge and truth out of the realm of immanence completely, away from the thinking 'subject,' and just restore it to the advent of traditions. Then—as Strauss and Popper realized—we could say the same for the history of Reason that Hegel said of history in general, that it is "the slaughter-bench" of individuals.[12]

It should be noted that Gadamer does claim at one point in *Truth and Method* that Heidegger criticized the theory of pure perception on the basis of an experience that is "pragmatic" (TM:91), one that he acknowledged risks the classicist's charge of conflating theory and practice.[13] Still there is, of course, more to Gadamer's story than this. There is what he referred to as the *freedom*—a certain autonomy, to speak with the Enlightenment—that traditions open up. On this showing traditions are not simply the limits of reason, interpretative contexts are not simply in Barthes's term, *facist*. They involve a certain free play (a factor that Barthes, too, recognized: we should avoid a strict antinomy here between poststructuralism and hermeneutics that is too often raised), as projecting possibilities of disclosure. Justification always belongs to the 'fore-structuring' of a tradition. But traditions both limit and open up possibilities, in Gadamer's narrative.

> Even though historical knowledge receives its justification from the fore-structure of Dasein, this is no reason for anyone to interfere with the immanent criteria of what is called knowledge. For Heidegger too historical knowledge is not a projection in the sense of a plan, the extrapolation of aims of the will, an ordering of things according to the wishes, prejudices, or promptings of the powerful; rather, it remains something adapted to the object, a *mensuratio ad rem*. Yet this thing is not a factum brutum, not something that is merely at hand, something that can simply be established and measured, but it itself ultimately has the same mode of being as Dasein. (TM:261)

There is truth, in short, not simply because there are traditions, but because traditions disclosively make possible the interpretations of texts and events.[14] Gadamer nonetheless often took this Heideggerean motif, that is, the phenomen-ological encounter as *a-lethic*, in a most positive sense. On this reading there would be commensurability among interpretations in the end to the extent and precisely to the extent that there is a fusion of interpretive horizons on what they disclose: that is, precisely and literally to the extent that they are interpretations of *the same world*. Even here the 'ambiguity,' if not the equivocity of the hermeneutic returns, however. As Merleau-Ponty (among others) had wondered early on with regard to the perspectivalism of phenomen-ology: "Do we know whether all perspectives are compossible (and) whether they can all be thematized together somewhere?"[15]

V

In fact Gadamer's commitments often seem to rely on such reserves, a patchwork concerning the antinomies of modernism his position hoped to avoid, but equally a patchwork in its reception and transformation of hermeneutics— both regarding the latter's complex connections with romanticism and his attempts to contest it. And if the *via media* between the antinomies of modernism are to be grasped, both shall need to be examined. The complex connection with transcendentalism becomes apparent, for example, as soon as one delves deeply into the status of the claims Gadamer's project hoped to achieve. In defending himself against 'linguistic relativism' in part III of *Truth and Method*, he stated:

> The verbal world in which we live is not a barrier that prevents knowledge of being-in-itself but fundamentally embraces everything in which our insight can be enlarged and deepened (*zu erweitern und zu erheben vermag*). It is true that those who are brought up in a particular linguistic and cultural tradition see the world in a different way from those who belong to other traditions. It is true that the historical "worlds" that succeed one another in the course of history are different from one another and from the world today; but in whatever tradition we consider it, it is always a human—i.e., verbally constituted—world that presents itself to us. (TM:447)

The notion of the 'world' however surely becomes 'figured' here, a figure whose diachrony within philosophical modernism remains still to be traced. Although it may be taken metaphorically, it should also be taken in a literal, even a logical sense. In the latter the 'world' would constitute the homogeneous ground in which all interpretations coalesce as interpretations of 'being in itself.' Thereby, it prolongs a synchronic role in the passage of transcendentalism that should not be missed: for Husserl also, the notion of the world was the unity of meaning delineating the appearance of any object in general.[16] This itself, moreover, involves a specific substitution on the phenomenological domain for Kant's notion of the transcendental object. In all three cases, to return to Kant: "The pure concept of this transcendental object, which in reality throughout all our knowledge is always one and the same, is what can alone confer on all our empirical concepts in general relation to an object, that is objective reality."[17] That Gadamer's understanding of the character of 'linguistic disclosure' of the world accomplished the same thing can be witnessed in the sentence that closes the preceding passage: "As verbally constituted, every such world is of itself always open to *every possible insight* and hence to every expansion of its own world picture, and is accordingly available to others."[18]

It is now perhaps clear that the notion of freedom that Gadamer coupled with traditionality was too quick in facilitating the reinstitution of truth as *mensuratio ad rem*. It was in a sense contradictorily effective: albeit conditioned, unrestricted. The bond with tradition is not a limit. And yet to be 'opened' to every possible insight does not imply, after all, that all possible interpretations can be encompassed or decided.

Here, at least, Adorno's brief against phenomenology may need to be affirmed. "If phenomenology ultimately seeks to restore totality and 'awaken' it out of the wreckage...[t]he formal unity of the world as constituted by transcendental subjectivity—that is all that remains from the system of Transcendental Idealism."[19] As soon as one attempts to exchange formal analytics for historical semantics, the underdeterminacy of condition and conditioned will result.

Whereas Gadamer was right in 'surpassing' Schleiermacher's divinatory method, what in effect happens in his own positive account of linguistic constitution is the reemergence of the classical grids. Subject and object, once split, again merge, fuse in the act of knowing. And whereas, when the notion of the fusion of discursive horizons was introduced, the underdeterminacy of interpretation seemed insurmountable, from this side, from the standpoint of its being open "to every possible insight," the questions of determinacy and relativism seemed to be less simply de-founded than perhaps dissolved.

VI

All of this may have satisfied the charge of Gadamer's critics (e.g., Habermas) that he locked understanding up in language, but it seems very strained from within the standpoint of hermeneutics, especially coupled, as we have said, with the advances Gadamer undoubtedly made.[20] The interpreter continues to be puzzled, for example, as to how the discourse of a *Principia* (Newton's or Russell and Whitehead's), that of Lewis Carroll, a seventeenth-century narrative about the witches of Salem, the physics of Einstein, and that of Aristotle, the arguments of Galileo and those of Bellarmine 'fit' into *one* 'world' in any but a trivial sense of that word—or how standing inside any of them, one might gain access to *all* the others. And, this is probably true whether we care about these discourses *as* 'expressions' or 'descriptions.' Even if we grant that they *disclose* something and remain within the Heideggerean advance, it is not clear that the problem ends. Why should they 'disclose' the same thing, or even relatable things, and finally, non contradictory things?

In fact, from the Heideggerean standpoint, the embedding of the hermeneutic *Sache* within the ontological differentiation inherent in interpretation, although avoiding relativism, likewise refuses ontological reductivism, inevitably binding together the *interpretandum* with the *interpretans*. Hermeneutic disclosure as the 'making present' of the *Sache* in question both makes the encounter with the *interpretandum* possible— and, at the same time, *qua hermeneutic*, withdraws its unconditional *presence* within all that conditions it, withdrawing once and for all the immediacy that was the *focus imaginarius* of classicism. The ensuing judgment (the apophantic) is overwhelmed in all that is depended on in its appropriation (contexts, practices, frameworks, 'perspectives,' etc.), all that rules out, in short, any simple reduction to a homogeneous foundation, to a world in which all interpretations might coalesce without conflict. The synthesis that results is instead heterogeneous: the identity it articulates differential and underdetermined. Gadamer's appeal to the Heideggerean position, consequently, would not bring about the resolution required by strict epistemic demands for univocal adjudication—neither from the neoclassicist standpoint nor those classically committed to univocal reflective critique of ideology.[21]

In his 1928 *The Essence of Reasons* where the question of 'world-hood' perhaps comes most directly to the forefront, Heidegger stated, "The totality [of the world] need not, in fact must not, be conceived in any explicit fashion; its range is variable."[22] Moreover, a move to the 'ontological' level will not remove this limit and its 'undecidability': "The manner in which ontological concepts apply to Being will always be limited to and circumscribed by a definite point of view (*Blickpunkt*)."[23] As Heidegger put it in his 1928 Marburg lectures on *The Metaphysical Foundations of Logic*, the world's 'universal character' in this regard is always "a totality relative to a dispersion."[24] Moreover Gadamer had not simply missed the point. *Truth and Method* realized (if not sufficiently) that neither the 'world,' nor *Wirkungsgeschichte*, nor the speculative structure of language as their medium (*Mitte*) could be made determinately present-to-hand, available for ultimate adjudication or final vindication (TM:455f). But the question then only becomes even more urgent: Does the denial of homogeneous foundations that could be counted on in advance make reason blind?

In one sense, of course, why should it? What it admits from the outset is that rationality is not guaranteed in advance. This is perhaps most easily recognizable in those domains in which the word *hermeneutics* became more generally invoked. As the authors cited earlier attest in appealing to 'hermeneutics,' even in their diversity, similar openings continually occurred. Kuhn refused to give up a use for the word *rational* simply because that experience is paradigm specific.[25] Rorty refused to separate values like 'rationality' and 'disinterestedness' from our practices but, like others, appealed to Kant's third *Critique* and its judgment of perception that transcend mere taste for a notion of rationality that is subjective without being relative.[26] Dworkin denied Hirsch's claim that validity in interpretative practices could be rigorously articulated, denied that we could articulate fixed ideas about necessary

and sufficient conditions of objectivity, and yet held that the interpretation of legal history "provides some boundaries" sufficient to deny
relativism.[27] If Fish still refused to separate a text from a community's
use of it, he claimed likewise that interpretations can be 'right' or
'wrong' *because* there is a practice that the community makes possible.[28]
As van Fraassen would put in his treatment of the hermeneutic circle,
in all these instances it would remain a question still of saving the
phenomena—but precisely as fragments within theory.[29]

Nor, it should be added would even the poststructuralists simply
deny it. Barthes called language (*langue*) *facist*, because one always
receives a practice and categories whose usage presupposes its 'mastery,'
but spent a career focusing on the possibilities of their transformation.[30]
And, Derrida appealed to a kind of metarationality that would embed
the metaphysics of presence within a textual play without losing the
necessity of what he called the *transcendental moment*, now deferred
beyond objective presence.[31] And, the list could go on. The point is that,
notwithstanding the underdeterminacy at stake, it still does not become
possible to make a text say what it does not say or an object be what
it is not.[32]

There remains, nonetheless, the negative formulation, the equivocity of the hermeneutical, the underdeterminability of interpretation—
Schleiermacher's problem, granting the justificatory shortfall, of
"avoiding misunderstanding." And the limits of such claims seem
equally obvious, incapable of subsumption within the grids of classical
and foundational paradigms. Heidegger realized from the outset in this
regard that if the positive potential of Dasein's *transcendens* had been
reopened in the hermeneutic circle, it was one that would, precisely
in establishing the complex relations between projection and finitude
('epistemic commitment' and 'empirical adequacy,' theory and practice),
"deny 'objectivism' any authority."[33] If, in principle, at least, we can
throw out bad interpretations, any timeless, iterative, demonstrative,
univocal 'adequation' or reduction would be out of the question.

The interpretative *mensuratio ad rem* that Gadamer quoted directly
in Latin, for all its classicism could not in the end simply be classical.
To miss the transformation would be to miss the theoretical fertility of
its event. Gadamer was right, certainly, to embed interpretations within
what he still called their *facticity*. And, he was right to see a certain free
play in what those conditions open up. Yet, this is as far as one can
go to satisfy both Nietzsche and Schleiermacher, neither of whom could
rest easy with this solution. Not Schleiermacher, who believed that a
science of interpretation was possible and perhaps that an objectivity
(albeit divinatory) could be had here just as the Enlightenment had

envisaged. Not Nietzsche, who would hear in the end too little of the problem of justification, but instead substituted for it the metaphysics of the will to power. And both did so at the expense of the requisites of legitimation that they hoped to surpass.[34]

VII

As Gadamer realized, the field of the 'hermeneutic' must extend beyond these classical antinomies. Rather than trying to confine the play of 'textuality' within the homogeneous foundations of the world and explicate it from within the 'superior vision' Gadamer claimed the notion of horizon entails, however we will likewise need to consider the heterogeneous synthesis risked thereby. We will need to consider— perhaps even respect—something like the free play of this transcendental foundation itself. Here the Derridean argument, too often assumed to be simply opposed to hermeneutics, becomes again relevant:

> This *play* thought as absence of the transcendental signified, is not a play *in the world*, as it has always been defined, for the purposes of *containing* it, by the philosophical tradition. . . .To think play radically the ontological and transcendental problematics must first be radically *exhausted*. . . .It is therefore *the game of the world* that must be first thought.[35]

What this would involve likewise perhaps may be found in the works of writers already noted who had appealed to the fecundity of hermeneutics in their own practices. By it in any case we lose neither the *mensuratio ad rem* nor even the immediacy of experience, if we have foreclosed any attempt to guarantee their 'explications' in advance by purging them of syntactic 'complication.' If Derrida's caveat, after all, combines, indeed runs together, aesthetic and formalist accounts of 'play' extending not only from Kant and Schiller to Gadamer, but also Hilbert and Poincaré to Wittgenstein and Cavaillès, it never simply denies what classical phenomenologist's could claim of the issues (and evidence) accompanying it. Even the classicist *de gutibus non est disputandum* could simply be sustained against it, if and only if our practices were simply defective *tout court*. Instead of a classical logic of demonstration, delivering us from relativism by rational purge and absconding us from the risks of rational adjudication, however, it would require a new understanding of things like texts, objects, perceptions, and so forth, one in that we return them from above the divided line by which they would be ideally separated from our interpretative practices.

By so doing we can give up what Gadamer has rightly referred to as what is 'vague and unreal' about 'the claim of superiority made by philosophic thought' to explicate the differences that are articulated and legitimated in the event of hermeneutic disclosure. But we may need as well to abandon what, perhaps not without a certain nostalgia, Gadamer likewise referred to as the transcendental belief (or rather, the guarantee) in "what is still and ever again real" (TM:541).

VIII

The difficulty in all this, it will be said, is that hermeneuts have too often acted as if their 'problematics' and 'explications' involved positive research programs providing answers in the strict sense. They would, in short, provide the ultimate foundation, solution, or clarification for something; the interpretation of texts, the methodology of the human sciences, the correction for the epistemic shortfall of phenomenology, an access to fundamental ontology, the retrieval of the science of Being 'as such,' and so on. Hermeneutics would, that is, be not only truth 'preserving,' but truth 'vindicating,' simply as it were abandoning method for the sake of truth. If hermeneutics is to be legitimated it must be absolved of such illusions. But, in fact, both the internal logic of its own conceptual resources and the archive on which it depends contests the possibility as well as the necessity of such affirmations.

To return once more to the Kantian archive to which Gadamer originally appealed in replying to Betti, if the former's construal of the *qaestio juris* relied on an Enlightenment or modernist account that aligned justification and the cognitive with the disputable and the decidable—invoking again the myth of the given, a science of pure facts for its validity conditions—even in order to ground the latter, it became necessary to admit that "we have an understanding (*einen Verstand*) of things that problematically extends further."[36] This extension, the latter's *conditio sine qua non*, could not, however, occur within the genre of the apodictic and the adequate. Rather than the unconditional field comprising the strictness of the deductive procedures thought to be its exemplars, problematic judgments are ones "in which affirmation or negation is taken as merely possible (optional)."[37] As Droyson would then put it with regard to the question of historical interpretation, what is required in this domain is not a logic of proof, but one of verisimilitude and "a discipline of the plausible."[38] Precisely in default of the objective rules for subsumption here judgment must proceed, in short, without prior keys for enquiry.

Still, lacking such criteria, Kant's general account of judgment in the first *Critique* becomes again a significant one:

(T)hough understanding is capable of being instructed and of being equipped with rules, judgment is a peculiar talent which can be practiced only, and cannot be taught. It is the specific quality of so-called mother-wit (*Mutterwitz*); and its lack no school can make good. For although an abundance of rules borrowed from the insight of others may indeed be profferred to, and as it were grafted on, a limited understanding, the power of rightly employing them must belong to the learner himself.[39]

If it is true in general, as Kant admitted, that "only seldom do [particular acts of judgment] adequately fulfill the requirements of the rule," so much the less is the case in the eventuality in which the 'rule' itself might be rendered problematic.[40] In all of this Kant was clear. And if he was in fact not uncomfortable with the question of this graft (*pfropfen*)—doubtless because of his own *credo* concerning the indisputable exemplars and heroes of pure reason—it is at least true, nonetheless, that he realized the risk of such grafting.[41]

Doubtless too, however, the risk of these examples themselves could not leave the *Critique of Pure Reason* and its account of reason unscathed. If Kant himself claimed that "sharpening of the judgment is indeed the great benefit of examples"—perhaps recalling that the whole critical enterprise depended on the good judgment of the examples of the Copernican turn—the benefits in question could not, after all, be objectively instituted in the requisite sense. Hence as Gadamer rightly pointed out, the pivotal importance of exemplarity in Kant, one however that ultimately calls into question the distinction between determining and reflective judgment (TM:39). The graft in question could not be demonstrably, but merely hypothetically and experimentally, inscribed—as Kant acknowledged, a matter of 'analogy,' one indicative of the perilous (and tenuous) distinction between the 'empirical' and the 'transcendental.'[42] And, like all questions of analogy in the critical system, the strictness of the enterprise could at best be regulative or ampliative, threatening to rupture the strict distinction between schema and example, sign and symbol Kant hoped to institute.[43]

IX

Against Hobbes, for example, who had thought reason to be calculative through and through, that 'wit' and 'reason' were in fact to be held in strict opposition, Kant was forced instead then to broaden and temper his commitments to philosophical modernism, precisely in the admission that the paradigm of mathematics ultimately failed here, that the appeal to the 'strictness' of the examples in this regard ultimately turned to naught.[44] Philosophy and science go separate ways. Although "the exactness (*Grundlichkeit*) of the mathematical rests on definitions, axioms, and demonstrations," that is, on a priori *construction*, "in philosophy the geometrician can by his method build only so many houses of cards."[45] The philosopher relies not on construction, but the discursive exposition of concepts. Concepts, however, are for a finite intellect merely finite horizons, discursive 'standpoints,' for Kant—as they had been for Chladenius before him at the dawn of modern hermeneutics. Unlike the latter, there would be for Kant no demonstrably ultimate horizon; the horizon of horizons, that is, precisely escaped our conceptual grasp. Consequently, "a multiplicity of suitable examples suffices only to make the completeness *probable*, never to make it apodeitically certain."[46]

Granted Kant's investment in this grounding, however, there perhaps could not help but be certain *lapsus judicii* concerning the contingency of the examples and the judgments ultimately required within the critical tribunal. These examples and their extensions remained themselves precisely grafts, analgons, imported for *Reason's* experimental and hypothetical purposes, ones that could at best be 'confirmed,' but not deduced and finally decided. As extensions (*Erweiterungen*) they lacked themselves ultimate *Erweiterungs-Grundsatze*.[47] And, as a result, Kant's appeal to *Mutterwitz* and the ensuing elevation of imagination at their source became paradigmatic in the texts of romanticism.[48] Kant realized, that is, that in the absence of strict rules judgment must become an 'art'—precisely the account hermeneuts from Schleiermacher to Heidegger and Gadamer have presented as the paradigm for hermeneutic 'judgment': that is, interpretation. The question is how this 'art' is to be interpreted.

X

Hannah Arendt, taking her point of departure from the early Heidegger, recognized perhaps better than others the importance of Kant's account of judgment in these matters. Arendt rightly saw in all this not only the elevation of romantic *Witz* but also a retrieval of an ancient art—perhaps even the art of all art—the art of discriminating (*techne diakritike*).[49] The question of judgment concerns, she claimed, first and foremost the issue of examples and exemplification, questions regarding "exemplary validity" in which reason is placed explicitly "at the service of imagination."[50] Moreover, she too affirmed that the issues involved extend beyond the examplar of demonstrability: "judgments are not arrived at by either deduction or induction, in short, they have nothing in common with logical operations."[51] And yet, in all this she became once more the foil for those like Habermas who saw her retrieval as merely ancilliary to an account of "the universal discourse" that all validity claims imply.[52] Instead, Habermas argued, fully recognizing the fallibilist turn in epistemology that would surpass the Enlightenment's foundationalism, the rationality of communicative action involves a set of background assumptions for the possibility of consensus that "appears as if it could never become problematic."[53] And thereby, it might be claimed, Habermas's account from the outset never fully escaped the positivism to which he opposed it.

Arendt's turn to the question of judgment was instituted precisely to acknowledge the 'problematic' character of the public realm, a realm in which the universal Habermas demands was de facto in question. What attracted Arendt to the third *Kritik* (and perhaps repulsed Habermas in his demand that the protocols of the critical tribunal regain what Kant quite straight-forwardly referred to as a "dogmatic procedure"[54]) was the recognition of an account of the rational in default of such proof, an account that might return to the appearances and the question of the reflective articulation of their significance within the singular. Against the dogmatic establishment of the critical tribunal, it involved the recognition that, strictly taken, decidability and Reason 'come to an end,' as Wittgenstein put it.[55]

Still, Habermas was right in this regard, that Arendt, like Kant, still too much excluded judgment from cognitive significance, as is evident *inter alia* in the strict opposition she delineated between the realm of judgment and "logical operations"—risking the appearance that ratiocination and argumentation had no effect at all here. But, *pace* Habermas, it was not to arrive at another, more secure realm in which reason and judgment were ultimately less 'problematic.'[56] Rather, like Kant, Arendt continued to limit the cognitive to the demonstrative, all the while overcoming it with an account of rationality as 'problematic.' Unlike rational practices that could be guided by the demonstrable, it involved a domain in which, once again, 'otherness' becomes meaningful without thereby becoming simply 'irrational.' From the outset, or at least since Fichte's claim that "the distinguishing characteristic of mankind" involves this reciprocal influence of each other through communication, "the giving and receiving of knowledge," it is true too that it was at best a reflective 'transcendental' extension without guarantee.[57] Or, if, as Arendt too put it "What saves the affairs of mortal men from their inherent futility is nothing but this incessant talk about them," it remains again true too that "all thought begins in remembrance"—and thereby what exceeds that talk.[58] In fact, if in this again she affirmed Kant's account of judgment over against its cognitive constraints—if, "In matters of taste we must renounce ourselves in favor of others (*Wir müssen uns gleischen anderen zu gefallen entsagen*),"[59] this renunciation, almost, to speak Levinasian, "respect for the other," could not legitimate itself by a simple graft, could not provide an affirmation in the strict sense, because that is precisely what has been precluded by the extension of judgment into the problematic in the first place. Here too consequently the critical archive from which hermeneutics emerges imparts a complex remainder: a site in which the intertwining between identity and difference, judgment and its limit, recognition and renunciation, remembrance and invention, the same and the other will again be irreducibly complicated.

XI

From the outset Gadamer's refusal of 'method' had in a sense acknowledged this. Gadamer too realized that hermeneutics originates with this question of the other—both that of the 'other' of tradition and the hermeneut's own 'otherness' in distinguishing him- or herself from it. And yet the 'otherness' in question often escaped the categories by which his patchwork enframed it. Instead, too often it involved for him a differentiation by which the 'otherness' could be overcome or reduced on the way to "the attainment of a higher universality" and finally a "return to self" (TM:306). All of this would presuppose the truth and the tribunal of representation—presuppose that the conflict of interpretation could be overcome, that the differences between interpretations could find a neutral criterion for adjudication and, thereby, a certain uncontroversial commensurability.

As Gadamer likewise recognized however—aptly in fact responding to Derrida—the hermeneutic event always involves "a potentiality of otherness (*Andersseins*) that lies beyond every coming to agreement about what is common," one that remains then irreducible to a transcendental logic and the unity of its account of judgment.[60] The outcome of the interpretative event, consequently, could not be simply the transcendental unity of the one, the propositional result of judgment, but rather, the indeterminate dyad, and the opening of dia-logue.[61] The field of the hermeneutic could not then be simply a matter of identity, foundation, and consensus, but equally difference, separation, and distinction—a matter of *Auseinandersetzung*, as Heidegger put it.[62] And yet even here Gadamer realized the extent to which, in his appeal to dialogue in understanding the positivity of tradition, "how deeply rooted I am in the romantic tradition"—acknowledging all the while the failure of the "myth" of its final justification (*Letzbegrundung*).[63]

If he recognized that to interpret is "to expose oneself and to risk oneself in the presence of the other," however, it did not prevent him from ultimately claiming—still in accord with Chladenius, Leibniz, and the preestablished harmony of perspectivism that seemed always to underwrite hermeneutics—that "the different standpoints, the separate horizons enter into one another."[64] But precisely thereby the Nietzschean (or Kantian) risk of discontinuity that Gadamer attributes to Derrida (and before him to Heidegger, and even to a figure such as Buber) may not have been faced. For example, in a portentous—and over-determined—letter written to Strauss soon after the publication of *Wahrheit und Methode* Gadamer stated forthrightly:

> I do not believe *at all* that we live "between" worlds. I can follow neither Heidegger nor Buber in this. Only the prophet who already sees the promised land would have, in my estimation, the possibility to say the like. I *remember* (*erinnere*) instead of this, the one world that I alone know, and which in all decay has lost far less of its evidence and cohesion (*Evidenz und Bindekraft*) than it talks itself into.[65]

The question, of course, is whether such a claim (in fact, again the Hegelian claim that essence is timelessly past Being) would not depend on an *Augenblick* no less prophetic concerning the truth of its past and whether there were the grounds to exclusively endorse that evidence— whether, that is, Gadamer's ultimate commitments regarding the homogeneity of the evidence, that is, the transcendental unity of such a world (or of the world-historical) did not in the end turn ultimately dogmatic, whether the extension of the hermeneutic 'promise' were not as inextricably illusory as it was necessary.

If that were true, it would not be Nietzsche but Hegel again who would provide not only the foil, but the solution for Schleiermacher's shortcomings (cf. TM:149f). But the question is whether we can so exclusively endorse the evidence of our world *without* turning dogmatic and without making the question of the difference in question, that is, the "between" that Gadamer refused, precisely to the contrary insurpassable, whether, in short, the *memoria* in question does not equally concern the *e-vidence* of the *Zwischen* of what escapes this world.[66]

Gadamer's appeal to the evidence doubtless remained in this sense correct, however; hermeneutics remained the recognition that, its risk notwithstanding, "(t)he Eikos, the verisimile, the 'probable'. . . belong in a series that defend themselves against the truth and certainty of what is proved and known." It is true moreover, as Benjamin realized, that the experience in question is one that "has fallen in value. And it looks as if it is continuing to fall into bottomlessness."[67] Here as Arendt likewise rightly saw, precisely in the a-lethic exposition of truth as 'revelation', as *Unverborgenheit*, Benjamin and Heidegger were—or should be seen as—of a piece.[68] But the event in question could be legitimated only by preserving the difference that withdraws them from the certainty of all proof, all representation and finality—and thereby the simple affirmation not only of the *Letztbegrundung*, but likewise the destiny of their *'Erstbegrundung'* (TM:484). Tradition (*traditio*), is not simply re-collection, but trans-mission, and its authority (*auctoritas*) inevitably a matter of augmenting (*augere*), a matter of extension.[69] The turn to tradition and to its *Bildung* remains then categorically distinct both from the mere reiteration of law as much as the mere imposition of dominion, requiring instead precisely the art, the risk, the auto-chthomy, and the autonomy of judgment.[70]

The evidence in question could not simply dissolve the under-determination on which it rested, could not turn its judgments 'determinate,' could not without hubris mimic either the strictness of science or the immediacy of myth. It remains too heterogeneous, too 'incoherent,' too exclusive, and in any case too 'complicated' for such a priori characterizations. If Benjamin too concurred with the Hegelian retrieval of Mnemosyne linking reason to its narratives, claiming again, that is, that "memory creates the chain of tradition," he realized also that no tradition is vindicated thereby—that its exclusions cannot simply be dissolved.[71] Indeed memory is by no means an ontic faculty, a faculty of reproductive synthesis, nor is the *Zwischen* it opens up simply one between worlds, but the opening of ontological difference itself (TM:15). Moreover, the demand for simple preservation becomes nascently historicist. As MacIntyre realized in this regard "every tradition. . . confronts the possibility that at some future time it will fall into a state of epistemological conflict."[72] And, being able to meet such conflict is precisely the condition for the "rational warrant for asserting such hegemony."[73] But, if such a confrontation becomes the condition for re-legitimating tradition, it requires equally that rationality not be ontically bound thereby, inherently necessitating an extension beyond and between traditions. If reason, that is, depends in this regard on the realm of the public good—not only for the limits of rational coherence, but as both a mode of representation and a mode of invention, as Arendt realized—rational warrant remains in this respect irreducible to it.[74]

What Gadamer taught us in the end—notwithstanding the foundational models he inherited—was that the critical moment in which the past becomes risked (*wird gereizt*) in this extension did not preclude the venture of the humanist tradition but was (and was from the outset, ever present in the question of translation) precisely its virtue, the legitimation that accompanies all application, inevitably removing it from simple repetition. Against the positivism that always accompanied hermeneutics, the humanities were not Comtean 'proto-human sciences,' but practices that instead extended beyond—and despite—such homologous models.[75] From the outset, the humanist tradition arose in this venture acknowledging the intimate bond between issues of translation and those of the rational, a site in which iteration and invention, memory and imagination, philosophy and literature were of a piece: a site, that is, in which tradition had become problematic. Not only de facto, but de juris, consequently, to understand is to understand differently (TM:297). Not simply because all events, to speak Husserlian, are clouded in the "shadings" (*Abschattungen*) of temporal removal, but because all historical interpretation requires the infinite task of renewed legitimation.

The problem then becomes almost our timidity before the demands of this excess, its risk, and its underdeterminacy. The problem, as Arendt wrote Jaspers, is that "Even good and, at bottom, worthy people have, in our time, the extraordinary fear about making judgments."[76] In interpretation the appearances—received or otherwise—can be saved only by acknowledging their fragility. It is precisely in this sense that the extension of tradition becomes (albeit inescapable) still viable, poised, that is, between iteration and transformation. Consequently, as Jean-Luc Nancy has put it, "the authentic decision is. . .the decision for *taking* a decision as such"[77]—requiring that is, the art of discriminating and perhaps too the art of the storyteller. But, the danger in all this perhaps is that, having fully recognized what it is not, we will have missed what is decisive—divided that is precisely between the danger and the fragility of interpretation.

Supplement: Quarreling Between the Ancients and the Moderns:
Gadamer and Strauss

Perhaps in this light nonetheless it becomes possible to begin to
articulate Gadamer's effect anew, especially regarding his commitment
to *both* the indispensibility and the dispensibility of tradition, one that
has shown itself again to be particularly recalcitrant in recent debates.
Of all the discourses that have circulated around the topic of politics
and interpretation in recent years perhaps none is more crucial, more
informed, and perhaps in the end more frustrating than the attempts
of Alain Renault and Luc Ferry to come to grips with the interface
between critical theorists and hermeneuts. The latters' polemics attempt
historically to trace the emergence of contemporary rifts, in particular
tracing again the impasse of modernity by returning to the ancients
and pointing to the critical archive at stake in German idealism for both
antecedents and resolution of the impasse. Strauss and Heidegger now
are selected as two antipodes of this impasse, but in a way that in the
end forces the undoing of both. Fichte, correctly seen as proto-
Habermasian on their account, becomes then posed as their 'sublation.'
Heidegger in this account becomes once more posed as an irrationalist
attempting to escape the failures of modernity—relativism, decisionism,
and historicism—by returning to a prephilosophical or at least
prerational call beyond the Greek horizon (or alternately, a quietism
regarding what has yet to be thought on its basis). Strauss on the other
hand is depicted as simply remaining convinced that we ought to
preserve what could still be maintained of ancient reason. Most of this
unhappily remains merely imputed. At one point Renault suggested
that Heidegger "appears to imply a denial of right insofar as he permits
suspicion of it."[78] Ferry however acknowledged that Strauss's naivete
"would surely have made Heidegger smile."[79]

In fact the debate, as significant as it is, never fully takes place;
never does the question of reason or its account ever come up in the
constructed *Auseinandersetzung* between Strauss and Heidegger. Nor in
the end did Ferry or Renault do much to attempt to deal with what
is at stake between their accounts, being more concerned themselves
with founding reason as a matter of decision procedures. They are in
this regard acquiescent, almost fatalistic, about the failure of all and
any 'substantialist' accounts and then simply silent about the conventional underdeterminacy, the finitude of constitutive accounts that
would, to use Rousseau's, term, bring forth a "second nature." Hence
adjudication never takes place. And, the point at stake in such an
adjudication, it should be said, may not be simply an attempt to defend

either natural law or natural right or their successors, but equally to trace the dispersion that ensues in the wake of their confrontation—and in the case of Renault and Ferry's strategies perhaps, the (transcendental) illusions that arise in proposing fallibilist replacements for such quarrels, simply retreating once more from fundamental ontologies to transcendental semantics.[80]

What should be realized to begin this task, however, is that this debate is better served by looking at Strauss and Gadamer where, as has become evident, a more developed account of the issues at stake emerges. This is a debate that concerns the contributions of the ancients, but ultimately it concerns the place the ancients and tradition can hold in articulating an account of the rational beyond the blinders of modernist and even romanticist protocols. Moreover, closer adjudication of the issues becomes possible, precisely because, if Heidegger is wrongly labeled an irrationalist (or an historicist), Gadamer developed more direct resources for dealing with such accusations, whereas they often remain in the background of Heidegger's *Denkweg*. As Strauss himself put it, Gadamer's "translation of Heidegger's question" more directly confronts these issues, being both more "traditional or academic" and at the same time arising out of a "certain common background" that he more directly shares with Strauss.[81] There is, as Gadamer agrees, "a strange overlapping of our positions along with a number of important divergences" (I:3). To speak to the point, however, the claim (made by Renault in focusing upon the fact-value distinction) that "the critique of reason, far from being as Heidegger thought the destruction of reason, permits one to assign new status to the requirements of reason following its critique"[82] all but begs the question. Renault never seems to allow that the question of justification, far from requiring that one change ground or paradigm with respect to the question of *Destruktion*, might better emerge from within Heidegger's own advance (or retrieval). The possibility does not arise, that is, that Heidegger's critique may contribute to an account of the rational—to quote Gadamer in this regard, the possibility that through *Sein und Zeit* "the problem of hermeneutics becomes universal in scope, even attaining a new dimension, through his transcendental interpretation of understanding" (TM:264).

It should be acknowledged at the outset—though we will need to return to it—this transcendental dimension nonetheless will not fulfill the classical requisites of transcendental theory, will not provide, that is, the methodological guarantor for the production of truth, will not proceed by or generate extrinsic criteria for adjudication. It will, in short, violate both Kant's conception of the critical tribunal and his hopes for the constitutive reformulation of "natural" or "inner right." Consequently, it will complicate the attempt to provide rational foundations for the original possession of nature (*possessio noumenon*), a matter whose ontic fictions had already been recognized by Maimon in confronting Kant's distinction between what the latter called modernist "fictions" concerning a *communio primaeva* and his own rational attempts to *demonstrate* a *communio fundi originera.*[83]

Instead, hermeneutics will indeed be suspicious concerning such conceptions of both *communio* and *natura* and will do so by denying the simple correlation between method and theory, deduction and right. Recall that if the hermeneutic *Seinsfrage* opens a new transcendental dimension, even a universal *Umriss*, if it openly confronts the limits of criteriologically sound method, it does so not by simply *abandoning* reason but only and precisely by denying that reason can be limited to such extrinsic methodological constructions, that instead there is a reason otherwise than the calculative. Rightly taken, that is, far from abandoning reason, Gadamer hoped still to advance it, formulating a theory of hermeneutic experience (*Theorie der hermeneutischen Erfarung*) (TM:264). It is here consequently that Gadamer, on the basis of Heideggerean protocols (on the basis of the critique of theory), would directly confront Straussian objections. Even on the strongest of readings, however, it cannot be claimed that what is at stake involves direct opposition. It was Strauss himself, after all, who declared that "the very disavowal of reason must be reasonable disavowal."[84]

Prefacing his own discussion of natural right and the distinction between fact and value in *Natural Right*, Strauss himself (like Betti), assumed the critical high ground: "There cannot be natural right if the fundamental problem of political philosophy cannot be solved in a final manner."[85] Instead this is the axiom of the tradition itself: "The whole galaxy of political philosophers from Plato to Hegel, and certainly adherents of natural right, assumed that the fundamental problem is susceptible of a final solution. This assumption ultimately rested on the Socratic answer to the question how man ought to live."[86] The quest for knowledge of the most important things or quest for wisdom is what underlies the foundation of natural right and it is this, consequently, that must be capable of resolution. But natural right in this respect becomes parasitic not only on the search for wisdom but on knowledge and in its decidability on *Erkenntnistheorie*, on the protocols of philosophy as strict science, as Strauss affirmed in his final years.[87]

Gadamer's *The Idea of the Good in Platonic-Aristotelian Philosophy* (1978) is many things, but among them it is a denial of the very idea, that is, the standard (*Masstab*) or criteria, of such a conception. Indeed the heart of its demeural with respect to such neo-Kantianism is in a sense precisely its 'neo-Platonism.' It is the denial that the Idea of the Good and the question of transcendence it inaugurates is simply calculable in any way that 'standard' accounts equate calculability (decidability) with knowledge or reduces questions of truth to those of demonstration. Hence the claim that the Marburg school's radicalization of Plato scholarship "has kept its attention focused all too much on science" resulting in Hegel's 'tranquil kingdom of laws (IG:101). Surely this is not only correct but equally, historically the common horizon from which both Gadamer and Strauss's work likewise emerge, the horizon of neo-Kantianism. The return to Plato and Aristotle for the latter accordingly was precisely a return to "classical social science."[88] Gadamer's claim was that these texts and their problem is much more complex and "Heidegger's great merit...to have broken through the aura of obviousness" in which the concept of Being became used (RAS:101).

Accordingly, in his own exposition of *Republic* 533ff., having applauded the demarcation of dialectic from the mathematical sciences, Gadamer paused before the claim that the idea of the Good (*idea tou agathon*) must be separated from everything else—that, as in a battle, one must be willing to endure all challenges at the expense of recognizing neither the good itself nor anything else that is good. "We must pause here. This 'in the same way' is a source of no small difficulty" (IG:84). No small difficulty indeed. This source of everything else will be difficult indeed to simply parse—and always a matter of interpretation.

It is important to note however that the first thing disclaimed by Gadamer is that this difficulty would entail an abandonment of reason: "Certainly one can comprehend that in the case of the good too, it is the procedure of the dialectician—giving justification—that alone can prevent our being confused by false similarities..." (IG:84–85). The problem is not only one of differentiating and reconciling the manifold of true reality with the unity of the true good, but likewise comprehending what lies beyond this differentiation, what gives *aletheia* to what is known (IG:87). Hence the ontological difference of the *analogia entis* that Aristotle too would acknowledge, notwithstanding his criticism of the schism between *empereia* and *eidos* (IG:131–32). Instead of any kind of simple reduction, what emerges here is that these realms, like the relation between the theory and practice, are "indissociably intertwined" (IG:171). Even in the *Nichomachean Ethics*, however, Gadamer pointed out, even following the critique of Platonic separation, "the paradigm of 'being that always is'—be it the being of the divine or of the heavenly bodies—remains the ultimate point of reference in treating the practical nature of the human being" (IG:172). The confrontation between Strauss and Gadamer would in this regard concern precisely the difference between Plato and Aristotle and not at all a denial that justice requires the Good and knowledge of the Good—whether it makes sense to speak of that knowledge in the end as one capable of simple *Augenblick* and adjudication: that is, resolution. Indeed at stake is whether claims concerning such a 'one' could ever overcome the differences of its indeterminacy, whether such a 'one' does not always imply an indeterminate two (*ahoristos dyas*), its assertion always 'heterological.' For better or for worse then these principles for Gadamer "were not meant to yield an ultimate determinacy" (HS:322). And, the last thing they authorize then is a return to a 'classical social science.'

All of this becomes critical, of course, granted the "special importance" granted Aristotle and the account of *phronesis* in *Truth and Method*. The dangers of the dependence on the practical were seemingly equally obvious. After all, there is prima facie a fallacy—as Heidegger's critique of the primacy of the will would realize—in simply asserting the pragmatic to be decisive for understanding hermeneutics. And, consequently, Heidegger's own reference to pragmatism in the now-published 1922 *Phenomenological Interpretation of Aristotle* was quick to deny its *relativismus*.[89] Short of such a distinction, the result would in fact—*pace* Ferry and Renault—be too Fichtean, substituting the primacy of practical reason for the demands of theoretical reason. Fichte's "It is so because I make it so" involves a move that is perhaps more than anything else the move that inaugurates historicism, relativism, and the condition for the possible elevation of the will (to power).

Now at one point, as has been noted, *Truth and Method* does affirm Heidegger's critique of pure perception as one undertaken on the basis of pragmatic experience (TM:91). If hermeneutics simply makes this move, if it simply turns pragmatic, the Straussian challenge would become insurmountable. When Gadamer introduced the Kantian account of natural dialectic in *The Idea of the Good*, he did so by citing *The Metaphysics of Virtue* and the question of the lure of sensibility, the seductive sophistry of the passions. Whereas this connection with the faculty of desire cannot be overlooked, especially its "special role in the matter of the good" (IG:97) it is decisive too, however, that Gadamer acknowledged that other side of Kantian dialectic, the sophistry of rationalization and the confusion of mathematical paradigms (*konstruktion*) with the discursive dialectic of (finite) philosophical rationality. Acknowledging both the demand for justification and its limitations becomes the inauguration instead of a critical hermeneutics, precisely, that is, a theory of interpretative rationality. If the primacy of application (or interpretation) is to be argued for in such a theory, however, Gadamer was absolutely clear that the primacy of practice is not: "the inclusiveness of human practice entails no subordination of theory to practice" (IG:176). Neither, is the subordination of theory to human interest affirmed, if it *does* entail the refusal to dissociate them.

This is not to say either that the logic of critical theory has gone unaltered or that Straussian (now precritical or at least prehermeneutic) objections are easily defeasible. In fact what must be argued, for reasons already evident, is that the infinite task or striving for the Good, that refuses to univocally possess it, that refuses to turn mathematical, will face such objections only in utter fragility. Indeed we should be specific: Gadamer's tack would not overcome the regulations of Kantian critique any more than the question—or the *Andenken*—of the Good could be reduced to the proof of practice. In this regard, if as Gadamer once put it, the result of Kantian critique is that "there remains rationality, but so to speak, in fragments" (HT:8), this fragmentation would not be overcome by the question of the Whole—not by the return to metaphysics, the narratives of the sacred, nor by the explications of the life world. Gadamer was right to point out that in none of these 'immediate' questions, undertaken in defiance of the concept, has rationality come to an end—not even in the Sartrean, existentialist appeals to the immediate against which Heidegger railed and to which Renault and Ferry still appeal (HT:13). The Sartrean doctrine of freedom will inevitably encounter the problem of abyss and withdrawal, involving from the outset "a freedom that is not its own foundation."[90] If Ferry and Renault may have been right to see in this the remnant of the subject, a Kantian autonomy irreducible to the prius of the will or the destiny of Being, and if Gadamer was right to see in it the interplay of hermeneutic rationality, in neither case would the demonstrability or the determinability of the mathematical be regained.

It is not quite right, consequently, then to say that "a hermeneutics of the human sciences certainly has nothing to learn from mathematical as distinguished from moral knowledge" (TM:314): the former will be precisely the sign of the limits of hermeneutics, the articulation of its 'syntactic failure' within modernist systematics. In this regard, if Gadamer could claim in 1986 that "I clearly am in much greater proximity to Schlegel than I had previously realized," referring directly to Schlegel's concept of the work, it is likewise because of his account of the work as (logically) aphoristic and fragmentary (HL:123). Far from being simply irrational—and without simply entailing falibilism—it remains part and parcel of such a recognition that the justificatory status of such ex-plications defy completeness. As he argued against Strauss,

"It is by no means settled (and can never be settled) that any particular perspective in which traditionary thoughts present themselves is the right one" (TM:535). The hegemony of theory in all cases, but especially here perhaps, in the case of an extension that defies all calculative resolution, requires that one be capable of placing ones own theoretical perspective into question.

The modalities of the hermeneutic will always be subjunctive, the domain of the dialectical, the justified narrative of the as if, the legacy of Aristotle's *orexis* (TM:312)—and it should be added, against Strauss's retrieval of *Strenge Wissenschaft*, Husserl's transition from static to genetic encounter with the *Sache*. Moreover it is just this distinction (separating if not Aristotle from Plato, then ultimately Gadamer from Strauss) that warrants the claim that the proposition, "all knowledge is historically conditioned" and "this piece of knowledge is true unconditionally" cannot simply be opposed to one another (TM:534). Not simply propositional relationships are at stake (TM:448)—and not, *pace* Husserl, simply lived encounters within the *lebenswelt*, but equally the dialectic in which the propositions become articulated in our rational narratives (TM:484).

Gadamer aptly appealed in this regard to Vico as having preserved what was at stake in the Aristotelean Idea of the Good, precisely in articulating the narratological extensions of the human 'sciences.' In this respect, Vico declared, *mythos* is not the realm of fable but of "true narration."[91] Still, what is at stake is not 'true' in the case of deduction, not then 'strict'—or as Heidegger realized, the strict does not restrict (that is, exclude) the equivocal and multiplicity—and the interrogation of the *analogia entis* always depended on it. But, on the other hand, neither does the latter guarantee it. The event remains fragmentary through and through. If Being can be said in a number of ways, it cannot be 'said' in just any way—nor can *mythos* just *mean* true narration; this is, after all, the problem of its interpretation. To use Nancy's term, if myth is inextricable, then, it is likewise inextricably interrupted or fragmented.[92] *Logos* is always at sea in the weaving of 'forms,' the weaving of the between. It remains to Gadamer's credit, when all is said and done, to have realized—perhaps better than others—that this weaving, fragile, limited, and ventured as it is, still remains justified, the highest virtue of what belongs to what is human: to be fragmented and yet not simply dispersed; to err and yet not to be closed off from the truth.

The closest Strauss ever came to such a recognition perhaps was to have glimpsed the importance of Machiavelli's acknowledgment of the equivocity of tradition. For Ferry it would also mark an *aporia* between natural right and fate.⁹³ Strauss, nonetheless, could view this equivocity only as the opening of a certain modern tragedy:⁹⁴ to use Gadamer's terms, a certain "contastrophe of modern times" (TM:533). Gadamer I think in the end cannot however simply join him there— nor can we. And in this we should be precise. If Strauss, for example (like Gadamer), could acknowledge a certain variance in the articulation of justice, the latter realized too that the Good was from the outset a *problem*, the hope for its unequivocal resolution, that is, for an unprob-lematic, unchallengeable, demonstrative—algorithmic or mathematical—foundation or resolution, something of a sham.⁹⁵ Gadamer was in this regard fully capable of realizing that the idea of the good as "neither capable nor in need of a justification (*Rechtfertigung*)" was indeed mythic, an old story (*alte Geschichten*) whose distance, the distance of all reflection in fact, requires legitimation, re-application (RAS:76–77). As Lefort similarly charged in this regard, Strauss's Machiavelli analysis, tossed between the ancients and the moderns, in the end simply ignores the interrogation of the origin of the political and the social, precisely as this 'indetermination'—and thereby, the fecundity which underlies democracy itself perhaps.⁹⁶

While Strauss was doubtless right in criticizing the failures of the modern, he remained both too modern, still thinking in terms of ultimate resolution, and not modern enough, not critical enough to see the problem that haunts the question of the Good. The difference between him and Gadamer, Strauss maintained, was simply the difference of the *querelle* itself.⁹⁷ The problem, however, as has been seen, is that the dispersion of that quarrel is overdetermined. Hence Strauss's continued concern both with Gadamer's relativism *and* his own demeurals concerning claims for the hermeneutic universal⁹⁸—all the while attempting to maintain, and "without logical difficulty," the perdurance of "an absolute moment" that "retains (its) binding power for every one who is not a brute"—and that, unlike the articulemes of Heidegger's *Seinsfrage*, remains adequately present to hand. "Above all, these things—in contradistinction to 'world' (cf. 432) and other *Existentialien*—are necessarily thematic within all 'horizons'."⁹⁹ But it is precisely this narrative whose re-iteration requires justification. And, here Strauss's story of the absolute moment tautalogously narrates again its own version of *Seinsgeschichte*. Despite the patchwork of *Truth and Method*, despite that is, the foundations to which Gadamer too often appealed to understand (and contain) it, here his 'appropriation' of Heidegger's advance becomes intransigent. By its means he was able to recognize tradition as more the venture of truth than its guarantor, and interpretation more the possibility of access to Being than its representation: more the opening of the horizons of difference than the simple fusion of their identity. The result is an opening that less precludes or preempts judgment than requires again the integrity of its discernment.

Instead of the simple assertion of right, we will need again to acknowledge its provisional indeterminacy, a narrative then of the one and the many, the absolute in the relative—a narrative that forms a certain rational *via media* between the ancients and the moderns. But it is just this that Strauss objected to in Gadamer's text, citing the latter's invocation of the Husserlian genetic—and differential—account of *Abschattungen*.[100] And, what is startling here is Renault and Ferry's own attempt to recur to this model *against* Heidegger, demanding both the sciences of infinite tasks and a critique of judgment and deploring their lack.[101] But it would be blind not to see Heidegger's concentration on the transcendental schematism as precisely that, to see it as the exposition of a critique of judgment as hermeneutic rationality—which is of course just the way Gadamer read it, realizing that the distinction between reflective and determining judgment could not ultimately hold up.[102] The 'middle way' could not count on a return to Kant—or Plato— but would require a route between the antinomies of spontaneity and receptivity, voluntarism and naturalism. In this regard, rather than being divided between the ancients and the moderns, what is at stake is the status of the quarrel itself. On its own terms, for Gadamer, the *querelle* is irresolvable. What is all important is the question of its remainder. Hence; "[T]he famous *querelle des anciens et des modernes* belongs to the prehistory of hermeneutics" (RAS:97). Moreover, what follows in this text is equally decisive: "insofar as it awakened a hermeneutical reflection on the ideals of humanism" (RAS:97). The humanities became reflectively viable only in the wake of, and precisely as a result of, the overcoming of this querelle—in default of, and in extension beyond, tradition. The famous *agon* in fact never took place. To put it bluntly, the humanities, already concerned with their own distance from origins and the issue of translation, from the outset already stepped beyond the univocal demonstrative demands of the modern. We will need then to see the quarrel between the *Geistes und Naturwissenschaften* equally without resolution.

Nonetheless, for all its demonstrative hubris, a hubris that short shrifts, indeed to use Husserl's term, 'decapitates,' the rational, the modern likewise remained mindful of the sham concerning demonstrability that reappears in theories of natural right. And, what needs to be retrieved in both destructions, that is, natural right and natural reason, *physis and logos*, is the 'rationality' that was at sake in both cases—that is what remains yet unfulfilled in the Enlightenment project, as Habermasians rightly realize. Still, this authorizes neither the abandonment of natural right, nor makes it feasible for us simply to reconstitute it—the 'Fichtean' option was contrived mathematically at the start, and transcendentally illusory.

To reconstitute is not to regain the universal, even if it may be a necessary condition of putting it into play. Precisely in acknowledging our distance with respect to it, the question of its interpretation instead provides an opening, to use Gadamer's term, for "the reawakening consciousness of solidarity of a humanity that slowly begins to know itself as humanity" (RAS:86). The 'solidarity' at stake is not however the 'solidity' of a 'natural' substance, but that of the difference wagered between and beyond 'substance,' that very difference that has been from the outset the venture of the 'humanities' beyond all 'humanism.' The *communio natura* in this regard will lie beyond the fictions of *communio primaeva*, but equally both the foundations and demonstrative myths of the *communio fundi originera*—as well as the founding spontaneous act in which reason gives itself the law, *natura naturans*.[103]

The critical demand for both enactment and constitution will remain an ever present requisite, a necessary but not sufficient condition for the articulation of justice. And, it may not suffice to claim, as does Ferry, that the charge concerning the nonfulfillment of sufficient conditions misses "the conception of humanity, the theory of communication, and the criticism of ideology that this thesis contains in nucleo."[104] As has been seen, to claim that the distinguishing characteristic of mankind, as Fichte's *Rechtslehre* declared, involved a practice of education (*Erzogen*) through *freie Wechselwirkung* of concepts, surely elevates the question of rational dialogue to its rightful and rationally necessary place. The significance of Fichte's work remains incontrovertible in this regard.[105] Still, that elevation neither solves the problem of reason nor on its own preserves truth. To know that the ideal depends on constitutive freedom, after all, does not warrant the univocal validity of its calculation, nor can it provide the necessary defeasibility concerning possible suspicion of its legislation.[106] Hence the return of the critique of critique. It is in this sense that natural right and jurisprudence will be inextricably complicated, as was immediately recognized to be the case in Fichte's wake, precisely insofar as the latter had dissipated the withdrawal of 'nature.' Hence the legacy of the *communio natura* . . .

Even if knowledge of the Good will be rule-governed as Gadamer put it, "there are no rules governing the reasonable use of rules" (RAS:121). Appeals to tradition equally of course cannot suffice here:

but the mediation required will not simply be provided in response to the demand for intelligent consensus, demanding equally the dialogue by which what is alien, unthought, or excluded always remains mediated. The difference between transcendental semantics and transcendental ontologies remains a transcendental difference, its articulation again the weaving of forms and once more the 'translation' of what always exceeds possible consensus. The dimension at stake then truly eludes the simple application of method, the opening of an *Umriss*, perhaps a certain prophetic hope concerning a justice whose articulation requires less the machinery of deduction or the constraints of calculative method than an art capable of uniting discernment and interpretation, recollection and invention. It is doubtless this art which lies at stake in the *Auseinandersetzung* between the ancients and the moderns—not only critically at stake in the rationality of *Wirkungsgeschichte*, but likewise at stake in articulating its remainder, the status of the "fundamental category" of the classical (TM:577).

Merleau-Ponty,
Transcendental
Imagination, and
Body-Schema: On
the De-lineation
of the Visible

In his decisive chapter in the *Phenomenology of Perception* introducing the synthesis of the lived body (*le corps propre*), Merleau-Ponty claimed that "the body is to be compared, not to a physical object, but rather to a work of art" (PoP:150). In fact, no more than the classical reduction of the body to a physical object, analyzable *partes ex partes*, could the body be reduced to a classical reflection: univocal, hierarchialized, instituted, and enacted from on high. Rather than the strict opposition between the sensible and the intelligible that both 'reductions' presuppose, the *schema corporel*, instead, would provide the Kantian "art hidden in the depths of the human soul" constituting their interstice (PoP:429).[1] Hence the privilege of the account of the body within the text of first philosophy. Moreover, even if Merleau-Ponty would later find it necessary to extend this account, without question it involved an affirmation from which he never relented. The latest lectures at the College de France still speak of "the body schema as a lexicon of corporeality in general" (Themes:129), fully consistent with the *Phenomenology's* description of the 'art' of the body, incommunicable by any other means than its own event, to be accessible, consequently, only to a descriptive delineation that was phenomenological.

Still, if, as is often recognized, the resulting account of the body as *das Organ des apriori* would doubtless yield a very rich description of intentionality, it has equally seemed troublesome.[2] To describe, after all, is not to *assert*, which is why 'descriptions' concerning the facticity of Reason and its *Masstab* have always verged on a peculiar form of psychologism, as neo-Kantians and logicians like Cohen and Frege have always objected. And doubtless, no one invokes the danger of this psychological moment more than Merleau-Ponty, who, after all, easily claimed that the *disciplines* of philosophy and psychology themselves 'verged' in accounting for this event—a claim problematic enough that it troubles even those within the phenomenological camp. Gadamer, for example, at one time claimed that Merleau-Ponty's impact was ultimately one of a 'moralist,' a claim that rested on, if nothing else, the latter's development of Scheler's account of the lived body and its retrieval of an insistence that countered the ambiguities traditionally haunting the Greek's conception of Reason (*Nous*).[3] Still, *pace* what Heidegger too had called the account's appeal to the theological language of personhood,[4] even Scheler's disclaimer against philosophical modernism that "we are not disembodied intellects," valorized from the outset by the problem of finitude and "finite consciousness," was not without epistemic consequences.[5] In fact, Scheler claimed, "just as the 'ego' must accompany all our (psychic) experiences (as Kant

observed), so must our lived body accompany all organic sensations, . . . the underlying form through which all organic sensations are
conjoined."[6] Moreover, the necessity of a similar 'transcendental'
aesthetic is by no means absent from the archive of hermeneutics itself.
No less a figure than Chladenius had claimed that what distinguishes
the specificity of our conceptual viewpoints are "the conditions
governed by our mind, body and even the person which make or cause
us to conceive of something in one way or another," a conditioning that
in a number of senses is itself identical with the origins of hermeneutics.[7]
Nor perhaps would it remain simply absent in the wake of hermeneutics, as critics such as Foucault have attested in claiming that the
archaeology of the human sciences remain still poised on the 'investments' of the body.[8]

II

    This 'turn' to the body by which Merleau-Ponty might be
claimed—by those both within and without the 'hermeneutic' tradition—to involve a certain culmination of modern transcendentalism,
then, is not new to philosophy, nor even unique to 'phenomenology,'
if it would involve an extension that would necessitate surpassing both.
In fact, the need to systematically attend to the faculty of Reason can
be traced at least as far back as Aristotle's treatise, *De Anima*. And, the
need to see in the imagination (*phantasia*), the faculty to which Kant
ascribed this secret art, a mediatory function in which the sensible and
the intelligible are 'meted out,' can equally be traced through Aristotle's
proclamation that imagination does not occur without sensation, nor
judgment without it.[9] Moreover, that Merleau-Ponty cited the Kantian
variant in the closing pages of the *Phenomenology* is perhaps neither
accidental in relating himself to that tradition and its modern, transcendental legacy, nor, for the same reason, unproblematic, granted the
conflict that prevails within Kant's own retrieval. And, for reasons that
will be seen to be essential, it is not accidental that the *Phenomenology's*
preface cites the protocols of Kant's account of teleological judgment
in the third *Critique* as a precursor of the overcoming it institutes in
relation to that past.
    What separates modern 'transcendentalism' from its ancient
archive, nonetheless, is precisely a conflict thought to be insurmountable, transforming the status of the mediation in question. In fact, the
modernist versions of *De Anima* proceeded *without* the teleological
assurance of the harmony of the faculties of Plato and Aristotle. In
accord with the new science, the inventory of the faculties à la Descartes,

Locke, Gassendi, or Leibniz (and thereby, Chladenius) led instead to what Kant himself recognized as a certain dispersion within the subject. After all, the demand that we trace the 'nature' of reason was now one by which it might be submitted to a science essentially opposed to its own *telos*, issuing in a series of antinomies that essentially undercut the classical account.[10] What separates Kant's account of the imagination from Aristotle's in this regard involves the disappearance of the unity of the mediation in question.

If in fact the synthesis of the sensible species, the *synthesis speciosa*, as Kant still continued to call it, remains a function of the imagination, the unity of those particulars—the universal—escapes, forcing Kant to acknowledge the underdeterminability accompanying their intellectual counterpart.[11] Instead, it is the spontaneity of imagination, its "originality [*Originalität*] (as distinguished from imitative production)" that reigns here, its function as *exhibitia originaria*—even to the extent that, notwithstanding Kant's demand that what ultimately justifies its products is their connection with objects of possible experience, the lectures on anthropology nonetheless define the *facultas imaginandi* as "the power of [producing] intuition even when the object is not present."[12] But if Reason depended on such a faculty, it could no longer in fact *solve* the problem of the link between the sensible and the intelligible as the Greeks had hoped. Instead, precisely because of this potential and the underdeterminability and 'laterality' that resulted, the problem of Reason was unresolvable, a faculty instead that required utmost restraint, because its products inevitably fell into conflict, heterogeneity, and irreconcilable polysemy.

Kant, consequently, bequeathed the space of this conflict to the practical realm, claiming that from the standpoint of the theoretical (i.e., granted the principles of pure reason), any account of 'observables' would of necessity deny Reason a 'place.'[13] Which is not to say, of course, any Being, granted the undecidability afflicting the problem of the noumenon.

III

As a result, the status of the 'place' to be occupied by Reason and the sphere it would entail became problematic immediately for those who came after Kant. Fichte, in fact, immediately questioned the implicit link between the productions (*Erzeugungen*) of imagination and those Kant had relegated and regulated within the sphere of the practical. The 1794–1795 *Wissenschaftslehre* in this regard had already emphasized the imagination as the site of an essential and insurmountable conflict and interplay between the founding and the founded, subject and object, the finite and the infinite—even between light and darkness (SK:293). Two years later, *The Science of Rights* confronted the issue of this conflict within the practical realm in a way that would not be without recoil on theory itself. Moreover, in so doing Fichte proceded wholly by means of the model of the aesthetic in delineating the art of this 'conjunction.' In a text that would have an impact both on those immediately (e.g., Hegel) and mediately (e.g., Cohen) in its wake, Fichte claimed:

> In contemplation (*Anschauung*), reason is the *productive power of imagination*. Through the seeing (*Schauen*), or contemplating, something is thrown out from the Ego, as it were, somewhat in the manner that the painter throws out from his eye the completed forms on the canvas (*looks them [hinsieht]*, so to speak on the canvas,) before the slower hand can draw their outlines. In the same manner the sphere is here posited, or contemplated. . .The Ego in contemplating itself as activity contemplates its own activity as a *line-drawing*. This is the original scheme of activity in general, as every one will discover who wishes to excite in himself the highest contemplation. This original line is the pure extension (*Ausdehnung*), the common characteristic of Time and Space, out of which Time and Space arise only by distinction and further determination. This line does not presuppose space, but space presupposes it; and the lines in space, that is, the limits of extended things in space, are something utterly different (*ganz anderes*). (SR:89–90)[14]

The space of this original alterity, the opening of this "formless form"—a certain transcendental reinstitution of Plato's *chora*—involves a play in the possibility of pure imagination.[15] In accompanying all our perception, Kant claimed, it remains an event whose existence "psychologists have hitherto failed to realize," sure nonetheless that psychology would never be scientific itself, being bound wholly to time.[16] What was at stake, as Hegel likewise would put it in writing three years after Fichte's text, involved an event in which Reason remains "immersed in extension and becomes intellect and category only as it separates itself out of extension."[17] And for all three thinkers, following Kant's recognition in the antinomies, it is the delineation of a conflict between subject and object, or the Ego and its World that remains inextricable.

The importance of Fichte's own account in concentrating on this conflict in which judgments become "destabilized" may be too often underestimated. In concentrating on this 'separation' and its difference in the margins of the Copernican revolution, Fichte doubtless announced the space of a reason that extended beyond the strict foundations of modernism, a reason that explicitly forced justification to turn 'circular' (SK:247)—perhaps even 'hermeneutic'—its facts and their interpretations always theory laden and without ultimate decidability. Explanation (*Erklären*), Fichte claimed, is consequently always a "finite affair," by definition not objectively and immediately certain, "but a progression from one thing to the next…and limitation or determination is simply the bridge we traverse to it" (SK:248). What results is a certain 'interdetermination' between judgment and understanding (SK:214). The act of understanding is, consequently, always a momentary stabilization in the manifold possibilities of conceptualization, an event in which the play of imagination becomes "arrested, settled" (SK:207), a certain "fossilization," to speak Wittgensteinian, by which what he too would call "the play of imagination" precludes the possibility of univocal and unconditional adjudication. Hence, Fichte claimed—granted the premises of the Copernican revolution—"the unattainable idea of determinability" (SK:194).

Doubtless under the sway of the foundationalism his account had challenged, however, Fichte still sought a way to resolve the conflict and the dispersion it portended. Notwithstanding his recognition concerning the ultimate underdeterminability of theoretical reason, still fully in Kant's wake, and by means of an argument that Hegel described as one that "twists and turns in all sorts of ways,"[18] he attempted to dissolve this strife in the sphere of the practical. Reason demanded, it was claimed, an endless search that might reintroduce the harmony of system—eliminating, thereby, the dependence of finitude on its conditions in every form (SK:220). Hence, under the protocol that "everything should conform to the self" (SK:232), it not only allowed but obligated in the practical sphere, "the constant extension (*Erweiterung*) of our limits to infinity" (SK:244), the dominion of freedom over nature.

Still, if the possibility of such an extension had been depended on since Kant's second *Kritik* and the conditions of its actuality at least assertorically posited, the event of its *realization* remained wholly undetermined, a dependent variable within the experiment of the Copernican turn. Whether the actuality of the possible world theoretically hypothesized and the reality (*Realität*) of our own coincided remained itself in fact undecidable. Hence the *experimentum crucis* concerning the incarnation of Reason, a question that divided the rational from within, hinged on the event of the transition between *quantum* and *quantitas*. What lies contested, then, Fichte claimed, is nothing other than the *"real existence (wirklichen Daseyns)"* that constitutes the distinctive difference of our "finitude" (SK:245).

Precisely in this regard, the *Science of Rights* (1796) inevitably extended the account of this conflict in explicating a sphere in which the ancient strife between the sensible and the intelligible, free will and determinism would be "played out." The condition for the occurrence of this antinomial event's resolution, it declared, is a specific extended thing itself within the realm of pure extension, one in which the purely formal ego is constituted within "a limited, but exclusively its own sphere of possible free acts." The extension involved is one in which, Fichte claimed, the Ego changes "from the absolute formal to a determined material Ego or to a person" (SR:88), an event that is the *conditio sine qua non* of its individuality (SR:87). At the end of its legacy Merleau-Ponty—perhaps more than any other thinker, the inheritor of its commitment—would wonder what had been accomplished thereby, questioning whether this 'concretization' did not transform—*de facto, if not de juris*—the matrix in question: "Is not Fichte's *Ichheit uberhaupt* simply Fichte?" (Themes:107). And, although it was an objection that had not gone unrecognized, Fichte always hoped he could simply deduce his way out of it, a hope doubtless not without effect for theory, but likewise *praxis*—let alone the political 'solution' it would attempt to inaugurate.

IV

The 'effect' of schematization is not simply a 'product,' it is likewise an event, an event, moreover, that itself *adheres* to space and time precisely in its 'production'—an event in fact in which space and time themselves would arise, as Fichte put it, only through differentiation (*Unterscheidung*) (SR:90). As a result, all that had remained 'excessive' within the conflict of theory becomes submitted to its other, readmitted in the play of its own *ekstasis*. The event of Reason's incarnation is itself, that is, the transcendental event in which the conflict of Reason becomes crystallized in its own embodiment, an event in which the ego is both actualization and product. Consequently, in the same way that the imagination figures the world as a line drawing, Reason quite literally is itself *figured*. Continuing the analogy between transcendental schematism and artistic schematism or *Linienziehen*, the *Grundlage des Naturrechts* affirms: "In the same manner the sphere [of free acts] is here produced in the form of lines, and thus becomes an Extended Something (*ein Ausgedehntes*)" (SR:90). It is on the originary basis of this pure 'extension' that the concrete *extenda* of space would become articulated, schematized precisely in the projection (*Enwerfung*) of an image (I:375).[19] Moreover, by means of this differentiation, and indeed, through the wavering of the imagination itself, he claimed, "there arises a time" [*eine Zeit entsteht*) (SR II:47). The 1794–1795 *Wissenschafslehre* described it more precisely, perhaps, as an event in which, by means of the imagination the condition of the self becomes extended to a moment of time (*zu einem Zeit-Momente ausdehnt*), convinced all the while that Reason itself remains timeless (SK:194). And yet, if the syntheses of these moments or 'points' would thus reduce time to 'space' (or, in any case, pure 'extensionality'), and this in turn to the presence of the subject's autoaffection, it would ultimately imply, nonetheless, a certain differentiation within the subject itself, because it occurs "in part with extension and subsistence, and in this respect it becomes a determinate body; in part with identity and duration in time, and in this respect it [the self] becomes a soul" (SK II:66). But, as the *Schauen* of this pure 'centrifugal' extension, that is, as a progressive sequence of points in which space and time are differentiated (SK:185), the self remains the unmoved mover in the sensible and intelligible worlds. In fact in a passage that alludes to Kant and the problem of conceptual horizons while stepping beyond him, Fichte claimed the self "stands precisely at the point joining the two worlds, from whence they can be further surveyed with a single glance" (SK II:42).[20] The certainty of this cyclopsean *Blick* and its *Uebersehen* was for Fichte unchallengeable. "[T]he philosopher contemplates himself, scans his act directly (*sieht der Philosoph sich selbst zu, er schaut sein Handeln unmittelbar an*), knows what he does, because he—does it." That is, "it is so, because I make it so (*Es ist so, weil ich es so mache*)" (SK:36).

Nonetheless, even for Fichte this account remained incomplete, at least in that it projected in the pure spontaneity of its linear analogue a 'schema' the *Wissenschaftslehre* itself admitted to involve a transcendental illusion. The model of geometrical construction in which the philosopher intuits him- or herself in constructing (*construi*) the concept of self (SK II:62–63) could be transferred only unmindful of the critical difference separating "absolute being and real existence" (SK:245n).[21] *Pace* Fichte's claim that *Wissenschaftslehre* would not be a "lifeless concept" (SK II:30), the 'line' depicted here, to reinvoke the earlier model, remains purely 'centrifugal,' an absolute act generated, as he said, on the figure of a congealed, mathematical point—one, "altogether where it is"; that is, fully self-enclosed. Hence its projection would arise self-deceptively, almost as if Reason itself, which Fichte still thought as 'simultaneous,' 'simple,' and self-gathered (SK:194), divinely generated its own embodiment, wholly an *intellectus originarius*. But such a conception, he admitted, would involve "a body without life or soul and not a self" (SK:241). If in fact Fichte's account of this upsurge, schematized in terms of pure extensionality threatened to turn Spinozistic in reducing thought to substance, *against* Spinoza, he had himself claimed that such a reduction wholly separating pure consciousness from empirical consciousness (SK:101), turned dogmatic, unable to account for its own emergence; Spinoza, that is, "could only think his philosophy, he could not believe it" (SK II:81).

Instead, what characterizes the event of the ego's 'living' incarnation involves its being "checked," necessitating that it "open itself (*offnet es sich*)" to its other and to "external influences (*Einwirkung von aussen*)" (SK:243). As such, the check (*Anstoss*) in question, originating in the recognition of its own centrifugal '*ek-stasis*,' provided the moment in which the series of the real became constituted—thus in fact grounding the claim that "*The Science of Knowledge* is therefore realistic" (SK:246). And, granted the self's "recoil" it necessitated, it forced equally the recognition of the self's 'linerarity' as 'centripetal.' Even if the self is modeled as a construction, as a series of points and the generation of lines, it still remains the case (as he would admit elsewhere) that the institution of the present 'now point' remains conditional on a certain receptivity, on a past point that does not in turn depend upon it (I:409).

Precisely in this regard the pure mathematical construction by which the Wissenschaftslehre had delineated its account of the self from its opening principle—"I am because I am" (SK:99)—missed the basis of its being qua *living*, an event that is equally as much passivity, and thereby, the basis of what the later Fichte would call—his earlier criticisms notwithstanding—the "revelation (*Offenbarung* [V:442])" of life itself. The basis of this upsurge, moreover, is not simply the reflective self-positing of the "I think" of consciousness, but the synthesis of transcendental schematism itself, that "act of imagination (which) forms the basis for the possibility of our consciousness, our life, our existence for ourselves, that is, our existence as selves. . ." (SK:202). It is, moreover, this opening of productive imagination that is even responsible for our 'experience' of the "interior to the body within the surfaces," the source of feeling, and thus, in turn, "the source of all our knowledge [since] without feeling, there can be no presentation at all of an external thing" (SK:275-76). Only here, consequently, could one delineate that moment in which the centripetal-centrifugal conflict intertwined and the possibility of the emergence of "the point of union...between the absolute, the practical, and the intellectual characters of the self" (SK:244).

The early Fichte, nonetheless, committed to the self as an absolute point of self generation, or as he put it, to thinking of the "pure self as absolutely self-active, not as determined by things, but as determining them" (SK II:41), demanded that the self be viewed—at least practically—as a self-active generation that would 'draw' itself together out of dispersion, an absolute freedom achieved not by transition but a leap [*Sprung*] (SK:262). Hence the practical (or pragmatic) solution to the *agon* of theory by which it would be posited equally as an extended something (a *quantum*) and at the same time, potentially at least, all reality (*quantitas*)—an event through which the self's opposed moment might be made, if only momentarily, to use his already loaded word, *aufgehoben* (SR:97). But the projection could occur only at the expense of being impelled by an illusion that doubtless Fichte held to be necessary and inevitable—"wholly oblivious," that is, "to the possibility of a check" (SK:244). In fact, notwithstanding Reason's reliance on the transcendental imagination, Fichte felt himself entirely unconditioned with respect even to its upsurge: "in the act of imagining the self is wholly free (*völlig frei*)" (I:379).

Accordingly—and doubtless proceeding precisely within this very oblivion—Fichte specifically deduced the requisite body for this substantial harmony, a specific body adequate for this dispersion's overcoming, in accord with the enactment of a synthetic harmony that constitutes the *Wissenschaftlehre's* definition of substance itself (SK:185). What resulted was a notion of the body by which it would be articulated, strictly available to the will, with higher and lower organs capable of 'organically' instituting the *Aufheben* in question—a composite by which "a material body becomes capable of expressing a conception" (SR:92), a *physis*, that is, fully capable of supporting and being subsumed by a *logos*.

As a result, Fichte claimed (in a manner that those who came after him would not miss), practical reason would be enabled to resolve the inherent conflict of Reason precisely in the infinite task that "expressly *realizes* freedom" (SR:100)—an event in which reflection would be invested in material garb, but in a manner in which its hierarchial dominion could not be endangered.[22] No less than Hegel himself, however, would recognize therein a "physico-theology that is directly opposed to the older tradition in its content, but [remains] grounded in the same principles with respect to its form": that is, a nature "absolutely unhallowed and lifeless."[23] In fact, Hegel wondered whether out of a certain "meritorious service that Kant and Fichte had rendered for Voltaire's argument,"[24] both had suffered from a certain abhorrence of nature, resulting in a notion of reason that was precisely "without a body"; that is, "soaring above the wreckage of the world."[25]

If Fichte had blinkingly recognized the inextricability of the question of embodiment, it still remained the case, after all, that the final pronouncement remained the same: "this body is not I" (V:237) but, instead, the sphere "in which we happen to be enclosed" (V:184) an undecidable to be strictly overlooked, if not overcome, in the demand of an 'ought.' Consequently, rather than de-lineating the *ekstasis* of imagination itself, Fichte's final move would be to mask its play in Reason's quest for unity, freedom and 'domination.' "To act, that is why we are here" (VI:345). And as Schelling would note in seeing things precisely to the contrary, Fichte's position always presupposed the very overcoming it was invoked to eradicate. The call to action presupposes, after all, that the answer to the question, "What kind of action?" has been attained.[26]

V

Doubtless, this initial entrance of the concept, if not the phenomenology of the lived body into the transcendentalist text remains overdetermined. And, much more would need to be said ultimately to clarify it as well as those who come after, recognizing, inter alia, that the history of 'the phenomenological movement' cannot be identified simply with discoveries in the 'science of phenomenology.'

Nonetheless, if Merleau-Ponty's distance from the origins of this classical archive seems *prima facie* clear, his proximity likewise remains undeniable. Its trace remains readily apparent in the closing chapters of the *Phenomenology of Perception*. In fact, precisely before appealing to the Kantian hidden art of schematism, Merleau-Ponty claimed:

> It is characteristic of idealism to grant that all significance is centrifugal, being an *act* of significance or *Sinn-gebung*, and that there are no natural signs. To understand is ultimately always to construct, to constitute, to bring about here and now the synthesis of the object. Our analysis of one's own body and of perception has revealed to us a relation to the object, i.e. a significance deeper than this. (PoP: 428–29)

What lies deeper involves a 'logos of the aesthetic world' already presupposed—as he quoted Husserl, an "other kind of intentionality"

already at work "beneath the intentionality of acts or thetic intentionality," which in turn is claimed to be "the condition of possibility"
of the latter (PoP:429).[27] Thereby, the nature of significance might once
more be claimed to be precisely "both centrifugal and centripetal"
(PoP:439). Now however, rather than the pure positing and unfolding
of the Absolute Self, the ground of this interplay is claimed to be the
always already presupposed stratum of the sensible world and the body
synthesis that has access to its presentation. That is, the *Anstoss* of
phenomenology rests on our nascent corporeal bond with the world,
"an autochthonous significance. . .which provides the ground of every
deliberate *Sinngebung*" (PoP:441).

The classical Husserlian may not have disagreed at first sight,
recognizing in all this the problem of passive synthesis, a matter that
has often led to a reading by which the commitments of Merleau-Ponty's
text to the analysis of the lived body could be seen as merely a matter
of regional ontology. But, in retrieving the archive of transcendental
schematism, Merleau-Ponty necessarily extended the phenomenological
account of the rational beyond the clairvoyant vision of the cogito. Rather
than affirming the cogito's access of the given as the principle of all
principles and the guarantee of the veracity of presence, the schematic
event that is invoked of necessity forced a certain differentiation and
re-move of the given and the denial of its strict recuperation and
adequation.[28]

What lies deeper than the representative acts of the "I think"
remains a "schema of all possible being, a universal setting in relation
to the world" (*une typique de tout l'être possible, un montage universel a
l'égard du monde*) (PoP:429). For Merleau-Ponty that typic involved a body
schema. The things emerge, that is, not insofar I constitute them but
insofar as the "I" in question is anchored and adheres to a world already
articulated and meaningful. In this regard, far from it being the case,
as Fichte had declared, that the body is "something external to the ego"
the '*Schauen*' by which the world arises occurs instead *only* "in so far
as I have a body and am able to 'look' " (PoP:240).

The ground sought by classical reflection could not then rest on
a pure or simple intellectual synthesis, but required an upsurge that
was incarnate. Hence, if the *Phenomenology* would concur that transcendentally space is existential, it would be necessary to add that
"existence is spatial, that is, that through an inner necessity it opens
on to an 'outside' (*un 'dehors'*)" and that, far from being reflectively
constituted, it arose only on the basis of our being in the world
(PoP:293). "The 'motion which generates space' does not deploy the
trajectory from some metaphysical point with no position in the real

world, but from a certain here towards a certain yonder" (PoP:387).[29] Hence time too could not simply be 'conceived' as a mere form of inner sense, but as the opening of this *'espacement'* itself, a dimension of the 'here-now.' In both cases, the specificity of reason's 'incarnation' would require a spontaneity that is constitutive of us (PoP:427) as much as we constitute it, one that, consequently dissolves the reflective I of the transcendental ego in the course of the enfolding and unfolding of time itself—a synthesis that always remains transitional, always distended and remade (*distendue et refait*) (PoP:240).

In fact, then, it is precisely by the incarnate upsurge of time through which the subject "is nothing but a general flight out of Itself, the one law governing these centrifugal movements" (PoP:419). As Schelling similarly put it in explicating the *ekstasis* of intellectual inituition that had fascinated those in Kant's wake: "It is not *we* who are in time, but time is in us."[30] The attempt to articulate time simply as an effect of reflective presence and the *Uebersehen* of space then remains illusory. The articulation of time cannot simply be limited to extension, but must admit a certain *dis-tention*, a transcendence that as constitutive of this *Schauung* is the condition anterior to positing itself. And, if, in accord with his phenomenological commitments, Merleau-Ponty still appealed ineluctably to "a unique structure which is presence" (PoP:430), it remains, he admitted, irresolvably a presence that is ecstatic, presumptive, detotalized, and lacking in completeness.

The appearance of time, the appearance and its origination, its schematism, is not simply an event that I differentiate, but is one that is differentiated *through* me. If it involves an event that adheres to a unique and individual subject, the opening of a gaze at the core of time (PoP:422), it is equally in this *ek-stasis* the re-moval of 'subjectivity'—a movement that marks the appearance as 'revelation' and only thereby the opening of the subject as *un sujet révélé* (PoP:361). Moreover, even if Merleau-Ponty would in this respect still tie temporality to a 'subject,' if, that is, "time is someone"—it is an adherence that could be traced, *pace* classical attempts to tie embodiment and personality, by admitting equally that this adherence occurs only by a certain "depersonalization" (PoP:215), which in turn traces its adherence and transcendence within Being.

The idealist attempts of Fichte, Scheler, and the rest to link the world of the Absolute to the metaphysics of embodiment, personhood, and the *dynamis* of a moral upsurge thus are placed in jeopardy.[31] If it is true that the Absolute and the relativity of subjectivity are *not* in principle at odds, it still remains the case that the split (or the *écart*)

between the ontic and the ontological is not thereby dissolved—
"appearance is not being, but the phenomenon" (PoP:296).

VI

Still, despite the ruptures he had traced between the reflecting
and the reflected, the centrifugal and the centripetal, Merleau-Ponty's
account of the lived body in the early works did not break with the
foundations of classical transcendentalism. In fact his appeal to the lived
body as a *body subject* in one sense retained its full transcendental rights
de juris within the sensible field—as has been seen, a schema of *l'être
universal*. Further, despite all that it invoked *against* the transcendental
Ich, the *Phenomenology* still claims its basic *Satz* to be fulfilled. That is,
despite all that he claimed mitigates against the subject of classical
thought here, Merleau-Ponty still added, precisely in the culmination
of the *Phenomenology's* time analysis: "Nothing said of the subject is
false: it is true that the subject as an absolute presence to itself is
rigorously indeclinable, and that nothing could happen to it of that it
did not bear within itself the lineaments" (PoP:426–27).

If Merleau-Ponty's account had undercut the *Ich* of transcendental
representation—as had Sartre in fact before him[32]—and if he had
eclipsed transcendental consciousness in submitting it to the event of
ontological synthesis—as Heidegger likewise had done before
him[33]—the art hidden in the human soul and the extended notion
(*notion élargie*) of intentionality Merleau-Ponty invoked in tracing the
body schema did not in this regard tread against the commitments of
his transcendentalist predecessors—as some commentators in fact have
affirmatively argued.[34] Indeed in one sense, the *Phenomenology* simply
retained the matrix of transcendentalism, only inverting its Fichtean
(and Kantian) past. In both instances, at least, the relation in question
remained wholly one of *Fundierung*. Whereas for Fichte—and Husserl,
who still saw phenomenology as the self-explication of the transcendental ego—what came first was irrevocably the absolute positing of
the *Ich*, the centripetal moment only appearing within an *Anstoss* or
noema, an in-itself-for-us whose 'objectivity' both admitted to be wholly
inexplicable, the *Phenomenology* exchanges this reflective stronghold
(*reduit*) for the guarantee of its sensible stratum without being able to
explain any more satisfactorily how the centrifugal moment arises out
of it to reconquer it. Hence, as Scheler put it, the "miracle" of the
phenomenological *Urdoxa* and its motivation.

Moreover, even granted the latter commitment, Merleau-Ponty's
text seemed always threatened by a certain disequilibrium in its attempt

to retrieve this foundation. On the one hand, by a certain *ekstasis*, it embedded reason in its centripetal moment *à la* Schelling, resolving the *Wechsel* of finitude in *Naturphilosophie*—appealing to what the latter called the *transcendental history of the I* [V:164][35] (or what Merleau-Ponty called its *prehistory* [PoP:240]) and risking perhaps thereby a certain self-alienation that Fichte early on had called the very principle of religion. (Critique:73). And yet, equally, in accord with the metaphysics of Reason's infinite extension and "domination," Merleau-Ponty turned to a metaphysics that would *à la* Hegel unite the pure act of the transcendental subject to substance by a movement of self-realization, a certain "blind plunge into doing" (PoP:382) by which it might overcome the dispersion of this "barbarous source" (Signs:178)[36]—thus enabling him to speak still of a for-itself that would be the body's culmination. But even here this culmination would occur only 'ambiguously.' This enactment itself arises through the experience of the body and thus depends on a work already done, precisely and paradoxically a founding that in fact never fully occurs. If it is true that I do not create time (PoP:427), that is, that "the body creates time instead of submitting to it," this foundation itself inevitably crumbles—an event, that is, in which there is a "summoning (*invocation*), but not the experience, of an eternal natura naturans" (PoP:240). What results, consequently, remains a *Hexenkreis* of the founding and the founded, a 'dialectic' of *naturans* and *naturata* that was itself to unveil the "primordial layer at which both things and ideas come into being" (PoP:219). Perhaps the most important discovery concerning the 'transitional syntheses' traced within the *Phenomenology of Perception* would remain in this regard their ultimate disequilibrium and opacity.

VII

Despite his flirtation with the classical responses, however, Merleau-Ponty still realized that the event in question could not be so easily leveled off. On the one hand, the attempt to view perception on the basis of a constitutive "act," in accord with the metaphysics of classical transcendentalism, would fail simply because our adherence within the world is the result neither of the encompassing unity of an 'act' nor its 'synthesis.' The latter, he claimed, is an event that is as much 'synopsis' as synthesis (PoP:276); not one, consequently, over which "a second force" might be added to its own 'dialectic' integrity (SC:202). Moreover, the belief that 'we' might simply reflectively or 'theoretically' coincide with perception and the perceived was equally untenable, in fact a break with the critical attitude that could occur only by turning 'precritical,' a retreat to Spinozism that from the outset threatened its archive from within. *The Structure of Behavior*, however, had already realized this failure:

The whole in the organism is an idea, as Spinoza thought. However, while Spinoza believed he was able to rediscover the unity of the body beyond the fragmented extension of the imagination in a law homogeneous with the law of physical systems, it does not seem possible to understand life by a regressive analysis that goes back to its conditions. It will be a question of a prospective analysis that will look for the immanent signification of life, the latter again being no more a force of attraction than cause is a force of propulsion. (SC:160)

The opening then could be reduced neither by a cause nor subsumed by a propulsive 'force' or end antedating it. Strictly taken, it involved an event that escapes the foundations of classicism, an event, that is, without *arche* or *telos*, one accessible only insofar as we ourselves 'witness' (*assister*) and trace it out. Unlike the parallel determinations of Spinozistic modes, the 'idea' or significance articulated here remains both theoretically irreducible and conceptually indeterminate, an event in default of the deductions and proofs of classical transcendentalism. Instead, the opening in question involved an underdetermination that forced a certain contingency and 'ambiguity' on interpretation—thus giving rise to a certain "wavering (*fluctio*) of the imagination" that Spinoza himself already claimed accompanied the contemplation (*contemplatio*) of the contingent and the temporally dependent.[37]

For Merleau-Ponty it is precisely the fragility of this opening onto an other that is 'constitutive' of intentionality and precisely "the novelty of phenomenology," to have seen with respect to it that "objectifying acts are not representations" (PoP:294). And yet, the delineation of this "purposiveness without a purpose" was ultimately not without a certain recoil on the origins of modern transcendentalism, a recoil that Merleau-Ponty in fact understood—in a manner that was often the case—by *overstating* the possibilities of Husserl's text:

What distinguishes intentionality from the Kantian relation to a possible object is that the unity of the world, before being posited by knowledge in a specific act of identification, is 'lived' as ready-made or already there. Kant himself shows in the *Critique of Judgement* that there exists a unity of the imagination and the understanding and a unity of subjects *before the object* and that, in experiencing the beautiful, for example, I am aware of a harmony between sensation and concept, between myself and others, which is itself without any concept. . . Husserl takes up again the *Critique of Judgement* when he talks about a teleology of consciousness. (PoP:xvii)[38]

Granted the indeterminacy of this event, phenomenology became the "ever-recurrent failure" (PoP:240) to explicate what remains in the wake of the constitutive guarantees of classical transcendentalism, a "gift (*don*) of nature that Mind was called on to make use of beyond all hope" (PoP:127), the *appearance* of a *logos*, a certain indemonstrable *beauté sauvage*[39] encountered within the world. What was at stake involved the possibility of an event in which imagination and concept, image-schema and image, sign and signified might not be totally disparate. Hence, rather than the constitutive act that might precede it, its event could be accessible only by means of an "operative reason" and a "logic lived through" (PoP:49–50). Moreover, if Merleau-Ponty, in accord with a certain Hegelianism that often structured his text, agreed with Hegel concerning the importance of reflective judgment in Kant, radically *unlike* the former, he claimed that what was at stake in this opening precisely *pre*cluded the affirmation of an *intellectus originarius* and the transcendental ego as either subject or substance.[40]

The 'radical reflection' based on the *logos* of the aesthetic world would instead force the logic of transcendental representation into ruin. Granted the very contingency of perspectives on which its differentiations depend, the opening in question required that no judgment or intuition could ever be ultimately affirmed—a point made by Merleau-Ponty precisely in again returning to Kant. Even if Kant himself had proceeded in the *Opus Postumum* by invoking the God of Spinoza as a paradigm for Reason's constitutive relation to the world,[41] such hopes concerning the efficacity and objectivity of Reason must ultimately fail.

[T]he transcendental aesthetic would be confused with the transcendental analytic only if I were a God who posits the world and not a man who finds himself thrown (*jeté*) into it and who, in every sense of the word, 'is wrapped up in it' (*tient à lui*). We do not therefore need to follow Kant in his deduction of one single space. The single space is the indispensable condition for being able to conceive the plenitude of objectivity, and it is quite true that if I try to thematize several spaces, they merge into a unity. . . . But do we know whether plenary objectivity can be conceived? Whether all perspectives are compossible?. . .There may well be, either in each sensory experience, or in each consciousness, 'phantoms' that no rational approach can account for. (PoP:220).

The transcendental unity in question could then not be deduced without begging the question. And, in Merleau-Ponty's reading, Kant himself already knew it: "The idea of a single space and a single time, being grounded on that of a summation of being...is precisely what Kant subjected to criticism in the Transcendental Dialectic" (PoP:220). Both Kant and Husserl—in what Merleau-Ponty aptly called his "Kantian texts" (PoP:276n)—achieved the absolute certainty demanded by the paradigm of *Wissenschaftslehre* only by conflating the realm of the reflective with the determinant, a conflation that rested on endowing the subject in advance with the keys to certainty. Both proceded, that is, by the logic of positing consciousness, "the supposition of a wholly determinate world" (PoP:273). But thereby, Kant's Analytic missed the possibility of accounting for the "appearance as appearance" (PoP:301). If the percept is always understood 'intentionally,' that is, as directed beyond itself, a percept 'of' the world, it does not follow that any (or all) percepts remain anything other than simply 'presumptuous': that is, apparent.

The foundation of Reason could be constituted neither "from above" nor, *pace* classical phenomenology—and perhaps even certain texts of the *Phenomenology of Perception* that still labored under the illusion of a certain cosmo-the-ology—could it be founded "from below." Even if, against all that had been admitted within the uncertainty of the "world's free play" (PoP:295), it appealed equally to the determinacy of my "absolute certainty of the world in general" (PoP:297), this assertion could find no unequivocal vindication, granted Merleau-Ponty's commitment to perspectivism and the multiplicity of *Abschattungen* to which his work had been likewise committed from the time of *The Structure of Behavior.*[42]

The indeterminacy accompanying the opening afforded by my 'point of view' and the ensuing (radicalized) reflective 'judgments' could not in the strict sense provide—either de facto or de juris—"a way I have of infiltrating into the world in its entirety" (PoP:329). What undercut the constructions of the subject-pole likewise deconstructed the investments of the object-pole and the *Anstoss* of intentionality. In both respects the reproach against Kant's transcendentalism would need to be made equally against those who stand within his lineage. What Kant learned in the Dialectic "he seems to forget in the Analytic" (PoP:304). And, if Merleau-Ponty invoked the teleological judgment of the third

Kritik in Husserl's name, he did so as much *against* the metaphysical unities of classical phenomenology, as he did simply in affirming Husserl's 'opening.'[43]

It would be mistaken, that is, to think that this opening could be encompassed or grounded either from above or below, either by appeal to an *actus* and its *energeia* or to *a subiectum* and *hypokeimenon*. The *Phenomenology's* attempt to restore the opening of the *scheme corporel* it traced to a *body-subject* occurred only by leaving the categories of the metaphysics it implied intact. The 'foundations' of the *Phenomenology of Perception* would not then need to be simply applied in the later works—but overcome. If the *Phenomenology* had attempted to redefine metaphysics in terms of this "opening out to another" (PoP:168), it could not contain the absolute Other (*un Autre absolu*) (PoP:326) that had been disclosed. *The Visible and the Invisible* consequently would speak more directly in this regard: *"la métaphysique reste coincidence"* (VI:127).

VIII

This is not to say that the itinerary that had led to the later work would force the abandonment of transcendentalism itself, but precisely, instead, that in overcoming the metaphysics which too had grounded the latter, Merleau-Ponty hoped to finally make "explicit" the event it sought to trace. In fact, if one must insist here on the rejection of the earlier work's 'solution,' one must equally insist on its continuity within the later work's project.

Granted the transformation involved, however, the extent to which these works remain in continuity is in some respects startling. If *The Visible and the Invisible* again opens in defending the *doxa* of *le foi perceptif*, it does so against the *Phenomenology* in finally denying the *telos* of identity and coincidence that structured the earlier work's investment of the intelligible within a *body-subject* and affirming the circularity, complementarily, and reciprocity of the elements of its investigation. Instead of trying to get behind or beneath the philosophy of reflection's centrifugal moment by *founding* it in an autochthonous and originary centripetal moment, Merleau-Ponty reinstated the circularity of condition and conditions that had provoked classical transcendentalism from the outset:

[T]here is no longer any philosophy of reflection, for there is no longer the originating and the derived; there is thought traveling a circle where the condition and the conditioned, the reflection and the unreflected, are in a reciprocal, if not symmetrical, relationship, and where the end is in the beginning as much as the beginning is in the end. . . . It is a question not of putting the perceptual faith in place of reflection, but on the contrary of taking into account the total situation, which involves reference from the one to the other. (VI:35)

The task of the philosopher's text could not be, as the *Phenomenology's* model of radical reflection still had conceived it, one of 'positivistically' embedding the reflective within the unreflective, a retrieval that would fulfill the quest for absolute knowledge precisely in restoring its perpetual beginning. In fact such an account could succeed only by invoking a 'recuperation' in which the body's 'dialectic' might be *resolved*, a coinciding between the reflecting and the reflection, between the 'personal' and the 'impersonal' that might be recovered, reinstituting, thereby, the *Ich* = *Ich* about which classical reflection had dreamed.

Beyond this metaphysics however—and in accord instead with the 'circularity', the *Wechsel*, of condition and conditioned—what would be required is an account of an event in which coincidence always remained at best 'partial', affirming thereby the 'discontinuity' and 'reciprocal relativization' of the in itself and the for itself (PNP:39). Here, beyond the myth of the return to the immediate, and the ideal of an epistemic zero point, this 'truth' and the method of its acquisition could no longer be regulated by coincidence. The *Phenomenology's* attempt to perceive the world at a stroke, even Merleau-Ponty's appeal to the single stone in the Tuileries's wall "entirely without history" (PoP:293), was in this sense doomed to the very failure—and the very history—it had itself outlined. In a sense it had itself already acknowledged that the 'horizontal' model of strata and foundation broke down. . . ."it is through the originated that the originator is made manifest" (PoP:394). The account of human finitude can be satisfied only if it is grasped that Dasein is not only thrown into the world but 'wrapped up' or 'intertwined' with it. . .

IX

What is at stake even in the final pages of *The Visible and the Invisible* remains, nonetheless, fully in line with the legacy of transcendentalism and the 'productive' upsurge attributed to the transcendental imagination: what is at stake, that is, remains "the formative medium (*milieu formateur*) of the object and the subject" (VI:147). If Merleau-Ponty still raised the classical question, however, what is required, he now claimed, is an entirely different answer. And yet, in stepping beyond the philosophy whose collapse the *Phenomenology* had foreseen, this overcoming emerges only in retracing the *écart* operative in the classical *Wechsel* itself, retrieving at the same time what *The Visible and the Invisible* called, in denying the strict (and metaphysical) opposition between the perceived and the imaginary, an "operative imaginary that is part of our institution" (VI:85), part of a finitude, that is, that remains "militant" (VI:251).[44] Nonetheless, this transformation became possible only by exchanging the neo-Platonic schemata that had structured the metaphysics of self and world, the dialectics of point, line, and plane—a dialectic that, Hegel too had argued, implicitly resulted in the *Ich=Ich*[45]— for the differentiation and decentered 'circularity' of the body and its world, a certain 'verticality' *sauvage*:

> There is reciprocal insertion and intertwining one in the other. Or rather, if as once again we must, we eschew the thinking by planes and perspectives, there are two circles, or two vortexes, or two spheres, concentric when I live naively, and as soon as I question myself, the one slightly decentered with respect to the other. . . (VI:138).

Although Merleau-Ponty could still conceptualize this event as a certain "self-manifestation" (VI:173), what was involved was neither the manifestation of an absolute spirit, nor an idealistic dialectic of self-consciousness and its *prise de conscience*, but the opening of Reason's corporeal adherence itself, an event more complex than had been conceptualized by the classical and logocentric teleology of act intentionality. Rather, what was at issue was the intertwining and the *écart* of intentional life within *and* beyond itself (VI:173). The event at stake could be understood only by explicating our belonging to it and the reciprocal envelopment of its 'incongruent counterparts' themselves, retracing thereby the 'circle' of the sensing and the sentient, the touching and the touched, the seeing and the visible, and ultimately, that of the sensible and the intelligible as a whole (VI:143). Against the *telos* of pure ideality that had structured classical metaphysics, consequently, it would need to admit, to speak Platonically, both a certain 'invisible' to the visible, but equally a flesh, a certain 'geography' to ideas, 'rechaining' them to their conditions, 'the visible' and the specificity, the historicity, of their 'opening'—precisely, that is, the specificity of their 'incarnation.'

In this regard it would be necessary to grant that there is—as Fichte had put it in the 1795 treatise, *Grundriss der Eigenthümlichen der*

Wissenschaftslehre—"no thing without an image *and* no image without a thing" (I:379). But precisely thereby it would likewise be *impossible* to say (as he likewise declared) that the self remains "wholly free in imaging." The freedom in question, this ability to posit 'otherwise' (I:374), is in fact not absolute but only the indeterminacy of this 'wavering' itself, a 'differential' freedom that remains contingent and temporally bound—that is, the conditioned freedom Merleau-Ponty had attempted to characterize since the concluding chapter of the *Phenomenology*. It is in this respect that Merleau-Ponty's account of incarnate ambiguity approaches Schelling, resuming once more the attempt to trace the event in which "life is the schema of freedom."[46]

Even in the later works, however, the body's privilege remains inextricable. It remains the case, as he still put it, "that 'my consciousness' is not the synthetic, uncreated, centrifugal unity of a multitude of 'consciousness of. . .' that would be centrifugal like it is, that it is sustained, subtended, by the prereflective and preobjective unity of my body" (VI:141–42). What 'subtends,' however, is not a substance and its *milieu formateur* is not the 'act' of a 'body subject' but the opening of this reversibility within the visible itself (VI:139). Consequently, it would need to surpass the reflective *réduit* that the *Phenomenology* still invoked tentatively, departing from the *Element des denken* as a self-contained moment before and behind the moment of its own rupture. Rather than the transcendental reduction yielding the stronghold of reflective interiority, it would be necessary instead to trace our participation in the event in which, by means of the play of imagination and its hidden art, "life becomes ideas and ideas become life" (VI:119).

Which is not to say that the critical moment had been left behind—on the contrary, as has been seen. In fact, the failure of coincidence is not accidental, simply a tragic fate accompanying the finite. Nor, on the other hand, is the necessity of this turn to the body simply a matter of including an account of Reason's intestines, as Heidegger put it.[47] Rather, it is a question of tracing the specificity of both Dasein's finitude *and* transcendence, both its *Geworfenheit* and its intertwining. The quest for a knowledge without such *Vor-Urteilen*, a free knowledge (*savoir 'libre'*), would miss the figurative potential of the symbolic function as resource for truth—*not* in so far as "we want to observe what underlies the 'symbolic function' " (PoP:128), but rather in so far as 'Being' (and its 'truth') is differentiated precisely *through* it; precisely, that is, insofar as it is itself the delineation of the play between life and idea.

If there remains an 'essence of truth,' consequently, it is not simply what escapes all presumption, but involves an opening that depends on an image not, as Merleau-Ponty put it, in "bad repute" (VI:77). Rather than barring the image from the realm of the visible, it would be necessary to risk the potential of the image precisely as its 'double,' affirming the potential of its *Zweideutigkeit* as 'revelatory'; that is, a schematism, or figuration, or trace (i.e., *Aspekt or revelateur*) of the visible itself. Hence, it would be necessary to invoke the possibility of a truth beyond coincidence, beyond adequacy, and a 'figured synthesis' that, precisely within this *fluctuatio* remains, *qua exhibitio originarius*, both the explication and de-figuration of a "good error"—the affirmation of a certain 'errancy' as the setting into work of truth itself and, thereby, a "transcendence of the phantasm" (VI:191).[48] And, it is just in this regard that Merleau-Ponty's turn to the body and the figuration of the visible, refusing its liberation from any but a lateral transcendence, marked the culmination of what Levinas called a certain anti-platonism in contemporary philosophy.[49]

X

This is not to say that in all this Merleau-Ponty had either solved or resolved the problem of metaphysics, the problem of the relation between the sensible and the intelligible, or that between the in-itself and the for-itself. In fact, if anything, exactly the opposite is the case. Despite all the richness of the phenomenological description that emerges in the final work, one fact remains: the moment of the conflict that opens modern transcendentalism is ultimately affirmed. Despite all that Merleau-Ponty had worked to complete in the hands of Schelling, or Blondel, or Bergson, or Husserl, towards the end of *The Visible and the Invisible* he was forced to simply reassert the locus of the antinomy that has spurred post-Kantian thought once more:

> To be sure, one can reply that between the two "sides" of our body, the body as sensible and the body as sentient (what in the past we called the objective body and phenomenal body), rather than a spread, there is the abyss (*plutot qu'un écart, l'abîme*) that separates the In-itself from the For-itself. It is a problem—and we will not avoid it—to determine how the sensible sentient can also be thought. (VI:136–37).[50]

Moreover, in the preface to *Signs* written about the same time, he asserted what any logician would see to be the paradox in this reply. The abyss in question, that is, is not only possible, on this account it is, strangely enough, the necessary condition for the possibility of

Reason itself. "There would be nothing," he stated, "if there were not that abyss of self" (Signs:14). No exploration of the invisible within the visible; nor thought of the visible within the invisible—both depend precisely on the possible 'exteriority' in question.

The solution then risks—deliberately perhaps—becoming a non-solution, a solution that remains inevitably equivocal (PNP:49), 'solving' the problem of *Fundierung* by affirming what remains instead ungrounded. Even if, as the *Phenomenology* had proclaimed, the body is the site of this metamorphosis of ideas and things, it cannot *ensure* it (PoP:164). It would be wrong, of course, to think that, because thought depends on what exceeds it, immediacy and coincidence have consequently been strictly removed, that thereby all phantasms are simply false: "the illusion of illusions is to think now that to tell the truth we have never been certain of our own acts" (VI:37), discounting the evidence of truth itself (PoP:295). Still, granted all that over-determines it, such a response may be easily misconstrued.

Fichte too invoked a similarly 'equivocal' argument, having likewise committed thought to the depths of transcendental imagination and its symbolic function. He claimed in fact that the act of the imagination that "forms the possibility of our consciousness, our life, our existence for ourselves. . .cannot be eliminated (and) hence the act is not a deception but gives us truth (*sie giebt Wahrheit*)" (SK:202)—substituting thereby the circle of *Wissenschaftslehre* and the possibilities of what he called the creative imagination for the *circulus vicioso* and undecidability that haunted it from the ground up (SK II:75ff). Strictly taken, however, Fichte would simply be mistaken, and so would Merleau-Ponty were we to read him to have argued similarly—invoking against the unities of metaphysics the uncertainties of the 'reflective,' in the recognition that "the external cannot be eliminated" (PNP:52) while depending on transcendental certainties and determinations for the 'faculty' of presentation. Such a solution is precisely that of bad ambiguity—as Fichte's eventual recourse to the mask of practical extension would underscore.[51] Hence the neo-Kantian claim that, *pace* Fichte (and those who come after), transcendental arguments demand the safeguard of criteria, the unspoken word of *Wissenschaft* itself, its inventory one that involves not the phenomena and presentation (a phenomen-ology), but the secured *logos* of pure reason itself, that is, the scientific presentation of truth (i.e., a logology).

Without recourse to sure foundations the veracity of the imagination's presentations cannot be assured to provide the only truth possible. There is, after all, as Nietzsche likewise realized, at least one other truth possible, namely, that all truth escapes this 'sphere'—or, that all truths are 'lies'. From the fact that we are inevitably 'conditioned,' that reason inevitably exceeds itself, it does not follow that those conditions are (*not* deceptive, but) true. Nothing precludes the possibility, as Fichte himself would realize in *The Vocation of Man* (1800) that the intuition to which he appealed "is dream (*der Traum*); [and] thought—the source of all the being and all the reality I picture, the source of my own being, my own powers, and my own purposes—is the dream of that dream" (VM:80).

There is admittedly, moreover, a certain 'Nietzschean' moment in Merleau-Ponty's appeal to the body, to what he aptly called its *intentional transgression* (Signs:94) and the swarming (*pullular*) of perceptions I can feel beneath my gaze (PoP:338). There remains, even it might be said, a certain Dionysian appeal to Merleau-Ponty's invocation of the *art* of the body. Indeed, the *Phenomenology* at one point claims that it is *only* the body's art—that is, the transfiguration of the body in dance—that is capable of escaping what it still Platonically calls our 'imprisonment,' accomplishing thereby, a certain 'de-situationizating' to which thought could not aspire—thus overcoming the very subject-object dichotomy itself (PoP:287n). Here, then, to cite no less a figure than Heidegger on Nietzsche, the "chaos of our region of sensibility that we know as the region of the body [would be] only one section of the great chaos that the 'world' itself is," one in which "our body is admitted into this stream of life, floating in it, and is carried out and snatched away. . ."[52] And yet, neither Fichte's appeal to '*praxis*' nor Merleau-Ponty's appeal to 'nature'—Nietzschean *or* Schellingian—would *solve* the problem of foundations and abyss. It would necessitate instead a step beyond it.[53]

Accordingly, in 1958, outlining his own lectures on the concept of nature, Merleau-Ponty insisted on reentering this maze to explicate it otherwise, radicalizing the account of this milieu and the antinomy that classically inscribed the conflict as well as dehiscence of subject and object. Having assented to the insurpassability of the realm of appearance that split Being before its doubles—precisely in recognizing, again, what the *Phenomenology* called the irreducibility of the phantoms of Being—he stated:

> Could we not find what has been called an "ontological diplopy" (Blondel), that after so much philosophical effort we cannot expect to bring to a rational reduction and which leaves us with the sole alternative of embracing it, just as our gaze takes over monocular images to make a single vision out of them? (Themes:90)

But what would be the nature of such an 'embrace'? Clearly, against the ultimate philosophical reductions of those immediately or mediately in Kant's wake, such an embrace could not be 'scientific'; could not provide the ultimate grounds for our rational practices. On the contrary, it would have to admit from the outset to the *Ab-grund* of all foundations—thereby opening the possibility of the play of reversibility, the *Ineinander* nature of the ground and the grounded.[54] And, only thereby might the end of philosophy be its 'fulfillment'; that is, only by affirming what, again in 1958, Merleau-Ponty called the *labryinth of first philosophy* (Themes:90).

XI

The Visible and the Invisible is inscribed precisely within these ruins, doubtless a text that intends to renew philosophy by the step beyond it. It became a philosophy, it has been said, *"sans absolu"*[55]—or as Merleau-Ponty himself put it, the absolute as chiasm (PNP:30), invoking an event in which the reciprocal relation at stake places this absolute at risk. Rather, between the visible and the invisible, "reversibility, is the ultimate truth" (VI:155). And yet, from the outset it involved the exploration of a domain whose certainty—the certainty it continued to explicate as perceptual faith—always remained in doubt, "a certitude, entirely irresistible as it may be, [which] remains absolutely obscure." What was at stake in this step beyond concerned, in the strict sense a *"certitude injustifiable* (VI:11). And yet, *The Visible and the Invisible* neither abandons it, nor attempts to surpass it for the sake of a sphere that might found it, nor even deduces or presumes the possibility of a world that might vindicate it. Rather, it is precisely in dwelling on this *milieu indecis* (VI:115), and the 'ambiguity' and the conflict of interpretation that it portends, that the issue of Reason's incarnation emerges. Having fully affirmed the abyss in question concerning the "accursed logic" afflicting the in-itself and the for-itself, Merleau-Ponty stated:

> But here, seeking to form our first concepts in such a way as to avoid the classical impasse, we do not have to honor the difficulties that they may present when confronted with a *cogito* that itself has to be reexamined. Yes or no: do we have a body—that is, not a permanent object of thought, but a flesh that suffers when it is wounded, hands that touch? We know: hands do not suffice for touch—but to decide for this alone that hands do not touch, and to relegate them to the world of objects or of instruments, would be, in acquiescing to the bifurcation of subject and object, to forego in advance the understanding of the sensible and to

deprive ourselves of its lights. We propose on the contrary to take it literally to begin with. (VI:137)

The 'proposal' remains fully problematic. Doubtless its appeal would (and did, in fact) open Merleau-Ponty to objections concerning its metaphysical nature, relying on the *bon sens* of the body as a metaphysical *hypokeimenon*, simply construing the 'flesh' as the "maternal bond" and unending resource for thought. Hence, perhaps not without a certain justification, the charges of Deleuze, Lyotard, Foucault, and Serres. In fact, then, if we see the project of *The Visible and the Invisible* as sustaining and solving the phenomenological quest, then these rocks are, doubtless, again to reinvoke the *Phenomenology of Perception* itself, simply the site of its ever recurrent failure.

If, however, we read the later work as de-lineating its 'phantasms' precisely in those ruins and their *écarts*, then perhaps it is a text radically displaced with respect to this failure in its extension beyond it. From the outset it remained, after all, a 'phenomen-ology' wholly *au delà des preuves*, the tracing of the unfolding and enfolding (the *explicatio* and *complicatio*) of a world that remains 'unfinished', an *Aussersein* lacking determinability and completeness (VI:48). Far from a retrieval and adequation of a foundation that always already escaped it, here the task of explication instead involved the tracing of an event, and an 'extension' *in indefinitum* that occurs wholly devoid of foundations, *une cohesion sans concept* (VI:152). It involved, that is, precisely a purposiveness without a purpose, as Kant consented in his critique of judgment—and who perhaps thereby already risked the possibility of a "philosophy which *might* be nonphilosophy" (PNP:44). The result is a 'fundamental' thought that is anything but foundational:

'Fundamental' because it is not borne by anything, but not fundamental as if one reached a foundation upon which one ought to base oneself and stay. As a matter of principle fundamental thought is bottomless (*sans fond*). It is if you wish an abyss (*abîme*). This means that it is never with itself, that we find it next to or setting out from things thought, that it is an opening out—the other extremity of the axis that connects us to ideas and things. (Signs:21)[56]

XII

Still, this entrance into the labyrinth—the 'extremeties' of the visible and the invisible—would always stir a certain dismay within the philosopher's text, raising the question of what had been accomplished by a commitment that arose admittedly *de facto* without a warrant *de jure* (PoP:396). Within the text of philosophy, the explication that would appeal instead to an ambiguity that would not be simply "a lack of univocity" (PNP:44) and an *écart* that would be the opposition of neither identity nor truth (PNP:40) all seems simply to beg the question, a circularity that again turns vicious. And accordingly, its appeal to the body—what Heidegger too called "the gathering of the gesture"[57]—would be only the ultimate gasp of its failure in the turn to psychologism.

Without question both are true, so long as *theoria* and *psyche*, ontology and ontogenesis, evidence and institution, 'theory' and observation can be strictly distinguished. Such charges would hold, that is, if (and only if) a *logos* and its *Masstab* could be irrevocably presupposed, grounded by "nothing other than itself."[58] In fact, the possibility of reinstituting such a 'leap' to an immutable necessity based now on the inextricability of *mathesis*, occurred with all too much ease in neo-Kantian appeals to *mathematischen Naturwissenschaften*.[59] It was, after all, a move that could be made only by transforming historical contingencies into transcendental necessities. And, that was the character of the 'transcendental risk' it incurred by invoking the paradigm of pure ideality and mathematical construction, a *Masstab* that was, Merleau-Ponty fully realized, a result of "productive imagination and not a return to the eternal idea" (PoP:386). In fact, the very nature of this risk lies in its 'return' to eternity and an absolute foundation, stepping beyond "the verificatory attitude and reflective operations" that might recuperate but equally underdetermine the given (PoP:241). If recourse to the 'purity' of productive imagination would contain its own step beyond, however, precisely in re-moving itself from the contingency (*la fragilité*) of our opening on the real (VI:40), it would likewise rejoin that other invocation of the eternal present Merleau-Ponty described, that is, the world of the dream (PoP:423), the realm of the pure imaginary, *l'imaginaire*.

Against this absolute and its logology, this other '*logos*' that refuses to surpass the appearances—this phenomen-ology—will, as Heidegger put it, always seem divided between anthropologism and psychologism, an ancillary discipline of mere illusion that has always both troubled and overdetermined its archive.[60] But if, on the contrary, such claims themselves inevitably turn metaphysical, and 'science' itself depends on attaining, as Hegel himself put it, a thoroughgoing *skepsis* regarding the Absolutes of metaphysics, if, that is, the conflict of interpretation remains inextricable and we stand in the ruins of the matrix on which these distinctions depend, then the institution of this conflict and its narratives—and in the end even its biographies[61]—is itself the interrogation of our own embodiment, a site irreducible to representation, an algorithm, a faculty, or a mode of presentation. Philosophy then will not unlock the problem of determination without becoming nonphilosophy, none of Spinoza's infinity of modes will become ultimately determinate, and consequently "there can be no question of distinguishing two elements of knowledge: one *a priori* and the other *a posteriori*" (PoP:220). What is demanded instead is the decipherment of an event that occurs in the strict sense "outside all criteriological control" (VI:40), an explication whose articulation reveals no surpassing, refusing to abandon its own equivocity, its own plurality and double meaning.[62] What results is a dialectic without synthesis, a hyperdialectic (VI:94–95) that rejoins but extends the *Phenomenology* in recognizing that radical reflection, never univocally adequate, is always hyper-reflection or sur-flexion (VI:38)—or as Cavaillès and Bachelard put it, that rationality always involves a certain sur-rationality.

The turn to the body consequently will not provide, as Fichte, Scheler, and the rest hoped, a solution or 'point' of union for "the unity of theory and practice."[63] It is instead the site in which the *problem* of theory and practice irresolvably arises, the site—like representation in general—in which reason is both event and figure, risk and virtue. And in this sense, beyond the foundations—and in retrospect the psychologism that strangely enough always accompanied the assurances—of metaphysics, the question of thought's incarnation erupts within the conflict between theories, between perspectives and their worlds, between the sensible and the intelligible, between self and other—and perhaps only thereby, between who we are and what we can become.

On the Right
to Interpret:
Beyond the
Copernican Turn

Your reason is never more plausible and on more solid ground than when it convinces you of a plurality of worlds.

— Montaigne[1]

I

The problem of interpretation from the outset accompanied the Copernican turn, both involving an event that necessitated the articulation of a fundamental decentering. As a result, both have been intimately linked within the complex history of the modern, a history in which assertion itself became inevitably problematic, a crisis in representation. It is a failure most directly encountered now as one in conceptual standpoints, that is, the failure of *theory* as representation. And, the ensuing crisis in adjudication it entails, in default of rational foundations, is seen most directly perhaps in terms of the threat of its result: that is, the failure of transcendental grounds and the threat of nihilism.[2] Still, we proceed perhaps too often as if the problem of interpretation were somehow distinct from that history both as 'Copernican' and modern.

Consequently, especially among those writing in Hegel's wake, which, as Foucault has argued, is just about everyone who would attempt historical narratives—and perhaps especially when historians have attempted to tell those narratives under blinders compelling them to defend the purity of the human sciences—the problem of historical interpretation and its rationality has in fact looked as though it were, rather than the delineation of a specific set of problems, a sequence of stages on Spirit's way. The resulting account, as Popper rightly pointed out, verged on tautologies that were, if not vacuous, then, at best perhaps, simply descriptive.[3] Moreover, in this regard, even the description of synchronic structures without connection, Foucauldian discontinuities or dispersions immune from causal account or linear explanation, was, as he too realized, perhaps still nascently Hegelian.[4]

The problem is not that such interpretative accounts are simply false, or even useless. Indeed it can be argued that it is precisely the status of their failure before the critical tribunal which marks the trace of their fecundity. Still, if we are to grasp their status as legitimate it will be necessary to see that the theoretical problem of interpretation arises in fact within a specific trajectory—that it interfaces the rise of science in the same moment that it extends the unresolved inheritance of its theoretical past. And it is this interface that still links such diverse occurrences as Ockham and Suarez's problem of divine creative transcendence to Nietzsche's will to power and the latter to an experimentalism by which nature might still be deciphered in its wake. Similarly, both meet in the failure of the appearances—now necessarily understood in an extended sense, that is, uncircumscribed within modern categories: epistemic, logical, or evaluative. If the problem of interpretation has thus been constantly connected with the problem of Reason's "destiny" within history or has constantly invoked the need for a critique of historical reason, it was first and foremost a participation within a specific history.[5]

II

It is precisely in this regard that the Copernican turn itself however becomes inextricably overdetermined—as various writers have attested. If it involves, on the one hand, an event that marks the emergence of a new science, it does so only insofar that it effects in the same advance a challenge to a metaphysics and its metanarrative that is ancient, precisely insofar as it effects, as Koyré put it, "the destruction of the Cosmos."[6] To use Blumenberg's apt characterization, what is at stake involves a rupture in which "man can no longer be the designated witness of the wonders of creation."[7] The Copernican revolution marks instead, as Habermas has noted, the rupture of pure 'visibility' by which the human had accessed the immutable—the destruction of the metaphysical matrix assuring the harmony of theory and practice, the human spectator and its contemplation of the universe, the harmony of *theoros* and *kosmos*.[8] Moreover, in thus destroying the hypothesis of visibility, it threatened not simply the metaphysical past, but the very possibility of *philosophia* as systematic science, a metadiscourse that might oversee the heterogeneity of discourse itself, precisely, that is, as the synthesis, the "jointure of heaven and earth."

Heidegger reminded us that the *Kosmos* and its discourse, its systematics, has been understood in terms of this jointure of heaven and earth from the outset: *systema ex ouranou kai ges*.[9] As such the Copernican transformation would be most properly metaphysical in impact, one, that is, not only of ontic but ontological implication.[10] Vico had already realized that what would be at stake in its lapse required, instead of a metaphysics of immanence, one that arose out of the fragmented unity of the finite: "a metaphysics sensed and built up by the imagination."[11] And yet, as Kant's transcendental dialectic likewise realized, precisely in turning all such attempts problematic (albeit by reemphasizing the imagination in the syntheses of the Copernican turn), the result would not be one whose *ekstasis* would find reappropriation in *noeisis*.

The experiment of Kant's *Dialectic*, proclaiming the absolute of metaphysics to be a *focus imaginarius*, is not only the application of the success story of theoretical modernism, the result or importation of the paradigm of the 'sciences properly and objectively so called so-called' into the realm of theory—denying thereby the legitimacy of its precursor, the science of being qua being.[12] It is also the recognition that to grant privilege to the critical moment is also to recognize the ultimate hetero-geneity and possible conflict of our rational practices—revalorizating the narratives from which it had long hoped to separate. Donning perhaps its full irony on its sleeve, the first 'positivist' venture into the arena of justification became at the same time the first to encounter the problem of possible 'incommensurability,' one with portentous transcendental returns. The possibility in question ultimately takes on an inextricable necessity—less because thought is necessarily subreptive, than only because nothing forbids that possibility. To affirm the poststructuralist charge here, a charge made still fully within the orbit of transcendental logic, a possibility that is always present is "in some sense universal, a necessary possibility."[13] The Copernican turn and the denial of the visible, that is, became de facto the mark of human finitude. And it was just in this sense that Kant understood it, in fact claiming that it marked an abyss.[14]

Accordingly, Kant's own transcendental turn was precisely *not* the simple reinvocation of the transcendental tradition whose testimony the critical tribunal still invokes. Rather, it remained entrenched in vindicating a fallibilist reply to Hume's onslaught and remained thereby equivocally transcendental. Moreover, it is the very notion of 'objectivity' itself that equivocates in this new Copernican turn, a turn by which both the canons and rights of reason became linked with the strictly determinate, the *more geometrico*, and yet withdrawn only to be subjec-tively constituted in the empty concept of an object in general—applicable, then (*pace* Heidegger) to no object in the ontological sense. In fact it may be the case that many of the controversies that have arisen in Kant's wake rest on this equivocation and the several senses of legitimation invested within it. We have yet perhaps to fully confront all that was at stake—historically, philosophically, and perhaps even politically and religiously—in the rise of this new notion, 'objectivity,' and all that had attempted by means of it to equate the rational with the demonstrative, timelessly replicated within the community of investigators. But if, in any case, Kant ultimately both appeals to and departs from the modernist commitment to the genre of the *non feigno*, he does so precisely in confronting the infinity of the modern with its finite past, ultimately calling the extension *in infinitum* of the space of reason into question—a space that is, after all, one in which, to cite Cusa's celebrated phrase, "the center is everywhere and the circumference nowhere."[15]

III

The analytic of Leibniz's *ars combineatoire* would be aptly credited with the consistent demarcation of this realm of homogeneous extension, an analytics rendering the space of reason wholly and demonstratably determinate. Still, it was perhaps in the same moment its most metaphysical outburst, providing even, Leibniz claimed, proof for the existence of God and thereby the fulfillment of *metaphysica rationis*. But if the eternal truths would again provide "the fixed and immovable point around which everything else rotates," their assertion equally raised again the problem of finitude, the question of its synthesis, and consequently, the site of its skeptical challenge.[16] Here as before him with Descartes, who, after all, also sought respite through recourse to a fixed Archimedean point, the problem of foundations still threatened.[17] Consequently, as Michel Serres has rightly pointed out, "The difficulty in Leibnizianism is the Labyrinth."[18] The problem, that is, remains the justification of the fixed point that might access this rational space,

In the space of the combineatoire we turn *ad libitum* around as many of the *capita* as there are elements. In metric space, the unity of reference is arbitrary or unknowable, itself referred or indefinitely divisible. In contextual space (*l'espace des situations*) there is only *situs inter se*. In perceptual space, the point of view and the spectacle, the scene and the center of vision are indefinitely exchanged. In phoronomic space, the poles of movement are arbitrarily assignable and substitutable at leisure. In gravitational space, distinguishable aggregates designate a common center of gravity, that varies by the contingencies of the distinction and thus the result.[19]

In all this the common space of the *combineatoire* presupposes a metaphysics, principles of nature and grace, as Leibniz still called it. But that is precisely the problem, the problem, that is, of the synthesis that unites (and assures) continuity within the space in which logic and metaphysics might be combined, thus igniting modernism's Homeric quest for origins. It is precisely in confronting the question concerning the status of this combination by which it defaults. Pascal had said it equally, "It is necessary to have a fixed point in order to judge."[20] And yet the appeal to this *Ordo* as the deploying of the adjudicable itself simply begged the question. In fact, even more radically, "before asking the question, 'What is the center of the world?' one must answer the question: 'Is the world centered or not?' "[21] The problem of conceptual discontinuity, that is, had neither been reached nor irradicated.

The difference between the conceptual and the real, transcendental ideality and empirical reality, the ontic and the ontological had not been confronted, the exhaustion of the Cartesian dioptrics. As was evident to Kant—already arguing in 1768 against what he described as "modern concepts" in this domain—the fulfillment of this *recherche* was as problematic and as incongruent as accounting for the mere appearance of a hand in space.[22] Moreover, Wittgenstein would again invoke this labyrinth in the wake of positivism, realizing the difficulties in question were as difficult to surmount as those affecting the mere epistemics of a hand as present.[23] As Merleau-Ponty would put it, in disarticulating transcendental presentation within phenomenology, it was both as simple and as complex as the chiasm of one hand touching another.[24] The very presence of Reason to its objects, both regarding the question of their logical concatentation and their appearance, the question of the interface between syntactics and semantics, thus remained unsolved. Moreover, in this regard it is perhaps fully intelligible why the question of the remainder of metaphysics became the question of what lies in general *Zu-handen*, that is, the status of presence and in general of the *Vorhandenheit*, to use Heidegger's term.[25] As Aristotle put it at the inception of metaphysics, the question of the status of thinking depends on the status of the analogy and the difference between the hand and the soul, the form of forms—and thereby the 'nature' of the movement that would unite them.[26] At the end of metaphysics, however, it would be a truncating of the difference at stake that would most characterize what Serres aptly called Kant's "vocation," one perhaps already nasently in place as early as 1768: "Let it be imagined that the first created thing were a human hand, then it must necessarily be either a right hand or a left hand."[27]

What remainded lacking within the space of philosophical modernism was precisely this Archimedean point of reference, rationalism's theoretically fixed point assuring the requisite determinability on which it relied.[28] Although Serres himself does not say it, the first explicit challenge to the doctrine doubtless should be found in Hegel, who had already claimed that such notions as subject and object could not be allayed as "fixed points," as he too called them, but were circularly linked, demanding an "expanded science" based on this movement.[29] In fact, Hegel claimed that every recourse to a causal account, in the strict sense, to the reduction of an entity to its external conditions, remained a move inextricably theory laden, a "formal method of explanation from tautological grounds"—precisely, that is, the circularity of condition and conditions.[30] The circularity that resulted however, he claimed, could be reduced again, now to the circle of *Nous* itself, a substance whose *telos*, instead of externally *grounding* the fixed point, would fulfill it, precisely as Subject.[31]

If Hegel thus saw the outcome of philosophical modernism as a failure of foundations, he sought respite from it—as so many would in his wake—by attempting to retrieve the very metaphysics it had itself irretrievably called into question. Instead, logically (and it is proof we will need more than logic) we are plunged into a network of presuppositions and consequences that can in the strict sense be vindicated neither in themselves nor in the requisite sense simply interdefined, as Serres put it, by inter-ference. The *ars combineatorie*, after all, had been from the outset 'labyrinthian,' only a space of infinite iteration. And yet throughout his accounts of its original formulation, Leibniz announced precisely what had most been depended on in steadfastly relying on its venue. As the *Monadology* proclaimed steadfastly: the virtual is not the void.[32] If it is necessary to have a fixed point in order to judge, then judgment, it would seem, will necessarily appear "disrupted," to speak Hegelian. But is this true? Or is it by abandoning this demand that judgment takes place—and perhaps only as this 'abandon'?

IV

Notwithstanding Kant's own institutions to the contrary, the *Critique of Pure Reason* opened in the recognition that the Copernican turn called into question the doxic homogeneity by which the appearances might be interconnected. In fact, if problems concerning the 'hypothesis' of naive visibility had provoked philosophy from the outset,[33] what is clear, in any case, is the extent to which that past would now be irrevocably challenged. In one sense, of course, in this transformation the heaven of ideas did become exchanged for the immutable laws of the appearances—and Kant's limitations on the conceptual depended on it, remaining, thereby both Copernican and Galilean.[34] But those appearances were categorically distinct from the phantasms of the 'manifest' image.

In fact, if the Copernican turn demanded this skepticism (indeed, as Husserl claimed, required its diplopia to accept the plausibility of its most stringent 'proof' that the telescope might provide a better 'view' of the real), the transferences and analogons on which it were modeled always remained contested. It remained divided between simply denying that the manifest image was real or, on the other hand, denying that that very image conflicted with the appearances of physics. Only Husserl would attempt, in a way from which even Dilthey's celebrated distinction perhaps still shied away, to draw a vital and necessary chiasm whose bridging would in fact be epistemically undesirable—but he too could do so (in fact thinking that he followed in Hume's wake) only by constructing a science of the very appearances he had hoped to exclude from the prerequisites of the objective sciences, all the while ascending to the Copernican turn in limiting even ideality itself to the specificity of its horizon, that is, the horizon of time.[35]

What Husserl continued to claim (a claim that eventually simply rendered his attempts in principle inconsistent) was that the science of the phenomenon and the *problem* of its horizon did not conflict. The problem of 'sameness' and 'otherness,' as Nicholas of Cusa had put it long before Hegel, could be overcome. The horizonal presentation of the given, however, marked instead the undecidable site of the thing's withdrawal and possible distortion. The great experiment denoted by the title of *Formal and Transcendental Logic*, combining pure apophantics with pure analytics, pure judgment with pure ontology, pure syntax with pure semantics, doubtless failed on a number of grounds. But it failed most directly and most manifestly in the very concept of the world logic it both posited and presupposed: "the *great* problems pertaining to a *world logic* that is to be grounded radically" starting "from the world that is given to us in fact."[36]

Husserl's "retrogression" presupposed from the start that such a principle of reducibility concerning the appearances could be legitimated.[37] He presupposed, that is, that the very 'objects' that were to be subsumed beneath pure apophantics and which might then be the subject of formal ontology were not themselves constituted from the start only through this very analytics, that the very *Spiel-Bedeutung* of syntactics that Husserl had loathed from the start was primitive and indeed constitutive with respect to the 'evidence' of 'intentionality.'[38]

But it was, at least, a very problematic assumption—let alone solution.[39] And it did not preclude Husserl—if not empirically, then unquestionably transcendentally, and probably metaphysically—from attempting to fulfill the protocols of *theoria* by regressing to the Ptolemaic world-view and an unshakable firmament that made its conception of the *kosmos* possible.[40] Moreover, although Husserl's concerns may appear idiosyncratic, in fact the problem of this *Spielbedeutung* ran deep, also accompanying philosophical modernism from the outset. Cusa himself had in a sense already anticipated it in transforming the medieval's account of *analogia* into mere comparative proportion. The opening lines of *De Docta Ignorantia* define the enquiry characteristic of finite understanding as one in which it is "comparative and uses the means of comparative relation"—and one, therefore, "which cannot be understood apart from number."[41]

Yet if understanding remained for Cusanus restricted in this sense, he still acknowledged the problem of its extension, of the relation between this relation and its foundation. As the *Docta Ignorantia* put it, the problem of the Absolutely great, the infinite insofar as "it escapes all comparative proportion," requires that we rely on the imagination for transcending the finite. Descartes too would similarly rely on the imagination as an "aid to our thinking," one through which our "knowledge is extended (*extendi*)" by means of *mathesis universalis* and the "image-making organ"—though he categorically denied the second move: "that does not show that we discover any new kind of entity."[42] Still, if the imagination provides the figures of figurate extension as such, notwithstanding all his Stoic admonitions concerning our need to withhold judgment about the ultimate nature of things, Descartes remained ultimately resolute in the end concerning the connection between figures and things. The imposition of reality through the senses remains strictly unmediated: the wax analogy, he assured us, "is no analogy."[43]

V

Husserl equally remained at pains to escape the paradox that attends the transformation of things into signs and first intensions into second. Portentously too Husserl's own admonitions concerning the reversal in question occur by reference to Johann Henrich Lambert's general account of semiotics and the problem of its interpretation or hermeneutic, as he already called it.[44] Husserl's argument, that is, remained poised precisely against semiotics, the "reduction of the theory of things to the theory of signs" and thereby "the game of calcuation" it depends on.[45] Whereas Husserl too was quick to admit that the *ars analytrice* bears endless fruit, the justificatory practices that are constitutive of it remained unconscious, in much the same way that Leibniz himself had claimed that in listening to music the proportions that render it beautiful remain unperceived: "Though our souls prevent us from noticing it, we are continually counting the strokes and vibrations of sounding bodies, that meet at certain intervals."[46] If Husserl's point, nonetheless, was that it is not enough to 'count' or infer in order to know, it is surely true too that to think we could know *without* it—to think that the return to the things themselves does not participate in 'inference' or in *mathesis* as much as 'constitute' it—surely remains in the end naive.[47]

Hence the ultimate failure of Husserl's own Ptolemaic epistemic proclivities. *Pace* the sublimity of the attempt, the manifolds of pure reason would remain as underdetermined for Husserl as they had been for Kant. Since the Stoics, as Montaigne too realized, the *epoche* was to provide the requisites for a firmature, the interruption and cessation of movement or a 'necessity' that might challenge consciousness from behind its back.[48] And, Husserl's renewal of its withdrawl inevitably faced the same contingency.

Even granting the admitted 'paucity' of standard transcendentalist claims, those who would issue the caveat of their simple failure, it might be objected, are perhaps no better off. If, after all, we have refused to guarantee the appearances, it has required ascending to what was at best a hypothesis—even for the most committed of scientific realists— even perhaps in the end a hope always constantly deferred into the indefinite future of scientific progress. We can, that is, grant to Husserl at least this much regarding the other domain of 'appearances.' It too involved a hypothesis that "in spite of its verification, continues to be and is always a hypothesis; its verification (the only kind conceivable for it) is an endless course of verifications."[49] And, it presupposed at the bare minimum that the harmony of scientific hypotheses was such that we could ultimately do without those other appearances and that the 'regions' of rational enquiry would by themselves still remain commensurable.

Granting this much, however, surely does not save the transcendentalist's strong program and its hope that the "disparaged *doxa* [might again] claim the dignity of a foundation for science."[50] It would not, that is, vindicate the project of *phenomenologia generalis* that had accompanied the descent of modern transcendentalism from its inception, one whose effects are overlooked often enough. Such a project in fact had already appeared in Kant's *oeuvre* at the time of the *Inagural dissertation* (1770):

The most universal laws of sensibility play an unjustifiably large role in metaphysics, where, after all, it is merely concepts and principles of pure reason that are at issue. A quite special, though purely negative science, general phenomenology (*phaenomonologia generalia*), seems to me to be presupposed by metaphysics. In it the principles of sensibility, their validity and their limitations, would be determined, so that these principles could not be confusedly applied to objects of pure reason, as heretofore almost always happened.[51]

Although this is a text dating from Kant's precritical writings, a time during which he would still grant metaphysical access to pure intuition of the real, in fact, as a purely negative science concerning the limitation of sensibility, it already coincides with the critical project. That is, as a negative science of phenomena, it outlines both a transcendental aesthetic and a logic of illusion (*Schein*).[52] Moreover, although other references to such a 'phenomenological' project occur within Kant's work (and as late as the *Opus Postumuum*),[53] it is significant that this early reference too should occur in a letter to Lambert. It is precisely in this regard that the encounter with Lambert becomes, to speak Kantian, perhaps both unavoidable and inextricable.

VI

Lambert's *Neues Organon* published six years previously to Kant's letter already contained a concluding section entitled *Phänomenologie oder Lehre von dem Schein*.[54] In this text—prior to both Kant and Husserl—Lambert granted positive epistemic status to the realm of the phenomenological in a fashion similar to the priority granted the delineation of the transcendental aesthetic: because knowledge is relative to sensibility, the problem of appearance is central to knowledge.

Still, Lambert had already realized too that these issues would demand that we step beyond the limitations of representational thought. That is, *Der Schein* is not simply false or illusory, but rather something intermediate, a *Mittelding* between the true and the false.[55] Rather than a domain in which the true and the false might be strictly distinguished, in a move that harkened back to traditional accounts of dialectic, the problem for Lambert became one of recognizing falsity by the truth that is in it. The problem of knowledge, that is, is "to reach truth through *Scheinung*,"[56] to distinguish, thereby, a task that would reach culmination in the grasping of truth in discourse, "hermeneutic or semeiotic *Schein*," as he in fact already calls it.[57]

The problem in grasping this event, Lambert had claimed, is that for too long the problem of appearance had been linked simply to sense knowledge. Only in optics had the doctrine of appearance been sufficiently treated. In phenomenology, consequently, it would be necessary for the articulation of this enquiry to undergo an extension

(*Erweiterung*) resulting in a discipline that Lambert described as "transcendent optics."[58] Hence it would be necessary to epistemically generalize the issues accompanying the investigation of perceptual dimensions or aspects [*Seiten*] of things and our point of view (*Sehepunkt*), "looking more closely at something," and clarifying (*Aufklären*)[59]—a point that, if already resonant with Husserl, is also not without analogy in Kant's claim that concepts are themselves points of view. Moreover, here too the imagination is reinvested with a privileged status that would not perhaps go without echo in Kant.

Kant's "Transcendental Dialectic" would similarly be instituted in relation to what it called the "empirical (e.g. optical) illusion. . .through which the faculty of judgment is misled by the influence of imagination."[60] In transcendental illusion, however, Reason would be categorically different, undergoing an influence from the faculty of synthesis by which it would be both better and worse off. On the one hand, unlike the empirical case of optical illusion, the distortions in question could not be overcome. Transcendental 'distortion' was ultimate and inextricable, the effect of Being's withdrawal from the faculty of representation, forcing knowledge endlessly to recur from ontology to transcendental analytics. On the other hand, the focal point of transcendental dialectic is transformed into vanishing point precisely "without foundations," a *focus imaginarius* instituted through the synthetic extensions of imagination by which reason attempts to recoup this loss, that is, through transcendental 'heuristics.'[61]

Nowhere is its effect more obvious than in the closing pages of the Analytic, in which Kant recounts the results of his Copernican experiment and its transformation of philosophical modernism. Against the very title of the dissertation of 1770, "On the Form and Principles of the Sensible and Intelligible World," Kant wrote:

In the writings of modern philosophers I find the expressions *mundus sensibilis* and *intelligibilis* used with a meaning altogether different from that of the ancients—a meaning which is easily understood, but which results merely in an empty play of words. According to this usage, some have thought good to entitle the sum of appearances, in so far as they are intuited, the world of the senses, and in so far as their connection is thought in conformity with laws of understanding, the world of understanding. Observational astronomy, which teaches merely the observation of the starry heavens, would give an account of the former; theoretical astronomy, on the other hand, as taught

according to the Copernican system, or according to Newton's laws
of gravitation would give an account of the second, namely, of
an intelligible world.[62]

There can be no such identification. "The division of objects into
phenomena and noumena, and the world into a world of the senses
and a world of the understanding, is therefore quite inadmissable in
the positive sense."[63] Still, even here the result remains overdetermined,
especially granted his reliance on the 'solution' of 'the two standpoints'
for the autonomies affecting practical reason.[64] Kant added the last four
words between the first and second editions. Although it remained the
case, certainly, that he had refused positive admissibility of such talk
within the critical tribunal, it remained true too that the claims could
not receive simple dismissal. Unlike both the ancients and the moderns,
Kant claimed (and it is perhaps what most characterizes his positive
response to Hume), we simply have no grounds to strictly decide these
doxatic claims—neither for nor against. Being able neither to subsume
nor to reduce one realm of knowledge into the other, the possibility
of both worlds remains both contested and problematic. They remain,
that is, merely *assertoric*—as the Dialectic, as well as the second and
third *Critiques* would elaborate, hypotheses problematically conjectured
within the remainder of the appearances following the critical turn.
Moreover, if what is ventured thereby lies *sensu stricto* beyond Kant's
restrictions concerning *Sinn und Bedeutung*, the usage of these metaphors
involves, he insisted, "a meaning [and an extension, albeit problematic]
that is easily understood." And yet, if the play involved is in this strict
sense "empty," its distortion is not in fact simply illusory, but the
opening of the imagination's power for transcending the limitations,
the 'optical illusions,' of representation itself. If the extension is carried
out by means of the faculty of synthesis, even Kant himself refused,
that is, to claim that the *focus imaginarius* involved merely an *ens
imaginarium*.

VII

The problem of this extension, however, from the outset remained
at risk within the Copernican turn. Even before Copernicus, Cusa had
pointed to the significance of imagination within the play of
cosmological standpoints—a play in which "wherever anyone would
be, he would believe himself to be the center." As a result, he asserted,
it is necessary "to aid oneself as best one can by means of the
imagination" in order "to fuse (*complicere*) each of the varying poles into

the other."[65] But clearly from the outset it put strong demands on imagination, ones to which Cusanus perhaps more than any figure before him, did not hesitate to ascede. It is precisely in this regard that, writing on the heels of the nominalist controversy that would elicit the demand for certainty in philosophical modernism, Cusa already affirmed the role of *coniectura* within the distance separating the finite and the divine, the possible and the real. The very 'feigning' of the imagination itself became a *virtû* in overcoming the finite through its capacity to step beyond its limits, the capacity to explicate all that the Divine enfolds (complicates) within Himself.[66] But it does so only to the extent that it no longer remains bound to imitation and 'reproduction.' Similarly, in the practical realm the hand of the craftsman could not be bound by imitation, as it produces an object "more perfect than one that imitates the [natural] forms of things and thus is more similar to infinite art."[67]

Still, in this reliance on the imagination (or, in any case, the simple assertion of the possibilities of *explication*) Cusa proceeded *more metaphysica*. Moreover, he relied on a specific metaphysics, metaphysics itself as onto-the-ological—and its corresponding cosmology, cosmotheology;[68] hence, the necessity of his citation of man as the image of God. The possibility that provoked this extension was theological through and through: the recognition that the 'reality' of this world was not a limitation on God's creative capacities. Despite Aristotle's arguments against the atomist's view concerning a plurality of worlds (*Kosmoi*), the condemnation of 1277 denied (among others) the article "that the First Cause cannot make many worlds (*plures mundos*)," already making way for this schism.[69] If, as Duhem argued, it was a decisive moment in the emergence of experimental or hypothetical reasoning, it is true too that its ultimate impart could not have been foreseen. The *male genie* had not in fact been met by Cusanus nor had it been confronted by Lambert (and probably not, as well, by Husserl).

The critical moment had not been confronted. As Kant put it to Lambert, for adjudication a measure (*Richtmass*) or criterion is needed. But strictly taken—in the sense in which truth and its appearance might be made wholly distinct—this is exactly what a phenomenology could not provide. The description remained not only conditional on an experience, but could not be extricated from it and remained indemonstrable apart from it. Hence Kant's claim: phenomenology would result in a "purely negative science." The problem at stake in fact can be specified through the difference that separates Leibniz before Kant from Nietzsche after him. If, after all, Leibniz had introduced perspectivism in noting the infinity of angles that meet at the monadic point, Nietzsche would transform its synthetic harmony into an unregulated infinite without totality.[70]

Nonetheless, if Kant's Dialectic was the stringent denial of the legitimacy of a logic of *Schein*, it was *not*, as has been seen, its simple negation, not even the "purely negative science" Kant foresaw in 1770, still in fact wholly confident about the possibilities of metaphysics. Since Plato himself it has been true, Kant claimed, that the Ideas of Reason "are by no means mere fictions of the brain."[71] Instead, Kant's Dialectic is itself, in the institution of the logic of the *Al ob*, recourse to the problem of transcendence—and, as the antinomies obviate, to the deferral of time as resolution. Moreover, in his only published reference on phenomenology, one limiting 'phenomenology' to external motion, that is, appearances in space and motion, Kant again concluded by denying the possibility of the *appearance* of the unconditioned, that "inasmuch as [Reason] can neither rest with the conditioned nor make the unconditioned comprehensible, nothing remains for it, when the thirst of knowledge invites it to grasp the absolute totality of all conditions, but to turn back from objects to itself and determine the ultimate boundary of the capacity given it. . ."[72]

If this turn back on itself involved an introversion and reflection, and thus, an *epistrophe* that was ancient, it was also a turn from the forms of external sense to the capacities of internal sense, and thereby to the beneficience of time—one that remains consistent throughout Kant's writings.[73] In fact, notwithstanding Kant's banning of such extensions beyond strict (i.e., representationally constitutive) rules of subsumption, the third *Critique* would instead risk the possibility that, as a result of native intelligence or *Witz*, such judgments might be put to good use as our ability to transcend the subjective (i.e., 'representational') conditions of thought. Moreover, it is the risk such judgments authorize that constitute what Kant called the "extended thought" constituting *sensus communis*.[74] Far from being simply the inextricable illusion of the rational, it was precisely the invocation of its peculiar virtue, indeed, Kant stated, its "talent."[75] In effect, Hume's skepticism would be overcome precisely in truncating the tolerance in the conditions that made 'belief' in his sense possible.

VIII

As Hegel brilliantly, if perhaps not sufficiently recognized, the result was overdetermined, both invoking the certainty of *repraesentatio* and depending on the moment of transcendence, regarding the Ego, as "a reference to something away and beyond."[76] Consequently, "[t]he Kantian philosophy must be accurately described as having viewed the mind as consciousness, and as containing the propositions only of a phenomenology (not of a *philosophy*) of mind."[77] Kant's 'limitation' of Reason was neither simply a vindication of the objectivity of science nor simply a question of making room for faith, all carried out at the expense of metaphysics, matters that could be invoked only were the latter 'simply at an end'—if, that is, either science or faith would find strict determinability. But that is exactly what Kant's venture could not affirm. In tracing instead the failure of representation and its *tabula rasa*, Kant's project involved a 'delimiting' (and not incidentally a vindication) of the rational precisely in relying on the underdeterminability, the free play in the extensions of imagination. Kant's Copernican turn depended for its plausibility, that is, precisely on the potential of time as deferral and the tolerance within appearances itself (that is, almost despite himself, beyond his own 'positivist' restrictions of *Sinn und Bedeutung*) and, hence, the phantasm as hinged between the actual and the possible.

Hegel, however, would again see this turn to imagination, the faculty of speculation, strictly along the modernist lines of the later Cusa, unmindful of the difference and the risk at stake and demanding precisely that its reference to "absolute otherness" be ultimately dissolved. Accordingly, rather than tracing the withdrawal of truth from the realm of certainty, for Hegel, phenomenology would rediscover it in the metaphysics of *Realizierung*, in the 'copula' combining subject and substance, thus completing the philosophy of Spirit. Similarly, the phenomenologies of both Fichte[78] and Hegel (like that of Husserl on other grounds) would miss the critical moment that had made the Kantian solution possible, threatening, as all three realized, to turn the extension of its revelation (*Offenbarung*) into "a gallery of images (*eine Galerie von Bildern*)," to use Hegel's phrase.[79]

In fact it had again been clear from the outset, as Cusa's *coniectura* had made evident. Only under the onslaught of the evil demon, faced fully with the consequences of the infinite power of creation would Descartes be forced to deny the *coniectura*, the ability of the will and the imagination to extend beyond the clear and distinct—but only by invoking in the same recognition the ever present threat of the imagination to appear not only as poetic or divine inspiration, but equally epistemic madness. Already in Cusa, after all, the extension in question not only opened hypothetical (and experimental) reasoning and the plurality of conceptual worlds, but likewise, as Duhem put it— precisely in the same event as an "imagination (that) knew no bounds"—

became the first to invoke the plurality of inhabited worlds.[80] Still, it marked in advance the failure of the *tabula rasa* of representation, tracing instead, in the same moment in which the appearances might become revalorized, a certain step "beyond the Copernican turn," as Marc Richir has quite rightly put it. And, beyond its substitution of the realm of appearance for the realm of essence,—beyond, that is, any simple reliances on the appearances, and ultimately the *Koinos* of the *Kosmos*—it would require instead the destruction of cosmology as a strict science.[81]

If philosophical modernism was the demand for a criterion of certainty, it was only because it was even more radically the opening of alterity, the interruption of the speculative narratives on which one could depend. Doubtless, it is by invoking this interruption that Heidegger's theoretical *Wege* as paths into the unknown became disjoined from the constituent elements of classical cosmology and the 'logical simples' of *ontologia generalis* (God, the world, and the soul).[82] Thereby, it might be said, à la Serres, first philosophy itself became turned into a labyrinth, a certain "acosmism" to which the delays and trajectories of Kant's dialectic form only the introduction. Reason becomes a practice without foundations carried on outside the homogeneous 'space' of *mathesis* as its ground, a series of extensions *in indefinitum*.[83] The space involved, consequently, is a space in which—in transforming its Copernican past—the periphery is everywhere and the center is nowhere,[84] a site in which all that Heidegger would explicate in the 'concept' of *Holzwege* perhaps becomes fully intelligible.[85]

IX

Still, to invoke this labyrinth, or, to claim with Serres, that this labyrinth now announces *our* modernity, is not to deny legitimation, nor simply to endorse a principle of indeterminacy and its relativism.[86] It is, however, to recognize that the difference between interpretation and adjudication has narrowed, a relation in play, to appeal to Kant's own logicism, between the condition and the conditioned. Moreover, it is to recognize that the metaphorics of Kant's logical critique, its appeal to the schematics of legal theory and the 'critical tribunal' are overdetermined. On the one hand, Kant doubtless reduced rationality to the exemplar of the 'objective' sciences, replacing the classical invocations of truth with the demonstrable, the objective, and the intersubjectively verifiable. But, on the other hand, granted the epistemic 'experiment' it involves, this reduction could not succeed by simply turning 'science' itself into a fetish, destroying the very fecundity on which Kant traded in replying to Hume. And, perhaps Kant ultimately realized it in granting freedom a certain privilege within the underdeterminacy of theory. Kant's metaphorics of the courtroom in any case became mixed. In the end, in fact, he understood the critical tribunal in the same way that he understood science: there is just so much science as there is mathematics in it. But, of course, that is false. Decidability and disputability go different ways both in the courtroom and human affairs generally.

The rationality it ultimately invoked instead remained on the order of the "pluralistic"; underdetermined, a series of extensions beyond and between the antinomies of theory.[87] If the critical moment nonetheless remains insurpassable—if, that is, the necessity of judgment and dialogue remain 'inextricable'—what has been given up in default are the strict foundations of ontology: that is, a domain of syntheses strictly founded in advance. In the ruins of ontology "Reason's task" remains, as Kant puts it, perhaps unknowingly invoking an ancient heritage, "the *exposition* [of appearances]," a task for which, it must be added, the understanding has no keys in advance.[88] Instead, it must rely on the hermeneutic capacities of judgment in the interpretation of what escapes, a domain—like the rules of analogy it ultimately invokes—that depends as much upon *poiesis* as *praxis* and more on the *ars inveniendi* than the canons of proof. As Wittgenstein concurred concerning the domains of Reason, it is the ana-logical, then, that extends our judgments.

> "How do we compare games? By describing them—by describing ones as variation of another—by describing them, and *emphasizing* their differences and analogies."[89]

But this is a task that almost escapes the critical tribunal that Kant set out to describe, more a matter of experiment than demonstration, and more perhaps a matter of the vagaries accompanying the common law than the civic. Instead, what is required is a practice that is as much art as reason, as much imagination as understanding—that is, the art of judgment (*di-judicare*) and its ability to perceive identity and difference. As Kant rightly put it, "it is the *order* of time, not the *lapse* of time, with which we have to reckon."[90] And what is at stake depends as much on exposition and anticipation than reconfirmation, consensus, mere custom, or constitution.

X

Montaigne's Copernican turn had from the outset seen the theoretical ambiguity of this turn and its reckoning: "Now if there are many worlds, as Democritus, Epicurus, and almost all philosophy has taught, how do we know whether the principles and rules of this one apply similarly to the others? Perchance they have a different appearance and different laws."[91] Most of philosophy has taught otherwise, of course, demanding that the very idea of the difference in question be seen as incoherent. Still, if those who have made such appeals have similarly been challenged as nonphilosophical or simply rhetorically with the worst of nonphilosophical outbursts, with simply being self-refuting, perhaps we are finally, if not ultimately in a position to see what was at stake in the difference between the transcendent and the transcendental—and the play of imagination that unites and separates both, the hinge between experience and judgment.

From the outset, after all, if the Copernican turn had involved a profound, even fundamental decentering, it too involved the hallucinatory projection of what escaped, of viewpoints that might not be fused, whose exposition escaped systematic reduction to either theoretical 'heavens' or 'earths.' Moreover, although empirically the feigning such questions provoked seemed simply a matter of science fiction, their transcendental and metaphysical proximity could not be so easily dismissed—as Husserl's continual worrying about this issue in *Experience and Judgment* still attested in generating anew a phenomenological science of the life-world:

> This world is, in the most comprehensive sense, as the *life-world* for a human community capable of mutual understanding, *our earth* which includes within itself all these different environing worlds with their modifications and their pasts—the more so since we have no knowledge of other heavenly bodies as environing worlds for possible human habitation.[92]

It would not be difficult to argue that it had in fact been (nascently or not) the bulwark of Husserl's (and Kant's) transcendental communcability, the transcendental foundation of the rationality and the commensurability of judgment, its *ekstasis* the inevitable paralogism resulting from a paradigm that had exchanged the experience of transcendence for the assurance of iterability.

The problem in fact for Husserl was already one of vindicating transcendental representation from the threat of this other that had always accompanied the Copernican turn. Moreover, if as those like Sartre and Levinas demanded, this recognition—the problem of recognition itself in fact—is not without ethical and legal impact, it is a question that arises for the Copernican and transcendental ego *prior* to the question of intersubjectivity and prior to whether there are, contingently, other possible worlds or even whether there are other people in this world—a question, to put it quite simply, of the foundation of its own evidence.

Husserl's descent into the *Lebenswelt* in the attempt to complete (by determining) the possibilities of *phenomenologia generalis* was the site of his most difficult struggle with the imagination, formulating it again and again as a problem of a passage between worlds (that of the actual to the possible or between possibles), thus turning its descriptions allegorical, precisely into anticipations.[93] From the outset, however, in accord with the demands of transcendental representation, Husserl remained absolutely convinced that their vindication could be had, that the question as to whether "complete heterogeneity is in general possible at all" had to be answered in the negative, de juris: *"things cannot enter into conflict that have nothing in common."*[94] Surely the whole phenomenological project of transcendental representation depended on this sorting of identity from difference, a point as he put it "of great importance for the theory of the hierarchical structure of ideas up to the highest regions."[95] As Hegelian as it was, it may have been his last word, one that prefigures a unity that "runs through the multiplicity of successive figures." The question is what remains in its denial or, in any case, the impossibility of its vindication. That Husserl and modern transcendentalism saw the lapse into the underdeterminacy of interpretation as its greatest threat, the disjunction of representation and adequation, testifies both to its most critical moment and its greatest failure. Transcendental 'representation' would instead depend less on a reduction than an extension both analogically and historically inscribed: between theory and observation, appearance and sedimentation, interpretation and sense, the scientific and the manifest image—without recourse to independent criteria for adjudication. The right to interpret must instead extend beyond its *Masstab* and, precisely as this extension, is itself the opening of an evidence before which it remains not simply fallible but both inevitably and inextricably at risk.

The Philosopher's
Text

The "rationality"—but perhaps that word should be abandoned for reasons that will appear at the end of this sentence—which governs a writing thus enlarged and radicalized (*élargie et radicalisée*), no longer issues from a logos. Further, it inaugurates the destruction, not the demolition but the desedimentation, the de-construction, of all the significations that have their source in that of the logos. Particularly the signification of *truth*.[1]

—Jacques Derrida, *Of Grammatology*

Cf. The Darwin Upheavel. One circle of Admirers who said, "Of course," and another circle (of enemies—R) who said, "Of course not." Why in the Hell should a man say 'of course?'[2]

—Ludwig Wittgenstein, *Lectures on Aesthetics*

But if you were to follow my advice, this hotter part of the day would be spent not in playing games (that inevitably bring anxiety to one of the players, without offering much pleasure to his opponent or to the spectator), but in telling stories (*novellando*)— an activity that may afford some amusement both to the narrator and to the company at large.[3]

—Giovanni Boccaccio, *Decameron*

I

It is a commonplace that one can (or at least that one must) clearly delineate the philosophical and the literary—that one can say once and for all that philosophy clearly does one thing and literature does something else. As a result, philosophers would, among other things, not be constantly plagued with the threat of the danger that they merely weave webs of belief (*doxa*), stringing the reader along without making him or her confess the belief's truth or falsity, virtue or vice. On the contrary, the philosopher's text would be *justified* and would once and for all signal the *exclusion* of mere opinion from the tribunal of reason. And its author (and likewise the demand for the philosopher's authorship) would be just as decisive, cut loose from the realm of shadows and the opinable, again once and for all. It is, after all, precisely the work of *logos*, to bring *muthos* to an end.[4]

The text is platonist, of course, perhaps not without just cause. Plato was in any case clearly and consistently able to delineate it already:

The man who cannot by reason distinguish the Form of the Good from all others, who does not, as in a battle survive all refutations, eager to argue according to reality and not according to opinion, and who does not come through all the tests without faltering in reasoned discourse—such a man you will say does not know the Good itself, nor any kind of good. If he gets hold of some image of it, it is by opinion, not knowledge; he is dreaming and asleep throughout his present life.[5]

Plato's text seems perhaps extreme—ideal, certainly, the exemplar, or 'idealization' of the philosophical text. And yet, this *agon* of Reason that demands that the philosopher survive all refutations reaches from Plato's dialectic to "the battlefield of metaphysics" of Kant's first *Critique*, Wittgenstein's "battle against bewitchment," and beyond.[6] The need to *exclude* here is absolute: the dogmatic, the unreal, the fictional, the imaginary, and ultimately their text, the literary. And Plato, as is known, was, consequently, strict in the need to regulate this eros of the literary: "One should be cautious in adopting a new kind of poetry and music, for this endangers the whole system."[7] That there is such a threat to the philosophical 'system' seems innocuous, perhaps. The philosopher, after all, is the one who sees the *things themselves*, as Plato was the first to say with the force of that reflexive autoclitic that indicates his certainty.

II

Equally commonplace however is the charge that philosophy and literature do mutually threaten one another. It is perhaps a recent *claim*, but not without ancient roots, a claim involving a controversy that is both as commonplace and as ancient as philosophy itself. It might be argued that the very foundation of philosophy necessitates this threat. The philosopher's text is, after all, a writing, a transformation or set of transformations in the system of signs. It is one text among others, one genre among others, with its own stylistic variants and good and bad stylists. In accordance, then, with the most ancient meaning of the word *literature*, philosophy is an architecture of signs, of letters. It is, in short, literature, a text whose lexemes are in fact idiomatic, 'philosophemes.' Moreover, this practice, the philosopher's *writing* is a practice among other practices with all the accompanying conditions, contexts, permutations, and perhaps dependencies. Still, the philosopher's text claims to be more than one text among others; it claims to be their meta-text, the text that provides the axis of their intelligibility and that orders and evaluates. Rather, it would institute a critical tribunal that itself *claims* to distinguish, to justify, to adjudicate: the real and the unreal, the true and the false, the literal and the fictional.

The problem has always been, however, that bad philosophical texts have often looked retrospectively like bad novels. The battlefield of metaphysics has always been a place of 'mock combat' (*Spielgefecht*), as Kant, again, put it.[8] Hence the response of empiricism and positivism committing all these bad novels to the flames. Artists, it is claimed, do better and more openly that to which metaphysicians would not admit, the result of their logical shortsidedness. And, at least the artist has the good *taste* not to couch his or her other delirium, *focus imaginarius* in the language of truth—or so went the response.

III

The threat, however, is the return of the constitutive difference itself. Although philosophy is built on particular classificatory schemata and strategies—those regarding the methodology for the differentiation and exclusion of the false, the imaginary, the fictional—literature affirms them. Unlike the irreal of the literary, the philosopher's text truly builds into its world the requirement that there be both logical and onto-logical order (*ratio*). As Kant put it in the construction of the transcendental Ideal of *metaphysica rationalis* only "one of every pair of possible predicates must belong to it."[9] The literary, on the other hand, turns all disjuncts into possible syntheses. That is, rather than excluding, the possibility of the literary *admits*. As Bloom declares in the midst of the Walpurgisnacht episode of *Ulysses*, that "metaphysics in Mecklenburg street," night of illusion, of unreason, or to use Joyce's words, "women's reason"—a declaration made precisely in relation to that *aporia* of *aporiae* for Western thought, the problem of time, of presence, and immutability: "I wanted then to have now concluded. . . .Hence this. But tomorrow is a new day will be Past was is today. What now is will then tomorrow as now was be past yester."[10] Fully cognizant perhaps of an *epos* and a *historia* and the archive of its overdetermination from Aristotle's own *aproiae* to Augustine's "thought that cannot be comprehended" and beyond—Joyce's text differs. Joyce refused to choose between theses, between affirmation and negation, real and irreal, refused to assume the propositional attitude. Rather he affirmed— without foreshortening—the phantasmagoria of time as dispersion, as contradiction, one before which "the center of gravity is displaced,"[11] as Stephen states. And, as such, the disparity in question introduces, as Harold Bloom, Jean-François Lyotard, Jürgen Habermas, among others, have agreed, a certain notion of the sublime and perhaps, thereby, a certain gnosticism that would dominate art of this century.[12]

This is not to say that all literature is built on 'disjunctive syntheses,' as Gilles Deleuze called them, or that there have not been times when literature was thought to be 'good' precisely when it avoided such possibilities.[13] As Adorno quite rightly pointed out, however, one of the distinctive features of art of this century is that "many modern works simply defy the question of how good or bad they are."[14] Rather, nothing 'fictional' excludes those possibilities. Literature, it is said, not without a certain risk, forges its own possible world. And (apparently unlike the philosopher's text) even if this should be an impossible world, it is still '*fictive*,' a commonplace that is perhaps forgotten when philosophers look at texts other than their own. And when philosophers attempt to de-limit this margin by simply denying that the literary constitutes a world, that there is strictly speaking no world at all to the literary, they face still the response of the margin itself: does one speak literally or figuratively here?[15]

The literary text doubtless occurs in that margin produced in bending language beyond the confines of strict reference, a *meta-phora* that demonstrates in its 'turning,' in its extending, if not its extensionality, the inherent 'meaningfulness'—the overdetermination—of language itself, a *Sinn* that surpasses *Bedeutung*. Kant was the first perhaps to make truth strictly a problem of meaning, a problem of *Sinn und Bedeutung*.[16] That signs were true only when they had *Sinn und Bedeutung* meant only that they could be cashed out in sensible intuition—a demand whose protocols would culminate in failures like those of Carnap's *Aufbau* and its commitments that empiricism could be brought to fulfillment by a stroke of absolute elimination.[17] Even Hume however, before Kant, had not made it strictly a question of meaning. Certainly all the signs of those old metaphysical *phantasmagoriae* remained 'meaningful' for him even when they were not true or even if their truth value could not be decided—which is what both Hume and Kant meant by the rejection of metaphysics. Hume even believed that "a criticism of the fictions of the ancient philosophy" could be useful in the same way that we "recollect our dreams in a morning"[18] its history being something like Joyce's "nightmare from which [we] are trying to awake."[19] This word, *meaningful*, and its vagaries both linguistic (e.g., grammaticality) and epistemic (e.g., adequacy, that is, meaning*ful*ness) nonetheless have proven especially recalcitrant for discussions in literary criticism, as was demonstrated in the exchanges between John Searle and Jacques Derrida on this issue.[20]

Even for Hume, however, it was perhaps hardly a question of 'meaning' in any but a conflated sense. We could still *read* all those 'fictions of the imagination' even if we could not validate them. If truth were to be limited, indeed *had* to be limited, what could limit the fictional? We can, after all, as Kant would admit, "think whatever we please."[21] And if, as Descartes before him argued, imagination is limited and it is only the will that "indicates to me that I am made in the image and likeness of God," still that act of willing presupposes a representation, that is, an image, a *Vorstellung* of the intentional object.[22] Confronting the issue of the 'meaningfulness' of the literary we come not to a problem of limits but to the problem of margins. In the Kantian idiom, we come to the problem of extension *in indefinitum*.

IV

Now in a sense all of this seems less than obvious. Recognizing the unlimited spontaneity of the imagination, the *libera facultas concipiendi* and its *virtus fingendi*, as Nicholas of Cusa had already put it in broaching the site of aesthetic modernism, Kant was quick at the same time to *ground* its link with receptivity.[23] In the *Anthropology*, the text in which he most fully probes this faculty, admitting again that, "imagination is creative, and being less subject than other powers to the constraint of rules (is) more apt for orginality,"[24] Kant was likewise quick to assure, to reintroduce order, and perhaps even the realist's text: "Imagination, however, is not so creative as we pretend. We cannot think of any form other than that of man as suitable for a rational being. So a statue or a painting of an angel or of a God always depicts a man."[25]

John Searle's recent work claiming that fictional discourse is always parasitic on the ordinary, the normal, the real, seems to concur. What distinguishes the fictional from its opposite is the illocutionary stance of the author. Doyle, for example, does not only pretend to make assertions in his text, but pretends to *be* John Watson, M.D. What obliterates the threat of the literary for Searle is the fact that what lies behind such utterances is already categorically distinguished—the intention to pretend and that on which it is in turn parasitic: that is, 'serious' intentions.

Morever, the imaginary is likewise equally *derived*, fictive variation on an original pre-text.

But how is it possible for an author to "create" fictional characters out of thin air, as it were?. . . Again, if Sherlock Holmes and Watson go from Baker Street to Paddington Station by a route which is geographcially impossible, we will know that Conan Doyle blundered even though he has not blundered if there never was a veteran of the Afghan campaign answering to the description of John Watson, M.D.[26]

And, just as the author's fiction is parasitic upon normal usage—pretending on serious usage—so his or her success is measured by how the text 'figures' vis à vis its real commitments, here its 'London.' That is, the fictional text finds its intelligibility outside it, in its coherence with the primitive, original text of the serious.

To the extent that the author is consistent with the conventions he has invoked or (in the case of revolutionary forms of literature) the conventions he has established, he will remain within the conventions. As far as the *possibility* of the ontology is concerned, anything goes: the author can create any character or event he likes. As far as the *acceptability* of the ontology is concerned, coherence is a crucial consideration.[27]

Like Kant, Searle looked almost as if he were willing to allow the fictional text the creative, that is, originary, function that he has subtracted from the realist's text. And yet 'acceptability' and 'coherence' still receive 'regulative employment' in this discourse, even with respect to revolutionary 'forms' of literature. Nonetheless, he admitted as well that 'coherence' when it comes to the fictional text remains an abstract criterion and—as Kuhn had discovered with science—somewhat problematic: "However, there is no universal criterion for coherence: what counts as coherence in a work of science fiction will not count as coherence in a work of naturalism. What counts as coherence will be in part a function of the contract between author and reader about the horizontal conventions."[28] Although the text remains internally unregulated, Searle again appealed to the illocutionary practices of author and reader to introduce a homogeneity into the play of fictions. That is, the realm of the fictional and the imaginary again *derives*—at least in its acceptability—from the real. 'Acceptable' fiction will not challenge that from which it ontologically derives. Still, the nature of this derivation and what it ultimately implies concerning the intentional relations between the literary and fictional, and more specifically, the imaginary and the serious intentions that underlie them, was not further elucidated. What Searle acknowledged, once more, was the ambiguity in the distinctions themselves. Literal meaning, for example, is not to be construed as a simple, 'classical', 'realist' text. While the distinction remains in force, the literal is in a sense itself in flux—relative to a background of assumptions and a context "that are not and in most cases could not also be completely represented as part of or as presuppositions of the representation."[29] Although literal meaning is thus relative, Searle stood fast: "Literal meaning, though relative, is still literal meaning."[30] And yet, if true, it was never clear whether it was in the end foundation or effect, the origin of meaning or the syntactic effect of positing. For Searle however it was clear: in the midst of these shifts, what orders, what differentiates and adjudicates—perhaps still—remains the meanings, the *'Protokollsätze,'* constituted within the *'Urtext'* of intentionality.[31]

V

This more 'obvious' view in one regard is still not without its own strangeness. Without simply denying either the literal or the intentional, the claim involves a strange view of language, after all: univocal and well ordered, an event in which discourse would be ruled by one of its texts. And it is a strange view in this regard of 'reality' and the realist text it stands on. It is strange that the play of signs, that fictive variations, that the *dis*order—the Babel—of language, in the end is a *chimera.* After all, it is a fact: there are competing accounts (*logoi*)—discourses, theories, practices, and literatures. Can one read Kafka in terms of coherence and decidability, the way one reads Doyle, the philosopher's novelist par excellence—deductive-nomological feigning?[32] It is strange, in any case, that in the midst of this play of differences one could seek a route back to an initial baptism (or intention) that would be clearly and distinctly nonlinguistic: an *Ursprung,* and its theory, and its observation.[33] It is after all a curious thing 'to put into words,' this *Wovon* of which one speaks, but itself remains silent. This brute index, this given, this tabula rasa of discourse seems anything but 'given,' seen from this side, seen as a figure of speech, if you will. For, it is, qua linguistic, *literature* too.

This *chimaira,* labyrinth that refuses a pure 'taking,' that refuses to separate the Same from the Other, as Joyce aptly caught, is perhaps a kind of 'she-monster' within the philosopher's text, a certain Greek variety of sphinx with all its mystery, its 'otherness' intact. It opens instead the other perhaps to all that is Greek that constitutes the philosopher's text, "the absolute absence of the Absolute."[34] This discursive monster, the labyrinth of fiction is akin—in fact, essentially related perhaps—to that other monster Plato guards against, which is uncontrolled because uncontrollable and which in the ninth book of the *Republic* must be governed, won over. This multiheaded beast threatens Reason from the other side, from below.[35] It is known, however, from the first book of the *Republic,* and would appear again and again thereafter, the threat that Socrates incessantly combats; namely, that we will only *seem* to be convinced, that the discourse, a mere *image* of *episteme,* would have been through and through an endless and uncontrollable "banquet of words."[36] And Gorgias would in the end then be right, words are inspired incantations, in their wizardry capable of saying or affecting anything, a Sophistic precursor of the principles of expressability.[37]

And finally, it is strange that confronted with this chimera the philosopher feels compelled to refute, to survive this battle with 'Otherness' intact. It is strange perhaps that this difference does not comfort, that as Nietzsche would have it, it not be welcomed as the philosopher's proper destiny, or even as Wittgenstein put it at the end of a similar confrontation, "[O]rdinary language is all right."[38] Or, to invoke a reference that is again archaic, it is strange that the philosopher does not affirm Plotinus' assertion made still within the ease of a certain metaphysical enthusiasm: "difference everywhere is good."[39] The philosopher's text nonetheless seems intrinsically a need to *appropriate*, to set language straight, to reduce its difference, to domesticate: if nothing else to *fix* a reference, to bestow a meaning, and finally, to express an Idea.

VI

Like Searle, but within a different context and perhaps a different notion of science, Edmund Husserl equally saw the problem of intentionality as the clearinghouse of meaning and truth. Husserl in many respects perhaps (already) more directly faces the problems inherent to the realist and here Cartesian text. The problem again is the content of the imaginary, the phantasm, and its incursion on the text of philosophy. For Husserl, as for Descartes (and for Searle, implicitly), it was from the outset hinged on a certain *logo-logy*, a question, that is, of science, truth, and the rational tradition from which both emerge in the mind's 'intentions.'

Now one will say that in the sphere that interests us here—that of science, of thinking directed toward the attainment of truths and the avoidance of falsehood—one is obviously greatly concerned from the start to put a stop to the free-play of associative constructions. In view of the unavoidable sedimentation of mental products in the form of persisting linguistic acquisitions, which can be taken over. . .by anyone else, such constructions remain a constant danger.[40]

The danger for Husserl, the phenomenologist of essences, is that language will get used without attending to the meanings or the essences it conveys—a failure then of re-collection in all its senses. Rather than reactivating the original sense of a sign, it will be used in a way that 'makes sense' without attending to all that went into its original meaning. For example, geometry would be leveled off to a mere play of signs that *constructs* semantic grids, rather than maintaining its original position in its emergence within conscious experience and the lifeworld (*Lebenswelt*). The danger however is that the *essence* of geometry, that which regulates its origin, its intelligibility, its order, its truth, and thereby, its meaning, will be lost.

This is a late text, *The Origin of Geometry* (1936), in which Husserl explicitly affirms that rational practices are constituted within a certain historical facticity, notwithstanding all that he previously had attributed to their ideality. Still, as early as the *Logical Investigations* (1900), the danger of the potential for transformation inherent in usage, its *Spielbedeutung*, as Husserl termed it, had already been the subject of analysis, an aspect of language that Husserl strictly distinguished as a parasitic or 'surrogate function,' the 'operational function' in which meaning is not determinate, is not intentionally "fixed."[41]

This question has by now a long history of interruptions. Sellars perhaps put forward the most direct challenge to its position on science, saying just point blank that Husserl got it wrong: science does not repeat the manifest image of the lifeworld, its 'essence' is not to recapture the givens of conscious experience, but to surpass them.[42] Doubtless in one sense this is true. Unlike Mach, who, shortly after the invention of the spinthariscope (making it possible to experimentally detect alpha ray scintillations), finally affirmed the *existence* of atoms, there is little evidence, for example, that Husserl would have regarded atoms as anything but theoretical entities derived from the 'original' ontological types of the lifeworld.[43] In this regard, as Bachelard had argued (before Sellars), science would instead extend phenomenology beyond simple intuitionism and its commitment to the analytic-synthetic distinction, forcing it to renounce its nostalgia for a return to 'the things themselves' preexisting methodological, hermeneutical, or experimental enquiry.[44] Derrida, on the other hand, perhaps even more directly demonstrated the problem in arriving either at an unbound ideality or a pure origin (the intention, or a pure index) once the issue of the factuality of the rational (linguistic) tradition has been raised, one that inevitably conditions it—openly admitting the event of Joycean equivocity.[45] The situation regarding meaning and intention is like the one that continually provoked Wittgenstein:

> The fundamental fact here is that we lay down rules, a technique, for a game, and that then when we follow the rules, things do

not turn out as we had assumed. That we are therefore entangled in our own rules. This entanglement in our rules is what we want to understand (i.e., get a clear view of). It throws light on our concept of *meaning* something (*Begriff des Meinens*). For in those cases things turn out otherwise than we had forseen.[46]

Far from being the repository of perceptual and intentional acts that would precede it, *founding* language and making all *imaginary* derivations parasitic, language and 'perception' would in this regard be already intertwined: "Uttering a word is like striking a note on the keyboard of the imagination."[47] Language, like our rational practices in general, offers no simple reflection of the real, but a route, or a schema, which no more belongs to the actual, to *the* real, than to *the* possible, *the* imaginary. But this, seemingly is precisely what the philosopher *needs* to deny, it seems—that the real, the 'essences' are somehow infused with the imaginary, their contrary, that they are in some respect 'fictive.'

In *Ideas I*, Husserl had, however, attempted to face the comparison head on:

(T)he parallel of feigning consciousness might still raise doubt, namely with respect to "existence" of essence. Is essence not a fiction as the skeptics would like to have it? Despite that, just as the parallelism of fiction and perception under the more general concept of "intuiting consciousness" prejudices the existence of perceptually given objects, so the parallelism [of essence and fiction] prejudices the "existence" of essence.[48]

Husserl had from the outset 'coordinated' fiction and perception within his conception of intuiting consciousness, but he fought with his whole philosophical archive the attempt to do anything but *co*ordinate. Imagination belongs to the acts of consciousness; perception, ultimately to the intending of real (or at least 'actual') objects. There could be no imagination to perception. No real danger: no real fictions. The danger is in fact defused a priori—and that is why it has failed to convince those who followed in Husserl's wake, wondering whether the 'phenomenological' experience ever fully escaped its imaginary margins.

VII

And, what if that 'Other' be admitted? What if the 'real' were in fact an 'effect' or as much a 'product' as a cause, the result of a figuration and a figurative synthesis? What if "imagination [were] a necessary ingredient of perception itself"?[49] The words, innocuous enough within the economics of his thought are again Kant's. But perhaps they bear rereading. *Perceptio*, the strict 'taking' of the real, the thing-in-itself, never takes place. It was already in some ways a 'postmetaphysical' view. And yet, the Kantian text, too—at least the first *Critique's* Analytic—remained seemingly unthreatened by this 'mixture.'

Kant in the end remained strict about the coordination between perception and imagination. Imagination would not be unleashed— nor could it even threaten, as it would Husserl, who took pains to separate them out. It is not, as the earlier-cited text indicates, 'so creative as we pretend,' our imagination being tied to 'real' origins in its manipulations. Although one might be tempted to align these products with the empirical or 'reproductive' imagination, in the *Anthropology* the contrary is the case. "Fantasy" is an "unintentional play of produc- tive imagination"[50]; in fact, "the imagination run riot," as Kant put it, in one of those assertions that almost anticipates Nietzsche. And yet Kant, again, remains strident about the nature of this rioting. Whereas genius gives the rule to art, it does not for all that, *pace* romanticism, become rule-less or lawless. Kant was specific, specific about the nature of its world, if not his own regulation of it:

> The offenses (*vitia*) of imagination consist in inventions that are either merely *unbridled* (*Blosszugellos*) or downright lawless [*regellos*] (*effrenis aut perversa*). Lawless inventions are the worst fault. Unbridled inventions could still find their place in a possible world (the world of fable); but lawless inventions have no place in any world at all, because they are self-contradictory....Unbridled fantasy can always be bent [to the artist's end] (like that of the poet whom Cardinal Este, when presented with the book dedicated to him asked: "Master Ariosto, where the deuce did you get all these absurdities?") It is luxuriant because of its richness. But lawless fantasy comes close to madness.[51]

Despite its downfall here, the 'schema' of the Ideal, of *metaphysica rationalis*, still carries its own weight. Fiction ('*phantasia*') must remain both lawful and consistent for Kant, though it need not be consistent with *our* world. Still, (again like Searle) fiction remains consistent as an imaginary 'bending' (*einbeugen*), the classical word for this trans- gression, from our world. Kant will not open the riot up further. The imagination cannot (*should* not?) give birth to fantasies that contradict. The lawless is not the realm of the fantastic. It is, apparently, the realm of the insane. This notwithstanding, both fantasy and insanity remain

vitia within the philosopher's text (contrary to the view of Nicolas of
Cusa stated earlier), occurring either by association off of the primal
ground of the real, or by a letting down of the rational guard—"mere
play is in keeping with the weakened state of our powers after the day's
work, while business suits a man strengthened and, so to speak, reborn
by a night's rest."[52] The 'turning' here is a turning away from business,
the philosopher's business, *Sinn und Bedeutung*. "Imagination is richer
and more fertile in ideas than sense (*Sinn*)."[53]

And yet, as many who may have lost Kant's realist commitments
may wonder, he was not above using the predicate, *lawless* to describe
things other than the insane. In fact, he provided again a quaint example
whose discussion is overdetermined. In reference to boring social
conversations he stated, "A lawless, vagrant (*herumschweifende*) imagination so disconcerts the mind by a succession of ideas having no objective
connection that we leave a gathering of this kind wondering whether
we have been dreaming."[54] Discourse itself it seems does not parse out
easily over the imaginary and the real.

VIII

One could perhaps say many things about this philosopher's
entrance into the realm of 'ordinary' language—the 'drift' of dialogue
into the indeterminate, to use Heidegger's phrase.[55] Having just talked
about the *vitia* of the imagination, Kant himself, nostalgic as ever for
the Platonic text, states, "an artist in the political sphere, like one in
the aesthetic knows how to guide and rule the world by dazzling it
with images in place of reality."[56] Consistently, it might have sufficed
for him merely to reinvoke the categorial distinction between the
subjective and the objective underlying his account of *Sinn und
Bedeutung* to end the matter. Kant nonetheless does not make this return
to the 'objective.' Instead, he immediately adds the following rider to
this discourse without objective connection (or apparent connection)
with the understanding and its truth.

Whether in silent thought or in conversation, there must always
be a theme on which the manifold is strung, so that understanding
too must be operative in it. In such a case the play of imagination
still follows the laws of sensibility, which provides the material,
and this is associated without consciousness of the rule but still
in keeping with it. So the association is carried out in *conformity
with* understanding, though it is not derived from understanding.[57]

Even here the manifold is gathered. There is a 'thema' a 'schematism,' even if Kant must appeal to 'associative,' or reproductive, or empirical imagination, as he described it in the first *Critique*—against his earlier outburst concerning its productive but 'unintentional play.' And yet, this 'schematism' is *not derived* from the *understanding*. Recall that Kant's example, nonetheless, remains discursive, that is, categorial, a particular significative—and consistent—'running along', to appeal to the significative past of 'ratio.'

When Kant proceeded to explicate the relationship further, it was not through recourse to the dichotomies of the constituted and the received, the sensible and intelligible, the orderly and the disorderly, the lawless and the lawful. Rather, what emerged was that mystery, that common root at the basis of the Kantian system, that third faculty that is the mediation between the other two.[58] But here it emerges in a simply 'formal' fashion (albeit by drawing, perhaps ironically on a chemical analogue):

> The word affinity (*affinitas*) suggests the chemical term: when understanding combines ideas in this way, its activity is analogous to the interaction of two specifically different physical elements working intimately on each other and striving toward a *union* that produces a third thing, with properties that can be generated only by the union of two dissimilar elements. Understanding and sensibility, for all their dissimilarity, join together spontaneously to produce knowledge (*Erkenntnis*), as intimately as if one had its source in the other, or both originated from a common root.[59]

Since its emergence (perhaps, its "re-emergence," as has been seen) philosophers have had trouble grasping this unwieldy event. Hegel—logician without arguments, it has been said—would speak of affinity as an 'external' relation, a relation to the outside, a relation of transformation from the quantitative (the Same) to the qualititative (the Other), a 'neutralizing' that is mediated through a third.[60] This third occurs in Kant's text by means of the spontaneous intertwining of sensibility and understanding through imagination, that indispensable element in perception. And, it is just this 'play of imagination,' when agreeable, that would provide the 'schematism' for the third *Critique's* narrative about the Beautiful, the sensible depiction of the infinite. It arises then as the degree zero of meaning, a syntax, a *schema*, which cannot be derived from the laws of understanding, but rather from the 'laws of sensibility,' the 'semantics' of a finite rational intellect.

The problem of the discourse in question, however, is not that it is 'lawless,' as Kant first stated, but that it submits to that other *vitia*, the wandering that departs from everything to which *Sinn* had become bound by Kant. It has—the best that Kant can do, granted the oppositions that organize the *Critique's* code—*another* law, the 'laws of sensibility.' Kant is fast, almost determined to move to the understanding's opposite here. An appeal to this 'other' law, classically that 'other' to understanding (and perhaps, thereby, other orders of 'knowing'), can involve no simple opposition.[61] It is not a question of opposition: "Understanding too must be operative in it"—because there is a thema that is present. And yet this *thema* simply *derives* from the understanding, that is merely 'in *conformity*' with it; that is, which merely *participates* in it.

If it is still pertinent here to appeal to a *logos*, an appeal must be made to a point at which the '*logos*' of the keyboard of the imagination, no longer derived from the understanding, proceeds on its own way, a meaningful— but for Kant boring—extension beyond the limits of *Sinn und Bedeutung*. Hegel, still at a loss for proof, if not exposition, was perhaps right to identify the faculty of this spontaneity, the imagination, this third that externalizes both roots in their other, as the faculty of speculative extension. He would be wrong, however, in thinking that this externalization could be harnessed, that this faculty of *ek-stasis* and the archaic threat it poses before the philosopher's text—assigned still to the vice of imagination—could be reduced and returned from its 'vagrancy' to harmony or ultimate adequacy.[62] He was, in short, wrong to think that this *logos* could ever simply be demonstrably harnassed. This '*logos*,' pre-text of *Sinn und Bedeutung*, of which the latter is—if not by the transcendentalist de juris, then de facto—but one thema, remains but one conceptual form, one mode, perhaps one idiom or genre, and hence, encompassable neither by a transcendental category nor an *Aufhebung*, indicative, rather, of a possibility, a 'play,' and a transgression that exceeds both.

Hegel's affinity, appropriately, is itself followed in the *Logic* by the "incomprehensible" externalized "leaps" of nodal lines.[63] If, however, it remains an event difficult (indeed impossible) to make conceptually determinate, it is apparent, in any case, that this '*logos*'—itself without ultimate grounds—was in some sense a *conditio sine qua non*, a primitive possibility of what Kant called the *facultas signatrix*. And yet, as such it remained the possibility of *Sinn und Bedeutung*, the possibility of grounds. Consequently, its introduction would always enforce a certain recognition of underdeterminacy within the play of significative practices, making their 'origins' irreducible to a pure or transcendental logic, concept, or possibility—introducing thereby a contingency that leaves their engagement always ultimately ungrounded and open ended, and the rationality involved in their participation always in a sense at risk. In fact, Wittgenstein perhaps said little else, if in saying it he 'said' as well that his own text is post-Kantian—and the text of a certain *Lebensphilosophie*.

> You must bear in mind that the language game is so to speak something unpredictable. I mean: it is not grounded: neither rational nor irrational.
>
> It is there—like our life.[64]

All of which should not forestall the recognition that this 'logos' from which Kant demurs cannot be *read* if it cannot be 'understood' in the 'pure' sense. In fact, its 'readability' is flagged with the same analogue that Hume's rejection of metaphysics had been—the rejection of the dream discourse. The difference is that fiction, narrative fantasy, and the play of the phantasm are not just seen here as parasites, derivations of the real, but rather as *haunting* its *possibility*, the *arche*, the "common root" of 'transcendental synthesis.'

IX

This unpredictability, this elusive heterogeneity, this under-determinacy would be inerradicable—the feigning of its alterity, the origin of truth, to speak classically. It would elude thereby the grids of a philosophical modernism and its strict commitments concerning the foundational, the rational, and the determinate—perhaps even its *virtu*, as has been argued by many in confronting the equivocity of Machiavelli's *Fortuna*, 'bitch goddess' of unpredictability on the margins of scientific modernism.[65] Moreover, if by invoking those margins Machiavelli fills out this story about reason and virtue, we too perhaps should look for the symptoms of regulation and closure within the same epoch. If Kant is, after all, perhaps the most direct about the 'regulative employment,' of the problem of *Sinn und Bedeutung*, opening up a conceptual grid that would inform linguistic inquiry after him, he was not the first (nor would he be the last) to assign the loss and impenetrability of its failure to the asylum. Again, Kant's position is in this regard complex, one that needs to be seen as the presentation of a certain inversion of—and perhaps, even 'reaction formation' against—a claim made on behalf of reason against madness that Hobbes, for example, could be seen already representing.

Hobbes in fact claimed that the madness affecting the social discourse that struck Kant blind belonged *only* to the philosophers, the "Schoole-men," to be precise. And, empiricist and yet Platonist through and through, he again classified their discursive extravagances as unruly passions. As has been seen, however, it occurs only by an assignment that returns once more on Plato and an exclusion of the sacred that was equally overdetermined.

> The common sort of men seldom speak insignificantly, and are therefore, by those other egregious persons counted idiots. But to be assured their words are without any thing correspondent to them in the mind, there would need some examples; which if any man require, let him take a School-man into his hands and see if he can translate any one chapter concerning any difficult point, as the Trinity; the Deity; the nature of Christ; transubstantiation; free-will, etc. into any of the modern tongues, so as to make the same intelligible; or into any tolerable Latin, such as they were acquainted withal, that lived when the Latin tongue was vulgar....When men write whole volumes of such stuff, are they not mad, or intend to make others so?...So that this kind of absurdity, may rightly be numbered amongst the many sorts of madness..[66]

In all this, Hobbes claims, the speaker "will find himself entangled in words."[67] It was precisely this entanglement, recall, from which Wittgenstein still believed we had to be liberated. And yet for him—in this sense like Joyce—this entanglement was the lot of all that was 'ordinary' and 'alright.' Indeed for Joyce it invoked an absolute—albeit a multiplicity—by which we are both entangled and infinite.[68] Hobbes and those after him however could see it only as a fateful loss, a failure (intentional or not) "to remember what every name [the speaker] uses stands for."[69] As has been seen, Husserl claimed that a similar recollection needed to be invoked to preserve language against the usurpation and syntactic surprise of *Spielbedeutung*. This view however not only stresses, as Gadamer has said, "the negative side of language," but limits its 'positivity' and its epistemic role to the domain of the determinate and the strictly demonstrable. Moreover, like its hope to exclude the complications of transcendence generally, "it condemns as heresy all knowledge that does now allow for this kind of certainty."[70] Perhaps only at the hands of those like Gadamer (or Benjamin or Joyce) and those generally willing to risk the venture of its fragmentation would this 'transcendence' regain effect.

What connects Kant and Hobbes, and those who follow them here, their 'opposition' notwithstanding, is precisely the 'modernist' version of the philosopher's text to which Hobbes appealed and the system of exclusions that it underwrites. It is a version in fact as 'modern' as the languages into which Hobbes demanded the 'old' philosophical concepts must be reducible or 'translatable.' Like the story concerning translation to which it appeals (unlike the stories about translation that preceded it and those which have come since Quine and Derrida to follow) it rests on the dream of a discourse that would be univocal. It required, that is, a discourse that was scrutable and ultimately grounded; an *ordo* capable of standing its ground before all that escaped, all that remained underdetermined, unpredictable, merely conditional, undecidable, uncircumscribable, or incommensurable—all that undercut the attempt to provide an ultimately adequate account of the real, its re-presentation. The result would be an image purged of all that exceeds the concept, enabling the construction of an epistemic *picture*, an *Abbildung* in the most literal of senses, purified into facts that were de facto 'logical.'

The failure of representation, on the contrary, forced a confrontation with the problem of deciphering all that exceeded simple adequation, requiring a discursive practice capable of encountering that for which there could be no simple rules of correspondence. It was a confrontation that the Wittgensteinian text (perhaps no less than the Gadamerian) disclosed in terms that were archaic, a confrontation involving a failure regarding the irreducibility of what it called *the variety of interpretation*.[71] The ensuing indeterminancy involved a threat, as the text states more directly, of *anders gedeuten werden*. And, its effect radically, inevitably displaced the marginal status of interpretation within the text of philosophy. Beyond the ideal of simple representation, of univocal adequacy, provoked instead by what Wittgenstein called, as did Kant before him, the *play of imagination*,[72] it outlined a domain in which justification would be more akin to the aesthetic than the ideals of classical rationality had decreed.[73] And its provocation, as a result, forced (as Wittgenstein's text, along with others, manifests) the question of style, genre, and form, to prominence, a provocation in which the propositional function of representation was turned back on itself, forcing it to rejoin its rhetorical past, to turn subjunctive, submitting its 'logical space' to a 'labyrinth' that undermined the clarity of simple assertion.[74]

As Beckett realized, it would not be accidental that Joyce's commitments regarding the rediscovery of language would find in a Dante or a Bruno antecendents for the metamorphoses he sought to trace.[75] Nor was it accidental that Joyce's retrieval of the mythic element of history would find resonance in Vico—if, as has been seen, rather than the latter's retrieval of the Homeric quest for Absolute Spirit, it acquired likewise the depth of a certain nightmare from which we are trying to awake and for which we lack ultimate creative resources. And yet, 'humanism' survives here precisely in the problem of the literary, of translation, invention, and inter-vention. It is, after all, a sense of the narration of truth that had been lost. If Boccaccio's *Decameron* seemed unconcerned about its genre, stating in its *Proemio* the intent to "narrate a hundred stories or fables or parables or histories or whatever you choose to call them"—it did not exclude, as a narrator of the third day put it, "a true story, demanding to be told."[76]

X

Far from being a mere appendage to truth, the problem of interpretation must be seen to arise necessarily out of the failure of the classical *recherche de la vérité*, the search for strict objectivity, or what Kant had called *determinate judgements*. It thus called forth a *Vor-urteil* that turned its predecessors into fictions, and their accounts, as Descartes half-saw, into 'fables.'[77] The domain that emerged was, as has been seen, more akin to the reflective: underdetermined, justified only by its practices, its "task," as the latter put it, but perhaps equally Wittgenstein's "use," and perhaps too, the experience accompanying it.[78] It was a domain in which the force of imagination could not be denied, nor could the productive character of its syntheses, nor finally the effect of imagination on the extensions of the literal—the *Einbeugen* of metaphor, to use Kant's word. But Quine perhaps has said little else:

> It is a mistake to think of linguistic usage as literalistic in its main body and metaphorical in its trimming. Metaphor, or something like it, governs both the growth of language and our acquisition of it. What comes as a subsequent refinement is rather, cognitive discourse itself, at its most dryly literal. The neatly worked inner stretches of science are an open space in the tropical jungle, created by clearing tropes away.[79]

The account of the literal as a rigorously delimitable set of propositions, thus, must be devalorized of its honorific privilege.[80] If it is true, obviously, that recognizing the 'conditional' past of the literal does not end the discourse of the literal—if it is true, as Searle put it, that the literal, though relative, is still literal—it remains equally true that it is never *fully* literal—as Derrida said—never unquestionably literal, not literal in the privileged, classical sense: not demonstrably and timelessly or 'strictly' real, and so forth. The literal is never in the classical sense 'objective'—not, that is, in the sense that it might, necessarily and finally, come through the philosopher's *agon* of refutation unscathed. As Michel Foucault put it in his study of madness (and reason) in the classical age, the latter account would have fortuitously provided "a serene division that makes truth possible and confirms it forever."[81] Within this matrix what escaped could no longer threaten—either as simple 'disease,' or as the Homeric poetic truth against which philosophy has seemingly always struggled. Rather, in accord with its paradigm, all that escaped the grids of simple representation and its evaluative methods, what showed, consequently, no promise of strict and univocal decidability, could have nothing to do with truth or its representational equivalent, 'truth value.' It could arise then only as a domesticated state of nonbeing: 'unreason'—like the transcendence of 'nature,' the imagination and discourse now might become subdued.[82] And yet, the breach opened up by Kant's text differs. Faced with all that makes up what he himself called an abyss (*Ab-grund*) here, he no longer *believed* the metaphysics of Descartes, Hobbes, and their successors, if he still tried to justify it. But in fact he did so only by opening up at the same time another account of the justificatory that undercut—by surpassing—all that had been excluded in committing the canons of rationality to the *more geometrico*, acknowledging, thereby, an event whose extension forced him precisely to admit the free play of imagination and, ultimately, the necessity (as well as the risk) of seeing even judgment itself as an art (*ars inveniendi*).

XI

Still, one might be tempted, as were many of Kant's followers, from Schelling to Foucault (at least in *Madness and Civilization*),[83] to claim that classical reason's altern, the affinity of the imagination, the locus of this abyss between genius and madness, indicates an *originality*, a primordiality, and the divine madness of Plato himself—a domain which was not only more than just 'other,' but privileged. One might be led to believe, then, that not only are fictions stranger than facts, but more true, the sign of a *poiesis* more primordial than the philosopher's, instead of the locus of an Other that eludes all strict grounds, all *homoiosis* or *adequatio*. Then one could simply place the philosopher's text *sur rature* and send the positivist to art school. One would have the romantic's text, perhaps as well, the text of the avante garde, the ultramodernist text. But the point is that both *fail* and for the same reason. The affinity, this *'logos,'* belongs to 'taste' no more than it belongs to 'reason.' The philosopher's text no more accounts for this exceeding than the artist's attempt to coincide with it. Rather, it is what puts this simple version of adequacy in question and forces the indeterminacy and the *agon* of interpretation—and what is specific to its rationality—on both.

If texts open themselves syntactically or semiotically to potentially infinite transformations they do not simply open themselves to an 'economics without reserve.' And if it remains impossible to reduce the heterogenity of the text, it still remains impossible to make it say what it does not say. If our 'hermeneutic prejudices" cannot be excluded as resources for truth, neither can they simply be exonerated from suspicion. As Kant put it in the *Logic,* the "prejudicial" and the "provisional" must still be distinguished.[84] We will need consequently to face the fragmented and problematic status of the remainder.

It is true: "Interpretations by themselves do not determine meanings."[85] Still, it is precisely the failure of meanings to stand their ground—beyond interpretation—that ruptures all ultimate determinacy, all foundations, and all attempts to surpass, thereby, the finitude of interpretation itself. Within the discourse of this *ek-stasis,* instead, philosophers no less than poets—and those who would intervene between them—all share the same fate, the inevitable straying to which Plato condemned his other, the interlocotor of the *Ion.* They are, that is, "interpretors of interpretors *(hermeneon hermeneis)."*[86]

On the
Rationality of
the Fragment

I

The preface to Nietzsche's *On the Genealogy of Morals* concludes with an aphorism claiming that we have not learned to read, a circumstance affecting, he believed, not only the most basic structures of argument but equally the deepest strata of communicative rationality itself. The very hope that one's writings will be understood by one's readers, as a result, is naive. What is excluded in this naïveté involves precisely the art of exegesis—the omission of a certain alternation or *Wechsel*, a certain backward and forward (*rück und vorsichtig*) movement that writing articulates and all intelligibility presupposes. The naïveté in question, moreover, remains in this regard quite complex, the result of a certain leveling-off of the sign, a reduction of expression and its rhetorical overdetermination, perhaps even its *grammatica speculativa* to the trivial. And this itself arises from the fact that "today this form [like all forms and all formalism it might be added] is *not taken seriously enough.*"[1]

The aphorism arises, perhaps especially in its modern manifestation (as writers from Bacon to Wittgenstein, Montaigne to Derrida attest), precisely when assertion has broken down: both in the uncertainty of expression and the occlusion of its referent—in both cases, to use Greimas's term, in the dispersion of the *seme.*[2] The aphorism erupts in the recognition that mere reading will not be enough. Instead "all aphorism, properly stamped and molded, has not been 'deciphered' when it has simply been read; rather, one then has to begin its *exegesis*, for which is required an art of exegesis (*ein Kunst der Auslegung*)."[3] And, evidently, much will be anticipated by this aphorism itself—one that will surely mimic itself in the paralogical status of the example that follows in Nietzsche's text. Genealogy is, after all, not just narrative (and reading). If it is these, it is also their substitute for *Erklärung*, genealogy being in this regard, to invoke the transcendental perfect, "always already" fragmentary.

Friederich Schlegel had in fact already claimed in the *Athenaeum Fragments* that "[t]o deduce a concept is to provide a genealogical proof of its descent. . ."[4] Nietzsche added however—still perhaps not far from him—that of this genealogy there would be no deductions, only interpretations, the play of deductive and inductive, disjunctive and conjunctive elements constitutive of all *semiosis.*[5] And for Nietzsche this is not without reason: "all concepts in which an entire process is semiotically concentrated (*semiotisch zusammenfasst*) elude definition; only that which has no history is definable."[6] Hence if Nietzsche writes off our failure to grasp this event to "the abyss of scientific conscience" and a certain failure of nerve, it involves too, he acknowledged "a certain weakness of demonstrability (*Beweisbarkeit*)."[7]

Although Nietzsche speaks strictly in this regard, still, that is, in the genre of the *non feigno*, perhaps his last debt to the *Wissenschaft* of his antecedents, surely the ascents and descents, the backward and forward glances elucidated in the "so-called experiences" by which we remain in all this strangers to ourselves both anticipates (and undercuts) much that is to follow.[8] If it delineates in advance the retentions and protentions of phenomenology or the factual 'relatedness backward or forward' of hermeneutics—perhaps too the poststructuralist distinction between the readerly and the writerly texts—unlike these, it acknowledges equally a 'dispersion' defying the simplicity of the assertoric— either in its transcendental or empirical mode.[9]

What emerges instead involved an inextricability—the new infinity—of the *interpretans*, one that remained fundamentally unthought within the classical model of truth and its procedural investments. In default of the overestimation of truth Nietzsche traced the denial of the *factum brutum*, of a science without presuppositions, invoking both the need to justify science anew and equally a critique of its will to truth.[10] This is, he rightly insisted, a denial of neither strict science (though perhaps the attempt to strictly distinguish the rigorous from equivocity and from its 'reading') nor its honest labor.[11] With respect to the historiographical in general in fact Nietzsche claimed disdain neither for the will to prove nor the need to play the judge, the absence of both being instead condemned as symptomatic of the failure of modern nihilism.[12] Only perhaps the pretence to have solved everything by it would be challenged, to have exchanged truth (or its will) for certainty in the dream of linear progress: in short, to have denied its 'art.'

Schlegel (after Fichte) again had already proclaimed in the *Fragments* that knowledge had remained too linear, requiring instead the figure—and the dispersion—of the circle (A § 43). Fichte had already indicated the economics of this circle, tracing the movement of its centripetal-centrifugal reciprocity, the *Wechsel* of the conditioned and the ensuing figural projection of the unconditional.[13] And yet the problem for Nietzsche was perhaps just how to subtract this line—this continuity—from the 'circle' with which it has been in fundamental complicity. Or, as Novalis had already realized perhaps, the problem involved a certain fictionalization concerning truth: "Everything is demonstrable=everything is antinomial. The sphere in which every proof is a circle—or an error—where nothing is demonstrable—this is the Sphere of the imagined golden age."[14]

II

The genre Nietzsche invoked without fulfilling is doubtless in this regard the text itself—and perhaps especially the philosophical treatise as syntactic-semantic *combineatoire* of truth functional completeness—in tatters. It is the recognition that strictly taken, there can be no scientific 'treatise'—any more than we can derive its univocal object language, no book of nature, no set of sentences whose connections and referents could be deductively-nomologically adequated. The very idea of a book in itself has broken down.[15] What is at stake instead would be something of the poststructuralist deployment of the writerly. It would involve, to use Barthes's terms, an event that is less the reiteration of truth-functional identity in "demonstrative oscillation"—one for which each text would be the "inductive derivative"—than the eternal return of what eludes such identification and derivation. It would involve "a difference which does not stop and which is articulated on the infinity of texts, of language, of systems: a difference of which each text is the return."[16] The scientific image, inextricably depended on, presupposed, and projected, would then be both an image of transcendental representation and transcendental defrayal at once, divided in the gap between a commitment always to be vindicated and the constraints of empirical adequacy.

It is in this sense, of course, that all 'texts' are fundamentally and foundationally incomplete, unavailing themselves to strict axiomatic enumeration. The difference in question is, to cite Heidegger on Leibniz's origination of the modern differential model of iteration, that is, *enumeratio*, precisely that point at which analysis with respect to identity as *idem esse* and identification is always already difference, *synthesis*: as much explication as complication, to reinvoke the ancient archive.[17] Or as Deleuze put it, having likewise delineated this expressivist archive with respect to Leibniz and Heidegger—all explicative analysis involves the enfolding of *"pli* upon *pli,"* a certain labyrinth of connectives.[18] Hence the requisite problematization of thought as *determinatio*.

The text of this *determinare* remains always incomplete, divided, determined by its background, one in the end fleshed out by assumptions unspecifiable in principle and underdetermined—or as Heidegger, Merleau-Ponty, Barthes, Polanyi, and Wittgenstein concur, a silence categorically different from an axiom: to speak neutrally, a 'practice'. But in any case it involves an event that marks the stumbling block to pure theory. Speaking transcendentally, transcendentally in Sartrean terms at any rate—but still those of *mathesis*—what is at stake involves then the in principle *nonequivalence* of consciousness to itself.[19] Ich ≠ Ich. The *Erlebnis* in question lies instead beyond all mathematical (Cartesian) constructions of the subject: a fixed point always less deductively reflected than 'presupposed,' precisely in a manner that rules out a reflection or simple axiomatic *enumeratio*—and consequently, an *adequatio*. The Sartrean text is therefore not only 'writerly' but aphoristic from beginning to end, both its Hegelian legacy and *plasticität* fully intact.[20]

Having truncated this difference, however, having traced justification's disappearance within the silence of practice, the inference seems always to be fast on its heels that lacking this ultimate word on the matter, "hence no reason," a charge found often enough in writers committed to a certain classicism of both form and content. What is lacking in all this, it is claimed, is precisely either the extrinsic criteria by which to procedurally endorse this 'silence' that remains "always unredeemed before its communication counterpart" or, lacking that, at least sufficient substantial criteria by which to definitively verify it.[21] And what the aphorism most lacks—in truncating this *enumeratio* as fragmented, as a *mimesis* without simple identity relation, and as a *semiosis* whose analogies remain irreducibly plural—is argument.

III

We should tread carefully. Even the most aphoristic of writers should have protested. "What's commonly called reason is only a subspecies of it," Schlegel had warned in his critical fragments.[22] As Foucault claimed, it may be that "no given form of rationality is reason," it being instead to speak Wittgensteinian, a question of when and under what conditions reason can be "circumscribed."[23] But this was precisely what philosophical moderism bequeathed us, the attempt to procedurally systematize, to rigorously delimit the rational, to model it on an exemplar, to invest a form with paradigmatic status. Hence the vagaries of demarcation: tossed between the deductive and the inductive, the procedural and the substantial: an event in all strictness de-limiting its mark.

What is true instead is that such demarcations remain experimental and hypothetical through and through. The fragment itself, Schlegel proclaimed, is a matter of historical experiment.[24] Even Nietzsche in this regard, far from being simply "irrational," claimed that what is at stake remained precisely experimental; an event in which we must recognize "ourselves as interpreters of our own experience"— even if it involves a matter before which we remain still too pious with regard to the experimental point of view.[25] In fact, Bacon's reliance on the aphorism from the outset intentionally involved a refusal to enumerate scientific results "as if they were complete in all parts and finished."[26] And of course, both Wittgenstein and Derrida would repeat Bacon's reliance in this regard—both invoking a certain *combineatoire* of the familiar and the unfamiliar, of the common and the uncommon, of the present and absent, the universal and the everyday.

What differentiates this 'modern' use of the aphorism from its more ancient protocols is the difference that intervenes regarding the rational, and consequently, as Bacon put it, the need for "passing beyond the ancient arts." Whereas the standard claim is that the aphorism derives from Hippocrates, who used the word *aphorismos* in a summary or classificational fashion to provide a medical listing of symptoms and their treatments, here it should be added that neither sign nor signified, symptom nor etiology remains clear. If a certain itinerary of this origin is preserved in writers such as Machiavelli, La Rouchefoucauld, Franklin, or Pascal (insofar as the health, political or moral, of individuals remains at stake), surely such is not simply the case when one approaches Nietzsche, his direct antecedents (e.g., Schlegel, Schopenhauer) or his successors (Wittgenstein, Derrida)— and even in those apparently 'literary' figures (e.g., Kafka, Joyce, Artaud, or Beckett) whom we often burden with the epithets *aphoristic* and *experimental*. Instead, as Adorno rightly realized with respect to the latter, the requisite transcendence becomes equally and openly paired with a certain disenchantment, one that would require the invocation and the experiment of form and the formal in the very surpassing it attempts.[27]

The fragment is thus the recognition that all that is at stake in this surpassing will not be integrated, resulting in a riddle "disclaiming to be a whole." Hence its peculiar "configuration of *mimesis* and rationality"—precisely insofar as what is at stake involves a question of "fragmented transcendence."[28] If, as Derrida realized, the aphorism is the reinvocation of form—the memory of form dirempted, the "ruin and monument" of totality—it is too (and was from the outset) the reinvocation of its promise.[29] And hence the complexity of the experience at stake and the experiment that would assist in its explication, the art of its exegesis.

IV

All that is ventured as 'experimental' within the trace of this 'experience' remains nonetheless still unclear. Granted, as has been seen, the priority of *enumeratio* within theoretical modernism, granted moreover the latter's epistemic and logical (classificatory) demand for completeness and finality, and granted then the complicity between what Schlegel had called the *combineatory spirit* (*kombinatorischen Geist*) underlying the fragment with mathematics—a *poiesis* uniting a certain constructivism and intuitionism—the result surely remains over-determined.[30] In fact in relying on the underdeterminacy that spurred its experimental venture, what was at stake ultimately involved less the *enumeratio* of the absolute than a deploying of the possible, precisely the recognition, as Leibniz had known, that *enumeratio* is in the end more a necessary than a sufficient condition, one itself fragmented in the difference between the empirical and the necessary, the real and the ideal. And it is perhaps just because of this weakness of demon-strability, that Nietzsche thought the problem of suspicion intervenes, the suspicion (or at least the possibility) that even a strong faith "does not establish 'truth', it establishes a certain probability—of deception."[31]

The fragment instead involves inextricably a certain principle of insufficient reason, one that unites the tentative formalisms of Novalis, Schlegel, and their followers with those of Brouwer and Poincaré, Wittgenstein, Cavaillès, and Derrida—indicative of the complexity, even a certain transcendental 'differential' at stake in the relations between the semantic and the syntactic.[32] To this it should be added that it is precisely in this sense that the risk inherent in Hegel's dialectic becomes intelligible, a risk that similarly invokes the formal grammar of *Aufhebung* while at the same time depending on the natural language for its 'fluidity.' The rhythm of the speculative proposition, that is, becomes intelligible only as a syntactic-semantic complex that will not be made determinate, a *glissement* between *semiosis* and *mimesis* that irreducibly remains, to use Hegel's term, figurative (*plastisch*). And it relied from the outset on what exceeds the conceptual unities of understanding.

In fact beyond the representationalism of the classical age one finds accordingly a similar renewal of the question of transcendence or infinity and its *grammatica speculativa*—as both Heidegger and Benjamin for example, claimed—for overcoming the shallowness, the illusory forms and totalizations of the experience of modern judgment.[33] There is, as Benjamin put it, a decisive moment in this occurrence of the retrieval of scholaticism—even in its most 'rationalist' instances, it should be added. Even if, as Aquinas had asserted, "we distinguish only in order to unite," it was true too that this unity is the unity of a certain 'differential,' for him an analogous unity with respect to what transcends and withdraws from the experiment of the finite, one that has confounded even the best of our accounts.[34]

And, Heidegger equally recognized that the origins of the experimental already exists in medieval thought. Here too, "The basic problems of modern philosophy remain completely closed to one who has no acquaintance with and understanding of these connections" with the medieval *scientia Dei*.[35] Nevertheless, if, by 1929 at least, he realized that the equivocity of the event at stake could be neither disciplined— nor demonstrated—by the rubrics of scholasticism (*Schülphilosophie*), he was perhaps too quick to think either then or now that the modern experiments that arose in its wake could simply be identified with its negation or inversion, nor the labyrinth of the calculative simply with a certain calculative control blinded by *techne*.[36] And, he remained, finally, quick to replace them ultimately with the poetic to which they seemed to be opposed.[37] Instead, as Adorno put it, having claimed that "in actual fact, art today is virtually impossible unless it is engaged in experimentation," it is true that rather than simply the will to control, "the need to run certain risks is actualized in experimentation."[38]

It is this risk, its extension, that remains perhaps too unthought in Heidegger's gloss, one that accompanies too the aphorism's strange complicity with experimentation. Rather than understanding it (baldly) as a change of grounds, or the move from *theoria* to *techne*, the origins of the experimental must be recognized to be much more complex, less the strategy for the infinite control or manipulation of the variable than an infinite (and contingent) extension into the unknown, into the still yet concealed: an event then brought about by need, to use Adorno's term. And this need is as complex as the institutions that would arise in its wake. Adorno, as has been seen, rightly connected it with the institutions of art:

As late as 1930 or thereabouts, 'experiment' referred to a procedure that had been screened by a critical consciousness and hence was the opposite of an unreflected attitude towards 'art as usual'. In the meantime something else has been added, which is that an experimental work must contain qualities that were unforseeable in its process of production; or to put it in subjective terms, the artist has to be surprised by what he creates.[39]

All of this is true however because experimentalism arises in the midst of the unforeseeable, precisely in the failure of reason to delineate the limits of thought. The experimental and the fragmentary go hand in hand, poised if you will between retention and protention.[40] "Conscious control over material," as Adorno called it, is what had been lacked from the outset. Neither science nor art controls the material. And hence perhaps the problem of nature itself as "determinate indeterminability (*Bestimmte Unbestimmbarkeit*)."[41] What has been added, the moment in which the experimental demarcates its contingency, its fundamental surprise—a certain 'oblivion of Being' and occlusion of the referent—is precisely what spurs the experimental from the outset.[42] As Bachelard realized about the same time, experimental reason—"aggressive, turbulant, fluid"—thus articulates and in this regard at least requires a certain surrationalism "like the experimental dream of Tristan Tzara surrealistically organizes poetic freedom."[43]

For either Adorno or Benjamin to say that the recognition of this moment of 'withdrawal' was 'added' is, however, something of a misnomer. What was missing was perhaps precisely the recognition of this surprise in the very origins of the experimental. It was in this sense that Adorno did realize elsewhere—like others have since—that "science requires aesthetics," its theoreticization linked essentially to art, imagination, and metaphor. And the complexity at stake moreover attests (again both in science and the arts) to the decisive impact of formalism on experimentalism in all its forms—from Malevitch or Kandinsky to Joyce or Pound, Poincaré to Gödel, Hjelmslev to Carnap.[44] On all accounts it might be claimed, what is attested to is both the dispersion and the experiment of form—and the elevation of what Cavaillès aptly termed the *syntactic imagination* in its wake.[45]

Moreover, it is perhaps an impact not simply absent from even Heidegger himself at that time—and what he would later call his own *experiment* or *attempt* (*Versuch*) with phenomenology.[46] All of his arguments against the experimental notwithstanding, surely Heidegger's own attempt to extend beyond the notion of thought as metaphysical remain precisely 'experimental' in this regard, not simply a matter of "archaicism," as Adorno had claimed, notwithstanding its liabilities.[47] From the outset Heidegger's endorsement of "the task of *liberating* grammar from logic" for the sake of a more primordial poetic discourse could occur neither naively nor without regard for the question of form—or its differential.[48] No less true of Heidegger's *Wege* was Adorno's claim that "potentially every work of art today is what James Joyce thought *Finnegan's Wake* was before he published it, namely work in progress."[49] Even the aesthetics (and epistemics) of genius on which Heidegger depended and from which even he (like Adorno) ultimately withdrew is not simply the reinvocation of "the construct of an absolute cognition" in accord with the mind of god, adequate to what it perceives clearly and distinctly.[50] Rather, far from being either simply creative or *konstruktiv*—as the itinerary of irony in this archive attests—it invokes the resources of a certain natural law that both divides that model from itself and provides the opening of its finite 'morbidity,' its 'diremption,' and *dis-tentio*. The result then, far from being a hallucinatory substitution of the phantasm for the real, would, in relying on the resources of *originalität*, risk this opening as the opening of a certain talent or character, the possibility, that is, of invention and extension.[51] And yet it does so only by affirming the complex relations that unite, not only the literary and the philosophical, but equally the scientific and the ideological, insofar as demonstration inherently turns into genealogy and narrative, and truth figuratively becomes laden in fiction. Hence again the scepter of reason's irrationality. . .

V

The failure of demarcating literature from philosophy was not the dissolution of either, however, but the opening of a narrato-logical rupture that underlies both, truncating the grammar (and consequently the 'reading', the "seeing as," to invoke the Wittgensteinian lexicon) of science.[52] All this, again, is not simply new, but to realize that the coherence of the rational is not simply the 'equivalent' of the demonstrative. Even John of Salisbury's twelfth century *Metalogicon* had seen this much in his defense of the trivium, claiming that "the scientific knowledge (which) is the product of reading, learning, and meditation" finds its own "basis and root" in grammar.[53] But to recognize the necessity of this extension, even to recognize with Nietzsche the history of truth as the history of fictions (i.e., the history of our readings) is (if it is to make them irreducible to structural form, logical syntax, or pure meaning) not to deny truth nor to affirm the failure of the rational and surely not a "surrender of the cognitive competency to art"—neither to the art of reading nor a reading of art.[54] Instead it invokes the acknowledgment of the cognitive competency of art—or more precisely the art of cognitive competency.

Even as 'aestheticization of reason' therefore, what Schlegel, Adorno, and the rest realized in the wake of Kant's third *Kritik*, is precisely in this regard the capacity for the 'artistic' to function as a rational reserve, one that could not without loss be converted into propositional structures, the well formed formulas of certainty. What had been relied on was a certain rupture regarding this model, risking instead the opening of alterity, and thereby the possibility of critique and dialogue—and if Schlegel and Gadamer are to be believed, a dialogue fully comic before the demand for consensus. It involved, precisely in accord in fact with Kant's aesthetic judgment, the recognition that, if decision procedures were necessary conditions for the rationality of political institutions, they would not be sufficient; if consensus ('scientific,' 'political,' or otherwise) might be truth preserving, it was not truth productive, dependent on a transcendence, a 'universal' that escaped. And hence the question of critique and ideology, even the ideology of consensus.

No more however could the hermeneutical *Wechsel* or 'bad infinite' that arises in its wake be defended to be truth productive, as Gadamer thought. Instead the hermeneutic or interpretative '*Kehre*' resulted in a dialogue of irony and a deferred infinity that remained, to use Adorno's apt term, "helpless" before the demand of certainty; in Sartrean terms, a dialogue of reciprocal inadequacies.[55] The point, as has been seen, is that one less defends this rupture than relies on it, presupposes it, extends the rational by means of it: an event whose interpretation functions then only by a kind of errancy. . .[56]

VI

Jean-François Lyotard was not far from all of this in characterizing the postmodern claims:

The postmodern would be that which, in the modern, puts forward the unpresentable in presentation itself; that which denies itself the solace of good forms, the consensus of a taste which would make it possible to share collectively the nostalgia for the unattainable; that which searches for new presentations, not in order to enjoy them but in order to impart a stronger sense of the unpresentable.[57]

Hence the priority of the essay for Lyotard over the fragment: "the essay (Montaigne) is postmodern, while the fragment (*The Athaeneum*) is modern)."[58] The essay is the attempt to present the unpresentable, not to make the unpresentable present, escaping thereby the *Wechsel* of finite and infinite. Whereas all this truncates the problem of categorization in general with regard to genre, its failure is perhaps more direct. Texts, as has become evident, are fragments and essays at once. And, theories involve both "the casting of metaphor against metaphor" and at the same time a certain wager on behalf of truth.

Hence the stillborn character of Lyotard's closing proclamation: "let us wage war on totality."[59] Doubtless this is what most troubles classical philosophers (so-called philosophers of identity) about all negative dialectics (modern or otherwise), the latter's Dionysian revel before Appollian horror—all of which seems to beg the question.

Granted the logic of the situation, fallibilism seems as appropriate as dispersion, propositions as appropriate as intensities, and so on. It does not, after all, follow that we are wrong about anything, just because we do not know everything. Nor does it follow that, because we might be wrong about anything (because we lack ultimate foundations) that we must be suspicious of everything—if it does follow, as Kant realized, that we have warrant, a right—and perhaps a 'duty'—to be. Even if, moreover, Lyotard is correct—albeit fast, as has been seen—to claim that "the continuous differential function is losing its preeminence" as a paradigm for the rational, it is true too that neither the demise of its functionalism, its extentionalism, nor its homogeneity (its '*Identitäts-logik*') simply result in the inverted world. Nor, finally, does it seem to follow, as Nietzsche declared, that "whoever tries. . .to place philosophy 'on a strictly scientific basis' first needs to stand not only philosophy but truth itself on its head."[60]

The problem remains much more complex. Instead since Kant, or in any case since Maimon, the explication of this 'differential' concerning the ideal and the real, the ontic and the ontological, has, far from being dissolved or inverted—or simply detotalized—been radicalized with the result that the thought of its *determinatio* has become much more complicated. It could not be simply a question of turning the issue into a pseudo-problem; neither by the dissolution of totality nor by simply changing grounds, a move Lyotard ultimately shares with Habermas's attack on the subject—hoping to avoid the antinomies of theoretical underdeterminability that attends all fallibilism. It remains true that if the transcendental presence of 'consciousness' has not been dissolved, neither has it been vindicated, its 'universals' inextricably 'fallible' or 'ontic.' And if on the other hand we have a right to defend fallibilism, we lack—infinitely and categorically—its guarantee. We lack inter alia its imperative. Both tacks in the end claim "more than we can know," the new empiricism in either case as 'detotalitarian' as the totalitarian. Rather than simply dissolving the metanarratives of metaphysics by a new empiricism, as both Lyotard and Habermas have affirmed, it becomes instead perhaps a matter of affirming narrative itself as both the extension and the fictionalization of truth: to use the former's Nietzschean term, paralogy.[61] But to dissolve the *issue* of truth (and its difference), to dissolve the narratological for its other—simply with Lyotard to wage war on the universal or with Habermas to dissolve the standpoint of the singular from which it arises—in the end waxes nostalgic.

Both positions simply seem, that is, to miss the point about the waging of such wars and their agonistics. On the one hand, how could we not? The post-modern extension, no less than any other, opened in the difference that unites synthesis to analysis, identity to difference, *homoiosis* to heterogeneity. For the same reason, however, the denial of totality is no less incoherent than its mere assertion, the problem of the one and the many, a relation that, again, as Leibniz and Hegel realized, culminates (albeit interminably) in attraction and repulsion, explication and complication. The rational will be 'fragmented' in either case—which is not to say that it has ended. If then as Nancy has put it, "philosophical discourse is today fragmentation itself,"[62] this attests both to its insufficiency and its necessity—there remains after all, both philosophy and critique.

Schlegel's ultimate claim that "fragments are the real form of universal philosophy"—a claim that philosophy and poetry, reason and imagination, immanence and transcendence, are inseparable—is in this respect unavoidable.[63] But this is not because the fragment provides the fulfillment of the speculative genre in which philosophy and poetry become one, but instead because its *combinatoire* of 'chaos' and 'wit' is itself an experimental necessity. Hence the appropriateness of Schlegel's claim, that if many works of the ancients have become fragments, many modern works are fragments as soon as they are written (A § 24).[64] We might say, it is precisely the sign of their modern itinerary, that is—as he put it in answering Schleiermacher's charge that the *Aetheneaum* was incomprehensible—that the fragmentary status of the modern was precisely in this sense critical, an experimentation on the possibilities and limits of the communicable.[65]

And yet even this, too, is not new. If *ratio* were, after all, a determined, even, it has been argued, a declining construal for the *logos*, the translation of the outside to the inside, *intus*, it was true too that it was equally the fracturing of transcendence, *dis-tentio*, a fragmentation that was perhaps anything but simple dissolution. Tracing "the disjunction between *arche* and *khora*," Derrida claimed, the aphorism is the "intersection between inner experience (the phenomenology of inner 'time or space consciousness') and its chronological or topographical marks, those so called 'objective' or 'in the world.' "[66] In this, as Lyotard too reminds us, Augustine's *extensio* already prefigured the modern account of experience, one submitted now to certain agonistics, a certain "sublime experimentation."[67]

What is 'sublime' in this event is precisely its re-move from origins, an event that, as Cavaillès aptly remarked about the dialectic of prediction, "involves both the refusal to abandon itself to time as dominant while situating itself within the rhythm of this time through which something takes place" and that, therefore, "risks departing from itself in an adventure toward the other."⁶⁸ Neither the fragmentation nor the withdrawal of transcendence it involved led simply to the dissolution of reason, invoking instead as much the risk of experiment as the ironies of analogy. And it is this that Bacon again truncated in extending the uncertain domains of the finite by experiment, not without irony opening the conceptual space of the modern and its demand for certainty. If, as he put it, "interpretation is the true and natural work of the mind when freed from impediments," and if this required a certain "scattering to the winds" of philosophical systems in order that "everything will be in more readiness, and much more sure," it remained true too that even the surety, the surety of cause and utility was itself but a sign of what escapes systematics.⁶⁹

This much, however, Bacon never denied, that the strategy of instrumental control for the sake of certainty remained both provisional and from the outset fragmentary and underdetermined with respect to the 'transcendence' at stake: undertaken, as he put it, out of "argument of hope."⁷⁰ What should have been denied in his wake was that these were the only resources for reckoning either with 'hope' or with 'transcendence,' that, moreover, the demand for certainty could not but be foreshortened (nor its shortfall ultimately "corrected or ammended by any felicity of wit or art"⁷¹). The demand for certainty could neither circumvent nor dissolve the fragmentation involved. Instead, granted the uncertainty involved, the interpretation required demanded much art and perhaps especially, to use Nietzsche's term, the art of exegesis. But that the form and content of the aphorism resulted from no other recognition perhaps can be evidenced already in its Hippocratean origins. It is perhaps just this that is conveyed in all that the famous first aphorism admonishes: "Life is short and the art long: the occasion fleeting, experience fallacious and judgment difficult."⁷²

Notes

Introduction

1. From the beginning, the humanists realized that their commitment to a retrieval of the ancients involved a remove from origins. Compare Petrarch's letter to Boccaccio (28 October 1366):

A proper imitator should take care that what he writes resembles the original without reproducing it. The resemblance should not be that of a portrait to the sitter—in that case the closer the likeness is the better— but it should be the resemblance of a son to his father.... Thus we may use another man's conceptions and the color of his style, but not his words. In the first case the resemblance is hidden deep; in the second it is glaring. The first procedure makes poets, the second apes (*la prima fà i poeti la seconda fà le scimmie*).

See Francesco Petrarch, *Letters From Petrarch*, ed. Morris Bishop (Bloomington: Indiana University Press, 1966), pp. 198–99.

2. On Hegel's discussion of the problem of theoretization, see the preamble to "observing Reason" in *The Phenomenology of Spirit*, trans. A. V. Miller (Oxford: Clarendon Press, 1977) Section 235f.

3. See Bernard Bolzano, *Theory of Science*, trans. Rolf George (Berkeley: University of California Press, 1972). Bolzano's criticism of his precursors (regarding Hegel, see Section 22), often taken to be decisive in this regard missed the problem of underdeterminacy that incites their accounts. Doubtless just for this reason the best treatments of Bolzano's legacy have a certain inevitable Hegelian return to them. In 'analytic' philosophy this occurs most forthrightly in the work of Quine and Sellars, whereas in the 'continental' tradition it is best witnessed in the work of Jean Cavaillès, whose effect can still be traced in French thinkers as diverse as Merleau-Ponty, Bachelard, Foucault, and Derrida.

4. Claude Lefort, "Outline of the Genesis of Ideology in Modern Societies," trans. John Thompson, in *The Political Forms of Modern Society* (Cambridge Mass: MIT Press, 1986), p. 201. Hence it becomes apparent, the 'postmodern' concern for what is excluded by the strategies of philosophical modernism in the quest for certainty, albeit one by which the question of 'alterity' remains inherent to the very idea of rationality itself.

5. It is ironic then that the inadequation demarcated by this excess has been focused upon, at least since Meinong, in terms of a certain capacity for human error with regard to truth, the construction of fictitious objects (golden mountains, centaurs, Godots). As a result it has been cited chiefly as a standard feature of the parody of truth rather than an excess at the heart of theory that

functions as something of a condition of possibility. Meinong at least, *pace* his intellectualism, realized that the formulation of explicit hypotheses was generically linked with art—and the art of theory. See Alexius Meinong, *On Assumption*, trans. James Heanue (Berkeley: University of California, 1983), Ch. 2.

6. Karl R. Popper, *The Poverty of Historicism* (London: Routledge & Kegan Paul, 1960), p. 151: "Historicism mistakes these interpretations for theories." Two examples of recent partisans of Popper's impact on these matters include Umberto Eco, *The Limits of Interpretation* (Bloomington: Indiana University Press, 1990), and Luc Ferry, *Rights—The New Quarrel Between the Ancients and the Moderns*, trans. Franklin Phillips (Chicago: University of Chicago Press, 1990).

7. See Hans-Georg Gadamer, *Truth and Method*, trans. revised by Joel Weinsheimer and Donald G. Marshall (New York: Crossroad, 1989), part II, and Jean-Luc Nancy, *L'Oubli de la philosophie* (Paris: Galilee, 1986), pp. 87f.

8. Martin Heidegger, *History of the Concept of Time*, trans. Theodore Kisiel (Bloomington: Indiana University Press, 1985), p. 1.

9. Ibid., p. 3. The *locus classicus* for the phenomenological account of this crisis remains Husserl's *The Crisis of European Sciences and Transcendental Phenomenology*, trans. David Carr (Evanston, Ill.: Northwestern University Press, 1970).

10. See Jean Cavaillès, "On Logic and the Theory of Science," trans. T. Kisiel (Evanston, Ill: Northwestern University Press, 1970), p. 409. For further discussion of Cavaillès's account of the *plasticité* of reason and its Hegelian antecedents, see my "Cancellations," *Research in Phenomenology* 17 (1987).

11. Martin Heidegger, *Being and Time*, trans. John Macquarrie and Edward Robinson (New York: Harper & Row, 1962), p. 1 See Plato, *The Sophist*, 244a.

12. Ibid., p. 26.

13. Ibid., pp. 54–55. Although, as will be seen, Heidegger relied on the positive (and indeterminate) potential of the circularity indicated by this 'doubling,' Kant, restricting legitimation to specifiable (or criteriological) determinacy, insisted on the inextricability of its limit and restricted in turn the transcendental moment of pure reason both to deductive standards and an enquiry that remained suitably regressive. Hence the necessity of the retreat (or the experiment) in the move from ontology to analytics and the negative impact of the latter on the former: "appearance can be nothing by itself outside our mode of representation. Unless...we are to move constantly in a circle, the word appearance must be recognized as already indicating a relation to something....Thus there results the concept of *noumenon*. It is not in any way positive, but signifies only the thought of something in general." See Immanuel Kant, *Critique of Pure Reason*, trans. Norman Kemp Smith (New York: Macmillan, 1973), pp. 269–70 (A 251f). On the relation between ontology and analytics see p. 264 (A247/B303).

14. See Heidegger, *Being and Time* p. 197.

15. Ibid., p. 201.

16. Compare Jacques Derrida, "White Mythology: Metaphor in the Text of Philosophy," in *Margins of Philosophy*, trans. Alan Bass (Chicago: University of Chicago Press, 1982), p. 254; "Philosophy, as a theory of metaphor, first will have been a metaphor of theory." Hence both the problem of its "elimination" and "the abyss of metaphor" (253).

17. See Rudolf Carnap, "The Elimination of Metaphysics Through the Logical Analysis of Language," in *Logical Positivism*, ed. A. J. Ayer (New York: The Free Press, 1965); See Ludwig Wittgenstein, *Tractatus Logico-Philosophicus* (London: Routledge & Kegan Paul, 1960), p. 189.

18. Martin Heidegger, *Zur Bestimmung der Philosophie* (Frankfurt am Main: Klosternann, 1987), Sections 19–20. The question of myth and science equally had been broached by this time. See Heidegger's discussion of the *Sophist*, p. 19.

19. See Martin Heidegger, *What Is Called Thinking?* trans. J. Glenn Gray (New York: Harper & Row, 1968), p. 10. Heidegger's 'mythic' invocation of the past must be separated, as will be seen, from the importance he rightly attributes to memory as "the gathering of thinking," a gathering hinged, as the language for this event of gathering attests, between imagination and memory. See ibid., p. 143.

20. See Karl R. Popper, "The Demarcation Between Science and Metaphysics," in *Conjectures and Refutations* (New York: Harper & Row, 1963), p. 275n.

21. See *Being and Time*, p. 492n.

22. Ibid., p. 318. Still, even these narratives were not without connection with the metaphysical past. On the 'Platonic' antecedents of the fourfold (*Das Geviert*), for example, see *Republic* 614f.

23. Compare in this regard Gadamer's description of the initial response to Heidegger's "The Origin of the Work of Art" as bewildered: "Metaphors? Concepts? were these expressions of thought or announcements of a neoheathen mythology?" See *Philosophical Apprenticeships*, trans. Robert R. Sullivan (Cambridge, Mass.: MIT Press, 1985), p. 51. Finally, on the question of the interruption of myth, compare Jean-Luc Nancy's "Myth Interrupted," in *The Inoperative Community*, trans. Peter Connor (Minneapolis: University of Minnesota Press, 1991), Ch. 2.

24. For further discussion of Heidegger's account of the rational, see my "Heidegger, Rationality, and the Critique of Judgment," *Review of Metaphysics* 41, No. 3 (1988).

25. See for example, Donald Davidson, "The Very Idea of a Conceptual Scheme," *Inquiries into Truth and Interpretation* (Oxford: Clarendon Press, 1984), p. 184. If Davidson is correct in claiming that "Tarski's Convention T embodies our best intuition as to how the concept of truth is used," and that consequently we ought to divorce the concept of truth from that of translation, likewise aborting the hope for a "ground" or a "single space within which each scheme has a position and provides a point of view," this recognition does not eliminate the task of what he calls the "off the cuff interpretation" involved in confronting other 'schemata' (195–96). Indeed it ought to be claimed that the rationality of such assumptions—if not the meaning—requires such confrontation.

Moreover, this strategy with regard to schematics is not without precedent, as already can be seen in Kant's similar attempts to brand talk about different worlds concerning the sensible and the intelligible as a sophistical twisting of words. See the *Critique of Pure Reason*, p. 273 (A257/B313). On the other hand, Kant himself maintained that the assumption that there remained an identity between the sensible and the intelligible was precisely illicit, being metaphysical itself. In fact, the very strategy that refused their determinate identity "in a positive sense" (A255/B311) forced the admission of alternative renderings of the 'world,' reopening in this regard the question of a plurality of standpoints, and hence the impossibility of limiting the intellible to any univocal schematic representation. That is, if knowledge remains limited to 'representation' and its truth conditions—the domain of *Sinn und Bedeutung*, as Kant already called it—"we have an understanding which *problematically* extends further" (A255/B310), a matter not simple absent from more classical intuitions concerning 'truth,' certainly. Still, again *unlike* Kant, Davidson's account of the imagination, crucial to grasping such an extension, remains pivoted between the false (and classical) dichotomy of the rationalists' pure intuition (Strawson's claim that we can imagine many different kinds of worlds other than our own) and the empiricist's atomism (Kuhn's limitation of the meaningful to the latter). And, in limiting Tarski's account of truth to the constraints of our own schema for the resolution of this dichtomy, Davidson doubtless united the worst features of both positions, a result not without repercussions in his follower's attempts to deal with interpretation.

It is doubtless just in this respect that even Habermas has been led to consign the philosophy of language "from Plato to Popper" (but equally including Husserl and "truth conditional semantics from Frege to Dummett to Davidson") to the Derridean cave of logocentrism, a fixation on assertion and the "fact-mirroring function of language." The question that remains is what to make of all that exceeds those constraints. See *The Philosophical Discourse of Modernity*, trans. Frederick Lawrence (Cambridge, Mass.: MIT Press, 1987), p. 311f. Finally, compare Gadamer's similar discussion of Davidson, *Truth and Method*, p. 314n.

26. See Hanah Arendt, *On Revolution* (New York: Penguin Books, 1986), p. 229. The peril, as she realized, was equally widespread: "The first essential step on the road to total domination is to kill the juridical person in man." See *The Origins of Totalitarianism* (New York: Harcourt Brace Jovanovich, 1979), p. 447.

27. See Gerard Granel, *Traditionis traditio* (Paris: Gallimard 1972).

28. Hans-Georg Gadamer, *Truth and Method*, p. 535. It should be added, however, that the same complexity stands behind Gadamer's claim, likewise made in reference to Strauss, which denies that the propositions, 'all knowledge is historically conditioned' and 'this piece of knowledge is true unconditionally' were contradictory. See *Truth and Method*, p. 534.

29. See Jean-Paul Sartre, *Being and Nothingness* trans. Hazel Barnes (New York: Washington Square Press, 1966), p. 604.

30. Maurice Merleau-Ponty, *Signs*, trans. Richard C. McCleary (Evanston, Ill.: Northwestern University Press, 1964), p. 10.

31. See Wilhem Dilthey, *Introduction to the Human Sciences*, trans Ramon J. Betanzos (Detroit: Wayne State University Press, 1988). Book 7.

32. See Kant, *Critique of Pure Reason*, p. 18 (B ix).

33. Hans-Georg Gadamer, "The Phenomenological Movement," in *Philosophical Hermeneutics*, trans. David K. Linge (Berkeley: University of California Press, 1976), p. 173

34. Jacques Derrida, *Of Grammatology* trans. Gayatri Chakravorty Spivak (Baltimore: John Hopkins University Press, 1976), p. 70.

35. See Michel Foucault, "The Subject and Power," afterword to Hubert L. Dreyfus and Paul Rabinow, *Michel Foucault: Beyond Structuralism and Hermeneutics* (Chicago: University of Chicago Press, 1982), p. 216.

36. See for example Michel Serres, *Hermes III: La traduction* (Paris: Minuit, 1974), p. 258. A knowledge, Serres claimed, "purified of all myth becomes mythic through and through." The creative function of imagination—and the alterity it opens up—remains instead a *conditio sine qua non* of science: "The duty of critique, in science, is second in relation to the right to dream."

37. Thus, although Barthes strictly claimed that the functionalist connections through which structuralism described "the simulacrum" could be analyzed neither in terms of the rational nor the real, doubtless this, again, attests as much to his tracing of their interconnection as their dissolution. See Roland Barthes, "The Structuralist Activity," *Critical Essays*, trans. Richard Howard (Evanston: Northwestern University Press, 1972), p. 218.

38. Hans Blumenberg, *Work on Myth*, trans. Robert M. Wallace (Cambridge, Mass.: MIT Press, 1985), p. 67.

39. Michel Foucault, *The Archaeology of Knowledge*, trans. A. M. Sheridan Smith (New York: Pantheon Press, 1972), p. 186.

40. See W. V. Quine, "After Thoughts on Metaphor," in *On Metaphor*, ed. Sheldon Sacks (Chicago: University of Chicago Press, 1978).

41. Hans-Georg Gadamer, "Philosophy and Literature," trans. Anthony J. Steinbock, *Man and World* 18 (1985): 257.

42. See Roland Barthes, "Introduction to the Structural Analysis of Narrative" [1966], in *The Semiotic Challenge*, trans. Richard Howard (New York: Hill and Wang, 1988), p. 129. Four years later, having, as he put it, "abandoned the structural *model*, and resorting to the infinitely different Text" (7), *S/Z* would still in fact attempt to formalize this distention's decipherment "morphologically." See Barthe's analysis of "the hermeneutic code, the voice of truth," in *S/Z*, trans. Richard Miller (New York: Hill and Wang, 1974) Section 89.

43. Karl R. Popper, "What Is Dialectic?" in *Conjectures and Refutations*, p. 316.

44. See Gadamer, "Philosophy and Literature," p. 258; Jean-Paul Sartre, *Mallarmé or the Poet of Nothingness*, trans. Ernest Sturm (University Park: Pennsylvania State University Press, 1988), p. 142.

45. See G. W. F. Hegel, *Phenomenology of Spirit*, pp. 33, 51.

46. Ibid., pp. 9f.

47. Hans-Georg Gadamer, *Hegel's Dialectic*, trans. P. Christopher Smith (New Haven, Conn.: Yale University Press, 1976), pp. 6–7, 32.

48. Ibid., p. 7.

49. Martin Heidegger, *Being and Time*, p. 47. On Heidegger's discussion of the *skandal* of philosophical modernism's demand for proof, see his response to the *Critique of Pure Reason*'s "refutation of idealism" and its recourse to "time as providing the basis for leaping into what is outside me," pp. 247f.

50. The question of analogy in this regard accompanies and over-determines Heidegger's thought from the outset, beginning with his 1916 *Habilitationschrift*. The problem of Being's *Doppelgesicht*, its *Zweideutigkeit*, its *Zwiefältiges*, its *Auseinandersetzung*, and finally, the problem of its *Differenz*, doubtless all are interrelated on this topic, one that in turn recoils on the critique of modernity and the conception of rationality as *determinatio, definitio*, and *certitudo* (*perfectio*). Heidegger's most detailed discussion of these matters available to date occurs in *The Basic Problems of Phenomenology*, trans. Albert Hofstadter (Bloomington: Indiana University Press, 1982), Ch. 2. For a comprehensive discussion of this problem see Jean-François Courtine, "Différence Ontologique et Analogie de L'être: Le Tournant Suarézien," *Bulletin de la Sociétié Française de Philosophie* 83, No. 2 (1989).

51. On the persistence of this abundance and its reliability in Heidegger, see "The Origin of the Work of Art," in *Poetry, Language, Thought*, trans. Albert Hofstandter (New York: Harper & Row, 1971), pp. 34f.

52. Plotinus, *Enneads* V. 7. 3.

53. See Kant, *Critique of Pure Reason*, p. 243 (A225/B272). More recent writers would reinstate Kant's move. Explicitly abandoning the myth of the given, Sellars would likewise argue for the theoretical fertility behind the notion of analogy, one that, he claimed, while both "obscure and difficult" is "nevertheless as essential to the philosophy of science as it has been to theology. . ." See Wilfrid Sellars, *Science and Metaphysics: Variations on Kantian Themes* (New York: Humanities Press, 1968), p. 18.

54. Popper, "What Is Dialectic?" p. 314.

55. See Jean Cavaillès, "On Logic and the Theory of Science," pp. 373–74.

56. In this regard modern dialectics was based on a metanarrative that extends from Vico and Fichte to Sartre, replacing deductive certainty with the ascertainment of enactment. As the latter put it: "[T]he dialectic must in the first instance be the immediate, simple lived *praxis*, insofar as it acts upon itself in the course of time so as to totalize itself, to disclose itself and progressively mediate itself through critical reflection." See Jean-Paul Sartre, *Critique of Dialectical Reason*, trans. Alan-Sheridan Smith (London: NLB: 1976), p. 56. Compare in this regard the claim of Vico's *Scienza nuova*, Section 349:

> [H]istory cannot be more certain than when he who creates the things also narrates them. Now, as geometry, when it constructs the world of quantity out of its elements, or contemplates the world, is creating it for itself, just so does our science [create for itself the world of nations], but with a reality greater by just so much as the institutions having to do with human affairs are more real than points, lies, surfaces, and figures are.

57. René Descartes, *Rules for the Direction of the Mind*, Section X.

58. Martin Heidegger, "Zeichen," *Aus Der Erfahrung des Denkens Gestamtausgable*, Book 13 (Frankfurt am Main: Klostermann, 1983), p. 212.

59. Stephen Toulmin, "The Construal of Reality: Criticism in Modern and Postmodern Science," in *The Politics of Interpretation*, ed. W. J. T. Mitchell (Chicago: University of Chicago Press, 1983), p. 115.

60. Hegel, *Phenomenology of Spirit*, p. 56. Compare p. 40: "[O]nce the dialectic has been separated from proof, the notion of philosophical demonstration has been lost." Instead, it should be argued, there is no such thing as *the* dialectic, but only perhaps the event in which dialectics becomes ventured.

61. See Edmund Husserl, *Experience and Judgment*, ed. Ludwig Landgrebe, trans. James S. Churchhill and Karl Ameriks (Evanston, Ill.: Northwestern University Press, 1973), Section 65.

62. Walter Benjamin, "Theoretics of Knowledge, Theory of Progress," *The Philosophical Forum* 15, Nos. 1–2 (Fall–Winter 1983–1984), p. 8.

63. Ibid.

64. Heidegger "Zeichen," p. 212. Still, in invoking a realm beyond *techne*, beyond all 'technicity,' Heidegger's project again flirts with the mythic.

65. Emmanuel Levinas, *Otherwise Than Being or Beyond Essence*, trans. Alphonso Lingis (The Hague: Martinus Nijhoff, 1981), p. 29.

66. See Jacques Derrida, "The Time of a Thesis: Punctuations," in *Philosophy in France Today*, ed. Alan Montefiore (Cambridge: Cambridge University Press, 1983), p. 38.

67. The posthumous working notes to Merleau-Ponty's final, incomplete work amount to an explication of these ruins. See *The Visible and the Invisible*, trans. Alphonse Lingis (Evanston, Ill.: Northwestern University Press, 1968). Here the order of the *urpräsentierbar* within the phenomenology of consciousness leads to the reposing of "the problem of the relations between rationality and the symbolic function," one that forces the reintroduction of "mythic time" along with its classical appeals to the transcendence of the phantasm. See p. 168f.

68. See Plato, *Rep. 525f., Aristotle, De Anima* 432a10.

69. The question that remains, as will be seen, is whether the event at stake should be understood, to use Deleuze's term, as "a free figure of difference" or, to use Gadamer's, the indeterminate duality (*ahoristos dyas*) that is the origin of hermeneutics. See Gilles Deleuze, *Différence et répétition* (Paris: Presses Universitaires de France, 1968) and its discussion of the image of thought, p. 189f; and Gadamer's discussion of this opening in *The Idea of the Good in Platonic Aristotelian Philosophy*, trans. P. Christopher Smith (New Haven, Conn.: Yale University Press, 1986), pp. 28f.

70. Maurice Merleau-Ponty, *The Phenomenology of Perception*, trans. Colin Smith [rev. Forrest William] (New York: Humanities Press, 1981), p. 344; and Cavaillès, "On Logic and the Theory of Science" p. 402. The classical emergence of this 'history' and 'genesis' can be found in the closing pages of Husserl's *Formal and Transcendental Logic*, trans. Dorian Cairns (The Hague: Martinus Nijhoff, 1978).

71. See Theador W. Adorno, "Introduction" to *The Positivist Dispute in German Sociology*, trans. Glyn Adey and David Frisbey (London: Heinemann, 1976), pp. 32f.

72. Karl R. Popper, *The Poverty of Historicism*, p. 159.

73. See, for example, Strauss's "Philosophy as Rigorous Science and Political Philosophy," in Leo Strauss, *Studies in Platonic Political Philosophy* (Chicago: University of Chicago Press, 1983).

74. Ibid., p. 150. Still, even Popper realized in this work (dating from the 1930s) that "This does not mean that we twist the facts until they fit into a

framework of preconceived ideas, or that we neglect the facts that do not fit" (ibid.). Moreover, his claim regarding the necessity of such a 'dialectical' step beyond formal analytics in history would soon be extended by philosophers like Toulmin to encompass scientific theory in general. See *Human Understanding*, Vol. 1 (Princeton, N.J.:Princeton University Press, 1972). Although as critical as Popper of a dialectic whose *telos* was conceived along the lines of logicism, i.e., as "conclusions of a Cosmic Argument which unfolds 'logical implications' operative throughout" (329), he nonetheless argued that the necessity of a step beyond mere analysis was not without dialectical import in dealing with Quinean issues in ontological relativity and underdeterminability (64), recognizing thereby that the pragmatic turn was—and was first and foremost— itself dialectical. Similar connections had been made in French philosophy of science (in addition to Cavaillès, noted previously), in the work of Gaston Bachelard. See, for example, *The New Scientific Spirit* [originally, 1934], trans. Arthur Goldhammer (Boston: Beacon Press, 1984).

75. Adorno, "Introduction" to *The Positivist Dispute in German Sociology*.

76. See, for example, Karl R. Popper, "On the Status of Science and Metaphysics," in *Conjectures and Refutations*, p. 195.

77. See Luc Ferry and Alain Renault, "D'un retour à Kant," in *Système et critique: essai sur la critique de la raison dans la philosophie contemporaine* (Brussels: Ousia, 1984). If Renault and Ferry were correct in their retrieval of the Kantian archive, they were naive to think that the 'retrieval' at stake could amount simply to a 'return.' It would be naive to think, that is, that its paradigm of rationality could be simply reinstated, resulting more in a problem than a solution. For further discussion of this issue, see my "On the Critical Tribunal," *Cordozo Law Review* 11, Nos. 5-6 (1990).

78. If the question of the extensions of reason becomes truncated in Kant's dialectic, it was present from the outset, indeed itself the origin of the critical system. From the outset the problem of speculative knowledge (like the problem of interpretation that would be fast on its heels) was recognized precisely as a question of extensions, its crisis provoking the search for principles of synthetic knowledge, *Erweiterungs-Grundsätzen*, which might transcend or extend beyond the demonstrative limitations of philosophical modernism. See Kant's *Critique of Pure Reason*, Introduction, p. 51 (A10/B13).
    If such 'bridging' principles would ultimately be validated (and restricted) through Kant's conditions of *Sinn und Bedeutung*, the latter in turn would be woven between the antinomies of analysis and synthesis, pure category and pure sensing, syntax and semantics. Disregarding (or at least regulating) the complications that result—appealing once more to a metaphysical argument regarding the unswerving character of natural forces—Kant claimed that we both sense and schematize, both intuit and represent, by nature, without error (*Irrtum*). Errancy, that is, remains always and only a matter of (ontic) judgment. See p. 297 (A293/B350). For further discussion of the 'natural laws' that underlie

Kant's epistemic constitutions, see my "Regulations: Kant and Derrida at the End of Metaphysics," *Deconstruction and Philosophy*, ed. John Sallis (Chicago: University of Chicago Press, 1987).

A more enlightened or complex view of the extension at stake doubtless arises in the third *Critique*'s discussion of the maxims of common understanding. Here, connected in fact both with the problem of enlightenment and the articulation of *sensus communis*, it likewise becomes openly connected with the problem of differentiating conceptual *Standpunkten* (connecting it in turn, as will be seen, with the archive of hermeneutics). The theoretical result is a more fertile account of judgment. Kant in fact then claims of *erweitereter Denkungsart* that it becomes the condition for reflecting from a standpoint other than one's own, indeed that it is itself in fact the opening of a universal standpoint. See the *Critique of Judgment*, trans. J. H. Bernard (New York: Hafner, 1951), Section 40.

79. Kant, *Critique of Pure Reason*, pp. 532f (A642/B671). The experimental (and overdetermined) status of the copernican turn in this regard will itself be the subject of analysis elsewhere.

80. Hegel, *Phenomenology of Spirit*, p. 12.

81. See Paul Ricoeur, *Time and Narrative* Vol. 1, trans. Kathleen McLaughlin and David Pellauer (Chicago: University of Chicago Press, 1984), p. 72. Compare Heidegger's discussion of the hermeneutic and aphophantic 'as' in *Being and Time*, p. 200.

82. See *Being and Nothingness*, p. 55. In this respect, Sartre claimed, Kant's regulative concepts already "caught a glimpse" of *négatités*—thereby a certain logic of *l'imaginaire* as transcendental analogy. See Sartre's *Psychology of Imagination*, trans. Bernard Frechtman (New York: Washington Square Press, 1966).

83. See Hans-Georg Gadamer, "Historical Transformations of Reason," in *Rationality Today*, ed. Theodore F. Geraets (Ottawa: Ottawa University Press, 1979), p. 7.

84. Martin Heidegger, *Hegel's Phenomenology of Spirit*, trans. Prvis Emad and Kenneth Maly (Bloomington: Indiana University Press, 1988), p. 146–47.

85. Heidegger, *Being and Time*, p. 63. In one sense only later in the 1930s and especially in the *Beiträge zur Philosophie: Von Ereignis* would Heidegger confront directly the very idea of systematicity, in more directly confronting the paradigm of *Wissenschaftslehre* generated in German idealism. In the *Beiträge*'s account of explication as *fuge*, an *Ordung* disclaiming totalization and certainty, more explicitly combining the necessity of truth with the freedom (and contingency) of its disclosure, Heidegger likewise more openly acknowledged the complexity of the rationality of this event (*Ereignis*). Still, if so, if, in effect, Heidegger had further realized the complications that unite syntax and semantics, *Sinn und Bedeutung*, overcoming thereby the nascent platonism (and

foundationalism) of *Being and Time's* focus on the *Sinn von Sein*, the latter doubtless lingers on in the account of this *Ordung* as a (univocal) logic of silence to which all of discourse would return. (See *Beiträge zur Philosophie*, ed. F. von Hermann (Frankfurt am Main: Klostermann, 1989). Likewise, from the same period, see the Schelling lecture's "What Is a System and How Does Philosophy Come to Build Systems?" *Schelling's Treatise on the Essence of Human Freedom*, trans. Joan Stambaugh (Athens: Ohio University Press, 1985), pp. 22ff.

86. Cf. *Posterior Analytics* 77: 25a; *Topics* 100b. Compare in this regard Gadamer's claim, fully aware of this ancient archive, that Strauss ignored the difficulties of understanding—and then the problem of the transcendence of the Good—"because he ignores what might be called the dialectic of assertion (*die Dialektik der Aussage*)." See *Truth and Method*, p. 535.

87. Hannah Arendt, "The Poet Bertolt Brecht," *Brecht*, ed. Peter Demetz (Englewood Cliffs, N.J.: Prentice Hall, 1962), p. 49.

88. See Francis Bacon, *Novum Organum*, Book I, Section XXVIff, in *The Works of Francis Bacon*, Vol. 8, ed. James Spiddig, Robert Ellis, and Douglas Heath (Cambridge: Cambridge University Press, 1863).

89. Ibid., Section LXXVI.

Abysses

1. Immanuel Kant, *Critique of Pure Reason*, p. 488 (A573/B601).

2. Ibid., pp. 490–93 (A576–79/B604–7).

3. Ibid., p. 56 (B22). See G. W. F. Hegel, *Faith and Knowledge*, trans. Walter Cerf (Albany: SUNY Press, 1971), p. 81.

4. Kant, *Critique of Pure Reason*, p. 163 (B149).

5. Ibid., p. 513 (A613/B641).

6. G. W. F. Hegel, *Science of Logic*, trans. A. V. Miller (London: George Allen & Unwin, 1969), p. 107.

7. Martin Heidegger, *Being and Time*, p. 262.

8. Kant, *Critique of Pure Reason*, p. 513 (A613/B641).

9. Ibid., p. 514 (A614/B642).

10. Ibid., p. 202 (A167/B209).

11. Immanuel Kant, *Anthropology from a Pragmatic Point of View*, trans. Mary J. Gregor (The Hague: Martinus Nijhoff, 1974), p. 55.

12. Ibid., p. 84.

13. F. W. J. Schelling, *Of Human Freedom*, trans. James Gutmann (Chicago: Open Court Publishing Company, 1936), p. 21.

14. F. W. J. Schelling, *Ideas for a Philosophy of Nature*, trans. Errol E. Harris and Peter Heath (Cambridge: Cambridge University Press, 1988), Introduction.

15. This transformation is perhaps most radically at work in *Die Weltalter*. See F. W. J. Schelling, *The Ages of World*, trans. Frederick deWolfe Bolman, Jr. (New York: Columbia University Press, 1942).

16. Kant, *Critique of Pure Reason*, p. 490n (A575n/B603n).

17. G. W. F. Hegel, *Science of Logic*, p. 483.

18. G. W. F. Hegel, *Lectures on the Philosophy of Religion*, Vol. 3, trans. R. F. Brown, P. C. Hodgson, and J. M. Stewart (Berkeley: University of California Press, 1985), p. 352.

19. Hegel, *Science of Logic*, p. 50.

20. Friedrich Nietzsche, *The Will to Power*, trans. Walter Kaufmann and R. L. Hillingdale (New York: Random House, 1967), p. 64.

21. Ibid., p. 300.

22. Ibid., p. 301.

23. Ibid., p. 278.

24. Immanuel Kant, *Critique of Pure Reason*, p. 451 (A511/B539).

25. Friedrich Nietzsche, *The Gay Science*, trans. Walter Kaufmann (New York: Random House, 1974), p. 336.

26. Friedrich Nietzsche, *Twilight of the Idols*, trans. R. J. Hollingdale (New York: Penguin Books, 1968), pp. 40–41.

27. Hegel, *Science of Logic*, p. 461.

28. Friedrich Nietzsche, *The Will to Power*, p. 330.

29. Friedrich Nietzsche, *Thus Spoke Zarathustra*, trans. R. J. Hollingdale (New York: Penguin Books, 1961), p. 233.

30. Friedrich Nietzsche, *On the Genealogy of Morals*, trans. Walter Kaufmann (New York: Random House, 1969), p. 45.

31. Nietzsche, *The Will to Power*, pp. 332–333.

32. Friedrich Nietzsche, *Beyond Good and Evil*, in *Basic Writings of Nietzsche*, trans. Walter Kaufmann (New York: Random House, 1968), p. 211.

33. Friedrich Nietzsche, *The Will to Power*, p. 334.

34. Friedrich Nietzsche, "On Truth and Lie in an Extra Moral Sense," in *The Portable Nietzsche*, trans. Walter Kaufmann (New York: Viking Press, 1954), pp. 46–47.

35. Nietzsche, *The Will to Power*, p. 340.

36. Nietzsche, *On the Genealogy of Morals*, p. 79.

37. Nietzsche, *The Will to Power*, p. 290.

38. Martin Heidegger, *Nietzsche, Volume I: The Will to Power as Art*, trans. David Farrell Krell (New York: Harper & Row, 1979), p. 74.

39. William James, *Pragmatism and Other Essays* (New York: Washington Square Press, 1963), p. 98. Likewise, on the classical debate regarding the distinction between truth and assertibility, see for example Bertrand Russell, *An Inquiry Into Meaning and Truth* (London: Allen Unwin, 1940) and John Dewey, "Propositions, Warranted Assertibility, and Truth" in *Problems of Men* (New York: Philosophical Library, 1946).

40. Schelling, *Of Human Freedom*, p. 24.

41. See, for example, "The Elimination (*Ueberwindung*) of Metaphysics Through Logical Analysis of Language," p. 60ff. Compare Heidegger's own description of "Carnap-Heidegger" as the "most extreme counter-positions" in the " 'philosophy' of our day" in "The Theological Discussion of the 'Problem of a Non-Objectifying Thinking and Speaking in Today's Theology'—Some Pointers to Its Major Aspects," in *The Piety of Thinking*, trans. James G. Hart and John C. Maraldo (Bloomington: Indiana University Press, 1976), p. 24.

42. Nietzsche, *The Will to Power*, p. 277.

43. Heidegger, *Nietzsche, Vol. I*, p. 132.

44. Nietzsche, *The Will to Power*, p. 279.

45. Ibid., p. 280.

46. Nietzsche, *Ecco Home*, trans. Walter Kaufmann (New York: Random House, 1969), p. 326.

47. Nietzsche, *The Will to Power*, p. 291.

48. Heidegger, *The Basic Problems of Phenomenology*, pp. 39ff.

49. Heidegger, *Nietzsche, Vol. IV: Nihilism*, trans. Frank A. Capuzzi (New York: Harper & Row, 1982), p. 191.

50. Ibid., p. 192.

51. See Martin Heidegger, "On the Essence of Truth," trans. John Sallis, in Martin Heidegger, *Basic Writings*, ed. David Krell (New York: Harper & Row, 1977), p. 127.

52. Martin Heidegger, *The Essence of Reasons*, trans. Terrence Malick (Evanston, Ill.: Northwestern University Press, 1969), pp. 127, 129.

53. Nietzsche, *Thus Spoke Zarathustra*, p. 191 (212).

54. Jacques Derrida, *Spurs: Nietzsche's Styles*, trans. Barbara Harlow (Chicago: The University of Chicago Press, 1979), p. 73.

55. Gilles Delueze, *Nietzsche and Philosophy*, trans. Hugh Tomlinson (New York: Columbia University Press, 1983), p. 229.

56. Derrida, *Spurs: Nietzsche's Styles*, p. 103.

57. Martin Heidegger, "Recollection in Metaphysics," in *The End of Philosophy*, trans. Joan Stambaugh (New York: Harper & Row, 1973), p. 79.

58. Derrida, *Spurs: Neitzsche's Styles*, p. 113.

59. Jacques Derrida, *Of Grammatology*, p. 61.

60. Derrida, *Spurs: Nietzsche's Styles*, pp. 119, 121.

61. Martin Heidegger, "The End of Philosophy and the Task of Thinking," in *On Time and Being*, trans. Joan Stambaugh (New York: Harper & Row, 1972), p. 70.

62. Ibid., p. 69.

63. Heidegger, *Being and Time*, p. 270.

64. See, for example, Nietzsche, *The Will to Power*, pp. 278ff.

65. Heidegger, *Being and Time*, p. 268.

66. Ibid., p. 271 (H229).

67. Martin Heidegger, "Recollection in Metaphysics," p. 78.

68. Martin Heidegger, "Overcoming Metaphysics," in *The End of Philosophy*, pp. 96-97.

69. Rudolf Carnap, "The Elimination of Metaphysics Through Logical Analysis of Language," p. 80.

70. See *The Piety of Thinking*, p. 24.

71. Kant, *Critique of Pure Reason*, A472/B500.

72. Heidegger, *Nietzsche, Vol. IV*, p. 201.

73. Phillipe Lacoue-Labarthe, *Le sujet de la philosophie* (Paris: Abbier-Flammarion, 1979), p. 127.

74. See Heidegger, *What Is Called Thinking?* Part II.

75. Heidegger, "Summary of a Seminar on the Lecture 'Time and Being,'" in *On Time and Being*, p. 45.

76. Heidegger, *What Is Called Thinking?* p. 71.

77. G. W. F. Hegel, *Enzyklopädie der philosophischen Wissenschaft* I, (Frankfurt am Main: Suhrkamp, 1970), p. 59.

78. Nietzsche, *Thus Spoke Zarathustra*, p. 177 (195).

79. Martin Heidegger, "Letter on Humanism," in *Basic Writings*, p. 223.

Aesthetics and the Foundations of Interpretation

1. Georg Wilhelm Friedrich Hegel, *Phenomenology of Spirit*, p. 19.

2. Martin Heidegger, "The Origin of the Work of Art," in *Poetry, Language, Thought*, trans. Albert Hofstadter (New York: Harper & Row, 1971), p. 79.

3. Quoted in ibid., p. 80. See G. W. F. Hegel, *Aesthetics*, Vol. 1, trans. T. M. Knox (Oxford: Oxford University Press, 1975), pp. 9–11.

4. Martin Heidegger, "Only a God Can Save Us: *Der Spiegel's* Interview with Martin Heidegger" trans. John P. Caputo and Maria P. Alter, *Philosophy Today* 20, No. 4 (1976), p. 283. Notwithstanding Gadamer's advances on Heidegger's aesthetics, he too has been prone to similar judgments. An October 1984 interview in *Flash Art* quotes Gadamer as claiming that "American art has been very ably puffed up by the media, but it has never produced anything of real significance, nothing that a hermeneutical analysis can't classify as pure imitation." See Klaus Davi, "Interview with Hans-Georg Gadamer," *Flash Art*, No. 136, (October 1987), p. 79.

5. Hegel, *Phenomenology of Spirit*, p. 19.

6. See Theodor W. Adorno, *Aesthetic Theory*, trans. C. Lenhardt (London: Routledge & Kegan Paul, 1984), p. 175.

7. Immanuel Kant, *Critique of Judgment*, p. 157.

8. Ibid., p. 158.

9. Ibid.

10. Ibid., p. 43.

11. Ibid., p. 47.

12. Ibid., p. 133.

13. Hegel, *Phenomenology of Spirit*, p. 16.

14. Plato, *Republic* (607b) trans. G. M. A. Grube (Indianapolis: Hackett Publishing Company, 1974). p. 251.

15. Plato, (534b) *Ion* trans. Benjamin Jowett (London: Oxford University Press, 1892), p. 288.

16. Hegel, *Phenomenology of Spirit*, p. 14.

17. The term *Augenblick* is used by Schelling to describe the work of art's revelation of *"reinen Sein"* in the 1807 lecture, "Uber das Verhaltnis der bilden Kunste zu der Nature," in F. W. J. Schelling, *Schelling Werke*, Vol. III, ed. Schroter (Munich, 1972), p. 403. Granted this elevation of the work of art, Walter Biemel's claim should perhaps be taken seriously: "Schelling's philosophy of art is the first, unprecedented philosophical acknowledgement of the significance of art." See his "Philosophy and Art," trans. Parvis Emad, *Man and World*, Vol. 12, 1979, p. 269.

18. Friedrich Schelling, "Letter to G. F. W. Hegel," 5 January 1795, in *Hegel: The Letters*, trans. Clark Butler and Christiane Seiler (Bloomington: Indiana University Press, 1984), p. 29.

19. Kant, *Critique of Judgment*, p. 12.

20. Ibid.

21. Ibid.

22. Compare Schelling's similar characterization and criticism of Hegel in his *Philosophie der Offenbarung*, *Schellings Werke*, Vol. 6, pp. 87ff.

23. Schelling, "Letter to G. W. F. Hegel," 2 November 1807, pp. 80–81.

24. F. W. J. Schelling, *System of Transcendental Idealism* [1800], trans. Peter Heath (Charlottesville: University Press of Virginia, 1978), p.1. All subsequent references to this text in this chapter will be parenthesized in the text.

25. See Friedrich Schiller's response to a conversation with Schelling, questioning what he calls the idealist's *"Bewusstlösen"*, detailed in a letter to Goethe, 27 March 1801, *Schillers Briefe* (Konigstein: Athenaum Verlag, 1983), pp. 400–1.

26. See Michel Foucault, "Foucault respond à Sartre," *La Quinzaine Literaire* 46 (1–15 march 1968): 20. For further discussion of the issue, see my "Kant and Foucault: On the Ends of Man," *Tijdschrift Voor Filosofie* Vol. 47, No. 1, (March 1985).

27. Immanuel Kant, *Critique of Pure Reason*, p. 61 (A 15/B 29).

28. Hegel, *Faith and Knowledge*, p. 80.

29. As Adorno has noted then (*Aesthetic Theory*, p. 244), the notion of genius in this regard is the *intellectus archtypus* of German idealism.

30. See Immanuel Kant, *Critique of Practical Reason*, trans. Lewis White Beck (New York: Bobbs-Merrill Co., 1956), p. 58. The notion of an *ästhetische Imperativ*, it may be noted, had been discussed by Friederich von Schlegel, without concern for its philosophical status, three years previously in his *Über das Studium der Grieschischen Poesie*. See *Kritishe Friedrich-Schlegle-Ausgabe*, Vol. 1 (Munich: Ferdinand Schoningh, 1979), p. 214.

31. Among Schelling's commentators Dieter Jahnig has perhaps best seen the importance of the concept of *Überraschung* in discussing the problem of certainty and transcendence in Schelling's deduction of art. Nonetheless, Jahnig's discussion remains limited to its status as a feeling under the rubric of "the empirical character of this condition" and is excluded from the discussion of what he called the problem of the condition's "metaphysical significance." See *Schelling: Die Kunst in der Philosophie*, Vol. 2, *Die Wahrheitsfunktion der Kunst*, (Pfullingen: Neske, 1969), pp. 38f.

32. See F. W. J. Schelling, *Philosophie der Kunst* [1802], *Schellings Werke*, Vol. 3, p. 393.

33. As Jean-Francois Marquet has stated, Schelling's *"Wo die Kunst sei, soll die Wissenschaft erst hinkommen"* obviously has certain anticipatory Freudian overtones. See "Schelling et Le Destin de L'Art" in *Acutalité de Schelling*, ed. G. Planty-Bonjour (Paris: Vrin, 1979), p. 77.

34. Friederich Nietzsche "The Birth of Tragedy" in *Basic Writings of Nietzsche*, pp., 19, 33.

35. F. W. J. Schelling, *On University Studies* [1802], trans. E. S. Morgan (Athens: Ohio University Press, 1966), p. 146.

36. Ibid.

37. Ibid., p. 147.

38. Ibid., p. 148.

39. F. W. J. Schelling, *Bruno or On the Natural and the Divine Principle of Things*, trans. Michael G. Vater (Albany: SUNY Press, 1984), p. 132.

40. Luigi Pareyson, *L'estetica di Schelling* (Turin: G. Giappichelli, 1964), p. 29.

41. The literature here and the various explanatory options are surveyed and adjudicated by Xavier Tilliette in a presentation to the French translation of Schelling's writings on art, *Textes Esthétiques*, trans. Alain Parnet (Paris: Klincksieck, 1978), pp. xxxviff.

42. Hegel, *Lectures on The History of Philosophy*, p. 527.

43. Ibid., p. 526.

44. Ibid. Kant's *Faktum* of pure reason too, it should be recalled, was one in which "the moral law is given, as an apodictically certain fact" whose reality "can be proved through no deduction." See my "Kant on Autonomy, the Ends of Humanity, and the Possibility of Morality," *Kantstudien* 77, No. 2 (1986).

45. Hegel, Ibid., p. 525.

46. "Das altes Systemprogram des deutschen Idealismus," translated in Norbert Guterman, "Introduction" to Schelling, *On University Studies*, p. xii. It should be noted that, whereas Guterman (and others) claim Schelling as the author of this document, this remains a disputed issue. What remains true, in any case, is that the passage cited here is at least not inconsistent with Schelling's writings during this period.

47. "Philosophical Letters on Dogmatism and Criticism," p. 157.

48. Hegel, *Lectures on The History of Philosophy*, p. 525.

49. "Philosophical Letters on Dogmatism and Criticism," p. 157.

50. Ibid., 162.

51. See, for example, Edmund Husserl, *Ideas Pertaining to a Pure Phenomenology and to a Phenomenological Philosophy, First Book*, trans. F. Kersten (The Hague: Martinus Nijhoff, 1982), pp. 106–7.

52. Edmund Husserl, *Cartesian Meditations*, trans. Dorian Cairnus (The Hague: Martinus Nijhoff, 1970), p. 22.

53. The argument presented here then rejoins Gadamer's claim that an adequate account of the foundation of hermeneutics must confront the history of aesthetics. See Hans-Georg Gadamer, *Truth and Method*, pp. 42ff, 474ff. Nonetheless, although Gadamer rightly emphasizes the role of the aesthetic here and acknowledges that what is involved is a phenomenon in which "what is evident has not been proved and not absolutely certain, but it asserts itself by reason of its own merit" (485), it may be necessary to depart from his account to the extent that it presents a conception of truth that remains perhaps recalcitrant with regard to the problem of incommensurability, remaining, as will be seen still "speculative,"—or as Kant put it in the first *Critique*, "hostile to heterogeneity" (A655/B683).

54. However the viewing of art as an inexhaustible *interpretandum*, as has been seen, is not the only, nor the final sense of Schelling's construal. In fact there is a sense as well in which there can be *no* interpretation of the work of art. Art can present *only* a sign for the infinite and not its symbol: one whose content remains fixed and determinate. In fact Schelling at one point, invoking

the metaphysics of exemplification, claimed that there can be *only one* work of art: "[T]here is properly speaking but one absolute work of art, which may indeed exist in altogether different exemplars (*Exemplaren*), yet it is still only one, even though it should not exist in its most original form (*Ursprunglichten Gestalt)"* (231, translation altered).

55. As Adorno asserted in *Aesthetic Theory* then: "Heterogeneity is inherent in works of art" (132). Consequently, understood classically, "[a]esthetics cannot hope to grasp works of art, if it treats them as hermeneutic objects. What at present needs to be grasped is their unintelligibility" (173); Adorno (still) operated here within an archaic view of interpretation and *Verstehen* as a reproduction of an original meaning, as "reenactment" or "reproduction" (177). He must affirm too that the work of art, precisely because of its enigmatic quality eluding simple *Verstehen*, still renders interpretation necessary: "Every single one opens itself to interpretive reason because its enigmatic quality is a deficiency, a condition of want" (186). Nonetheless, the interpretation called forth must remain a respect for what escapes the concept. "Achieving an adequate interpretive understanding of a work of art means demystifying certain enigmatic dimensions without trying to shed light on its constitutive enigma" (177).

56. Hegel, *Science of Logic*, 402.

57. Ibid., p. 408.

58. Hegel, *Aesthetics, Vol. I*, p. 300.

59. See Walter Benjamin, "Surrealism: The Last Snapshot of the European Intelligentsia" in *Reflections*, trans. Edmund Jephcott (New York: Harcourt Brace Jovanovich, 1979), p. 189. For Benjamin himself this aesthetics suffered from a certain inconsistency. It was in the end 'undialectical,' refusing to extend the mystery it ascribes to art equally to the 'everyday world.' For related discussion of these matters see Benjamin's doctoral dissertation, *Der Begriff der Kunstkritik in der deutschen Romantik* [1919] (Frankfurt-am-Main: Suhrkamp, 1973).

60. See Plato, *The Republic*, 508b.

61. See Michel Foucault's discussion of a similar issue in "The Discourse on Language," in *The Archaeology of Knowledge*, p. 235.

62. Jacques Derrida, *Of Grammatology*, p. 160. Gadamer too recognizes the event of this surprise as fundamental to the hermeneutic experience, again without confronting its ultimate philosophical implications. See his "Aesthetics and Hermeneutics," in *Philosophical Hermeneutics*, p. 101: "But [the communicative intent] that holds for all speaking is valid in an eminent way for the experience of art. It is more than an anticipation of meaning. It is what I would like to call surprise at the meaning of what is said."

63. Cf. Aristotle's claim that all enquiry proceeds out of wonder (*Thaumazein*) *Metaphysics* (983b).

64. Adorno, *Aesthetic Theory*, p. 99.

65. Ibid., p. 55. Xavier Tilliette quite rightly contrasted the ultimate serenity and harmony of Schelling's final account of art and the beautiful with Breton's "Beauty will be convulsive or it will not be at all." See the latter's *What Is Surrealism?* (London: Faber & Faber Limited, 1936) and Tilliette's presentation to Schelling's *Textes Esthétiques*, p. xxviii. Nonetheless, to the extent that the work of art accomplishes its serenity only by a struggle with the *Unbegrieflich* by which it is an opening out onto a higher domain, a surreality, the principle of the latter is perhaps already nascent.

66. Ibid., p. 118–19. Cf. Plato's description of the experience of shudder (*Ephrixe*) before the beautiful in *Phaedrus* 251a, a shudder that commentators have linked to the sacred past of Greek mystery cults and the daimonic.

67. See Friedrich von Schlegel, *Über das Studium der griechischen Poesie* [1797] quoted and commented on by Wladyslaw Tatarkiewicz, *A History of Six Ideas* (The Hague: Martinus Nijhoff, 1980), p. 151.

68. See Adorno, *Aesthetic Theory*, p. 75; see Nietzsche, "The Birth of Tragedy," p. 42.

69. Cf. Hegel, *Aesthetics* Vol 1, p. 71: "[T]he work of art...is essentially a question, an address to the responsive breast, a call (*Anrede*) to the mind and the spirit."

70. See Heidegger, *Being and Time*, p. 51.

71. Julie Kristeva, "Événement et Révélation," *L'Infini* 5 (Winter 1984): 3–4.

72. See Schelling, *Philosophie der Offenbarung*.

73. Compare Schelling's own indications of such an extension in the *Philosophical Letters on Dogmatism and Criticism*, p. 159, considered there in relation to practical reason: "Thus your theoretical reason would become a quite different reason; with the help of practical reason it would be broadened (*erweitert*) so as to admit a new field alongside the old."

Hermeneutics and the Retrieval of the Sacred

Abbreviations of Hegel's Works

(I, II, III)　　*Lectures on the Philosophy of Religion* [1824, 1827, 1831], ed. Peter C. Hodgson (Berkeley: University of California Press, 1984).

(HP)　　*Lectures on the History of Philosophy* [1833], three volumes, trans. E. S. Haldane and Francis H. Simpson (New York: Humanities Press, 1955).

(WdL)   *Science of Logic* [1812], trans. A. V. Miller (New York: Humanities Press, 1969).

(PhS)   *Phenomenology of Spirit* [1807], trans. A. V. Miller (Oxford: Oxford University Press, 1977).

(Ency)   *The Logic of Hegel* [1831], trans. William Wallace (Oxford: Oxford University Press, 1968).

(Let)   *Hegel: The Letters*, trans. C. Butler and C. Seiler (Bloomington: Indiana University Press, 1984).

(Eth)   *System of Ethical Life and First Philosophy of Spirit* [1802, 1803], trans. H. S. Harris and T. M. Knox (Albany: SUNY Press, 1979).

(FK)   *Faith and Knowledge* [1802], trans. Walter Cerf and H. S. Harris (Albany: SUNY Press, 1977).

(Aesth)   *Aesthetics: Lectures on Fine Art* [1835], trans. T. M. Knox (Oxford: Oxford University Press, 1975).

(Nat)   *Natural Law* [1803], trans. T. M. Knox (Philadelphia: University of Pennsylvania Press, 1975).

(Dif)   *The Difference Between Fichte's and Schelling's System of Philosophy* [1801], trans. H. S. Harris and Walter Cerf (Albany: SUNY Press, 1977).

1. On *relegation*, in this sense as "binding over," see the work of Samuel Taylor Coleridge, who, it can be argued, similarly wrote from Hegel's archive or, in any case, in the wake of Kant and Schelling. The term occurs, for example, in a letter dated 27 April 1814. See *Collected Letters of S. T. Coleridge*, ed. E. L. Griggs (Oxford: Clarendon Press, 1959), vol. 3, p. 479.

2. See for example Habermas's attempts to find in the Hegelian notion of reconciliation of community and self—purportedly Christian in origin—as "a way of construing things [which] might have given impetus to a communication-theoretic retrieval," Lecture II, *The Philosophical Discourse of Modernity*. Jean-François Lyotard's treatment of speculative reconciliation, on the other hand, questions its elevation of the *Uns* into a *Selbst* for the sake of a certain paganism of the narrative, a discourse deprived of the event in which the gods are "the masters of the word." See Jean-François Lyotard, Jean-Loup Thébaud, *Just Gaming*, trans. Wlad Godzich (Minneapolis: University of Minnesota Press, 1985), pp. 37f. Even to begin to adjudicate such differences—and certainly the status of the interpretations invoked—requires that we articulate what is at stake regarding the rationality and the metaphysics of the speculative in Hegel, a matter in turn only begun here, but not without, as will be seen, contemporary effect. Moreover the ultimate significance of Hegel's emphasis on 'religion' itself

doubtless will be contestable. Despite the apparent obviousness of the term, as will be seen, one can equally say of it what Nancy and Lacoue-Labarthe claim of Schlegel, namely that for Hegel too "religion is not religion...and especially not Christianity." To neutrally articulate the account of the relation will then carry with it all the excess of the speculative itself. As Nancy and Lacoue-Labarthe quoted Schlegel on *Witz*, if "no occupation is so human as the one that simply completes, joins, fosters" things become overdetermined—or 'ironical,' to use their term, precisely reinvoking again the problem of Kant's extensions, the speculative synthesis, or Schelling's *symballein*. Hence as they likewise saw: "And what if 'religion' should be understood in the proper meaning of the word? As *re-ligion*, the possibility of 'linking together'?" It is then perhaps wholly a question of deciding how this binding together—theoretical or practical—is to be understood. See Philippe Lacoue-Labarthe and Jean-Luc Nancy, *The Literary Absolute*, trans. Philip Barnard and Cheryl Lester (Albany: SUNY Press, 1988), pp. 75ff.

3. J. G. Fichte, "The Way Towards the Blessed Life or the Doctrine of Religion," in *The Popular Works of Johann Gotlieb Fichte*, Vol. 2, trans. William Smith (London: Trubner & Co. 1889), p. 314. (cf Let:73).

4. Hence inter alia, the difference in the treatment of religion in the *Phenomenology* and in the Berlin lectures. See the analysis of Walter Jaeschke, *Die Vernunft in der Religion* (Stuttgart and Bad Cannstatt: Frommann-Holzboog, 1986), pp. 198ff; and André Léonard, *Le foi chez Hegel* (Paris: Desclée, 1970), pp. 313f.

5. Compare Hegel's description of the incarnation of the divine Being as "the simple content of the absolute religion," construed as one in which the divine Being is revealed, known. "But it is known precisely in its being known as Spirit, as a Being that is essentially a *self-conscious* Being." (PhS: §759).

6. See J. G. Fichte, *The Science of Ethics*, trans. A. E. Kroeger (New York: Harper & Row, 1970), p. 258. Fichte's argument had been premised with the claim that rationality demands that each one open him or her self up to reciprocal influence (248), that only through intercommunication can I attain security and certainty (259), and that all must "start from common principles" (248), ones he immediately connects with the sacred as a rational community: "Such a reciprocity, which each one is bound to enter, is called a Church, an ethical commonwealth; and that about which they all agree is called their symbol" (248). It is in this respect that the division occurs concerning the symbolic origin, whether, that is, it be taken as ultimate, or whether the question of its legitimation demands transformation "as the minds continue to influence each other more and more."
While the Fichtean premises are, as others have noted, Habermasian in effect, the economy of the apparent antinomy they originate are not without hermeneutic impact—and perhaps not even without connection with the sacred. If Gadamer would by means of hermeneutics attempt to overcome the

Enlightenment by retrieval of traditions, he would do so by invoking the name of Schleiermacher, claiming in this regard that "the primary thing is application." MacIntyre on the other hand would do so by invoking the name of Newman, stressing the concept of development and pronouncing traditions as truth preserving. In fact the truth perhaps lies in what is risked between them—if they differ at all on this issue. Gadamer would, after all, immediately add that "neither jurist nor theologian regards the work of application as making free with the text," proclaiming instead precisely the encounter with tradition as the condition for 'freeing up'—and legitimating—the text, whereas MacIntyre, in fact following Wittgenstein and having exchanged the question of meaning for use, would admit that the commitment to the tradition itself can maintain rational warrant if and only if one can in the process of 'application' or 'problem solving' be willing to give it up: "Only those whose tradition allows for the possibility of its being put in question can have rational warrant for asserting such hegemony." See Hans-Georg Gadamer, *Truth and Method*, p. 332; and Alisdair MacIntyre *Whose Justice? Which Rationality?* (Notre Dame, Ind.: University of Notre Dame Press, 1988), p. 388.

7. F. W. J. Schelling, *Philosophy of Art*, trans. Douglas W. Stott (Minneapolis: University of Minnesota Press, 1989), pp. 67, 72–73.

8. Friederich Schlegel, quoted in Thomas F. O'Meara, *Romantic Idealism and Roman Catholicism* (Notre Dame, Ind.: University of Notre Dame Press, 1982). p. 31.

9. Schelling, *Philosophy of Art*, p. 70.

10. This is true even in Hegel's case, of course, where, as has been intimated, 'Protestant' and 'Catholic,' 'tradition' and 'emancipation,' have become 'theory laden'—inter alia distinguishing his account from all simple theological construal and anticipating doubtless what came to be called *Ideologiekritik*. See Laurence Dickey's account of Hegel's theological origins in *Hegel: Religion, Ecomonics, and the Politics of Spirit* (Cambridge: Cambridge University Press, 1987).

11. Immanuel Kant, *Religion Within the Limits of reason Alone*, trans. T. Greene and H. H. Hudson (New York: Harper & Row, 1960), p. 100.

12. Ibid., p. 100–1.

13. These debates began in fact as early as Schiller's letters. See *On the Aesthetic Education of Man in a Series of Letters*, trans. Reginald Snell (New York: Frederick Ungar, 1965). Schiller claimed that while Fichte's account of oscillation (*Wechsel*) "admirably expounded" the relation between form and matter, the sensuous impulse and the rational impulse, feeling and intellect, both must be limited and a partnership instituted, that of the play impulse itself (77). It is, wrong, in any case, to think the material simply as a hindrance. "Certainly such a mode of thinking is by no means in the *spirit* of the Kantian system,

but it may very well be found in the *letter* of it" (68n). Fichte, accused of adhering to the spirit and not the letter here, roundly replied in his "Ueber Geist and Buchstab in der Philosophie" (1794) and in an exchange of letters. In one of the latter (24 June 1795) he summed up his position in a way that would anticipate Hegel's decree concerning the dependency of interpretation on its spirit: "Originally philosophy has nothing at all of the *letter*; it is pure spirit."

14. Schelling, *On University Studies*, p. 96.

15. Fichte, "The Way Towards the Blessed Life," p. 382.

16. Gadamer, *Truth and Method*, p. 295.

17. Fichte, *Attempt at a Critique of All Revelation*, trans. Garrett Green (Cambridge: Cambridge University Press, 1978), p. 73. Hegel's *Phenomenology* affirms the necessity of this *Entäusserung* not only for religion but for science itself. See PhS:491F.

18. Edmund Husserl, *Logical Investigations*, Vol. 2, trans. J. N. Findlay (New York: Humanities Press, 1970), p. 452.

19. F. D. E. Schleiermacher, *Hermeneutics: The Handwritten Manuscripts*, trans. J. Duke and J. Forstman (Missoula, Mont.: Scholars Press, 1977), p. 43.

20. Schleiermacher, *On Religion*, trans. J. Oman (New York: Harper & Row, 1958), p. 43.

21. Ibid., p. 38.

22. Ibid., p. 53.

23. Ibid., pp. 40, 55–56.

24. The problem of the status of this revelation, as has been seen, extends from the 1800 *System* to the later works and the 1842–43 *Philosophie der Offenbarung*.

25. See the analysis of Richard Crouter, "Hegel and Schleiermacher at Berlin. A Many Sided Debate," *Journal of the American Academy of Religion* 68, No. 1.

26. Hegel, "The Frankfurt Sketch on 'Faith and Being' (1798): *Glauben ist die Art*," translated in H. S. Harris, *Hegel's Development: Toward the Sunlight* (Oxford: Oxford University Press, 1972), p. 512.

27. Ibid., p. 513.

28. Compare Schelling's similar remarks in *On University Studies*, pp. 100f.

29. Moreover, even in Hegel's own work the origin of this cleavage is complex. While the 1801 *Differenzschrift* revealed certain antecedents concerning

this *Entzweiung,* an 1802 essay whose authorship remains ambiguously divided between Hegel and Schelling is perhaps more direct. This essay claims that, even though the unity of *logos* and *mythos* for the Greeks "can be viewed as a still undissolved (*unaufgehobene*) identity," it now appears—like the unity of mythology in general, as has been seen—irrevocably lost: "The task of Christianity already presupposes absolute *Entzweiung.*" See "On the Relationship of the Philosophy of Nature to Philosophy in General" in *Between Kant and Hegel,* trans. George di Giovanni and H. S. Harris (Albany: SUNY Press, 1985), p. 376 and Dif:90–04.

30. See Pierre Duhem, *Medieval Cosmology,* trans. Roger Ariew (Chicago: University of Chicago Press, 1985). Likewise see *The Aim and Structure of Physical Theory* trans. P. Wiener (Princeton, N.J.: Princeton University Press, 1954), Chap. 2.

31. See Hans Albert, *Treatise on Critical Reason,* trans. Mary Varney Rorty (Princeton, N.J.: Princeton University Press, 1985), pp. 134f; and Duhem, ibid., pp. 273ff.

32. See "Schelling's Aphorims of 1805," trans. Fritz Marti, *Idealistic Studies* 14, No. 3: 245. The position had in a sense been prepared in Kant's retrieval of analogy in answering Hume. See the former's analogies of experience in the *Critique of Pure Reason.* Although the move is in its full-blooded version however a post-Kantian one, it is perhaps, too, simply 'post-formalist.' Compare, for example, Helmut Peukert's similar argument in *Science, Action and Fundamental Theology: Toward a Theology of Communicative Action,* trans. James Bohman & Cambridge, Mass.: MIT Press, 1984). Peukert, relying on the Benjamin-Horkheimer 'debates,' argued for a similarly 'theological' moment in Habermas's appeal to the regulative ideals of consensus, one which recalls the inevitability of Kant's postulates of pure practical reason. Similar remarks were made by Emmanuel Levinas, who has pointed out that the liberal state is not a purely empirical notion but:

> . . .an ethical category in which, placed under the generality of laws men conserve the meaning of their responsibility. [It involves] a messianic hope, an important moment in which the future as the *ekstasis* of a to-come (*à-venir*) is signified originally starting from the concrete response to the other man. In their unicity, uniqueness, and in themselves they find the resources of a charity irreducible to preexisting universal formulae, non-deducible resources which are able nonetheless to be joined with the justice of the liberal state in bringing about a better justice.

Levinas's remarks occur in a discussion transcribed in *Autrement que savior,* ed. Pierre Jean Labarriere (Paris: Editions Osiris, 1988), p. 62.

33. If the background of hermeneutics is doubtless (ontically in any case) a theological one, as Jean-Luc Nancy has rightly seen it is likewise onto-theological in origin. "[F]rom the Greek Fathers to Schliermacher and then to

Bultmann (hermeneutics) has been possible only in the space of philosophy and according to a fundamental hermeneutic determination of philosophy." See *Le partage de voix* (paris: Galilee, 1982), p. 17. The opening and the status of hermeneutics as will be seen remains infinitely complicated (both logically and ontologically) by this complexity. Still this is not to endorse Heidegger's 1929 reduction of the latter to an ontic, positive science ultimately then to be grounded in fundamental ontology, but to recognize the complexity at stake in their difference. See Martin Heidegger, "Phenomenology and Theology," *The Piety of Thinking*, pp. 5–21.

34. Compare in this regard Habermas's remark that Hegel "ought first to *demonstrate*, and not simply to *presuppose* that a kind of reason which is more than an absolutized understanding *can* convincingly reunify the antithesis that reason *has to* unfold discursively." See *The Philocophical Discourse of Modernity*, p. 24.

35. See Jean-Luc Nancy, "Of Divine Places," *The Inoperative Community*.

36. Cited by Nancy, ibid., p. 112. And yet, as Nancy also noted, granted the protocols of philosophical modernism, it was likewise "tantamount to proving the opposite" (113)—or tantamount to proving the fragmentation of the divine within modernity.

37. See Levinas's account of "the rationality of transcendence," based on revelation in the Jewish tradition and yet, as he realized, not unrelated to, if different from, that of the romantic ideal in "Revelation in the Jewish Tradition." *The Levinas Reader*, ed. Sean Hand (Oxford: Blackwell, 1989), p. 207. I have discussed the disequilibriuum of this account in my "Reason and the Face of the Other," *Journal of the American Academy of Religion*, Vol. 44, No. 1, 1986.

38. See Martin Heidegger, "...Poetically Man Dwells..." in *Poetry, Language, Thought*, p. 220f.

39. See Soren Kierkegaard, *Philosophical Fragments*, ed. Howard V. Hong and Edna H. Hong (Princeton, N.J.: Princeton University Press, 1985).

40. Hence the failure of Habermas's attempt in *The Philosophical Discourse of Modernity* to simply 'translate' Hegel's critique of the Enlightenment and its reliance upon the unwieldy concepts of 'life' and 'love' into a "communication-theoretic retrieval," one that would now be consensus theoretic. The move had been cut off from the outset. Hegel's extension depended, as has been seen, on acknowledging the underdeterminability of theory, that is, on acknowledging the difference between the Absolute and its hermeneutic criteria, a difference that is continually missed by Habermas's fallibilism—precisely, for Hegel himself, that is, the difference between law and justice. The question becomes the status of the remainder—once rationality has been (ontically) limited to "the disposition of speaking and acting subjects to acquire and use fallible knowledge" (314), the question of how this stands vis-à-vis the (ontological) implications Hegel's invocation of the Absolute sought to sustain.

41. See Georges Bataille, "The Sacred" in *Visions of Excess*, trans. Allan Stoekl (Minneapolis: University of Minnesota Press, 1985), p. 242. Compare Hegel's claim previously cited that what *les sciences exactes* as paradigms of enlightenment lacked was precisely this substantialization, each being "a system on its own account but without solid substance" (1:103). The point is, rather, that the problem is more complex, that, granted the *plasticity* of speculative exposition, the 'cleft' between 'syntax' and 'semantics,' 'system' and 'substance' will not be determinately resolved.

42. Compare the force or at least the modality of Hegel's claim in the *Aesthetic*: "[T]heologians distinguish between what God does and what man accomplishes by his folly and caprice; but the plastic ideal is lifted above such questions because it occupies this milieu of divine blessedness and free necessity, and for this milieu neither the abstraction of the universal nor the caprice of the particular has any validity or significance" (Aesth:II:719).

43. Elsewhere I will more fully develop Hegel's account of plasticity, in particular the plasticity of virtue and its impact on his account of character.

On the Agon of the Phenomenological

Abbreviations of Husserl's Works

(CM)   *Cartesian Meditations* [1931], trans. Dorian Cairns (The Hague: Martinus Nijhoff, 1970).

(EJ)   *Experience and Judgement* (1939), trans. Spencer Churchill and Karl Ameriks (Evanston, Ill: Northwestern University Press, 1973).

(EP)   *Erste Philosophie, Erster Teil* (1923) (The Hague: Martinus Nijhoff, 1956).

(FTL)   *Formal and Transcendental Logic* [1929], trans. Dorian Carins (The Hague: Martinus Nijhoff, 1978).

(I, II)   *Logical Investigations*, Vol. I [1900] and Vol. II [1901], trans. J. N. Findlay (London: Routledge & Kegan Paul, 1970).

(Id)   *Ideas Pertaining to a Pure Phenomenology and to a Phenomenological Philosophy* [1913], trans. F. Kersten (The Hague: Martinus Nijhoff, 1982).

(ILI)   *Introduction to the Logical Investigations*, trans. Philip J. Bossert and Curtis H. Peters (The Hague: Martinus Nihhoff, 1975). A draft of a Preface to the second edition of *Logical Investigations* [1913].

(IP)   *The Idea of Phenomenology* [1907], trans. William P. Alston and George Nahknikian (The Hague: Martinus Nijhoff, 1964).

(PP)   *Phenomenological Psychology* [1925], trans. John Scanlon (The Hague: Martinus Nijhoff, 1977).

1. Willard Van Orman Quine, *Word and Object* (Boston: M.I.T. Press, 1960), p. 221.

2. Ibid., pp. 4, 24, 26, 28.

3. See, for example, Roderick M. Chisholm, "Sentences about Believing," in *Minnesota Studies in the Philosophy of Science*, Vol. 2, ed. H. Feigl, M. Scriven, and G. Maxwell (Minneapolis: University of Minnesota Press, 1958). See also Roderick M. Chisholm and Wilfred Sellars, "The Chisholm-Sellars Correspondence on Intentionality," in the same volume.

4. Compare Karl-Otto Appel's similar remarks in Chapter 3 of *Understanding and Explanation*, trans. Georgia Warnke (Boston: M.I.T. Press, 1984).

5. Compare the distinction between "recognized or thought truths" and "truths in themselves" in Bernard Bolzano, *Theory of Science*, p. 32. See Husserl's discussion in I: 222–24; FTL: 277; Id: 230n.

6. Moritz Schlick, *General Theory of Knowledge* (New York: Springer-Verlag, 1974), p. 92. The English translation is taken from the second corrected edition [1925]. Changes from the first edition with regard to Husserl (a matter of a few paragraphs, pp. 120–21) will be noted later. As Schlick rightly states, however, these changes leave their differences intact.

7. Ibid., p. 138.

8. Ibid., p. 139–40.

9. Ibid., p. 140.

10. Ibid., p. 141.

11. Ibid.

12. Ibid., p. 86.

13. Ibid., p. 92.

14. Ibid., p. 168.

15. Moritz Schlick, *Allegemeine Erkenntnislehre* (Berlin: Springer Verlag, 1918), p. 121 (the first edition of this work).

16. Moritz Schlick, *General Theory of Knowledge*, p. 139n. As is evident from a statement already cited, Schlick did not completely purge this mistake from the second edition. He continued to argue against Husserl that "Logical structures are not real" (139–40). But Husserl has already agreed.

17. Ibid., p. 141.

18. See John Stuart Mill, *A System of Logic* (Toronto: University of Toronto Press, 1974), p. 851. Likewise see Gottlob Frege, "Review of Dr. E. Husserl's Philosophy of Arithmetic," trans. E. W. Kluge, in *Husserl: Expositions and Appraisals*, ed. Frederick A. Elliston and Peter McCormich (Notre Dame, Ind.: Notre Dame University Press, 1977).

19. See FTL:189: "Whoever has a judicial meaning or opinion and, in explicating it to himself, sees any analytic consequence, not only judges the consequence in fact but *cannot do otherwise [er kann nicht anders]* than judge it."

20. Paul Ricoeur was quite right in saying the problem of interpretation (*Auslegung*) and of the 'divergence' of hermeneutics within Husserl's work emerges in the later texts when phenomenology must account for experience *as a whole* with the emergence of the problem of the alter ego. See his analysis of the fifth of Husserl's *Cartesian Meditations* in this regard in "Phenomenology and Hermeneutics," in *Hermeneutics and the Human Sciences*, trans. John B. Thompson (Cambridge: Cambridge University Press, 1981), p. 124. Nonetheless, as this passage demonstrates, the problem is implicit already within the *Investigations*. While 'the hermeneutic turn' certainly becomes explicit in the problem of the alter ego, it does so precisely because of the character of phenomenological evidence. The other is not then a contingent problem but a necessary one for phenomenology, regardless of the contingency of there being 'other' people in the world or not . . .

21. *Republic*, 510b.

22. Compare Jacques Derrida's discussion of the same matter in his *Edmund Husserl's Origin of Geometry: An Introduction*, trans. John P. Leavey (Stony Brook, N.Y.: Nicolas Hays, 1978), p. 138. "It is not by chance there is no phenomenology of the Idea. The latter cannot be given in person, not determined in an evidence, for its only possibility of evidence and the openness of 'seeing itself.'"

23. See Karl Popper, *The Logic of Scientific Discovery* (London: Hutchinson & Co., 1959), p. 40.

24. See Paul Ricoeur "Conclusions," presented at a conference on *Vérité et Verification* in September 1969 and published under the same title (The Hague: Martinus Nijhoff, 1974), p. 208. The reference occurs in affirming Derrida's discussion referred to earlier in footnote 22.

25. Popper, *The Logic of Scientific Discovery*, p. 43.

26. Ibid., p. 40. Husserl's claim in *Ideas* that "to every cogito there belongs a counterpoint which precisely corresponds to it" (Id:269), the *conditio sine qua non* of "free variation"—and hence *Wesensschau*—has ironical consequences. Phenomenology begins on the basis of a suspension, "a certain having-

something undecided standing there" (Id:258) from which it never returns, never ultimately being able to decide, to completely determine the "standing there" of the evidence of the *protodoxa*. Hence the risk of its rational "extension."

27. See Richard Rorty, *Philosophy and the Mirror of Nature* (Princeton, N.J.: Princeton Unversity Press, 1979), p. 194. Rorty himself proceeded by a turn to the social:

> In particular, we would expect him to say that the reasons normally given for translating languages one way rather than another (or for ascribing one set of beliefs and desires rather than an odd alternative which would predict the same linguistic behavior) are justified simply by their internal coherence, and that such practices as translation and ascription of intentional states are justified by their social utility.

Nonetheless, this turn to the social may not be the only response to Quine's failure here and may in fact still be embedded within it: the need for objective, public, univocally decidable explanations for events. In this regard "Rorty commits an objectivistic fallacy," as Jürgen Habermas, among others, has pointed out. See the latter's "Questions and Counterquestions" in *Habermas and Modernity*, ed. Richard J. Bernstein (Cambridge, Mass.: M.I.T. Press, 1985) pp. 94ff. Popper, too, claimed still within the ease of a certain neo-Kantianism that the words *objective, justifiable,* and *scientific* were all exclusively interrelated, and he distinguished them, consequently, from the subjective, that which remains 'dependent upon particular whims': and hence remains unjustifiable, *The Logic of Scientific Discovery*, p. 44. Nonetheless, although true for neo-Kantianism, such was not the case for Kant himself, notwithstanding Popper's references to Kant. Both in the dialectic of the first *Critique* and the third *Critique* Kant was forced to overcome this ban on the subjective by means of reflective judgment. The 'overcoming' has in fact been recognized by Rorty himself in following Kuhn and trying to overcome the antinomy of taste and reason (336ff). Rorty realized that the locus of this overcoming is precisely the reflective judgment (338n), though he leaves its implications undeveloped in treading too lightly against Quine and opting still for the 'objective unit of the social' for his analysis. In this regard the 'theoretical' accounts of phenomenology would always be closer to 'reflective' judgments, carrying a weaker sense of justificatory commitment and warrant, than those of the 'exact' and strict science it was supposed to ground and on which it falsely modeled itself. It is in this sense perhaps not coincidental that a number of features of phenomenological 'experience' merge into the justificatory archive of the aesthetic.

28. Perhaps in the end the differences between the two research programs turns precisely on this issue. In a later article (1930), Schlick remarked:

> Is it the expression of a remarkable *Gasetzmassigkeit des Soseins* (lawful structure of essences), which forbids a green surface to be at the same time red, or forbids a tone to exist unless it has a determinate

pitch?. . .Fortunately, however, the matter is quite otherwise. . . .Our "materially" *a priori propositions* are in truth of a purely conceptual nature, their validity is a logical validity, they have a tautological, formal character. . . .Red and green are incompatible, not because I happen never to have observed such a joint appearance, but because the sentence "This spot is both red and green" is a meaningless combination of words. The logical rules which underlie our employment of color words forbids such usage, just as they would forbid us to say "Light red is redder than dark red." "Is There a Factual a Priori?" trans. Wilfred Sellars, in *Readings in Philosophical Analysis*, ed. Herbert Feigl and Wilfred Sellars (New York: Appleton Century Crofts, 1949), p. 284.

Doubtless Husserl's consideration on language did not take this tack—which Schlick attributed to Wittgenstein—and consequently, he did not focus on the fact that "such concepts as color have a formal structure just as do numbers or spatial concepts and that this structure determines their meaning" (ibid., p. 285). This much certainly Husserl need not have denied. He would have denied, however, the force of Schlick's ultimate claim: not only does this formal structure determine their meaning but it "determines their meaning without remainder." Here the phenomenologist must balk, wondering whether the 'Wittgensteinian' contribution, if necessary, can also be seen as sufficient, wondering, in fact as Wittgenstein himself ultimately did, whether the claim to analyticity could be "self-sufficient," and whether its supposed 'analytic' and tautologous truth did not return on a kind of synthetic a priori truth. See, for example, *Remarks on the Foundations of Mathematics*, trans. G. E. M. Anscombe (Cambridge, Mass.: M.I.T. Press, 1967). Here the proposition, "There is no such thing as reddish-green, "Wittgenstein stated, "can understandably be called a synthetic a priori proposition" (125).

The force of Wittgenstein's "a priori" became less and less a matter of tautology, to be linked instead to a (synthetic) practice, to use, and consequently, to a necessity that was without strict "logical" grounds. And if, then, Wittgenstein had found a solution to the problem of synthetic a priori judgments, as Schlick and his contemporaries claimed, it was not one that was any less 'mysterious' perhaps. In fact in light of Schlick's claim that the Wittgenstein solution (i.e., the solution of the *Tractatus*) had solved the "mystery of synthetic a priori judgments" (280)—that is, in their elimination—it might be said that the viability of both research programs, logical empiricism and phenomenology alike, as neo-Kantianisms, depended precisely on their being purged of transcendental illusions concerning ultimate grounds. In this regard it is perhaps remarkable to note the extent to which Schlick's final justification of his account repeated the protestations of Husserl's claims: "In the last analysis no one doubts this, and what difficulty there is consists merely in coming to see that the matter is a purely logical one, and with this insight the whole issue is disposed of, and gives rise to no further problem" (284–85).

29. In this regard this Husserlian "remainder" rejoins the fallibilistic consequences of Popper's position: "there can be no ultimate statements in science," *The Logic of Scientific Discovery*, p. 47. Nonetheless this is not to say

that phenomenological "exhibition" (*Aufklärung*) and empirical explanation (*Erklärung*) by default enter into a certain bivalence. On the contrary the exhibitions of Husserlian description will always be formally distinct from the explanatory purports of empirical science, as Husserl realized from the outset.

30. Compare Martin Heidegger's statement in his "Editor's Foreword" to Husserl's *The Phenomenology of Internal Time-Consciousness*, trans. James S. Churchill (Bloomington: Indiana University Press, 1964), p. 15: "Even today, this term 'intentionality' is no all-explanatory word but one which designates a central problem."

31. Hence perhaps the reluctance of Husserl's followers before the language of essences. Compare, for example, Maurice Merleau-Ponty's Preface to the *Phenomenology of Perception*, p. xivf:

> [T]he essence is here not the end but a means. . . .The need to proceed by way of essences does not mean that philosophy takes them as its object, but, on the contrary, that our existence is too tightly held in the world to be able to know itself as such at the moment of its involvement, and that it requires the field of ideality in order to become acquainted with and to prevail over its facticity.

32. Popper, *The Logic of Scientific Discovery*, p. 50. For further discussion, see Imre Lakatos "Falsification and the Methodology of Scientific Research Programmes," in *Criticism and the Growth of Knowledge*, ed. I. Lakatos and A. Musgrave (Cambridge: Cambridge University Press, 1970).

33. Max Scheler, "Phenomenology and the Theory of Cognition," in *Selected Philosophical Essays*, trans. David R. Lachterman (Evanston, Ill.: Northwestern University Press, 1973), p. 139.

34. See Max Scheler, *Formalism in Ethics and Non-Formal Ethics of Values*, trans. Manfred S. Frings and Roger L. Funk (Evanston, Ill.: Northwestern University Press, 1973), p. 50.

35. Jean Cavaillès, "On Logic and the Theory of Science," p. 409.

36. Ibid.

The Dispersion of Dasein

1. See my "Heidegger, Rationality, and the Critique of Judgment," *Review of Metaphysics* 41, No. 3 (March 1988). For further discussion of the textual status of Heidegger's writings, see my "Reading Heidegger," *Research in Phenomenology* 15 (1985).

2. Martin Heidegger, *Being and Time*, p. 83. Further references to this text in this chapter will be placed in parentheses within the text.

3. The question of this dispersion stands at the center of the transcendental deduction and the attempt to ground *Wissenschaft* by means of the institution of a "thorough-going identity of the apperception of a manifold." It required a pure synthesis that would overcome the indeterminacy of the "empirical consciousness which accompanies different representations" and that, Kant claimed, "is in itself disperse and without relation to the identity of a subject (*ist an sich zerstreut und ohne Beziehung auf die Identität des Subjets*)." See Immanuel Kant, *Critique of Pure Reason*, p. 153 (B 133).

4. In this regard, as the Dialectic manifested and ultimately perhaps admitted, if the transcendental deduction was aimed at sublating the dispersion of the finite, the *Critique of Pure Reason* would need to readmit it in granting the failure of the grand ediface of *Wissenschaftslehre*, precisely in reconfronting the problem of application and the plurality of narratives:

> The bold undertaking that we had designated is thus bound to fail through lack of material, not to mention the babble of tongues, which inevitably gives rise to disputes among workers in regard to the plan to be followed, and which must end by dispersing them all over the world (*in alle Welt zerstreuen musste*), leaving each to erect a separate building for himself...(A 707/B 736)

5. On the 'Fichtean' character of Heidegger's account of temporality and 'world entry,' see, for example, Martin Heidegger, *The Metaphysical Foundation of Logic*, trans. Martin Helm (Bloomington: Indiana University Press, 1984), p. 209: "The ecstematic temporalizes itself, oscillating as a worlding (*Welten*). World entry happens only insofar as something like ecstatic oscillation (*Schwingung*) temporalizes itself as a particular temporality."

6. Aristotle, *Metaphysics*, 1006b.

7. Pierre Aubenque, *Le problème de l'être chez Aristote* (Paris: Presses Universitaire de France, 1962), p. 204, cited in Paul Ricoeur, *Freud and Philosophy*, trans. Denis Savage (New Haven, Conn.: Yale University Press, 1970), p. 24. Here Ricoeur likewise connected this issue to the problem of polysemia and the nature of interpretation and traced it equally to the history of metaphysics, to "Platonism, Neoplatonism, and the philosophies of the analogy of Being" (17)—as will become necessary also in the treatment that follows. Still, as will become evident, Ricoeur's treatment of what he called the hermeneutics of suspicion ultimately missed the mark.

8. See Suarez, *Disputations metaphysicae Vol. II* (Hildesheim: Georg Olms, 1965), p. 224; and Heidegger's discussion in *The Basic Problems of Phenomenology*, pp. 81f.

9. Martin Heidegger, "Die Kategorien—und Bedeutungslehre des Duns Scotus," in *Frühe Schriften* (Frankfurt am Main: Klostermann, 1972), pp. 199, 348. This book has since been attributed to Thomas of Erfurt.

10. Ibid., p. 350. See the later Heidegger's discussion of the relation between the *Habilitationschrift* and *Being and Time* in "A Dialogue on Language," in *On the Way to Language*, trans. Peter D. Hertz (New York: Harper & Row, 1971), p. 6f. We should in this regard take more seriously the later Heidegger's retrieval of the *Habilitationschrift* in connection with *Being and Time*'s 'context of discovery,' one which included not only Aristotle (by means of Brentano), the medievals, and Hegel, and likewise not only the work of Husserl or Dilthey, but also Höderlin and Trakl—all written as he put it, "in those days of expressionism." His best readers (which included both Gadamer and Deleuze, as will be seen) have always recognized this complexity.

11. See *Hegel's Science in Logic*, pp. 81ff.

12. See *Hegel's Lectures on The History of Philosophy*, Vol. III, pp. 170ff.

13. See Michel Foucault, "Nietzsche, Freud, Marx," trans. John Anderson and Gary Hentzi in *Critical Texts* 3, No. 2 (Winter 1986): 4.

14. See Michel Foucault, "Theatrum Philosophicum," in *Language, Countermemory, Practice*, ed. Donald Bouchard, trans. D. Bouchard and S. Simon (Ithaca, N.Y.: Cornell University Press, 197), p. 165.

15. See Gilles Deleuze, *Différence et répétition*, pp. 52ff.

16. See John Duns Scotus, *Opus Oxoniense* I, D. 8, q. 3. Compare *Différence et répétition*, pp. 52ff.

17. Spinoza, "The Ethics," in *Works of Spinoza, Volume II*, trans. R. H. M. Elwes (New York: Dover, 1955), pp. 51 (I.X.), 45 (I.VI).

18. Ibid., pp. 11 (II.XL) and letter XL, 395 (January 1675).

19. Ibid., p. 80.

20. Gilles Deleuze, *Spinoza et le problème de l'expression* (Paris: Minuit, 1968), p. 164. Nonetheless, as Deleuze pointed out, Spinoza's account of expression still makes manifest substance—precisely qua expressed. In fact whereas the *Short Treaties* uses the Dutch equivalent of "to express" (*uytdrukken-uytbeelden*), it 'prefers' *vertoonen* (meaning both to express and to demonstrate). See *Spinoza et le problème de l'expression*, p. 11.

21. Deleuze, *Différence et répétition*, p. 59.

22. See Friedrich Nietzsche, "On Truth and Lie in an Extra-Moral Sense," p. 46.

23. Deleuze, *Différence et répétition*, p. 71.

24. Ibid., p. 165.

25. Ibid. Likewise see Gilles Deleuze, *Nietzsche and Philosophy*, p. 48.

26. Friederich Nietzsche, *Beyond Good and Evil*, p. 200; and Deleuze, *Nietzsche and Philosophy*, p. 9.

27. *Différence et répétition*, p. 82.

28. Kant, *Critique of Pure Reason*, p. A660/B688. See Deleuze's 1963 exposition *Kant's Critical Philosophy*, trans. Hugh Tomlinson and Barbara Habberjam (Minneapolis: University of Minnesota Press, 1984), which should be read both in light of its (later) preface, as well as the detailed discussions of *Différence et répétition*, especially Ch. 4.

29. Ibid., p. A 156/B 195.

30. *Différence et répétition*, p. 178.

31. Ibid., p. A179f/B222f. Accordingly, in his doctrine of religion Kant would speak of analogy itself as a "schematism of analogy." Moreover, in accord with his account of teleological judgment, this schematism is identified as one "with which (as a means of explanation [*Erlauterung*]) we cannot dispense"— albeit one that unlike "the schematism of objective determination" cannot be rendered constitutive without resorting to "anthropomorphism." See *Religion Within the Limits of Reason Alone*, p. 58n.

32. See *Hegel's Lectures on The History of Philosophy*, Vol. III, pp. 124f.

33. See Preface (1984) to *Kant's Critical Philosophy*, p. viii.

34. See Deleuze, *Différence et répétition*, pp. 82ff.

35. Gilles Deleuze, "Simulacre et Philosophie Antique," in *Logique du sens* (Paris, Minuit, 1969), p. 302.

36. Deleuze, *Différence et répétition*, p. 77.

37. Deleuze, *Logique du sens*, p. 303. On the importance of Schelling in this regard see *Différence et répétition*, pp. 246f. In fact Deleuze used a version of this argument against Heidegger's attempt to rethink identity as the same that we can articulate "only if we think difference." Here "the same gathers what is distinct into an original being-at-one" [whereas] "the equal on the contrary disperses them into the dull unity of mere uniformity." See Martin Heidegger, ". . .Poetically Man Dwells. . ." in *Poetry Language Thought*, pp. 218–19. For Deleuze, this declaration still remains itself part of "the history of the greatest error, the history of representation, the history of icons, (f)or the Same, the Identical (still) contains an ontological meaning." On the contrary, it matters little if identity is thought as the same or as identity. What matters instead is whether identity is recognized as itself a "second potency" of difference, one in which repetition perdures now as the repetition of Nietzsche's eternal return and identity becomes itself "the image of resemblance as the effect of the disperse," a repetition by which "the Same is always decentered." See *Différence et répétition*, pp. 384–85.

38. See *Logique du sens,* p. 293; and *Différence et répétition,* p. 82.

39. Plato, *The Republic* (524d).

40. Ibid. (528e).

41. Ibid. (524e).

42. Ibid. (525ff).

43. In fact the word *Explikation* occurs only once in *The Critique of Pure Reason* (A730/B758) where, along with other Latin-based terms, it becomes subsumed under the German *Erklärung,* a construal, doubtless, with portentous consequence that has troubled polemics in its wake. If, as has been seen, Kant drew on the archive to which 'explication' belongs, he adjudicated its warrantability wholly in terms of the modernist paradigm of the objective and the demonstrable. But he admitted, likewise, that discursive concepts for a finite intellect remained always partial. Because the only concepts that can be completely defined are ones that have been invented, only in mathematics can there be definitions, strictly taken. In the strict sense neither empirical nor a priori concepts can be defined, but only "made explicit (*explicirt*)" and hence this allows us to make its "completeness probable, never to make it apodeictically certain" (A 727–28/B 756–57).

44. Hans-Georg Gadamer, *Truth and Method,* pp. 502, 505. A similar affirmation occurs in Gadamer's *Hegel's Dialectic,* p. 32:

> Plainly, the concepts of exposition and expression, which properly define the essence of dialectic, the reality of the speculative, must, like Spinoza's *exprimere,* be understood as referring to an ontological process. "Exposition, "expression," being stated, demarcate a conceptual field behind which lies the grand tradition of Neoplatonism. "Expression" is not a matter of subjective choice, i.e. something added on after the fact and by virtue of which the meaning in the private sphere is made communicable. Rather it is the coming into existence of spirit itself, its "exposition." The Neoplatonic origin of these concepts is not accidental.

45. Hegel, *Lectures on the History of Philosophy,* Vol. II, p. 407.

46. Ibid., p. 412.

47. Ibid., p. 429.

48. See Deleuze, *Spinoza et le problème de l'expression,* Ch. 11.

49. Jasper Hopkins, *Nicholas of Cusa on Learned Ignorance: A Translation and an Appraisal of De Docta Ignorantia,* (Minneapolis: Arthur J. Banning Press, 1981), p. 94 (translation altered).

50. Gadamer, *Truth and Method,* p. 435.

51. Nichols of Cusa, *Apologia Doctae Ignorantiae* 18:26f. Cited in Hopkins, *Nicholas of Cusa on Learned Ignorance*, p. 15.

52. See Michel Foucault, *The Order of Things: An Archaeology of the Human Sciences* (New York: Pantheon Books, 1970), pp. 17–45.

53. Ibid., p. 30. Compare in this regard Cusa's *On Learned Ignorance*, p. 94: "[T]here is one explication of all things. The explication of substance, the explication of quality or of quantity, and so on, are not distinct explications" (Translation altered).

54. Ibid., p. 29–30.

55. See Michel Foucault, *Madness and Civilization* (New York: Pantheon Books, 1967), pp. 285ff. Compare Deleuze's similar account of "the absolute privilege of art" in *Proust and Signs*, trans. Richard Howard (New York: George Braziller, 1972), Chapter 4.

56. Foucault, *The Order of Things*, p. 44. Compare Gadamer's discussion of the *verbum creans* as "the first hint of the speculative interpretation of language," *Truth and Method*, pp. 483f.

57. Ibid., p. 42.

58. The shortcoming of Foucault's account in this regard should be contrasted with the version of hermeneutics in his earlier paper, "Nietzsche, Freud, Marx," a paper published a year after *Les mots et les choses*, in 1967. Having delineated the set of characteristics that underlie the "system of interpretation" (1) of the sixteenth century (an analysis similar to *The Order of Things*, pp. 17–25) he proceeded to contrast it with the writings of Marx, Nietzsche, and Freud, who "have put us back into the presence of a new possibility of interpretation; they have founded once again the possibility of a hermeneutic" (2). And, they have done so precisely in questioning the representationalism of classical Cartesianism "according to a dimension which could be called a depth (*profondeur*), as long as this is not taken to mean interiority, but on the contrary exteriority" (2). It is a hermeneutic that, unlike the 'homogeneity' of the sixteenth century, remains always an infinite task and incomplete, one by which "there is in the sign an ambiguous and somewhat suspicious form of ill will and malice" (4) that remains insurmountable. In fact, here too, Nietzsche (and, in particular, Deleuze's reading [4]) are invoked as models. But in this sense, far from being either condemned to a specific episteme that is now past, or simply retrieved in the form of the 'literary,' Foucault here argued, precisely to the contrary, that hermeneutics is an endless task in which "in opposition to the age of the dialectic, which is linear in spite of everything, we have an age of interpretation that is circular" (5). And, in all this hermeneutics and semiology, the 'belief in the absolute existence of the sign,' "are two ferocious enemies" (ibid.). For further discussion of this issue see my "Kant and Foucault: On the Ends of Man."

59. See Heidegger, *The Basic Problems of Phenomenology*, p. 82.

60. Compare Jacques Derrida's similar claim that the distinction between the 'implicit' and the 'explicit' is presupposed in Heidegger's defense here—although he understands the distinction as an 'opposition' that is 'phenomenological.' See "The Ends of Man" in *Margins of Philosophy*, p. 126: "If one looks closely it is the phenomenological opposition "implicit/explicit" (*"implicite/explicite"*) that permits Heidegger to reject the objection of the vicious circle..."

61. Deleuze, *Différence et répétition*, p. 91. Inter alia this is a difference that hangs on the notion of the first intelligible for Aquinas and Scotus. Whereas both in fact claim that the proper object, the first intelligible of the intellect is Being, for Aquinas, 'being' designates what has been abstracted from the sensible species, whereas for Scotus it designates existence in itself, without any determination whatsoever, and taken in its pure intelligibility—or to speak Heidegerrean, wholly devoid of its remnant of the ontic.

62. Deleuze, *Logique du sens*, p. 303.

63. See Roland Barthes, *S/Z*, pp. 5; 209. Barthes identified the following 'hermeneutemes': (1) thematization, (2) proposal, (3) formulation of the enigma, (4) promise of an answer, (5) snare, the pretense to be defined, (6) equivocation, (7) jamming, the insolubility of the enigma, (8) suspended answer, (9) partial answer, and (10) disclosure, decipherment.

64. See Michel Serres, *Jouvences sur Jules Verne* (Paris: Minuit, 1974), p. 235. Serres similarly blocks interpretation as a movement of truth:

> The idea of *explication* slides along a phantasm. It gives the illusion that there exists an inside and an outside, a higher and a lower, a latent and a patent of the implied to be explicated.... It accompanies the hallucination of the foundation and of form, as if precisely there were a foundational (*fond*) and profound (*profonds*) readings of interpretations. The explication-implication couplet is this strange nonsense that a text is not written on a flat page and readable *à la catonade*.

65. In fact Jean-Paul Sartre already marked this 'diaspora' explicitly. See *Being and Nothingness*: "In the ancient world the profound cohesion and dispersion of the Jewish people was designated by the term 'Diaspora.' It is this work which will serve to designate the mode of being of the for-itself; it is diasporatic" (197). And yet this diaspora was always in fact understood by Sartre in a Hegelian manner, precisely, that is, *as a* "being for-itself (*L'etre pour soi; Für-Sich Sein*)" and, thereby, still in accord with the requisites of representationalism and a transcendental logic. Moreover, if he likewise was willing to admit that its unity was always de facto de-totalized, a polyvalent negation (262) whose presence was in fact impossible, never "a pure given appurtenance," it remained true too that its unity was to be instituted wholly in a Hegelian manner, "the necessity of *realizing* (*realiser*) the diaspora by making itself

conditioned there outside within the unity of the self" (277). Deleuze, on the other hand, contested this attempt to restore the diaspora involved to a unity, even if "detotalized." Rather, he returned to Sartre's 1937 ejection of the transcendental ego from the field of the diasporatic to affirm an impersonal field no more individual than personal and in which the 'subject' is never able to resemble that which it founds, one of which it does not suffice to say that it is simply another history. "It is also another geography." See *Logique du sens*, pp. 120–21.

66. Deleuze, *Nietzsche and Philosophy*, p. 1.

67. Hence the later Heidegger would be more direct about the shortcomings of analogical thought. He charged in fact that in analogical thinking "one [still] thinks and explains with regard to correspondence, similarities, universals." See the excerpts from seminar notes 1941–43 in his *Schelling's Treatise on the Essence of Human Freedom*, p. 192. In the thought of Being, on the other hand, " 'analogy' no longer has any basis," precisely because the thought of the 'ontological' difference has called the homogeneity that regulated it (as well as pantheism) into question. Still, Deleuze would not be convinced that Heidegger had ultimately separated himself from the analogical, precisely to the extent that a homology between thinking and what is thought is retained. See *Différence et répétition*, p. 188n.

68. Heidegger, "On Time and Being," p. 21.

69. Ibid., pp. 22–23.

70. See for example "The Origin of the Work of Art" in *Poetry, Language, Thought*, p. 64.

71. *Différence et répétition*, p. 189.

72. Compare in this regard Heidegger's discussion of the differentation and "holding apart the between (*halten auseinander das Zwischen*)" of ontological difference in "The Onto-Theo-Logical Consititution of Metaphysics," in *Identity and Difference*, trans. Joan Stambaugh (New York: Harper & Row, 1969), p. 97.

73. See Heidegger, *The Basic Problems of Phenomenology*, p. 209.

74. See Michel Foucault, "Theatrum Philosophicum," p. 179, and *The Order of Things*, p. 328. The latter immediately claims that "Sade, Nietzsche, and Bataille have understood this on behalf of all those who tried to ignore it; but it is also certain that Hegel, Marx, and Freud knew it."

75. Compare the close of Heidegger's 1963 "My Way to Phenomenology," in *On Time and Being*, p. 82: "The age of phenomenological philosophy seems to be over. . . . But in what is most its own phenomenology is not a school. It is the possibility of thinking, at times changing and only thus persisting, of corresponding to the claim of what is to be thought."

76. See, for example, *Anti-Oedipus*, coauthored with Felix Guatarri, trans. R. Hurley, M. Seem, and H. Lane (New York: Viking Press, 1977). Here Deleuze defended Reich and Marcuse, Lawrence and Miller, against the often raised reproach of "Rousseauism" and "naturalism." If a society is identical with its structures, then "desire threatens its very being," as it is intrinsically revolutionary: "Desire does not 'want' revolution, it is revolutionary in its own right" (16).

Between Truth and Method

Abbreviations of Hans-Georg Gadamer's Works

(HT)   "Historical Transformations of Reason," in *Rationality Today*, ed. Theodore F. Geraets (Ottawa: University of Ottawa Press, 1979).

(IG)   *The Idea of the Good in Platonic-Aristotelean Philosophy* [1978], trans. Christopher Smith (New Haven, Conn.: Yale University Press: 1986).

(TM)   *Truth and Method* [1965], 2 rev. ed., rev. trans. Joel Weinsheimer and Donald G. Marshall (New York: Crossroad Publishing Company, 1990).

(PA)   *Philosophical Apprenticeships* [1977], trans. Robert Sullivan (Cambridge, Mass.: MIT Press, 1985).

(RAS)   *Reason in the Age of Science* [1976], trans. Frederick G. Lawrence (Cambridge, Mass.: MIT Press, 1981).

(HL)   "Hermeneutics and Logocentrism" [1987], in *Dialogue and Deconstruction*, ed. Diane Michelfelder and Richard Palmer (Albany: SUNY Press, 1989).

(HS)   "The Hermeneutics of Suspicion" [1981], *Man and World* 17 (1984).

(I)   "Gadamer on Strauss: An Interview," *Interpretation*, Vol. 12, No. 1 (1984).

1. F. D. E. Schleiermacher, *Hermeneutics: The Handwritten Manuscripts*, p. 111.

2. Bacon, *Novum Organum*, Book I, XXXVI.

3. Wilfred Sellars, "Empiricism and the Philosophy of Mind," in *Minnesota Studies in the Philosophy of Science*, ed. Herbert Feigl and Michael Scriven (Minneapolis: University of Minnesota Press, 1956). Likewise see Jacques Derrida, *Speech and Phenomena*, trans. David Allison (Evanston, Ill.: Northwestern University Press, 1973).

4. Friedrich Neitzsche, *The Will to Power*, p. 300.

5. Ibid., §479ff.

6. René Descartes, *Méditations Metaphysiques* (Paris: J. Vrin, 1978), p. 3.

7. Betti, "Hermeneutics as the General Methodology of the Geisteswissenschaften," in *Contemporary Hermeneutics*, trans. Josef Bleicher (London: Routledge & Keegan Paul, 1980), pp. 73ff. See Immanuel Kant *Critique of Pure Reason*, p. 655 (A836/B864).

8. Gadamer reprinted parts of his letter in Supplement I of *Truth and Method*. The supplement first appeared as "Hermeneutik und Historismus," *Phil. Rundschau* 9 (1962).

9. Cf. Betti, p. 84.

10. Martin Heidegger, *Being and Time*, p. 194.

11. See Hannah Arendt, "What Is Authority?" in *Between Past and Future* (New York: Penguin Books, 1968), p. 126.

12. Georg Wilhelm Friedrich Hegel, *The Philosophy of History*, trans. J. Sibree (New York: Dover, 1956), p. 21. See Leo Strauss, *Natural Right and History*, part VI; Karl Popper, *The Poverty of Historicism*. The seductions of Heidegger's own account of destiny, fate, resoluteness, and the problem of 'the hero' in *Being and Time* have been often pointed out. See *Being and Time*, §74.

13. Compare Heidegger's *Being and Time*. Despite Heidegger's account of meaning and significance as grounded pragmatically (97), despite his account of circumspective practices as grounded pretheoretically (99), and despite his exemplificatioan of these practices by means of craft in opposition to the leveling of mass production (100), Heidegger's account of the *Sinn von Sein* remained irreducible to such practices, trading as would Pierce before him in fact on the medieval account of analogy and transcendence—but without being able to simply reinstate it. Although these evaluations would overdetermine Heidegger's understanding of the leveling of the public realm in *Being and Time*, even in this work neither meaning nor truth would remain reducible to the realm of the pragmatic—or, to speak the language of the later Heidegger, to *techne*.

14. That Gadamer was correct in his reading of *Being and Time* can be read in Heidegger's elaboration of Dasein's forestructure. In discussing *Vorsicht* he said: "In such an interpretation, the way in which the entity we are interpreting is to be conceived can be drawn from the entity itself, or the interpretation can force the entity into concepts to which it is opposed in its manner of Being" (191).

15. Maurice Merleau-Ponty, *The Phenomenology of Perception*, p. 220.

16. Edmund Husserl, *Ideas Pertaining to a Pure Phenomenology*, pp. 128ff.

17. Kant, *Critique of Pure Reason*, p. 137 (A 109).

18. Gadamer, p. 447. I have stressed the text.

19. Theodor Adorno, *Against Epistemology*, trans. Willis Domingo (Cambridge, Mass.: MIT Press, 1982), p. 212. Compare Strauss's charge—notwithstanding his claim that Heidegger remained an historicist—that Husserl "seems to have taken it for granted that there will always be a variety of *Weltanschauungsphilosophien* that peacefully co-exist within one and the same society," "Philosophy as Rigorous Science," p. 31.

20. It is not entirely successful at this either. See Jürgen Habermas, "A Review of Gadamer's Truth and Method," in *Understanding and Social Enquiry*, ed. F. Dallmayr and T. McCarthy (Notre Dame, Ind.: University of Notre Dame Press, 1977), p. 358: "Gadamer's prejudice for the rights of prejudice certified by tradition denies an answer of reflection. The latter proves itself, however, in being able to reject the claim of tradition. Reflection dissolves substantiality because it not only forms, but also breaks up, dogmatic forces."

21. As Gadamer rightly realized, Brentano's "objectivating reflection, traceable to Aristotle," was not the same nor reducible to the mythic "coercion free" reflection stemming from German idealism that underlies that of the critique of ideology. See, for example, *Philosophical Apprenticeships*, p. 186.

22. Martin Heidegger, *The Essence of Reasons*, p. 83.

23. Ibid., p. 25.

24. See Martin Heidegger, *The Metaphysical Foundations of Logic*, p. 172.

25. See Thomas Kuhn, "Reflections on My Critics," in *Criticism and the Growth of Knowledge*.

26. Richard Rorty, *Philosophy and the Mirror of Nature*, p. 338. Still, Rorty's turn remained in this regard simply undeveloped because he opted (unlike the account that follows here) for a 'macro-level' analysis, concentrating, as has been seen, in accord both with pragmatism and positivism, on the level of the social and the 'objective.'

27. See Ronald Dworkin, "Law as Interpretation," *Texas Law Review* 60, No. 527 (1982).

28. See Stanley Fish, "Demonstration vs. Persuasion," in *Is There a Text in This Class?* (Cambridge, Mass.: Harvard University Press, 1980).

29. Bas C. van Fraassen, *The Scientific Image* (Oxford: Clarendon Press, 1980), p. 56f.

30. See Roland Barthes, *Leçon* (Paris: Editions du Seuil, 1978), p. 12.

31. See Jacques Derrida, *Of Grammatology*, p. 61.

32. See in this regard Umberto Eco, "Joyce, Semiosis, and Semiotics," in *The Limits of Interpretation*.

33. *The Essence of Reasons*, p. 97.

34. If Nietzsche's 'critique of truth' is well known, it is not in this regard so far from Schleiermacher's claim that comparisons such as true and false are inappropriate to religion. See the former's *On the Geneaolgy of Morals*, the latter's *On Religion*, pp. 53f.

35. *Of Grammatology*, p. 50. Kuhn similarly noted that Copernicus, Newton, Lavoisier, and Einstein "each transformed the scientific imagination in ways that we shall ultimately need to describe as a transformation of the world within which scientific work was done." Cf. the Introduction to *The Structure of Scientific Revolutions* (Chicago: University of Chicago Press, 1970), p. 6. The importance of imagination should be noted here. At the same time, the transformation inscribed on the notion of 'worldhood' finds a hesitancy later in his text. He stated: "the world does not change with a change in paradigms" (12). And, although realizing that the view of knowledge as an interpretation of already given neutral sense data is undermined by this standpoint, he stated that he finds it "impossible to relinquish entirely that viewpoint" (126).

36. Immanuel Kant, *Critique of Pure Reason*, A 255/B 310. And yet granted Kant's commitments to modernism and its paradigm of rationality modeled on the decidability of deduction, even this *conditio sine qua non* would of necessity be an object of suspicion:

> For there are so many ungrounded claims to the extension of our knowledge through reason, that we must take it as a universal principle that any such pretension is of itself a ground for always being mistrustful, and that, in the absence of evidence afforded by a thoroughgoing deduction, we may not believe and assume the justice of such claims, no matter how clear the *dogmatic* proof of them may appear to us. (A 209–10/B 255)

37. Ibid., A 274/B 100.

38. Johann Gustav Droyson, *Historik. Vorlesgunen über Enzyklopadie und Methodologie der Geschichte*, ed. Rudolf (Munich, 1937) cited in Hayden White's review of this work in *History and Theory* 19 (1980): 88.

39. Kant, *Critique of Pure Reason*, A 133/B 172.

40. Compare in this regard Jacques Derrida's discussion of grafting (*greffant*) and the *force de rupture* it necessitates for semantics in "Signature Event Context," in *Margins of Philosophy*.

41. *Critique of Pure Reason*, A 34/B 173.

42. Ibid., B xvii.

43. The distinction between these terms, as well as their 'opposition,' to use Kant's description, remains enframed by his account of the rational as objective and demonstrable. See Kant, *Critique of Judgment*, §59. Here the distinctions are introduced by means of the problem of "establishing the reality of our concepts." If the concepts are empirical, the intuitions are termed *examples*. On the other hand, all intuitions that are a priori are either *schemata* or *symbols*, of which the former contain direct, the latter indirect presentations of the concept. And, Kant claimed, the "former do this demonstratively; the latter by means of an analogy."

Likewise, see Kant's *Anthropology from a Pragmatic Point of View*, §38. Here, in delineating the products of the *facultas signatrix*, Kant correlatively distinguished between signs and symbols. The latter remain "figurate" and their use involves a "poverty in concepts," whereas with the former the concept is arrived at not mediately but directly. "The sign (character) accompanies the concept when the occasion arises." In the event that this strict 'opposition' would break down, the direct relation between sign and concept would become problematic and the function of the imagination in its figurate content could then not be excluded from any but a merely reproductive role; the relation involved could no longer be direct, and hence devoid of the necessity of interpretation.

44. At first glance the similarity between Kant and Hobbes on the question of judgment is in fact striking. See Leviathan, Volume 3 of *The English Works of Thomas Hobbes*, ed. Sir William Molesworth (London: Bohn, 1839). In both cases judgment and wit seem to be originally opposed: wit being, as Hobbes defined it, the natural form of intellectual virtue: judgment, the acquired (56ff). The lack of the former consequently, "stupidity," cannot be overcome. Good wit, for Hobbes is a person's ability to "observe differently the things that pass through their imagination," observing their similitudes: good judgment, the ability to distinguish between "thing and thing." Reason and science, or "acquired wit," for Hobbes, remain strictly opposed to natural wit and modeled on the *more geometrico*, the knowledge of consequences in proceeding from elements (35). Hence the ancient problem of the basic premises, or as Hobbes understood it, of starting with correct definitions, the "apt imposing of names" (35) a matter which becomes for Kant problematic in a finite intellect.

Of the *Mutterwitz* at the heart of judgment, Kant, too claims that its lack cannot be overcome, and that the result is stupidity, "a failing for which there is no remedy" (B 173). Still, although there are no rules for judgment itself, the transcendental doctrine of judgment provides rules of a priori synthesis and unification by means of the categories and the schemata, accomplishing, thereby, the work of Hobbes's basic elements in the *Leviathan*. In this regard, as the *Anthropology* acknowledged, "wit . . . provides understanding with material for making its concepts general . . . (it provides) flashes of inspiration." Judgment, on the other hand "strives for discernment" and "limits our concepts and contributes more to correcting than to enlarging them" (ibid., p. 90). Nonetheless, whereas this description holds for determinate judgment, an event in which properly speaking imagination (and wit) itself furnished no content, carrying out the synthesis in accord with the requirements of the concept (an *exhibitio originaria*), reflective judgment occurs quite otherwise, as a matter in which imagination and judgment combine without recourse to any (definite) concept. Still, that reflective judgment is viewed *as* objective and ratiocinative (albeit not in a way that can be decided) forces the recognition that judgment in this sphere is in fact ampliative in a way that extends our 'knowledge,' albeit only problematically. The danger in all this for Kant, nonetheless, is that the mind might become "a mere plaything of the imagination" (51). And yet, granted the question of the examples and exemplification that underwrites the transcendental deduction, there is in a sense a risk that is unavoidable, a risk, as Gadamer implied, that forces us to think the belonging together of the *quid facti* and the *quid juris*.

45. Ibid., A 726/B 754. Compare, B xxii: "This attempt to alter the procedure which has hitherto prevailed in metaphysics, by completely revolutionizing it in accordance with the example set by the geometers and physicists, forms indeed the main purpose of this critique of pure speculative reason."

46. Ibid., A 729/B 757.

47. Ibid., A 10/B 13.

48. See, for example, Friederich Schlegel, "Dialogue on Poetry," in *German Romantic Criticism*, ed. A. Leslie Wilson (New York: Continuum, 1982), and §220, p. 129: "wit is the principle and organ of universal philosophy. . ."

49. See Hannah Arendt, *Lectures on Kant's Political Philosophy*, ed. Ronald Beiner (Chicago: University of Chicago Press, 1982), p. 37. It is doubtless in this respect that the best phenomenologists realized that what was at stake involved less a reflective inventory of essences than the art of learning how to see. . .

50. Ibid., p. 85.

51. Ibid., p. 4.

52. See Jürgen Habermas, "On the German-Jewish Heritage," *Telos*, No. 44, (Summer 1980): 131. In this article Habermas credited Arendt with providing "a first approach to a concept of communicative rationality" (130), a view that perhaps declares that the success of the project depends on returning from the protocols of the third *Kritik* to the first.

53. Ibid., p. 129.

54. Immanuel Kant, *Critique of Pure Reason*, B xxxv. "This critique is not opposed to the *dogmatic procedure* of reason in pure knowledge, as science, for that must always be dogmatic, that is, yield strict proof from sure principles

a priori." The question perhaps is whether Kant's model of strict proof as the *nomos* for the rational did not itself harbor a certain dogmatism.

55. See, for example, Ludwig Wittgenstein, *On Certainty*, trans. G. E. M. Anscombe and G. A. von Wright (New York: Harper & Row, 1972), §564: "*Begundung hat ein Ende.*" While Wittgenstein understood this end ultimately in terms of pragmatics, "use," and "forms of life," to use his terms, it still did not prevent him from describing it in the more classical terms of judgment, as is evident from §124: "I want to say: We use judgments (*Urteile*) as principles of judgment." Still, the case in which reason comes to an end is not one in which it simply dissolves, but, again, problematically extends further. Even in the case in which two principles cannot be reconciled, and "each man declared the other a fool and a heretic," Wittgenstein claimed, "wouldn't I give him reasons? Certainly, but how far do they go? At the end of grounds (*Grunde*) comes *persuasion* (*Uberredung*)" (§611–12). What is at stake even regarding propositions that I regard as "certainly true," Wittgenstein declared, is the characteristic of language games to provide "my interpretation of experience (*meine Interpretation der Erfahrung*)" (§145).

56. See "Hannah Arendt's Communications Concept of Power," trans. Thomas McCarthy, *Social Research* (Spring 1977). Habermas claimed that this exclusion of the cognitive in fact presumes "an antiquated concept of theoretical knowledge that is based on ultimate insights and certainties (which) keeps Arendt from comprehending the process of reaching agreement about practical questions as rational discourse" (p. 22). Still, if Habermas was right about the problem of this antiquated account of the distinction between argumentation and ultimate norms, it does not follow that by moving beyond it the realm at stake becomes rationally transparent and decidable, nor that the conflict of interpretations can be put to rest and the arguments involved reduced to simple decidability, let alone decision procedures. Gadamer's *Truth and Method*, it might be said, was motivated from the outset by this insight.

57. See J. G. Fichte, *The Science of Right*, trans. A. E. Kroeger (New York: Harper & Row, 1969), p. 61. Doubtless, the importance of both dialogue and education in modern 'hermeneutics' is in part traceable to this origin. Yet, as will be seen, it is precisely the underdeterminability that results which bars the Fichtean position as a solution to the agonistics of political theory.

58. Hannah Arendt, *On Revolution*, p. 222.

59. Arendt, *Lectures on Kant's Political Philosophy*, p. 67. Arendt referred here to Kant's "Reflexionen zur Anthropologie," no. 767, in *Gesammelte Schriften*, Prussian Academy ed., XV, p. 334–35.

60. Hans-Georg Gadamer, "Text and Interpretation," trans. Dennis J. Schmidt, in *Hermeneutics and Modern Philosophy*, ed. Bruce Wachterhauser (Albany: SUNY Press, 1986), p. 384.

61. See for example, Hans-Georg Gadamer, "The Hermeneutics of Suspicion," *Man and World* 17 (1984): 322. Still, the question becomes one of understanding dialogue beyond the fragmentated infinites of romanticism.

62. See Martin Heidegger, excerpts from 1941–1943 seminar notes, *Schelling's Treatise on the Essence of Human Freedom*, p. 189. Moreover it could not preclude thereby a certain 'errancy' to all extension, one whose very possibility involved a "drifting away into the undefined." See "A Dialogue on Language," in *On the Way to Language*, p. 28.

63. "Text and Interpretation," pp. 381, 387. Especially, it should be noted, how close Gadamer's position perhaps remains to Schlegel, both on the potentials of dialogue and its underlying metaphysics.

64. Ibid., pp. 383, 396.

65. See Leo Strauss and Hans-Georg Gadamer, "Correspondence Concerning *Wahrheit und Methode*," in *The Independent Journal of Philosophy* 2 (1978): 10. This letter dates from April 1961. The status of 'worldhood' itself as will be seen remains ultimately contested here, the status, that is, of a transcendental articuleme and the requisites of interpretation. A later interview perhaps softens this divergence with Heidegger somewhat: "I do not follow Heidegger at all when he talks about new gods and similar things. I follow him only in what he does with the empty or extreme situation." While he could still claim "that there is no city in the world in which the ideal city is not present in some ultimate sense," he likewise admitted the position to be "somewhat overly conservative" (I:10).

66. Notwithstanding a certain complicity with this temptation regarding *memoria*, the status of the withdrawl from the 'worldly' runs throughout Arendt's work—and in its earliest version. See, for example, her discussion of a memory antedating even the world to which, as being 'of the world' humans "belong" in her 1929 thesis, *Der Liebesbegriff Bei Augustin* (Berlin: Springer Verlag, 1929), pp. 44f. Memory, like 'the gatherings' of imagination with which it is in fundamental complicity, is in the end however anything but simply a reproductive faculty here.

67. See Walter Benjamin, "The Storyteller" in *Illuminations*, trans. Harry Zohn (New York: Schocken Books, 1969), pp. 83–84.

68. See Hannah Arendt, "Introduction" to Benjamin, *Illuminations*, p. 41. Compare Nancy's similar remarks in *L'oubli de la philosophie*, p. 89.

69. Arendt, "What Is Authority?" p. 121f. A similar recognition concerning the 'translations' of tradition seemingly occurs in the *Relevance of the Beautiful* where Gadamer is intent on demonstrating the continuity between the artistic avante garde and tradition (RB:49). We are in fact just beginning in this regard to see the profound continuity between 20th century attentiveness to the found,

the everyday, the ready-made, and the ordinary, and its most tumultuous ruptures, for example in dadaism and surrealism—the continuities at work, for example in Wittgenstein, Emerson, and Heidegger (as Cavell for example has noted), but equally, Benjamin, Joyce, or Duchamps, as Gadamer attempts to argue (and thereby the perdurance of tradition, *mimesis*, and *aletheia*). Still, if this continuity makes itself felt, the rupture with tradition (and the question of legitimacy it provokes) must equally be recognized, the event in which coherence becomes deformation, reading both rereading and counter-reading. If, as Emerson put it, "tradition supplies a better fable than any invention can," it remains, as his claim likewise indicates, recognizably now figurative, less a foundation (*arche*) than an invention devalorized of the harmony between *mythos* and *logos*. About all this, as has already been seen, Gadamer's analysis of the work of art remains too silent—and consequently too silent about the 'translations' at stake that are as much interruption and discontinuity as iteration. See Stanley Cavell, *In Quest of the Ordinary* (Chicago: University of Chicago Press, 1988) and Ralph Waldo Emerson, *Representative Men* (Boston: Houghtin Mifflin, 1891), p. 187.

Even Cavell's retrieval cannot be simply affirmed however. Having rightly connected Emerson (or Wittgenstein or Heidegger) to the extensions of postkantian philosophy, the default of certainty and "the recovery from skepticism" (26), he likewise all but misses the complication which results regarding appearance and illusion, the ordinary, the received, and the dogmatic. Poe's horrors, as he puts it, are the "other side" to Emerson's ecstasies. The former, however, he too quickly assimilates to the foibles of analysis, to Moore and the early Heidegger and their centering upon "abstract, specialized, and highly refined examples" (176). In this respect the recognition of the problem of the appearance and dogmatism is lost, the recognition that mere reading will not be enough, requiring the interpretation of the originary—exemplification, judgment and counterexample. It is not of course that the 'everyday' or the 'ordinary' are not to be endorsed, the point is that they cannot be endorsed precritically.

70. Ibid., p. 119.

71. Benjamin, "The Storyteller," p. 98.

72. MacIntyre, *Whose Justice? Which Rationality?* p. 364.

73. Ibid., p. 388.

74. See Hannah Arendt, *On Revolution* and the *ars inveniendi* of representation, pp. 226ff.

75. Rightly understood then, the 'humanities' were neither scientific nor on the way to becoming scientific: neither reducible to nor replacable by something 'scientific.' Claims to objectivity or critique limited to the latter's constraints, consequently, would look equally suspicious before the rational warrants at stake.

76. Hannah Arendt, letter to Karl Jaspers, 29 December 1963. Cited in Elizabeth Young-Bruehl, *Hannah Arendt: For Love of the World* (New Haven, Conn.: Yale University Press, 1982), p. 338.

77. Jean-Luc Nancy, *L'expérience de la liberté* (Paris: Galilée, 1988), p. 205.

78. Alain Renault, *Le system du droit: Philosophie et droit dan la pensée de Fichte* (Paris: Presses Universitaires de France, 1986), p. 7.

79. Luc Ferry, *Rights—The New Quarrel Between the Ancients and the Moderns*, p. 3.

80. Renault, *Le system*, p. 171.

81. Strauss and Gadamer, "Correspondence, " p. 5. It is significant in this regard to note that *Truth and Method* likewise footnotes Strauss in introducing its famous discussion of prejudice (*Vorurteil*) and enlightenment. See TM:271n.

82. Renault, *Le system*, p. 11.

83. Immanuel Kant, *The Metaphysical Elements of Justice*, trans. John Ladd (Indianapolis: Bobbs-Merrill, 1965), p. 58. The difficulties in Kant's attempts to rationally ground right on the science of morality became immediately controversial. By 1795 Maimon, aware as always of problems of determinability, in fact had claimed that natural right was simply distinct from morality. Schelling's 1796 *New Deduction of Natural Right* went perhaps even further in truncating the excess that results from transcendental considerations: "Ethics solves the problem of the absolute will by identifying the individual will with the general, the science of right by identifying the general will with the individual. If both had completely solved their task, they would cease to be contrasting sciences" (para. 72). See F. W. J. Schelling, "New Deduction of Natural Right," in *The Unconditional in Human Nature*, trans. Fritz Marti (Lewisburg, Penn.: Bucknell University Press, 1980), p. 232. Schelling's response then revolves around the excess of freedom: "The general will exists no longer as soon as there is need to save freedom," p. 244.

84. Strauss, *Natural Right and History*, p. 36.

85. Ibid., p. 35.

86. Ibid., pp. 35–36.

87. Strauss, *Studies in Platonic Political Philosophy*, Ch. 1.

88. Leo Strauss *On Tyranny* (New York: The Free Press, 1963), p. 189. Strauss's discussion of Herman Cohen in "Jerusalem and Athens" is likewise relevant here. See *Studies in Platonic Political Philosophy*, pp. 167ff.

89. *Phänomenologische Interpretation zu Aristotles* (Frankfurt am Main: Klostermann, 1985), p. 135. Still it is doubtless significant to note that, notwith-

standing the proximity of pragmatists to instrumentalism and behaviorism, even Dewey, for example was able to acknowledge the complexity in the relation between pragmatism and 'tradition':

> Adoption of the experimental method does not signify that there is no place for authority and precedent. On the contrary precedent is. . .a valuable instrumentality. . . .But precedents are to be used rather than to be implicitly followed: they are to be used as tools of analysis of present situations, suggesting points to be looked into and hypotheses to be tried. . .

John Dewey, *Ethics*, p. 364–65, cited in *The Moral Writings of John Dewey*, ed. James Gouinlock (New York: Hafner, 1976), p. 252.

90. See *Being and Nothingness*, p. 623f.

91. J. B. Vico, "The First New Science," in *Selected Writings*, ed. Leon Pompa (Cambridge: Cambridge University Press, 1982), 139.

92. See Jean-Luc Nancy, *The Inoperative Community*, Ch. 2. Nonetheless—and notwithstanding both the criticisms made earlier and the profundity of Nancy's analyses—it will be necessary to deny the oppositions that underwrite the analysis of Gadamer by Jean-Luc Nancy in *Le partage de voix*, parts of which are translated in *Transforming the Hermeneutic Context*, ed. Gayle Ormiston and Alan Schrift (Albany: SUNY Press, 1990). Nancy is surely right to truncate the distinction between hermeneutics and the *Hermeneuein* that underlies it, right then to separate the event at stake in *Sein und Zeit* even as Dasein's *Vor-aussetzung* from epistemological presuppositions, the presupposition of premises, from simple hypotheses, or even a received preunderstanding: all of which it makes possible (223). Still, if Nancy is doubtless right in resisting what he calls the 'brutality' involved in subsuming the Heideggerean experiment under the presupposition of meaning or communication (or legitimation) (212f), no more, as he realized, can it be seen to be their denial. The *Seinsfrage* is not in short the simple inversion or dissolution of *apophansis* or rationality, if it is endlessly as has been seen, the complication of both. We will need in this regard to consider further the rational status of what elsewhere Nancy described as a "fragmented argument." See *The Inoperative Community*, p. 114.

93. Ferry, *Rights*, p. 59; cf. 199–200.

94. Strauss, *Studies*, pp. 210ff.

95. Strauss, *Natural Right*, p. 102.

96. See Claude Lefort, *Le travail de l'oeuvre machiavell*, (Paris: Gallimard 1972), Ch. 8. As a result, perhaps better than any one else, Lefort was able to see this opening of indeterminacy as the positive origin of democracy:

> The distinguishing feature of democracy is that, whilst it inaugurates a history which abolishes the place of the referent from which the law

once derived transcendence, it does not thereby make law immanent within the order of the world, nor, by the same criterion, does it confuse the rule of law with the rule of power.

See "Human Rights and the Welfare State" in Claude Lefort, *Democracy and Political Theory*, trans. David Macey (Minneapolis: University of Minnesota Press, 1988), p. 39.

97. Strauss and Gadamer, "Correspondence," p. 11.

98. Ibid., pp. 5, 11.

99. Ibid., p. 7. The latter issue, as has been claimed earlier, is crucial. In *On Tyranny*, arguing against Alexander Kojéve's similar Hegelian concerns regarding underdeterminacy, the problem of subjective certainty—the problem then of ideology and the relativity of the 'republic of letters'—Strauss claimed that he preferred the sect to the republic of letters, but immediately denied the choice had to be made. The problem of subjective certainty can be overcome in the recognition that "one cannot know that one does not know without knowing what one does not know" (209). Obviously this is false and misses the problem (of interpretation). One can, after all, know both that no actual theory fulfills adequate criteria for truth—and that more than one does...The question then is knowing whether Strauss's objectivist claims do not turn simply sectarian in the end.

100. "Correspondence," p. 7. See also TM:447–48.

101. Luc Ferry and Alain Renault, *Heidegger and Modernity*, trans. Franklin Philip (Chicago: University of Chicago Press, 1990), p. 96.

102. TM:39. See Luc Ferry and Alain Renault, *La pensée '68* (Paris: Gallimard, 1988), p. 332.

103. Cf. Ferry, *Rights*, p. 111.

104. Ibid., p. 55.

105. It will likewise be critical however to realize the complications at stake in the Fichtean account of dialogue, one by which truth became reduced to communicability and iteration, and validity claims linked to the (modernist political) issue of recognition. If Fichte was correct in importing the question of communication and the intersubjective iterability of validity into the practical domain, such communicability itself likewise became quickly reduced, that is, equated with 'truth' under the aegis of 'objectivity'.

Bacon for example could say of friendship in his essay on this topic (which since Aristotle was the virtue in question—both with respect to community and communicability) that it supports judgment by virtue of "faithful councel". See "Of Friendship," *The Works of Francis Bacon*, Vol. VI, p. 441. Kant would not be far behind in claiming that the communication between friends is "a human necessity for the correction of our judgments." See *Lectures on Ethics*, trans. Louis Infield (Indianapolis: Hackett Publishing, 1979), p. 206. Still, neither of them had simply equated truth with communicability, as would Fichte's demand in the practical realm. Moreover, the equation would in fact lead Fichte into a dilemma, committed both to the importance of conscience ("conscience never errs and cannot err") and the demand that the fallibilism of finitude must give way to the constraints of intersubjective communication insofar as "the more extended this intercommunication is, the more does truth (objectivity considered) gain and I likewise". See *The Science of Ethics*, p. 183; 260.

The Fichtean equation of intercommunication with certainty and security (and, as has been seen, this in turn with the Church of reason) is perhaps one step away from the dissolution of private judgment—not only in those cases for which demonstrable, 'public' adjudication is lacking but equally in those cases which motivate Kant's (protofoucauldian) admonitions concerning "man's...fear of the abuse which others might make of this disclosure of his thoughts" in the public sphere. See *The Metaphysical Principles of Virtue*, trans. James Ellington (Indianapolis: Bobbs-Merrill, 1964) sect. 47. Without openly asceding to the requisites of dialogue, Kant had perhaps realized what was at stake in turning against the classical metaphysics of friendship based upon similarity. As he put it in the *Lectures on Ethics*, not identity but "difference of thought is a stronger bond for friendship, for then the one makes up for the deficiencies of the other" p. 207. Even Fichte himself was however not simply unaware of the irony awaiting. In advance of Sartre he admitted that the issue was not merely a prudential but an epistemic matter: "from the standpoint of transcendental consciousness...it is quite possible that philosophizing individuals do not agree on a single point." See *The Science of Ethics*, p. 254. It is in this sense that dialogue, as hermeneuts realized (again after Schlegel), is less the site in which truth is circumscribed than ventured, its vindication ironically defrayed in the transcendental difference between the posited regulative ideals of 'objectivity' and the (finite) conditions under which its evidence emerges. For further discussion of this issue see my "On the Errancy of Dasein," *Diacritics*, Vol. 19, No. 3–4, Fall-Winter, 1989.

106. For further discussion of this issue, see my "On the Critical Tribunal."

On the De-Lineation of the Visible

Abbreviations of Merleau-Ponty's Works

(SC)   *The Structure of Behavior* [1942], trans. Alden L. Fischer (Boston: Beacon Press, 1963).

(PoP)   *Phenomenology of Perception* [1945], trans. Colin Smith (revised by Forrest Williams and David Guerriere) (London: Routledge & Kegan Paul, 1962).

(Themes)   *Themes From the Lectures at the College de France* [1968], trans. John O'Neill (Evanston, Ill.: Northwestern University Press, 1970).

(Signs)   *Signs* [1960], trans. Richard McCleary (Evanston, Ill.: Northwestern University Press, 1964).

(PNP)   "Philosophy and Non-Philosophy Since Hegel" [1974–1975], trans. Hugh J. Silverman, *Continental Philosophy*, No. 1 (1988).

(VI)   *The Visible and the Invisible* [1964], trans. Alphonso Lingis (Evanston, Ill.: Northwestern University Press, 1968).

(SNS)   *Sense and Non-Sense* [1942], trans. H. L. Dreyfus, P. A. Dreyfus (Evanston, Ill.: Northwestern University Press, 1964).

Abbreviations of Fichte's Works

(I-XI)   *Fichtes Werke* (in eleven volumes following the edition of I. H. Fichte) (Berlin: Walter de Gruyter & Co., 1971). The standard extent English translations will be abbreviated as follows.

(SK)   *Science of Knowledge* [a translation of the 1794–1795 *Wissenschaftslehre*, together with the first and second Introductions (1797), designated as SK I and SK II]. trans. Peter Heath and John Lachs (Cambridge: Cambridge University Press, 1982).

(Critique) *Attempt at a Critique of All Revelation* [1793], trans. Garrett Green (Cambridge: Cambridge University Press, 1978).

(VM)   *The Vocation of Man* [1800], trans. Roderick M. Chisolm (Indianapolis: Bobbs-Merrill, 1956).

(Religion) "The Way Towards the Blessed Life or The Doctrine of Religion" [1806] in *The Popular Works of Johann Gottlieb Fichte*, Vol. 2, trans. William Smith (London, Trubner & Co. 1889).

(SR)   *The Science of Rights* [1796], trans. A. E. Kroeger (New York: Harper & Row, 1970).

(VS)   *The Vocation of the Scholar* [1794], in *The Popular Works of Johann Gottlieb Fichte*, Vol. 1, trans. William Smith (London: Trubner & Co., 1889).

1. See Immanuel Kant, *Critique of Pure Reason*, p. 183 (A 141/B 180): "*Dieser Schematismus unserus Verstandes, in Ansehen der Erscheinungen und ihrer blossen Form, ist eine verborgene Kunst in den Tiefen der menschlichen Seele.*"

2. This characterization is taken from a similar neo-Kantian critique of Fichte by Hermann Cohen. See the latter's *Kants Begrundung der Ethik 2te Auflage*

(Berlin: Cassirer, 1910), p. 291. Compare Merleau-Ponty's own claim that each organ of sense "is the agent of a certain type of synthesis" (PoP:223). That this position, too, is not without its own ancient roots, however, can be seen already in Aristotle's claim that sense perception is the act of a bodily organ. See *De Sensu et Sensibili* 1, 436, b.7.

3. See Hans-Georg Gadamer, "Die phänomenologische Bewegung," in *Kleine Schriften III* (Tubingen: J.C.B. Mohr: 1972), p. 159.

4. See Martin Heidegger, *Being and Time*, pp. 73f.

5. See Max Scheler, *Formalism in Ethics and Non-Formal Ethics of Values*, p. 403. Compare Merleau-Ponty's similar claim that "the problem we have set ourselves [is] that of sensorality, or finite subjectivity" (PoP: 240–41).

6. Ibid.

7. Johann Martin Chladenius, "On the Interpretation of Historical Books and Accounts," in *The Hermeneutics Reader*, ed. Kurt Mueller-Vollmer (New York: Continuum, 1985), p. 67.

8. See, for example, Michel Foucault, "Body/Power," *Power/Knowledge*, trans. C. Gordan, L. Marshall, J. Mephan, and K. Soper (New York: Pantheon Books, 1980).

9. See Aristotle, *De Anima* 457.

10. See Kant, *Critique of Pure Reason*, p. 474 (A 550/B 578):

[W]hen we consider these actions in their relation to reason—I do not mean speculative reason, by which we endeavor *to explain* their coming into being, but reason insofar as it is itself the cause *producing* them—if, that is to say, we compare them with [the standards of] reason in its *practical* bearing, we find a rule and order altogether different from the order of nature.

11. Ibid., p. 164 (B151).

12. See Immanuel Kant, *Anthropology from a Pragmatic Point of View*, pp. 48, 44. See Heidegger's similar discussion of this passage in his *Phänomenologische Interpretation von Kant's Kritik Der Reinen Vernunft* (Frankfurt am Main: Klostermann, 1977), p. 278. A similar definition occurs in *The Critique of Pure Reason*, p. 165 (B151).

13. Both Fichte and the phenomenologists would deny this thesis concerning observables in the human realm, though without, as will be seen, being ultimately able to demonstrate their possibility, *pace* appeals to the 'strictness' of their descriptions.

14. The motivation for Fichte's line-drawing 'schema' also is not without Kantian origins. Indeed, the necessity of such a 'transcendental' figuration arose,

it might be claimed, precisely as an effect of acknowledging the antinomial conflict concerning origins, that is, a conflict in which the identity of the appearing and the appearance could not be guaranteed, enforcing, thereby, the inextricable link between thought, thinkability, and appearance. With respect to time, the universal form of appearance, however, it becomes precisely in this respect *overdetermined* in the Kantian text, in fact a question of presenting the unpresentable, the condition of the conditioned. Having tied all appearances to time, Kant could not make time, the condition of appearance itself, appear except as phantasm, that is, as the distortion of an effect. The event of time's representation, this figuring of the *figürlich*, already a certain distension of the present, hence became itself figured only 'figuratively'—precisely in the pure generation of a line:

> We cannot think a line without *drawing* it in thought, or a circle without *describing* it. We cannot represent the three dimensions of space save by *setting* three lines at right angles. . . . Even time itself we cannot represent, save insofar as we attend, in the *drawing* of a straight line (which has to serve as the outer figurative representation of time), merely to the act of synthesis of the manifold whereby we successively determine inner sense. . .(p. 167/B154)

Fichte's text doubtless reflects also a transformation of this schematism, one now more aesthetic than mathematical, already privileging in this regard the free play of imagination.

15. Compare in this regard Plato's account of cosmological origin and its "formless form" in which both Being and becoming would be differentiated in *Timaeus* 50f.

16. Kant, *The Critique of Pure Reason*, p. 144n (A121n.). Kant's ejection of psychology from the realm of science can be found in a 1786 text whose similar appeal to a linear analogue is not perhaps without impact on those in his wake, See *Metaphysical Foundations of Natural Science*, trans. James Ellington (Indianapolis: Bobbs-Merrill, 1970), p. 8.

17. See G. W. F. Hegel, *Faith & Knowledge*, p. 89, and Hegel's description of the event whereby Reason separates itself out of extension, an intuitive activity that, he claimed, as the unity of the intellect itself "is at bottom nothing but the *same Idea* of the transcendental imagination."

18. G. W. F. Hegel, *Lectures on The History of Philosophy,* Vol. 3, p. 496.

19. This citation is from the 1795 treatise, *Grundriss de Eigenthümlichen Wissenschaftslehre.* The process of schematization is further described as a transition (*Uebergehen*) from a state in which the self finds itself distinguished from an object that is originally confused. Precisely through its own vacillation and by means of the application of arbitrary schemata regarding figure, size, and color, the object is ultimately able to be brought to image and to complete

determination (*zu der völligen Bestimmung*) (I:374), an act whereby, he claimed, it becomes my product (*Es wird mein Product*) (I:375). If in this 'recollection' Fichte antedated Hegel's account, the account of transitional fulfillment perhaps likewise antedates Husserl's account of the fulfillment of phenomenological intuition.

20. As commentators such as Joachim Widmann have claimed, the concept of projection Fichte invoked, requiring a three-dimensional figure or plane, remains Euclidean (in accord, too with a model at work in Kant's Transcendental Aesthetic, as has been seen). See Joachim Widmann, *Analyse der formalen Strukturen des Transzendentalems Wissens in Fichtes 2. Wissenschaftslehre in dem Jahre 1804* (Munich, 1961), p. 153.

21. In fact in appealing to a certainty that we would prove by *making*, Fichte had in the Kantian sense already exchanged discursive exposition for mathematical intuition. As Kant put it in the first *Critique*: "Whereas. . . mathematical definitions *make* their concepts (*den Begriff selbst machen*), in philosophical definitions concepts are only explained (*nur erklären*). See p. 588 (A370/B759).

22. The account of embodiment surely then is not without impact on the political theory of the *Rechtslehre* itself. Whereas Fichte's theory remains innovative not only with respect to its articulation of embodiment but equally to the primacy granted to the category of the social, what results, granted his account, is still a view of the political as a conglomerate of Cartesian subjects who freely interact on one another in "reciprocal causality. . .through conceptions and after conception, only this giving and receiving of knowledge" (SR:61). Like all principles of analogy, however, matters of reciprocal causality, as Kant had declared in the third analogy of experience, are always matters of existence and relation and cannot be constructed by a concept (or an intention), being indeterminately regulative. See *Critique of Pure Reason*, p. 210 (A 179/B 222).

Doubtless Fichte's transformation of the transcendental (epistemic) de juris into political right suffers in this regard and suffers almost immediately with respect to questions concerning the natural, the right that is "to the continuance of our free influence upon the whole sensuous world" (SR:169). Setting aside the various analyses of embodiment, gender, and power that have arisen in Merleau-Ponty's wake, furthering complicating intentional analyses, even in limiting considerations (as we have done here) to epistemic question, Merleau-Ponty's response is forthright:

Idealism (like objective thought) bypasses true intentionality, which is *at* its object rather than positing it. Idealism overlooks the interrogative, the subjunctive, the aspiration, the expectation, the positive indeterminacy of these modes of consciousness, for it is acquainted only with consciousness in the present or future indicative, which is why it fails to account for class. (PoP:446)

Although, as will be seen, Merleau-Ponty remained 'Fichtean' in all this in describing freedom as both centrifugal and centripetal (PoP:439), Fichte himself, enframing the indeterminacy of this upsurge in the categories of *Wissenschaftstheorie*, doubtless missed the implications of its indeterminacy—and consequently what Hegel recognized as the problem of subjective certainty—or Marx ideology (though both would be similarly mystified perhaps concerning Fichte's elevation of praxis). Instead both consciousness and its law remain fully transparent, the phenomenology of embodied freedom still mystified in the illusions of determinacy constructed in the transference of theory to practice. The '*Wechsel*' between moral law, the extensions of imagination, and civil legislation will be more complex. See Marc Richir's analysis in "Révolution et transparence social, présentation et notes de J. G. Fichte," *Considerations sur la révolution française* (Paris: Payot, 1974). Nonetheless, this much must be acknowledged, notwithstanding what Merleau-Ponty would call the "high altitude thinking" that prevades Fichte's thought; Fichte's discovery opened the modern space of reflection on embodiment and the political. In the 1794 *Vocation of the Scholar* when he began his meditation on Society, openly invoking the *Wechselwirkung nach Begriffen* as Kantian, he likewise originated his reflection by asking the question, "By what authority (*Befugniss*) does man call a particular portion of the physical world *his body*?" (VS:160). Moreover, its implications were recognized to be immediately political: a question "which must be answered...before any natural right is so much as possible" (ibid.).

23. G. W. F. Hegel, *Faith and Knowledge*, p. 177.

24. Ibid., p. 178.

25. Ibid., p. 174.

26. F. W. J. Schelling, *On University Studies*, pp. 12–13:

Action! action! is a call that resounds on many sides, but is uttered most loudly by those who cannot get ahead with knowledge...We ask: What kind of action is it in relation to which knowledge is a means, and what kind of knowledge in relation to which action is an end? What grounds can be advanced for so much as the possibility of such an antithesis?

27. See Edmund Husserl, *Formal and Transcendental Logic*, p. 292.

28. The problematic character of this 'schematism' can be seen in Husserl's *The Crisis of European Sciences and Transcendental Phenomology*. If Husserl had conceived the life world as governed by a transcendental ontology, that is, as obeying an "essentially lawful set of types" (173), its transcendentality likewise always turned its "exhibiting" provisional, i.e., horizontal. The kinesthetic hold, the "holding sway" of consciousness on its body (107) is, after all, not without its own indeterminacy—horizonal and hypothetical. As Husserl too put it, within the system of altering kinestheses I recognize a hidden art: "I recognize that a hidden intentional 'if then' relation is at work here" (161).

29. This reference to a motion that would transcendentally generate space, in fact, is not only a concern of Merleau-Ponty's, but in French commentators of Kant preceding him. See, for example, Pierre Lachieze-Rey, *L'idéalisme kantien* (Paris: Alcan, 1932), pp. 264ff. Lachieze-Rey too refers the issue back to Kant himself, who in the Transcendental Deduction claims in explicating the synthesis of the *Figurlich* that "motion, as an act of the subject (not as a determination of an object), and therefore the synthesis of the manifold in space, first produces the concept of succession." See *The Critique of Pure Reason*, p. 167 (B154).

30. F. W. J. Schelling, "Philosophical Letters on Dogmatism and Criticism," p. 181.

31. See, for example, Max Scheler's analysis of the moral upsurge, "the *dynamis* through which the inmost personal Self strives" in *The Eternal in Man* (New York: SCM, 1960), p. 89. Compare Husserl's similar rejection of the 'Mythology of activities' in defining 'act' instead as intentional experiences, not as mental activities in *Logical Investigations*, Vol. 2. p. 563n.

32. See Jean-Paul Sartre, *The Transcendence of the Ego*.

33. See Martin Heidegger, *Being and Time*, pp. 23ff.

34. See, for example, Guenter Schulte, "Von Sinn der Wahrnehmung: Die Wissenschaftslehre Fichtes und Merleau-Ponty's *Phänomenologie der Wahrnehmung*," *Tijdschrift voor filosofie* 21 (December 1969): 742.

35. F. W. J. Schelling, "Zur Geschichte der neueren Philosophie" [1827], *Werke*, Vol. 5, p. 164.

36. Merleau-Ponty explicitly referred this notion of *le principe ''barbare''* to Schelling. (Themes:75; cf VI:30).

37. See Spinoza, "The Ethics," in *Works of Spinoza*, p. 117 (II.XLIV.I).

38. Already in *The Structure of Behavior* Merleau-Ponty in fact had claimed that his criticism of transcendentalism and neo-Kantianism were "not [applicable] to Kantian philosophy, which particularly in the *Critique of Judgment*, contains essential indications concerning the problems of which it is a question here" (SC:248n.41).

39. The term is Marc Richir's. See the latter's *Phénomènes, Temps, et Êtres* (MontBonnot and St. Martin: Editions Jerome Millon, 1987), p. 28. For further discussion of the issue of the "latent conflict of the phenomenological and the systematic" in the third *Kritik*, see Jacques Taminiaux, *La nostalgie de la grèce a l'aube de l'idéalisme allemand* (The Hague: Martinus Nijhoff, 1967), Ch. 2.

40. See, for example, G. W. F. Hegel, *Faith and Knowledge*, p. 86. Compare Kant's own introduction of the *intellectus archetypus* within the domain of teleological judgment in section 77 of *The Critique of Judgment*, pp. 256f.

41. See, for example, Immanuel Kant, *Gesammelte Schriften, Vol. XXI [Opus Postumuml* (Berlin: Walter De Gruyter, 1936), pp. 13f. Taken in itself, however, Kant still realized that Spinoza's concept of God remained illusory, precisely a *conceptus fanaticus.* Compare Merleau-Ponty's discussion in Lachieze-Rey's wake (PoP:372).

42. Cf. SC:212. Likewise compare the account of the later Merleau-Ponty's critique of reflection:

(W)e all reach the world, and the same world, and it belongs to each of us, without division or loss, because it is *that which* we preceive, the undivided object of all our thoughts....This unity suffices and it untangles every problem, because the division that can be opposed to it, the plurality of the fields of perceptions and of lives, are as nothing....This movement of reflection will always at first sight be convincing: in a sense it is imperative, it is truth itself, and one does not see how philosophy could dispense with it. The question is whether it has brought philosophy to the harbor, whether the universe of thought to which it leads is really an order that suffices to itself and puts an end to every question. (VI:31)

43. Compare in this regard Merleau-Ponty's affirmation of the act of perception in the wide sense, "which at one stroke cuts through all possible doubts to stand in the full light of truth *(en plein verite)*" (PoP:40) with the recognition later that we can provide a successful account of the rationality of perceptual consciousness "only by removing apodeitic certainty from perception and full self possession from perceptual consciousness" (PoP:343).

44. See VI:251. Paul Ricoeur previously claimed of the imagination that it is "perhaps primarily a militant power in the service of a diffuse sense of the future by which we anticipate the actual-to-be as an absent actual at the basis of the world." See *Freedom and Nature* [1950], trans. Erazim V. Kohak (Evanston, Ill.: Northwestern University Press, 1966), p. 97.

45. See G. W. F. Hegel, *Philosophy of Nature,* trans. A. V. Miller (Oxford: Oxford University Press, 1970), pp. 31f (Ency:§255f).

46. F. W. J. Schelling, "New Deduction of Natural Right" §9, p. 222.

47. Heidegger, *Phänomenologische Interpretation von Kants Kritik der Reinen Vernunft,* p. 399.

48. Compare Heidegger's own phenomenological transformation of the transcendental imagination as *exhibitio originaria* and the dovetail between spontaneity and receptivity within the Kantian *Figurlich,* ibid., pp. 412f. Heidegger's account here, however, must likewise be considered ultimately in relation to his later 'aesthetic' writings, most notably "The Origin of the Work of Art," in *Poetry, Language, Thought.* See especially the latter's discussion of the problem of figure and 'figuration' (69f) of art as "the setting into work of truth" (77)—one "beyond the deliberate action of the subject" (67).

49. See Emmanuel Levinas, "Meaning and Sense," in *Collected Philosophical Papers* (The Hague: Martinus Nijhoff, 1987), pp. 83ff.

50. The recognition is already nascently present in *The Structure of Behavior*:

[T]he life of consciousness outside of self. . .on the one hand, and, on the other, the consciousness of self and of a universe, which we are reaching now—in Hegelian terms, consciousness in-itself (*en-soi*) and consciousness in-and-for-itself (*en et pour soi*)—cannot be purely and simply juxtaposed. The problem of perception lies completely in this duality. (SC:176)

51. If this 'play' is irreversible and unsurpassable, judgment remains instead dependent on an 'opening' that extended beyond it, resulting in a truth that inevitably risked being 'one-sided' or 'partial'—or to use Merleau-Ponty's already loaded term, *deferred*. Hence, as Jacques Derrida would aptly put it— in fact, fully consistent with Merleau-Ponty's premises—"the phenomenological model (is) itself constituted, as a warp of language, logic, evidence, fundamental security, upon a woof that is not its own." See *Of Grammatology*, p. 67. The commitment to consciousness could not, therefore, simply avoid the possibility that archaically threatened the transcendental moment, a threat, moreover, Fichte himself—even more stringently attached to that commitment—had already raised, still hoping to conquer it on practical grounds. Granted reason's dependence on conditions that escape it, Fichte claimed—granted, that is, the ambiguity and underdetermination that occurs regarding the *Wechsel* of interpretation—there remains the risk that 'understanding' (like explanation, as has been seen) remains a "dormant inactive power of the mind, the mere receptacle of what imagination brings forth" (SK:207).

In this regard, only in those writing in Fichte's wake would an attempt be made at wholly determining the unity of reason and imagination. Compare in this regard Novalis's "Fichte Studies" [1795–1796] in his *Schrifen*, Vol. 2 (Stuttgart: W. Kohlhammer, 1960), and its search for a *"höhere Wissenschaften,* in which the ego is wholly an art (*Kunst*)" (294).

52. Martin Heidegger, *Nietzsche* Vol. 3, trans. Joan Stambaugh, David Farrell Krell, and Frank A. Capuzzi (San Francisco: Harper & Row, 1987), pp. 80–81.

53. If a Nietzschean reading of the later Merleau-Ponty inextricably gains a certain force (as it had for Heidegger before him), for each the importance of Schelling should not be underestimated. See, for example, Merleau-Ponty's Schellingian gloss on the problem of the abyss in the 1957 lecture course on "The Concept of Nature" (Themes:74f). Even the title of VI itself is not without its overtones. In concluding the introduction to *Ideas for Philosophy of Nature*, Schelling wrote: "Nature should be Mind made visible, Mind the invisible Nature" (42). Nonetheless, as has become evident, the elements of VI can no more be reduced to the 'metaphysics' of Schelling's idealism than to the 'empiricism' of Nietzsche's transgression.

54. In fact Scheler in the *Ethics* had already utilized the model of this *Wechsel* in describing the "levels of existence" within the lived body (422), only, as has been seen, to resolve what he called the distinction between the "schema of our lived body" (411) and the ego, the *Wechsel*, that is, between its *Ineinandersein* and *Aussereinandersein* (413) à la Fichte. That is, like Fichte, the account remains in the end logocentric, ultimately invoking the unity of the personal act and reinstituting again the account of the mental as a harmony between opposites—precisely, for Fichte, a substance.

55. See, for example, the article of Xavier Tilliette by the same name: "Une Philosophie Sans Absolu," *Etudes*, No. 342 (September 1961). Likewise see Rudolf Boehm, "*Chiasma*: Merleau-Ponty und Heidegger," in *Durchbliche: Martin Heidegger zum 80. Geburtstag* (Frankfurt am Main: Klostermann, 1970).

56. It is perhaps anything but accidental that Arendt would rejoin Merleau-Ponty precisely at this point, affirmatively citing this passage. See Hannah Arendt, *The Life of the Mind: Thinking* (New York: Harcourt Brace Jovanovich, 1978), p. 23.

57. Martin Heidegger, "A Dialogue on Language," p. 18.

58. See again Cohen, *Kants Begrundung der Ethik*, p. 139.

59. Ibid., p. 290.

60. The classification is in fact that of Hegel's of the *Encyclopedia*, as described in the text which was the subject of Merleau-Ponty's last lectures. See Martin Heidegger, *Hegel's Concept of Experience*, trans. Kenley Royce Dove (New York: Harper & Row, 1970), p. 145.

61. Cohen, *Kants Begrundung der Ethik*, p. 291. In fact the problem of the 'incarnation' of the rational forces precisely an account that refuses to strictly separate the rational from the 'biographical.' What has been at stake in the archive that extends from Fichte onwards concerning the circularity of assertion and context, imagination and judgment is precisely the demand for the recognition of the 'reciprocal envelopment,' the exchange or transformation between 'biography' and 'narrative.' It is in fact this 'circularity' that characterizes the underdeterminability *and* the warrant of reason *as* 'hermeneutic.'

62. The result of this double meaning is complex, a logic Merleau-Ponty had attempted to capture from the outset. In 1946 articulating *la rêverie herméneutique* of Freud, for example, he began by articulating a domain that extends beyond proof:

> Whatever is arbitrary in Freud's *explanations* (*explications*) cannot. . . discredit psychoanalytic intuition. . . . For if the suggestions of the analyst can never be proven, neither can they be eliminated: how would it be possible to credit chance with the complex correspondences which the psychoanalyst discovers between the child and the adult?. . .Unlike the

natural sciences, psychoanalysis was not meant to give us necessary relations of cause and effect but to point to motivational relationships which are in principle simply possible. [SNS: 24]

Still, if the connectives involved lack sufficient explanation to deny the charge of arbitrary interpretation, it is not the case that they lack rationality or cognitive competency. Indeed it is perhaps precisely the mark of their rationality that the decipherment takes place, transforming contingency into necessity. Merleau-Ponty accordingly cited Cezanne's response to the charge that the painter merely interprets: " 'J'entends que le peintre l'interprete' Cezanne says, 'le peintre n'est pas un imbecile' " (SNS:15).

63. See Max Scheler, *Gessammelte Werke*, Vol. 9 (Späte Schriften [Aus kleineren Manuskripten zu *Sein und Zeit*], herausgegeben von Manfred S. Frings (Munich: Franke, 1976), p. 297. In fact Scheler's aborted argument for this solution occurred while likewise convincingly arguing that Heidegger's account of care as Dasein's essential structure already presupposes it.

On the Right to Interpret

1. Michel de Montaigne, "Apology for Raymond Sebond," in *The Complete Essays of Montaigne*, trans. Donald M. Frame (Stanford, Calif.: Stanford University Press, 1965), p. 390.

2. The characterization doubtless appears overly Nietzschean. And yet Nietzsche was perhaps preeminent in the recognition of the overdetermined character of the Copernican turn. Far from being restricted to the arts and letters or the "human sciences," the *problem* of interpretation for Nietzsche arises in the modern period as an everpresent accomplice to (or step beyond) the upheavals in the 'sciences' generally. See *On The Genealogy of Morals*, p. 155: "Since Copernicus, man seems to have got himself on an inclined plane—now he is slipping faster and faster away from the center into—what? into nothingness? into a '*pennetrating* sense of his nothingness'?"

3. Even Popper, however, admitted a fundamental continuity or analogy— or perhaps more precisely, a reinstitution of analogy fundamental to each— between description and myth. See, for example, "Towards a Rational Theory of Tradition," *Conjectures and Refutations*, pp. 130f.

4. See Michel Foucault, "The Discourse on Language," in *The Archaeology of Knowledge1*. Cf. G. W. F. Hegel, *Philosophy of Nature* (Encyclopedia, part II), p. 11: "All revolutions, in the sciences no less than in world history, originate solely from the fact that Spirit, in order to understand and comprehend itself, has changed its categories. . ."

5. See G. W. F. Hegel, *The Philosophy of History*, Introduction; see W. Dilthey, *An Introduction to the Human Sciences*, p. 146.

6. Alexandre Koyré, *From the Closed World to the Infinite Universe* (New York: Harper & Brothers, 1958), p. 43.

7. Hans Blumenberg, *The Genesis of the Copernican World*, trans. Robert M. Wallace (Cambridge, Mass.: MIT Press, 1987), p. 632.

8. See Jürgen Habermas, "Knowledge and Human Interests: A General Perspective," appendix to *Knowledge and Human Interests* (Boston: Beacon Press, 1971), pp.301f.

9. See Heidegger's discussion, "What Is a System and How Does Philosophy Come to Build Systems?" in his *Schelling's Treatise On The Essence of Human Freedom*, pp. 22ff.

10. See Heidegger's *Kant and the Problem of Metaphysics* trans. Richard Taft (Bloomington: Indiana University Press, 1990), § 3.

11. Giambattista Vico, Section I of Book II (Poetic Metaphysics) in *The New Science*, pp. 116ff.

12. Kant, *Critique of Pure Reason*, p. 18 (B ix); see Aristotle, *Metaphysics* 1025b.

13. See Jacques Derrida, "Signature Event Context," trans. Samuel Weber and Jeffrey Mehlman, *Glyph I*, p. 189. Derrida's point is made in response to Austin's turn to contextualization, precisely to show that the move to context, or to history, or to conceptual framework and practice, in default of classical foundationalism, will not solve its strong (and valid) justificatory demands.

14. Kant, *Critique of Pure Reason*, p. 490n (A575n/B603n): "The observations and calculations of astronomers have taught us much that is wonderful; but the most important lesson that they have taught us has been by revealing the abyss of our *ignorance* which otherwise we could never have conceived to be so great."

15. *De Docta Ignorantio* II.11.

16. Leibniz, letter to Sophie, August 1696, quoted in Michel Serres, *Le système de Leibniz et ses modèles mathématiques* (Paris: Presses Universitaires de France, 1968), Vol. 2, p. 660.

17. René Descartes, *Meditations on First Philosophy*, meditation II.

18. Michel Serres, *Le système de Leibniz et ses modèles mathématiques*, Vol. 2, p. 791. Compare Russell's solution for this problem in his conclusion to a *Critical Exposition of the Philosophy of Leibniz* (London: 1900) and its claim that Leibniz's philosophy is grounded in ethics, or practical reason, a view that qua critical, repeats Fichte's response to Kant—as much as it foretells Wittgenstein's of the *Tractatus*.

19. Ibid.

20. Pascal, quoted in Serres, *Le système de Liebniz*, Vol. 2, p. 659.

21. Ibid., p. 662. Compare Heidegger's similar argument concerning Leibniz in *The Metaphysical Foundations of Logic*, pp. 100ff.

22. See Immanual Kant, "Concerning the Ultimate Foundation of the Differentiation of Regions in Space," in *Selected Pre-Critical Writings*, trans. G. B. Kerferd and D. E. Walford (Manchester: Manchester University Press, 1968), pp. 41f. Against the "modern concept" of space that would reduce reality to external relation or extension, Kant argued for "an internal difference [which] remains..."

23. See Ludwig Wittgenstein, *On Certainty*, p. 2 (§1): "If you do know that *here is one hand*, we'll grant you the rest." Contrast this on the other hand with the optimism—and the pragmatics—of Schelling (more exuberant than even Moore himself on such 'pure-takings'): "Whoever is absorbed in research into Nature, and in the sheer enjoyment of her abundance, does not ask whether Nature and experience be possible. It is enough that she is there for him: he has made her real by his very *act*, and the question of what is possible is raised only by one who believes that he does not hold the reality in his *hand*." See *Ideas for a Philosophy of Nature*, p. 9.

24. See Maurice Merleau-Ponty, "The Intertwining—the Chiams," concluding chapter to *The Visible and the Invisible*.

25. See Martin Heidegger, *Being and Time*, pp. 102f. Likewise see the analysis of Didier Franck in *Heidegger et le problème de l'espace* (Paris: Minuit, 1986), Ch. 7, "L'Entrecroisée des Mains."

26. On the analogy of the hand and soul see *De Anima* 432a: on the status of the 'movement which unites', 433b. Here too the problem of this difference and the joint between the sensible and the intelligible is not absent, though it is one that remains homogenously resolvable—for Aristotle, not a difference *de re*. Speaking of the 'instrument of appetite' and the bodily effect of the psychic, Aristotle claimed: "(T)hat which is the instrument in the production of movement is to be found where a beginning and an end coincide as e.g. in a ball and a socket joint; for there the convex and the concave sides are respectively an end and a beginning (that is why the one remains at rest, the other is moved): they are separate in definition but not separable spatially."

27. Kant, "Concerning the Ultimate Foundation of the Differentiation of Regions in Space," p. 42.

28. See Michel Serres, third part of *Le système de Leibniz*, Vol. 2, and his extension of this account in *L'Interférence* (Paris: Minuit, 1972).

29. Hegel, *Phenomenology of Spirit*, p. 34.

30. See Hegel, *Science of Logic*, pp. 463f. The point in fact is already nascent in Kant's "all analysis presupposes synthesis"—or at least in Fichte's gloss, "no synthesis is possible without a preceding antitheses". . . See the latter's critique of analysis in his 1794 *Science of Knowledge*, pp. 111f.

31. Ibid., p. 13. Hence, he claimed, "Spirit, on the contrary, may be defined as that which has its centre in itself." See Hegel's lectures on *The Philosophy of History*, p. 17. Doubtless this 'center' extended throughout Hegel's thought, invoking consistently "the right of action to evince itself as known and willed by the subject as thinker," the "right of the objectivity of action" as he put it in *The Philosophy of Right*, trans. T. M. Knox (Oxford: Oxford University Press, 1967), p. 82.

32. See *Monadology* § 69 and Serres's discussion, *Le système de Leibniz*, p. 800.

33. Compare, for example, Plato's account of perception in the *Republic* 524d. The articulation of perception in terms of the enumerable and *mathesis*, the question of the one and the many, is one that accompanied it from the outset and one to which it will be necessary to return.

34. See Evandro Agazzi, "From Newton to Kant: The Impact of Physics on the Paradigm of Philosophy," *Abba Salama* 9 (1978).

35. See the Husserl-Dilthey correspondence in *Husserl: Shorter Works*, ed. Fred Elliston and Peter McCormack (Notre Dame, Ind.: University of Notre Dame Press, 1981).

36. Edmund Husserl, *Formal and Transcendental Logic*, p. 291.

37. See Husserl's account of this "retrogression" in *Experience and Judgment*, p. 41 (§10), and the analysis of Jean Cavaillès in "On Logic and the Theory of Science," p. 398.

38. The problem of such a *Spielbedeutung*, denying Husserl's reduction of all meaning to the foundations of intentional experience occurs as early as the 1900 *Logical Investigations*, Vol. 1 § 20 and persists—axiomatically—throughout his work. It will be the subject of further discussion in the essay that follows.

39. Hence the inevitable objection in contemporary thought that the crisis was less a crisis in 'philosophy' than the failure of one of its paradigms, i.e., 'epistemology.' See, for example, Richard Rorty, *Philosophy and the Mirror of Nature*, and more specifically regarding Husserl, Michel Serres, *L'Interférence*, p. 46.

40. See Edmund Husserl, "Foundational Investigations of the Phenomenological Origin of the Spatiality of Nature," trans. Fred Kersten, in *Husserl: Shorter Works*. Here Husserl claimed: "Perhaps phenomenology has supported Copernican astrophysics—but also anti-Copernicianism according to which God

had fixed the earth at a place in space" (229). Transcendentally, in any case, "the earth does not move" (225). Rather, "its orientation-center (is) in me" (227).

41. See Nicholas of Cusa, De Docta Ignorantia I.

42. René Descartes, Regulae XIV.

43. Regulae XII.

44. See Johann Heinrich Lambert, Philosophische Schriften, Vol. 2: Neues Organon. (Hildesheim: Georg Olms, 1965). 'Semiotic' for Lambert concerns the relation between thoughts and things and is expressly and essentially connected by him with questions of 'phenomenology,' as will be seen.

45. See Edmund Husserl, Logical Investigations, Investigation Vol. 1 §20.

46. See G. W. Leibniz, Principles of Nature and Grace § 17.

47. Compare Edmund Husserl "On the Concept of Number," trans. Dallas Willard, Husserl: Shorter Works. If from the outset, or since The Philosophy of Arithmetic (1891), in fact, Husserl had claimed "the concept something" is "more primitive" (117) with respect to acts of conceptual exposition or combination in identity and difference—which are in turn "reciprocally conditioning functions" (107), it is still true that, qua differentiation with respect to identity, number and the enumerable remain an essential condition of knowledge, insofar that, as a concrete instantiation of multiplicity, it is the expression of a pure form of synthesis, that is, "the empty form of difference" (107). Moreover, although the direct antecedent of Husserl's solution here is doubtless Bolzano, the proximity of Hegel's discussion of the antinomies of intensive and extensive magnitude, should not be missed. See the discussion of Quantum in The Science of Logic, pp. 217ff.

48. See Montaigne, "Apology for Raymond Sebond," p. 374. As Herman Weyl likewise realized, Husserl's invocation of the epoche had modern overtones, modeled more geometrico with antecedents that were equally Hobbesian. "Hobbes in his treatise De Corpore starts with a fictitious annihilation of the universe (similar to Husserl's 'epoche') in order to let it rise again by a step by step construction from reason." See Philosophy of Mathematics and Natural Science, trans. Olaf Helmer (Princeton, N.J.: Princeton University Press, 1949), p. 112.

49. Edmund Husserl, The Crisis of European Sciences and Transcendental Phenomenology, p. 42. Compare Foucault's similar argument against 'hermeneutics' in The Order of Things, pp. 44f.

50. Ibid., p. 155.

51. Immanuel Kant, Letter to Marcus Herz, 1772. Philosophical Correspondence, trans. Arnulf Zweig (Chicago: University of Chicago Press, 1967), p. 59.

52. Compare the analysis of Paul Ricoeur in his "Kant and Husserl," in *Husserl: An Analysis of His Phenomenology*, trans. Edward G. Ballard and Lester E. Embree (Evanston, Ill.: Northwestern University Press, 1967).

53. See, for example, Kant, *Akademieausgabe*, Vol. 21 (*Opus Postumum*), p. 174.

54. J. Heinrich Lambert, *Philosophische Schriften*, Vol. 2 (1965).

55. Ibid., p. 217.

56. Ibid. Compare in this regard Hegel's attempt to 'ontologize' the equivocity of appearance as the illusion-appearance of essence (*das Scheinen des Wesen*) in his *Science of Logic*, pp. 479f.

57. Ibid., p. 236.

58. Ibid., p. 220.

59. Ibid.

60. Kant, *Critique of Pure Reason*, p. 298 (A295/B352).

61. Ibid., pp. 532f (A642f/B670f).

62. Ibid., p. 273 (A256–57/B312–13).

63. Ibid., p. 273 (A265/B255).

64. See for example Immanuel Kant, *Foundations of the Metaphysics of Morals*, trans. Lewis White Beck (Indianapolis, 1959), pp. 69f. For further discussion of this issue, see my "Kant on Autonomy, the Ends of Humanity, and the Possibility of Morality," *Kantstudien* 77, No. 2 (1986).

65. Nicholas of Cusa, *De Docta Ignorantia* II, 11.

66. Nicholas of Cusa, *De Ludo Globi*, 219.

67. Nicholas of Cusa, *Idiota de Menta*, c. 2.

68. Whereas the use of these terms is Heideggerian, they are Kantian in origin. See Heidegger's "The Onto-theological Constitution of Metaphysics," in *Identity and Difference*, and Kant's *Critique of Pure Reason*, p. 525. (A632/B660).

69. See Pierre Duhem, *Medieval Cosmology*, pp. 449f.

70. See Leibniz, "Principles of Nature and Grace," § 2, and Nietzsche, *The Gay Science*, p. 336.

71. See Kant, *Critique of Pure Reason*, p. 311 (A314/B371). Compare Kant's invocation of the plurality of standpoints precisely in the denial that "morality is a phantom of the mind" in the *Foundations of the Metaphysics of Morals*, p. 64.

72. Immanuel Kant, *Metaphysical Foundations of Natural Science*, p. 134.

73. In fact the strategy for resolving "if not ending" the undecidability involved in antinomial conflict by relying precisely on the deferral of play operative in the sequential synthesis between homogeneous and heterogeneous elements; that is, the "time order in the connection of the condition and the conditioned" already emerges with the problem of astronomical theory in the precritical writings. See *Universal Natural History and the Theory of the Heavens*, trans. W. Hastie (Ann Arbor: University of Michigan Press, 1969), pp. 72f. On the issues of "cosmological inference" and the problem of "time order" in the "Transcendental Dialectic," see the first *Critique*, pp. 444–45 (A499f/B527f). Finally, compare Blumenberg's discussion, *The Genesis of the Copernican World*, pp. 588f.

74. Immanuel Kant, *Critique of Judgment*, p. 137 (translation revised).

75. Ibid., pp. 136f.

76. G. W. F. Hegel, *Philosophy of Mind*, trans. William Wallace, together with the Zusatze in Baumann's text (1845) trans. A. V. Miller (Oxford: Oxford University Press, 1971), p. 156 (§415).

77. Ibid.

78. See Fichte's account of phenomenology in the 1804, *Wissenschaftslehre*, *Fichtes Werke* Vol. 10 (Berlin: de Gruyter, 1971), pp. 195f.

79. See Hegel's *Phenomenology*, pp. 492f. Compare Husserl's similar description of the gallery of images and the transformation of all mental events of "phantasyings into phantasyings" in *Ideas Pertaining to a Pure Phenomenology*, p. 246.

80. See Duhem, *Medieval Cosmology*, pp. 509f.

81. See Marc Richir, *Au delà du renversement copernicien* (The Hague: Martinus Nijhoff, 1976), p. 31.

82. Ibid., p. 33.

83. Michel Serres, *Le système de Leibniz*, Vol. 2, p. 810.

84. See Richir, Ch. 5, "L'articulation de l'au-dela du renversement copernicien."

85. See Martin Heidegger, *Holzwege* [1935–1946] (Frankfurt am Main: Klostermann, 1963).

86. Serres, *Le système de Leibniz*, Vol. 2, p. 810. Compare Merleau-Ponty's similar claims concerning the "labyrinth of first philosophy" in "The Concept of Nature I," *Themes From the Lectures at the College de France*, p. 90. Although Merleau-Ponty too borrows the phrase from Leibniz, now, he claims, it is to

be taken "in the strict sense." Serres himself would attempt to defend relativism on its basis. See for example, *L'Interférence*, pp. 40, 64.

87. Immanual Kant, *Critique of Judgment*, p. 119.

88. Kant, *Critique of Pure Reason*, p. 264 (A247/B303). Still, compare, as has been seen, Kant's positivist reduction of 'exposition' 'explication' 'declaration', and 'definition', to *Erklärung* on p. 587 (A730/B758).

89. Ludwig Wittgenstein, *Remarks on the Foundations of Mathematics*, p. 61. It is doubtless important to recall in this regard that having denied justification to assertions lacking publically endorsable criteria of identity, in particular whether I might be justified before myself in using the words 'I am in pain,' Wittgenstein notes, "To use a word without a justification does not mean to use it without right." See Ludwig Wittgenstein, *Philosophical Investigations* §289.

90. Kant, *Critique of Pure Reason*, p. 228 (A203/B245).

91. Montaigne, "Apology for Raymond Sebond," p. 390.

92. *Experience and Judgment*, p. 163.

93. Ibid., p. 40.

94. Ibid., p. 346. The claim again is evident as early as *The Philosophy of Arithmetic's* account of synthesis in which distinguishing and identifying are held to be reciprocally conditioning functions and the concepts of multiplicity and unity generated (by reflection) out of them as mutually interdependent concepts. See *Husserl: Shorter Works*, p. 107. Nonetheless if such claims are transcendentally 'true', it surely does not follow that this holds true of the concept of 'something' in general. To think such is the case would be to conflate certainty with truth, the ontic and the ontological.

95. Ibid., p. 341.

The Philosopher's Text

1. Jacques Derrida, *Of Grammatology*, p. 10.

2. Ludwig Wittgenstein, *Lectures & Conversations*, ed. Cyril Barret (Berkeley: University of California Press 1967), p. 26.

3. Giovanni Boccaccio, *The Decameron*, trans. G. H. McWilliam (New York: Penguin Books, 1986), p. 68. (Pampinea, Giornata J.).

4. See Hans Blumenberg, *Work on Myth*, p. 628.

5. *Republic*, (534c).

6. Immanuel Kant, *Critique of Pure Reason*, p. 21 (B xv). Ludwig Wittgenstein, *Philosophical Investigations*, trans. G. E. M. Anscombe (New York: Macmillan Company, 1953), § 109, p. 47.

7. *Republic* (424c).

8. Kant, *Critique of Pure Reason*, p. 21.

9. Ibid., pp. 488–89 (A573/B601).

10. James Joyce, *Ulysses* (New York: Vintage Books, 1961), p. 515; cf. pp. 432, 504.

11. Ibid., p. 589.

12. On the sublime in modern art, see, for example, Jean François Lyotard, "Presenting the Unpresentable: The Sublime," *Artforum* 20 (April 1982); T. W. Adorno, *Aesthetic Theory*, pp. 280ff. On the gnostic in modernism, see, for example, Jürgen Habermas, "Modernism Versus Post-Modernism," *New German Critique* 22 (1981); Harold Bloom, "*Agon*," *Towards a Theory of Revisionism* (Oxford: Oxford University Press, 1982). Neither of these concepts can be 'borrowed' from their classical site unchanged, however.

13. See, for example, Gilles Deleuze, *Logique du sens*, pp. 325ff.

14. Adorno, *Aesthetic Theory*, p. 470. Examples at the extreme were works such as Cage's 'silent' compositions, Reinhardt's black paintings, Dadaist writing, etc. But there is a sense as well in which 'good' and 'bad' are perhaps derivative questions for modern art.

15. See, for example, Nelson Goodman, "Fiction for Five Fingers," *Philosophy and Literature* 6, Nos. 1 and 2: 163–64. Compare on the other hand Paul Veyne's remark in *Did the Greeks Believe in Their Myths?* trans. Paula Wissing (Chicago: University of Chicago Press, 1988), pp.21f: "According to a certain program of truth, that of deduction and quantified physics, Einstein is true in our eyes. But if we believe in the *Iliad*, it is no less true according to its own mythical program."

16. Kant, *Critique of Pure Reason*, p. 163 (B149).

17. See Rudolf Carnap, *The Logical Structure of the World and Pseudoproblems in Philosophy*, trans. Rolf A. George (Berkeley: University of California Press, 1967).

18. David Hume, *A Treatise of Human Nature* (Oxford: Oxford University Press, 1968), p. 219).

19. Joyce, *Ulysses*, p. 34.

20. Derrida, in fact, at one point suggested that their entire disagreement rested on equivocations on this point and the implications of the relations obtaining between this term's grammatical-institutional sense and the possibilities of epistemic 'incommensurabilities' which haunt it (between traditions, but also between speaker's meaning and language meaning, to use Gricean terms). See Derrida, "Limited Inc. a b c. . .," trans. Samuel Weber, *Glyph* 2 (1978): p. 203.

21. Kant, *Critique of Pure Reason*, p. 27n. (B xxxvi).

22. René Descartes, *Meditations on First Philosophy*, trans. Laurence J. Lafleur (Indianapolis: Bobbs-Merrill Co., 1960), p. 55.

23. See Nicholas of Cusa, *De Ludo Globi*, 219.

24. Immanuel Kant, *Anthropology from a Prgamatic Point of View*, p. 93.

25. Ibid., p. 53.

26. John R. Searle, "The Logical Status of Fictional Discourse," *New Literary History* 6, No. 2 (Winter 1975): 329–31.

27. Ibid., p. 331.

28. Ibid.

29. John R. Searle, "Literal Meaning," *Erkenntnis* 13 (1978): 219.

30. Ibid., p. 220.

31. Compare Searle's discussion of the character of the intentional origin of the speech action, "What Is an Intentional State?" *Mind* 78, No. 349 (1979): 89.

The mind imposes Intentionality on entities that are not intrinsically Intentional by intentionally transferring the conditions of satisfaction of the expressed psychological state to the physical entity. The double level of Intentionality in the speech act can be described by saying that by intentionally uttering something with a certain set of conditions of success, those that are specified by the essential conditions for the speech act, I have made the utterance Intentional, and thus necessarily expressed the corresponding psychological state.

32. Such theoretical completeness remains, as Michel Serres realized, a function of the classical novel in the same way that it was a posit of classical physics: "The classical novel is determinist and determined. It is a system with a hierarchy, a closed narrative, homogeneous, open to evaluation on all points, regulated locally as it is globally." *Jouvences dur Jules Verne*, p. 241.

33. As Umberto Eco rightly saw in this regard, "Fictional worlds are the only ones in which sometimes a theory of rigid designation holds completely." See *The Limits of Interpretation*, p. 80.

34. Samuel Beckett, "Dante...Bruno...Vico...Joyce," *Our Exagmination Round His Factification for Incamination of Work in Progress* (Paris: Shakespeare and Company, 1929), p. 22.

35. See *The Republic* (588).

36. Ibid., (354b).

37. Gorgias, "Encomium of Helen," trans. George Kennedy, in *The Older Sophists*, ed. Rosamund Kent Sprague (Columbia: University of South Carolina Press, 1972), p. 52.

38. Ludwig Wittgenstein, *The Blue and Brown Books* (New York: Barnes & Noble, 1969), p. 28.

39. Plotinus, *Enneads* (V.7.3.)

40. Edmund Husserl, "The Origin of Geometry," in *The Crisis of European Sciences and Transcendental Phenomenology*, p. 362.

41. Edmund Husserl, *Logical Investigations*, Vol. 1, p. 305. And yet in one sense at least, in the same text Husserl admitted the failure of the project, the impossibility of carrying out the task of determination. "Strike out the essentially occasional expressions from one's language, try to describe any subjective experience in unambiguous, objectively fixed fashion: such an attempt is always plainly vain" (I, 322). On the problem of "games meaning" (*Spielbedeutung*), "unconscious equivocation," and the "surrogative function" of the sign, see § 20, pp. 304f. The reference to Lambert's *Neues Organon* and its semiotics should be noted.

42. See Wilfrid Sellars, *Science, Perception, and Reality* (London: Routledge & Kegan Paul 1963), pp. 25–28. Similarly for the Sellarisan 'syntactic' reversal on intentionality, see "Empiricism and the Philosophy of Mind," in the same volume.

43. See John T. Blackmore, *Ernst Mach: His Work, Life, and Influence* (Berkeley: University of California Press, 1972), pp. 319f.

44. See, for example, the introduction to Gaston Bachelard's *Le matérialisme rationnel* (Paris: Presses Universitaires de France, 1953), pp. 19f. Bachelard's commitments to French Hegelianism and the solution of *realization* or "phenomotechnics" however brought him close to the failures of instrumentalism.

45. See Jacques Derrida, *Edmund Husserl's "Origin of Geometry, an Introduction*," p. 101. Still, if for Derrida it was necessary to acknowledge this equivocity "which grows in the very rhythm of science," it could not be a question of dissolving the latter or of simply choosing against Husserl. In fact the opposite is true:

> Absolute univocity is inaccessible, but only as an Idea in the Kantian sense can be. If the univocity investigated by Husserl and the equivocation generalized by Joyce are in fact *relative*, they therefore are not so *symmetrically*. For their common *telos*, the positive value of univocity, is immediately revealed only within the relativity that Husserl defined. Univocity is also the absolute horizon of equivocity. (104).

These implications regarding this interplay between reflection and determination, the univocal and the equivocal, judgment and its excess should perhaps be taken as paradigmatic for the Derridean construal of the rational.

46. Wittgenstein, *Philosophical Investigations*, § 125.

47. Ibid., p. 4e (§ 6).

48. Edmund Husserl, *Ideas Pertaining to a Pure Phenomenology*, pp. 43-44.

49. Kant, *Critique of Pure Reason*, p. 144n. (A 120n).

50. Kant, *Anthropology*, p. 55.

51. Ibid., p. 56.

52. *Anthropology*, p. 56. This reference to the business of the philosophical, the cognitive, and the serious also makes a crucial entrance in the third *Critique* in defusing the play of imagination in poetry and rhetoric. See Immanuel Kant, *Critique of Judgment*, p. 165:

> The arts of speech are *rhetoric* and *poetry*. Rhetoric is the art of carrying on a serious business of the understanding as if it were a free play of the imagination; *poetry*, the art of conducting a free play of the imagination as if it were a serious business of the understanding.
>
> The *orator*, then, promises a serious business, and in order to entertain his audience conducts it as if it were a mere *play* with ideas. The *poet* merely promises an entertaining play with ideas, and yet it has the same effect upon the understanding as if he had only intended to carry on its business.

53. *Anthropology*, p. 55.

54. Ibid., p. 52.

55. See "A Dialogue on Language," *On the Way to Language*, p. 28.

56. Ibid., p. 56.

57. Ibid., p. 52.

58. Kant, *Critique of Pure Reason*, p. 61 (A15, B29).

59. Kant, *Anthropology*, pp. 52-53. In fact Kant states immediately about this "as if" that "this cannot be—at least we cannot conceive how heterogeneous things could sprout from one and the same root." (52). Nonetheless, a note accompanying the statement explicates the result. Even lacking an account of origins, the task of exposition is not lost: "It is true that we arrive at knowledge of this nature by experiencing its operations; but we cannot reach the ultimate cause and the simple components into which its material can be analyzed" (53n). This is, it should be added, precisely his account of the unwieldy event of freedom in the *Religion*, distinguishing it from the miraculous. See *Religion within the Limits of Reason Alone*, p. 129n-130n. It is moreover equally true of the ethical union of individuals: "All we know is the duty which draws us toward such

a union" (130n). The same event, finally, might be claimed for the unwieldy account of discourse here, one again not without decipherable laws. Indeed the *Anthropology* already provided hermeneutic protocols for explicating the ungroundedness of ordinary discourse: "So, in starting a social conversation we must begin with what is near and present, and then gradually go on to more remote subjects, if they be of interest" (52n).

60. *Science of Logic*, pp. 354ff.

61. Cf. Kant's statement in the *Anthropology*: "Unreason (which is not mere lack of reason but something positive) is, like reason itself, a mere form into which objects can be fitted, so that both reason and unreason are ordered to the universal," pp. 87–88.

62. Hegel, *Faith and Knowledge*, p. 80.

63. *Science of Logic*, p. 368.

64. Ludwig Wittgenstein, *On Certainty*, p. 73e (§ 559), translation altered.

65. Compare, for example, similar discussions by MacIntyre and Arendt in this regard. See Alasdair MacIntyre, *After Virtue* (Notre Dame, Ind.: Notre Dame University Press, 1981), p. 89; Hannah Arendt, "What Is Authority?" *Between Past and Future*, p. 136ff. Likewise as has been seen, the importance of Lefort's discussion of Machiavelli and indeterminacy should be noted. See *Le travail de l'oeuvre de Machiavel*, Ch. 6.

66. Thomas Hobbes, *Leviathan*, pp. 69–70.

67. Ibid., p. 23.

68. See in this regard Hélène Cixous, *The Exile of James Joyce*, trans. Sally A. S. Purcell (New York: David Lewis, 1972), Conclusion.

69. *Leviathan*, p. 736.

70. See Hans-George Gadamer, *Truth and Method*, pp. 350, 476.

71. See Ludwig Wittgenstein, *Philosophical Investigatons*, § 28, 215.

72. Ibid., § 216.

73. The position emerges at least as early as the *Brown Book's* declaration that "What we call 'understanding a sentence' has, in many cases, a much greater similarity to understanding a musical theme than we might be inclined to think" (167).

74. Compare Ludwig Wittgenstein, *Tractatus Logico-Philosophicus*, § 1.13 p. 31, and *Philosophical Investigations* § 203, p. 82. See Gadamer's discussion of what he calls "the interpenetration of interpretation and rhetorics" in "On the Scope and Function of Hermeneutical Reflection," in *Philosophical Hermeneutics*, pp. 21ff.

75. See Beckett, "Dante. . . Bruno. . .Vico. . .Joyce."

76. See Giovanni Boccaccio, *The Decameron*, pp. 47, 294.

77. See René Descartes, *Discourse on Method*, trans. Donald A. Cress (Indianapolis: Hackett, 1980), p. 2.

78. This is not of course to say that such an experience or its 'phenomenology' might become foundational. Despite his flirtations with a phenomenology of pure grammar, a project which reunites him with the transcendentalism of both Kant and Husserl, Wittgenstein's epistemological break in the *Investigations* equally transforms the project of both: "Justification by experience comes to an end. If it did not it would not be justification." See *Philosophical Investigations* § 485.

79. W. V. O. Quine, "A Postscript on Metaphor," in *On Metaphor*, p. 201.

80. Compare Wolfgang Stegmüller, *The Structure and Dynamics of Theories* (New York: Springer-Verlag, 1976), pp. 170–80, and Richard Bernstein's discussion of this issue in *Beyond Objectivism and Relativism* (Philadelphia: University of Pennsylvania Press, 1983), pp. 56ff.

81. Michel Foucault, *Madness and Civilization: A History of Insanity in the Age of Reason*, p. 110.

82. Ibid.

83. See Foucault, ibid., p. 288:

After Sade and Goya, and since them, unreason has belonged to whatever is decisive, for the modern world, in any work or art. (285). . . [T]hrough madness, a work that seems to drown in the world, to reveal there its non-sense, and to transfigure itself with the features of pathology alone, actually engages within itself the world's time, masters it, and leads it. . . (288)

84. See Immanuel Kant, *Logic*, trans. Robert S. Hartman and Wolfgang Schwarz (Indianapolis: Bobbs-Merrill, 1974), p. 83. Kant also realized that "(O)ccasionally prejudices are true provisional judgments." The point, however, is that their truth always remains to be vindicated and "it is wrong. . . (if) we should let them pass as principles or *determining* judgments" (83). On the contrary "(P)rovisional judging is therefore a consciously problematic judging" (82). The question is when the problematic of judgment, that is, its 'hermeneutic,' can simply be discarded.

85. Ludwig Wittgenstein, *Philosophical Investigations*, § 198.

86. Plato, *Ion* (535a).

On the Rationality of the Fragment

1. Friederich Nietzsche, *On the Genealogy of Morals*, p. 23 (Preface § 8).

2. Algirdas Julien Greimas, *On Meaning*, trans. Paul J. Perron and Frank Collins (Minneapolis: University of Minnesota Press, 1987), pp. 50f.

3. Nietzsche, *Genealogy*, p. 23 (Preface § 8).

4. Friederich Schlegel, "Athenaeum Fragments," in *Lucinde and the Fragments*, trans. Peter Firchow (Minnesota: University of Minnesota Press, 1971), p. 239 (§ 443).

5. See Greimas, Ch. 3.

6. Nietzsche, *Genealogy*, p. 80 (II § 13).

7. Ibid., p. 148 (III § 24).

8. Ibid., p. 15 (Preface § 1).

9. See Edmund Husserl, *Zur Phänomenologie des inneren Zeitbewusstseins* (1893–1917), ed. Rudolf Boehm (Husserliana, Vol. 10: The Hague: Martinus Nijhoff, 1966); Likewise, See Martin Heidegger, *Being and Time*, p. 28; also see Roland Barthes, *S/Z*.

10. Nietzsche, *Genealogy*, pp. 151, 153 (III § 24).

11. Ibid., p. 147 (III § 23).

12. Ibid., p. 157 (III § 26).

13. Schlegel, "Athenaeum Fragments," p. 166 (§ 43). See J. G. Fichte, *Science of Knowledge*, § 5.

14. Novalis, *Schriften*, Vol. 3, p. 227.

15. Nietzsche, *Genealogy*, p. 143 (III § 22).

16. Barthes, *S/Z*, p. 3.

17. See Martin Heidegger, *The Metaphysical Foundations of Logic*, pp. 65ff.

18. Gilles Deleuze, *Le pli: Leibniz et le baroque* (Paris: Minuit, 1988), Ch. 3.

19. Jean-Paul Sartre, *Being and Nothingness*, trans. Hazel Barnes (New York: Washington Square Press, 1966), p. 120.

20. Even when in the *Critique of Dialectical Reason* Sartre had seemingly reduced this ambiguity by means of dialectic and the event through which "the experimenter must see his own life as the Whole and the Part, as the bond between the Parts and the Whole, and as the relation between the Parts in the

dialectical movement of Unification"(52), he likewise realized that its synthesis was only at best regulative (46), and that the difference between totalization and totality was unsurmountable, opening in an event where all ultimate synthesis is impossible.

21. T. W. Adorno, *Aesthetic Theory*, p. 165 (VI:7).

22. Schlegel, "Critical Fragments," *Lucinde and the Fragments*, p. 155 (§ 104).

23. See Michel Foucault, "How Much Does it Cost for Reason to Tell the Truth?" *Foucault Live*, trans. John Johnson (New York: Semiotexte 1989), p. 251. Compare Wittgenstein's 'dismantling' of the notions of extension and multiplicity in the *Philosophical Investigations'* articulation of the (formally) uncircumscribed notion of language game:

> For I *can* give the concept 'number' rigid limits in this way, that is, use the word "number" for a rigidly limited concept, but I can also use it so that the extension of the concept is not closed by a frontier. And this is how we do use the word "game" (§ 68).

Hence the fragmentation of the Wittgensteinian 'treatise', articulating and articulated at the same time: "Each of the sentences I write is trying to say the whole thing, i.e. the same thing over and over again; it is as though they were all simply views of one object seen from different angles." See Ludwig Wittgenstein, *Culture and Value*, trans. Peter Winch (Chicago: University of Chicago Press, 1980), p. 7.

24. Schlegel, "Athenaeum Fragments," p. 234 (§ 427).

25. Nietzsche, *The Gay Science*, pp. 253 (§ 319), 280 (§ 344).

26. Francis Bacon, *Novum Organum* § XXVI.

27. Adorno, *Aesthetic Theory*, p. 117 (V:2).

28. Ibid., pp. 184–85, (VII:9).

29. Jacques Derrida "Cinquante-deux aphorismes pour un avant propos," *Psyché* (Paris: Galileé, 1987), p. 517, § 46.

30. See Friederich Schlegel, "Lessing: Vom kombinatorischen Geist," in *Schriften und Fragmente* (Stuttgart: Kroner, 1956).

31. Nietzsche, *Genealogy*, p. 146 (III:23).

32. On the origins of the problem of a transcendental differential, one again that arguably depends on a certain dissonance between the modern demand for certainty and the medieval archive (in this case, perhaps especially Maimonides), see Solom Maimon, *Versuch uber die Transcendentalphilosophie* (Berlin' Christian und Sohn, 1790). The importance of Maimon, from Fichte

to Deleuze is apparent in this regard. See for example the latter's *Différence et répétition*, pp. 221ff.

33. See Walter Benjamin, "Program of the Coming Philosophy," trans. Mark Ritter, *The Philosophica Forum* 15, Nos. 1–2 (Fall–Winter 1983–1984): 45. Heidegger's own discussion of the significance of the retrieval of the medieval account of transcendence that is "at the same time the source of multiple oppositions and the richest source of lived experience," as has been discussed, dates to his *Habilitationsschrift* on the problem of *grammatica speculativa*. There is some evidence, moreover, that Heidegger's early work was not unknown to Benjamin.

34. See *Summa Theologicae*, I.Q. 13 (On the Names of God).

35. Heidegger, *The Metaphysical Foundations of Logic* p. 43.

36. See Martin Heidegger, "What Is Metaphysics?" in *Basic Writings*. Benjamin equally of course realized the conceptual failure of the 'retrieval' of this sphere of transcendence.

37. See Martin Heidegger, *What Is a Thing?* trans W. B. Barton, Jr., and Vera Deutsch (Chicago: Henry Regnery, 1967), p. 67.

38. Adorno, *Aesthetic Theory*, p. 55.

39. Ibid. Adorno was himself however quick to admit that this surprise has always been present in art "but was not emphasized until recently (by Mallarme)." Indeed, he cites in this regard the infiltration of medieval music by the *ars nova* and later the Dutch developments which likewise "probably exceeded the subjective ideas of the composers" (55–56). What became characteristic of the avante garde instead was the "welcoming" of this surprise, an event in which, as he puts it in relation to Stockhausen, "indeterminacy is built right into determinacy as its moment." Still, Adorno in the end remained unable to interpret this event otherwise than by means of the rubrics of 'control,' claiming "only when it is dominated does that moment bear witness to the existence of freedom" (56).

40. The invocation of the "pure schemata" of phenomenology is deliberate. In his 1925 lectures on the concept of time, Heidegger charged that "what phenomenology took to be intentionality and how it took it is fragmentary," requiring the *Sorge* structure to complete it, Dasein's "being-ahead-of-itself-in-already-being-involved-in." But what could be more fragmented or distended than this? See *History of the Concept of Time*, pp. 303f.

41. Ibid., pp. 105f.

42. In other words, to use Heidegger's terms, the *Stellen* of the *Ge-Stell* "from which the latter stems" was at work from the outset—but conversely the latter a necessary accompaniment of the former's articulation. There can be

neither pure form nor pure *poiesis*. Compare Heidegger's *The Question Concerning Technology and Other Essays*, p. 21. 'Science' from the beginning remained hinged between the 'calcuable' and the 'incalcuable.' See "The Age of the World Picture," p. 135.

43. Gaston Bachelard, "Le surrationalisme," *L'engagement rationaliste* (Paris: Presses Universitaires de France, 1972).

44. See Michel Foucault's discussion of formalism as "in general one of the most powerful and complex forces in 20th century Europe" in "How Much Does It Cost for Reason to Tell the Truth?" p. 234.

45. See Jean Cavaillès, "On Logic and the Theory of Science," p. 380.

46. The word occurs in connection with Heidegger's later attempt to 'explain' his use of language, and ultimately hermeneutics in *Being and Time*. See "A Dialogue on Language," in *On the Way to Language*: "As I do [it], I would like to start from the etymology of the word [hermenetics/*hermeneuin*]; it will show you that my use of the word is not arbitrary, and that it also is apt to clarify the intention of my experiment (*Versuch*) with phenomenology" (28).

47. See T. W. Adorno, *Negative Dialectics*, trans. E. B. Ashton (New York: Continuum, 1973), p. 118; and *The Jargon of Authenticity*, trans. Knut Tarnowski and Frederic Will (Evanston, Ill.: Northwestern University Press, 1973).

48. Martin Heidegger, *Being and Time*, p. 209. Hence the necessity, Heidegger declared, of emancipating phenomenological evidence from the logicist theory of the proposition in Bolzano and Husserl (493–94). The 1925 lectures on the concept of time were more direct in this regard in claiming that phenomenology is indeed opposed to such axiomatics and closer to the intuitionism of Brouwer and Weyl for whom "the differentiation of the specific structure of the objects themselves" precedes analysis. See *History of the Concept of Time*, p. 3. Without adjudicating Heidegger on the foundations of mathematics, this much is true, that the syntactic-semantic event which results, devalorizing the privilege of the proposition in favor of its synthesis, is what transforms phenomenological *Auslegungen* into *positiven phänomenologischen Interpretationonen*. See *Being and Time*. Weyl, it should be noted, likewise had been specific about the transformation that results in his *Philosophy of Mathematics and Natural Science* (Princeton, N.J.: Princeton University Press, 1949)—most of which dates from the 1920s. Although mathematics still preserves an urge toward totality, it reveals too "that that desire can be fulfilled on one condition only, namely, that we are satisfied with the symbol and renounce the mystical error of expecting the transcendent ever to fall within the lighted circle of intuition" (66). If he retained Husserl's conception of formalism, what he retained is in one sense only the act, as Cavaillès put it ("On Logic and the Theory of Science," p. 367)—or more precisely the connection between evidence and the act, denying at the same time its formalist bond to immanence. Finally, Weyl was in fact

specific about the transformation that ensues for the rational. Justification becomes both "subjective-absolute" while at the same time "objective-relative," a pair of opposites whose metonymic juxtaposition expresses, Weyl claimed, "one of the most fundamental epistemological insights which can be gleaned from science" (116)—and a fragmentation that could be plotted perhaps as the biconditional of interpretation.

49. T. W. Adorno, *Aesthetic Theory*, p. 39.

50. See ibid., p. 43.

51. See Kant's discussion of talent, character, and *Originalität* in his *Anthropology from a Pragmaic Point of View*, §56f. Compare in this regard Jacques Derrida's discussion of Kant's inventions in *Psyche: Inventions de l'autre*, an analysis that (rightly) calls the *Anthropology*'s distinction between invention and discovery (like that between analysis and synthesis that underwrites it) into question. Nonetheless, Derrida again verged on the Heidegerrean naiveté in reducing the experiment—the extension—of 'invention' to simply a matter of *techne* and the creation of forms, and thus incapable of acknowledging the other. Consequently, having in an 'analysis' of Schelling's extension on Kant deconstructed the latent 'ontotheological metaphysics' of invention, Derrida almost lost the 'trace' of this event by reduction. Just, as Derrida realized, that Schelling was wrong to claim that philosophy might (indeed must) experiment with all form, in order to "arrive at the absolute form" so too to think that writing or its 'deconstructive' trace could simply escape form, or its institution—or its experiment—would be naive. The point instead, *pace* Kant and Schelling (and those in their wake), is that experiment is itself this invocation of the other—precisely that is, as the deformation of form—and the recognition that Absolute form will be neither (absolutely) formulated nor formalized. Hence, as Derrida put it, beyond the metaphysics of discovery and invention, receptivity and spontaneity, the original and the derived, "the necessity of reinventing invention" (59).

52. See Wittgenstein, *Philosophical Investigations*, pp. 192f.

53. *The Metalogicon of John of Salisbury*, trans. Daniel D. McGarry (Gloucester, Mass.: Peter Smith, 1971), pp. 64–65. Hence then the persistence of both the liberal arts and the humanist tradition, precisely, that is, in the readings of the fragmentary.

54. See Jürgen Habermas, *The Philosophical Discourse of Modernity*, p. 68.

55. See Sartre, *Being and Nothingness*, pp. 552f.

56. See Heidegger's account of the errancy of truth in "On the Essence of Truth" and my "On the Errancy of Dasein," *Diacritics* 19, Nos. 3–4. Perhaps in this regard, moreover, it becomes possible to further specify the status of Heidegger's insight. Doubtless, that is, it was Heidegger's great recognition to

have realized against "modernity," as his 1956 *The Principle of Reason* states, that "Being does not mean ground/Reason." If however, rather than simply 'meaning' reason, "being is experienced as ground/reason"—interpreted, that is, *as ratio, as* account, it must equally be insisted that, for the same 'reason,' neither can appeal to Being (or Being's 'appeal') simply replace *ratio*. This is, after all, precisely what Leibniz's failure implies: the failure of reduction, the failure of substitutability. The issue will be more complicated—and, I am arguing, it is precisely this complication to which the fragment attests in its particular exposition of the *ars inveniendi*. See Martin Heidegger, *The Principle of Reason*, trans. Reginald Lilly (Bloomington: Indiana University Press, 1992), pp. 128–9.

57. Jean-François Lyotard, "Answering the Question: What Is Postmodernism?" trans. Regis Durand, appendix to *The Postmodern Condition* (Minneapolis: University of Minnesota Press, 1984), p. 81.

58. Ibid.

59. Ibid., p. 82.

60. See Lyotard, *The Postmodern Condition*, p. 60; and Nietzsche, *Genealogy*, p. 152 (III § 24).

61. See Nietzsche, ibid., and Lyotard, p. 60, "Legitimation by Paralogy."

62. See Jean-Luc Nancy, *L'expérience de la liberté*. See § 14, "Fragments," p. 191.

63. Schlegel, "Athenaeum Fragments," p. 199 (§ 259).

64. Ibid., p. 164 (§ 24). The often commented on fact that only the romantics could abide the fragmentary remainders of ancient 'relics' without needing to recreate them is then perhaps anything but accidental.

65. See Schlegel "On Incomprehensibility," in *Lucinde and the Fragments*, p. 249:

Of all things that have to do with communicating ideas, what could be more fascinating than the question of whether such communication is actually possible? And where could one find a better opportunity for carrying out a variety of experiments to test this possibility or impossibility than in writing a journal like the *Athenaeum* oneself or else taking part in it as a reader?

66. Derrida, "L'aphorisme à contre temps," *Psyché*, p. 253.

67. See Jean François Lyotard, *L'assassinat de l'experience par la peinture, Monory* (Paris: Astral, 1984), pp. 7ff.

68. Cavaillès, "On Logic and the Theory of Science," p. 402.

69. *Novum Organum* § CXXIV, CXXX.

70. Ibid. § CIX. For a similar reading, complicating Bacon's role as the philosopher of power and industrial technology, see for example Michèle Le Doeuff, "L'homme et la nature dans les jardins de la science," *Revue Internationale de Philosophie*, No. 159 (1986).

71. Ibid. § CXVIII.

72. Hippocrates, *Aphorismoi*, § 1.

Index of Proper Names

Adorno, T., 7, 17, 13, 14, 20, 49, 64, 66, 148, 228, 251, 253–256, 268, 275, 277, 279–280, 302, 330, 336, 338–340
Albert, H., 82, 285
Althusser, L., 121
Andre, C., 66
Anselm, 76, 82
Appel, K-O., 288
Aquinas, T., 252, 298
Arendt, H., 7, 11, 23, 145, 154–156, 158–159, 170, 264, 271, 301, 305–309, 321, 334
Aristotle, 17, 19, 22, 77, 94–95, 117–118, 142, 144, 148, 163–164, 166, 174–175, 207, 215, 227, 279, 293–294, 309, 311, 314, 324
Artaud, A., 130, 251
Augustine, 117, 145, 227, 258
Aubenque, P., 293
Austin, J. L., 323

Bachelard, G., 200, 233, 254, 261, 269, 332, 339
Bacon, F., 23–24, 27, 66, 89, 119, 139, 141, 247, 251, 259, 271, 300, 311, 337, 342
Barthes, R., 13–15, 145–146, 265–266, 298, 302, 336
Bataille, G., 83, 287, 299
Beckett, S., 66, 241, 251, 331, 335
Benjamin, W., 10, 18, 63, 66, 84, 158, 240, 252, 254, 267, 279, 285, 307–308, 338
Bergson, H., 194
Bernstein, R., 335
Betti, E., 141–144, 152, 162, 301
Beuys, J., 66
Biemel, W., 276, 280
Blondel, M., 194, 196
Bloom, H., 330

Blumenberg, H., 14, 204, 265, 323, 328–329
Boccaccio, G., 225, 242, 261, 329, 335
Boehme, J., 119, 321
Boethius, 128
Bolzano, B., 4, 90, 261, 288, 326, 339
Brecht, B., 271
Brentano, F., 19, 87, 89, 294, 302
Brouwer, L., 252, 339
Bruno, G., 59, 241, 331
Buber, M., 157
Bultmann, R., 84, 286
Burke, E., 177

Cage, J., 66, 330
Carnap, R., 9, 19, 21, 35, 43, 228, 254, 263, 273–274, 330
Carroll, L., 148
Cavaillès, J., 6, 17, 19, 109, 151, 200, 252, 254, 258, 261–262, 267–269, 292, 325, 341
Cavell, S., 308, 339
Cézanne, P., 332
Chagall, M., 66
Chladenius, 154, 157, 174, 175, 314
Chisholm, R., 288
Cixous, H., 288
Comte, A., 14
Cohen, H., 173, 176, 309, 313, 321
Coleridge, S., 83, 281
Copernicus, N., 214, 303, 322
Courtine, J-F., 266

Dante, A., 241, 331
Darwin, C., 225
Davidson, D., 11, 246
Deleuze, G., 39, 113, 120–129, 131, 133–135, 198, 227, 249, 268, 274, 294–300 330, 336, 338
Democritus, 220

Derrida, J., 7, 9, 10, 13, 19, 35, 39–41, 45, 64, 121, 139–140, 150–151, 156–157, 225, 228, 233, 241, 243, 247, 251–252, 258, 261, 263, 265, 268, 270, 274, 279, 289 298, 300, 302–303, 320, 323, 329–330, 332, 337

Descartes, R., 17, 96, 118, 139, 141, 144, 174, 206, 210, 217, 228, 232, 242–243, 267 301, 323, 326, 331, 335

Dewey, J., 273, 310

Dilthey, W., 12, 13, 15, 141–142, 209, 265, 294, 325

Droyson, J., 303

Duchamps, M., 308

Duhem, P., 81–82, 215, 217, 285, 327–328

Dummet, M., 264

Duns Scotus, J., 118, 120, 293–294, 298

Dworkin, R., 140, 149, 302

Eco, U., 140, 262, 303, 331

Einstein, A., 148, 303, 330

Emerson, R., 308

Epicurus, 220

Erasmus, D., 6

Euclid, 27

Ferry, L., 160–161, 164–166, 168–169, 262, 269, 309–310

Feyerabend, P., 10

Fichte, J. G., 7, 72–74, 78, 156, 160, 169, 175–186, 192, 195–196, 200, 217, 248, 267, 281–284, 306, 309, 311–317, 320–321, 323, 328, 337

Fish, S., 140, 150, 302

Foucault, M., 7, 10, 13, 14, 54, 64, 120–121, 129–130, 134, 174, 198, 203, 243, 250, 261, 265, 276, 279, 294, 297, 299, 314, 322, 326, 335, 337, 339

Franklin, B., 251

Frege, G., 4, 7, 90, 99, 173, 264, 289

Freud, S., 131, 293–294, 297, 299, 321

Gadamer, H-G., 5, 7, 11, 13, 15, 17, 21, 78, 127–128, 139, 141–170, 173, 240, 255–256, 262–263, 265–266, 268, 270–271, 275, 278–279, 282–284, 294, 296–297, 300–302, 305–311, 314, 334

Galileo, G., 27, 90, 148

Gassendi, P., 175

Gödel, K., 254

Goethe, 276

Goodman, N., 330

Goya, F., 335

Granel, G., 265

Greimas, A., 247, 336

Guatarri, F., 300

Habermas, J., 7, 11, 84, 155, 204, 227, 257, 264, 281, 285–286, 290, 302, 305–306, 323, 330, 340

Heidegger, M., 6–10, 13, 15–17, 19, 21, 22, 28, 34–45, 49, 52, 62, 66, 113–118, 120, 125–127, 129–135, 145–146, 149–150, 154, 157–158, 160–161, 163–168, 173, 185, 193, 196, 199, 204–205, 207, 218, 236, 249, 252–254, 262–263, 266–268, 270–271, 273–275, 280, 286, 292–295, 297–299, 301–302, 307–309, 314, 318–324, 327–328, 336, 338–341

Hegel, G. W. F., 3, 15, 17, 18, 21, 28, 30, 32–33, 44, 49–55, 57, 59–60, 63–64, 66, 71–84, 119–120, 124, 127–128, 145, 157, 162–163, 176–177, 181, 186, 188, 192, 199, 203, 207–209, 216–217, 237–238, 252, 258, 261, 266–267, 270–272, 275–276, 278–287, 294–296, 299, 301, 313, 315–319, 321–322, 324–328, 334

Hempel, C., 88
Herz, M., 326
Hilbert, D., 151
Hippocrates, 251, 342
Hirsch, E. D., 149
Hjelmsley, L., 254
Hobbes, T., 154, 239–243, 304, 326, 334
Hölderlin, F., 130, 294
Horkheimer, M., 285
Home, D., 109, 205, 209, 214, 216, 219, 228, 239, 285, 330
Husserl, E., 4, 6–7, 13, 16, 18–20, 44, 61, 78, 89–109, 114, 119, 126–127, 131–132, 147, 166, 168, 182, 185, 187–190, 194, 208–213, 215, 217, 220–221, 232–235, 240, 262, 264, 267–268, 278, 284, 287–289, 291–292, 294, 301–302, 316–318, 325–328, 332–333, 335–336, 339

Irigaray, L., 84

Jacobi, F. H., 73
Jaeschke, W., 282
Jahnig, D., 277
James, W., 35, 273
Jaspers, K., 159, 309
Joyce, J., 227–228, 231, 241–242, 246, 251, 254, 303, 308, 330–331, 334

Kafka, F., 231, 251
Kandinsky, V., 254
Kant, I., 7, 13, 14, 16, 17, 20–22, 27–33, 36–38, 40, 42, 44–45, 50–57, 60–61, 73, 76–78, 88, 90, 93, 109, 114, 116–118, 121, 123–124, 126, 130–131, 134, 142–144, 146, 149, 151, 153–156, 161–162, 168, 173–177, 179, 182, 184, 187–189, 197–198, 204–205, 207–208, 211–220, 226–230, 235–244, 255, 257, 262, 264–265, 267, 269–272,

274–278, 281–283, 285, 290, 293, 295–297, 301–306, 309, 311–316, 318–319, 323–331, 333–335, 340
Kierkegaard, S., 83, 116, 286
Klee, P., 66
Kojéve, A., 331
Koyré, A., 204, 323
Kristeva, J., 66, 84, 280
Kuhn, T., 10, 104, 149, 230, 264, 290, 302, 303

Lacan, J., 121
Lachieze-Rey, P., 318–319
Lacoue-Labarthe, P., 44, 274, 282
Lakatos, I., 292
Lambert, J. H., 17, 210, 212–213, 215, 326–327, 332
Laplace, P., 29
LaRouchefoucauld, F., 251
Lavoisier, A., 303
Lawrence, D. H., 300
Le Doeuff, M., 342
Lefort, C., 4, 167, 261, 310–311, 334
Leibniz, G., 109, 157, 175, 206, 208, 210, 215, 249, 252, 258, 323–324, 326–328, 334, 341
Léonard, A., 282
Lessing, G., 81
Levinas, E., 19, 84, 194, 220, 268, 285–286, 320
Locke, J., 175
Luther, 6
Lyotard, J-F., 84, 198, 227, 256–258, 281, 330, 341

Mach, E., 19, 109, 233, 332
Machiavelll, N., 166–167, 239, 251, 334
MacIntyre, A., 158, 283, 308, 334
Maimon, S., 162, 257, 309, 337
Maimonides, M., 337
Malevitch, K., 254
Marcuse, H., 300
Marion, J-L., 83

Marllarmé, S., 15
Marquet, J-F., 277
Marx, K., 54, 131, 294, 297, 299, 317
Meinong, A., 261-262
Merleau-Ponty, M., 7, 12, 19, 146, 173-174, 178, 182-199, 207, 249, 261, 265, 268, 292, 301, 312, 314, 316-322, 324, 328
Mies van der Rohe, L., 66
Mill, J. S., 99, 298
Miller, H., 300
Montaigne, M., 203, 211, 219, 247, 256, 322, 326, 329
Moore, G. E., 308, 324

Nancy, J-L., 5, 82, 140, 159, 166, 258, 262-263, 282, 285-286, 307, 309-310, 341
Natrop, P., 7, 9
Newman, J. H., 283
Newton, I., 27, 90, 148, 214, 303, 325
Nicolas of Cusa., 17, 128-129, 206, 209-210 214-215, 217, 229, 236, 296-297, 326-327, 331
Nietzsche, F., 6, 16, 17, 21, 23, 31-39, 42-43, 66, 82, 113, 122-124, 131-132, 140-142, 150-151, 157, 195-196, 204, 215-516, 232, 235, 247-252, 255, 257, 259, 272-275, 277, 280, 294-295, 297, 299, 301, 303, 320, 322, 336-337, 341
Novalis, 248, 252, 320, 336

Ockham, 203

Pareyson, L., 59, 277
Pascal, B., 206, 251, 324
Petrarch, 261
Peukert, H., 285
Philo, 124
Plato, 7, 8, 15-17, 19, 22, 27, 51, 56, 58, 80, 102, 125, 134, 162-164, 166, 168, 174, 176, 216, 225-226, 231,

240, 243-244, 262, 264, 268, 276, 279-280, 296, 315, 325, 335
Plotinus, 16, 127, 232, 266, 332
Poe, E. A., 308
Poincaré, J., 151, 252, 254
Polanyi, M., 249
Popper, K., 5-6, 9, 15-16, 20, 88, 103-104, 107, 145, 203, 262-264, 266-269, 289-292, 322
Pound, E., 254

Quine, W. V. O., 14, 43, 87, 104, 106, 241-242, 261, 265, 288, 290, 335

Rahner, K., 84
Reich, W., 300
Reinhart, A., 330
Reinhold, K., 21
Renault, A., 160-161, 164-165, 168, 269, 309, 311
Richir, M., 218, 317-318, 328
Ricoeur, P., 21, 104, 121, 270, 289, 293, 319, 327
Rorty, R., 104, 140, 149, 290, 302, 325
Rothko, M., 66
Rousstau, J-J., 160
Russell, B., 19, 148, 273, 323

Salisbury, John of, 255
Sartre, J-P., 7, 12, 15, 17, 21, 185, 220, 265-267, 270, 276, 298-299, 312, 318, 336, 340
Scheler, M., 108, 173, 184-185, 200, 292, 314, 318, 321-322
Schelling, F. W. J., 14, 29-30, 33, 35, 51-67, 71, 73, 75, 77-79, 81-83, 127, 182, 184, 186, 193-194, 243, 271-273, 276-278, 280-285, 295, 299, 307, 309, 317-320, 323-324, 340
Schiller, F., 54, 151, 276, 283

Schlegel, F., 65, 74, 144, 165, 247–248, 250–252, 255, 258, 277, 280, 282–283, 305, 307, 312, 336–337, 341
Schleiermacher, F., 12, 77, 79, 139, 141, 148, 150, 154, 157, 258, 283–285, 300, 303
Schlick, M., 19, 95–98, 100, 103–104, 106, 109, 288, 290–291
Schönberg, A., 66
Schopenhauer, A., 251
Searle, J., 228–232, 235, 242, 331
Sellars, W., 139, 233, 261, 267, 288, 291, 300, 332
Serres, M., 13, 121, 133, 198, 206–208, 218, 265, 298, 323–325, 328, 331
Shakespeare, 74
Socrates, 231
Sophocles, 74
Spinoza, B., 59, 71, 115, 121–123, 131, 180, 187, 200, 294, 296, 318–319
Stegmüller, W., 335
Stockhausen, K., 338
Strauss, L., 11, 20, 145, 157, 160–168, 265, 268, 271, 300–302, 307, 309–311
Strawson, P., 264
Stumpf, K., 19
Suarez, 293

Taminiaux, J., 318
Tarski, A., 264
Tatarkiewicz, W., 280
Thébaud, J-L., 281
Thomas of Erfurt, 293
Thucydides, 22
Tilliete, X., 59, 277, 280, 321
Toulmin, S., 18, 267, 269
Trakl, G., 294

van Fraassen, B., 140, 150, 302
Veyne, P., 330
Vico, G., 166, 204, 242, 267, 310, 323, 331
Voltaire, F., 182

Warhol, A., 66
Weyl, H., 326, 339–340
White, H., 303
Whitehead, A., 148
Wittgenstein, L., 4, 10, 35, 151, 155, 219, 225–226, 232–233, 239–242, 247, 249, 251–252, 263, 283, 291, 306, 308, 323–324, 329, 332–335, 337, 340
Wundt, W., 19, 105